THE ROOTS OF JEWISH CONSCIOUSNESS, VOLUME ONE

The Roots of Jewish Consciousness, Volume One: Revelation and Apocalypse is the first volume, fully annotated, of a major, previously unpublished, two-part work by Erich Neumann (1905–1960). It was written between 1934 and 1940, after Neumann, then a young philosopher and physician and freshly trained as a disciple of Jung, fled Berlin to settle in Tel Aviv. He finished the second volume of this work at the end of World War II. Although he never published either volume, he kept them the rest of his life.

The challenge of Jewish survival frames Neumann's work existentially. This survival, he insists, must be psychological and spiritual as much as physical. In Volume One, *Revelation and Apocalypse*, he argues that modern Jews must relearn what ancient Jews once understood but lost during the Babylonian Exile: that is, the individual capacity to meet the sacred directly, to receive revelation, and to prophesy. Neumann interprets scriptural and intertestamental (apocalyptic) literature through the lens of Jung's teaching, and his reliance on the work of Jung is supplemented with references to Buber, Rosenzweig, and Auerbach. Including a preface by Nancy Swift Furlotti and editorial introduction by Ann Conrad Lammers, readers of this volume can hold for the first time the unpublished work of Neumann, with useful annotations and insights throughout.

These volumes anticipate Neumann's later works, including *Depth Psychology and a New Ethic*, *The Origins and History of Consciousness*, and *The Great Mother*. His signature contribution to analytical psychology, the concept of the ego–Self axis, arises indirectly in Volume One, folded into Neumann's theme of the tension between earth and YHWH. This unique work will appeal to Jungian analysts and psychotherapists in training and in practice, historians of psychology, Jewish scholars, biblical historians, teachers of comparative religion, as well as academics and students.

Erich Neumann (1905–1960) was a student of C. G. Jung, a philosopher, psychologist, and writer. Born in Germany, he moved to Israel in 1934, where he became a practicing analytical psychologist. His previously published works, including *Depth Psychology and a New Ethic*, have never been out of print.

Ann Conrad Lammers, Ph.D., received her Master of Divinity from The General Theological Seminary in New York and her doctorate in theology and psychology from Yale University. A Jungian psychotherapist and marriage and family therapist, she retired from practice in 2015 to edit *The Roots of Jewish Consciousness*.

"'The Jewish problem and my work on it ended for me precisely at a time when it became conspicuous in the world in an indescribably ghastly way' (Neumann in 1945, at the end of World War II). I was the living witness of this ghastliness when I met Neumann in 1948. Being a survivor of Auschwitz with my whole family murdered, my god had only one face, and I was in dire need of help. Help came in the compassionate form of Erich Neumann, whose god had two faces.

It is an extraordinary experience to trace the development of Neumann's early thoughts from revelation to the actualization of messianism in this remarkable book. Many cornerstones of Neumann's opus are already in his *Roots of Jewish Consciousness:* the covenant between God and his people; God holding the opposites together; the ego–Self axis; the transcendent function; secondary personalization; and, foremost, the emphasis on a strong ego as the *conditio sine qua non* for moral man. In this thoughtful and profound publication, Neumann shows himself to be the independent thinker he was, vis-à-vis the first generation of Jungians who were fascinated by the unconscious.

At a meeting between Erich Neumann and Gershom Scholem in 1959, in Neumann's flat in Tel Aviv, he asked me to just listen to their conversation. What a conversation! The atmosphere in the room was charged, with both men evidently in the grip of strong emotions. They had a long and rather loud discussion. Would Neumann have changed something in his writing if destiny had given him more time?"

—Dvora Kutzinski, Jungian analyst; friend and supervisee of Dr. Erich Neumann, Tel Aviv, Israel

"Unsurprisingly, Volume One of this previously unpublished work of Erich Neumann delivers exactly what the title states in clear, and scholarly, labored depth and breadth. For me, a Jewish reader, it stirs my Jewish soul and roots. But it is much more than a history and analysis of the roots of Jewish consciousness. To those familiar with Jungian theory, this work puts additional meat on the structural bones of some of Jung's theories, most particularly his theory of the collective unconscious. And beyond that, for those who will give a reflective reading of this profound work, it does throw light in evolutionary terms on the eruption of the shadow and psychic chaos in today's world. Neumann's analyses of the historical and psychic influence not only his Jewish roots, but those of the spirit of the times as reflected in Gnosticism and Christianity, as well as a radical view of the responsibility of the Jewish individual in today's world as the carrier of those roots as compared with Judaism itself. I can think of no other contemporary work on the evolution of the Jewish psyche and its footprint in the world than this work."

—Jerome S. Bernstein, M.A.P.C., NCPsyA, Jungian analyst

THE ROOTS OF JEWISH CONSCIOUSNESS

Volume One: Revelation and Apocalypse

Erich Neumann
Edited by Ann Conrad Lammers

TRANSLATED BY MARK KYBURZ AND ANN CONRAD LAMMERS

LONDON AND NEW YORK

First published 2019
by Routledge
2 Park Square, Milton Park, Abingdon, Oxon OX14 4RN

and by Routledge
52 Vanderbilt Avenue, New York, NY 10017

Routledge is an imprint of the Taylor & Francis Group, an informa business

British Library Cataloguing-in-Publication Data
A catalogue record for this book is available from the British Library

Library of Congress Cataloging-in-Publication Data
Names: Neumann, Erich, author.
Title: The roots of Jewish consciousness / Erich Neumann.
Description: New York : Routledge, 2019. | Includes bibliographical references and index.
Identifiers: LCCN 2018055761 (print) | LCCN 2019010908 (ebook) | ISBN 9781315149905 (Master eBook) | ISBN 9781351369121 (Adobe Reader) | ISBN 9781351369107 (Mobipocket) | ISBN 9781351369114 (ePub) | ISBN 9781138556195 (v. 1 : hardback) | ISBN 9781138556201 (v. 1 : pbk.) | ISBN 9781138556218 (v. 2 : hardback) | ISBN 9781138556225 (v. 2 : pbk.)
Subjects: LCSH: Psychology—Religious aspects—Judaism. | Judaism and psychology. | Consciousness—Religious aspects—Judaism. | Revelation. | Eschatology. | Hasidism.
Classification: LCC BM538.P68 (ebook) | LCC BM538.P68 N4813 2019 (print) | DDC 296.3—dc23
LC record available at https://lccn.loc.gov/2018055761

ISBN: 978-1-138-55619-5 (hbk)
ISBN: 978-1-138-55620-1 (pbk)
ISBN: 978-1-315-14990-5 (ebk)

Typeset in Bembo
by Swales & Willis Ltd, Exeter, Devon, UK

Visit the eResources: www.routledge.com/9781138556201

In memoriam Erel Shalit

Erich Neumann (1905–1960) was born and raised in Berlin, the second son of a successful merchant family. At university in Erlangen, where he began his study of psychology, he wrote a dissertation on the "mystical linguistics" of Johann Arnold Kanne, a "forgotten Romantic." Neumann entered medical school in 1928, intending to be a psychiatrist and psychotherapist. That year, too, he married Julie Blumenfeld. Their son, Micha, was born in June 1931.

Eighteen months later, as Neumann was finishing medical school, Hitler came to power. Jews were immediately barred from many positions, including medical internships. Recognizing the dire significance of the moment, Erich and Julie, Zionists since their teens, left for Palestine/Israel in the fall of 1933 with two-year-old Micha. On the way, however, they stopped in Zurich, where Erich underwent eight months of analytic training with C. G. Jung.

After settling in Tel Aviv in 1934, Neumann began to practice as a Jungian analyst and also to write the present work. A daughter, Rachel (Rali), was born in May 1938. In 1940 Neumann finished the first part of *The Roots of Jewish Consciousness*. In 1945, as the war was ending in Europe, he finished the second part. Then, for reasons that are imperfectly known, he laid the whole work aside.

Erich Neumann's previously published writings are read worldwide, including *The Origins and History of Consciousness*, *Depth Psychology and a New Ethic*, *The Great Mother*, *Amor and Psyche*, *Creative Man*, *The Fear of the Feminine*, *The Child* (published by Julie Neumann in 1963), and his many Eranos lectures, delivered from 1948 until his death in 1960. An important early essay, *Jacob and Esau*, edited by Erel Shalit and published in 2015, brings a missing piece of his thought to light. His correspondence with Jung, *Analytical Psychology in Exile*, also appeared in 2015. The two volumes of the present work represent not only the young author's thorough integration of Jungian theory with Jewish religious symbolism, but also his early development of profound theoretical insights, now recognized as the hallmarks of his psychology.

Ann Conrad Lammers, Ph.D., received her Master of Divinity from The General Theological Seminary in New York and her doctorate in theology and psychology from Yale University. A Jungian psychotherapist and marriage and family therapist, she retired from practice in 2015 to edit *The Roots of Jewish Consciousness*. In addition to journal articles and book chapters, her published works include *The Jung–White Letters* (co-editor, Routledge, 2007) and *The Jung–Kirsch Letters* (editor and co-translator, Routledge, 2011/2016).

CONTENTS

List of illustrations   *x*
Preface, by Nancy Swift Furlotti   *xi*
Acknowledgments   *xvi*
Abbreviations   *xx*
Introduction to Volume One, by Ann Conrad Lammers   *xxiii*

Introduction to the work, by Erich Neumann   1

The discovery of mythical prehistory 1
The new orientation given by depth psychology 3
The Jewish situation 5
The theme 7

The problem of revelation in Jewish antiquity

1   The YHWH–earth relation and prophecy   15

1. Moses and the revelation on Sinai 15
    The Near East and the significance of the Mother Goddess 15
    The revelation on Sinai and the people's failure 17
        The phenomenology of YHWH's irruption 21
        The Tablets of the Law 23
        The Golden Calf 23
    Moses as rescuer from the danger of the unconscious 24
        Plague, ordeal, murder by the Levites 24
    The elevation of Moses and the introduction of prophecy 27
        The latent prophetic capacity of the individual 27
        Prophetic law-giving and the healing function 30
        Prophecy, false prophecy, pagan prophecy 32

2. YHWH and the earth-principle 36
The affirmation of nature and nature's purity 37
Earth as threat 41
YHWH as lord of fertility 43
3. YHWH and prophecy 44
The nature of YHWH 44
Distance, paradox, unconditionality 44
The nature of prophecy 46
Prophecy, mysticism, divination 46
The depth of the revelatory layer and the conscious attitude 47
*Ego-stability and its religious significance: Partnership with
YHWH and morality 49*
The individual as a bearer of revelation 53
Prophecy, cult, and law 56
Prophecy as protection against the unconscious 57
Law and cult as protection against the unconscious 60
The primacy of consciousness and its dangers 61
YHWH and the Mother Goddess 62
Author's note 64

2   The apocalypse: Heightening the YHWH–earth tension   75

1. The new worldview and alienation from salvation 75
The Exile and the end of the primitive collective 76
Judah-ism and subjective religiosity 77
The end of direct revelation 79
2. The psychological meaning of eschatology 82
The historical form of the certainty of salvation 83
Eschatological psychic space 86
Messianism and apocalypse 87
The eschaton and the archetype of rebirth 90
Apocalypse and alchemy 95
3. Apocalypse and redemption in time 96
YHWH's working in time 96
Time as the working level of the unconscious 98
Destiny as the possibility of archetypal experience 99
The messiah as a symbol unifying heaven and earth 100

3   The dangerous ending of the YHWH–earth tension   115

1. Breaking the tension between YHWH and earth 115
The Gnostic threat 115
The danger of intuition 116
Gnosticism and Judaism 118
2. Shrinking the tension between YHWH and earth:
The anti-Gnostic threat 123
The exclusion of inner experience 124
Law and rabbinism 125

The loss of earth, inner and outer 128

3. *The secret victory of the mother archetype 131*
   The dominance of rational consciousness 131
   The Torah and the mother archetype 132
   How the principle of YHWH became latent 132

4   Author's appendices   137

Appendix I: Methodology 138
Appendix II: The foundation stone and the waters of the deep 140
Appendix III: The composition of the Pentateuch 144
Appendix IV: Earth and the symbols of the elements 147
   Wind symbolism 148
   Body-soul and blood 150
   Earth and bull 153
   Circumcision and Passover 155
   Lilith 157

Editorial note   *172*
Bibliography   *176*
Index   *188*
Scriptural index   *199*

ILLUSTRATIONS

Figure P.1   Erich Neumann at home in Tel Aviv   xiii
              Photograph: c. 1945 (photographer unknown)
              Courtesy of the Erich Neumann Estate
Figure I.1   Erich and Julie Neumann, Berlin   xxiv
              Photograph: © 1931, Tim Gidal
              Courtesy of the Erich Neumann Estate
Figure 1.1   Moses and the revelation on Sinai   18
              Watercolor: © Erich Neumann (date unknown)
              Courtesy of the Erich Neumann Estate
Plate 2.1   Vision of the Holy Land
              Watercolor: © Erich Neumann (date unknown)
              Courtesy of the Erich Neumann Estate
Plate 2.2   Joseph's dream
              Watercolor: © Erich Neumann (date unknown)
              Courtesy of the Erich Neumann Estate
Back cover   Erich Neumann at 40
              Photograph: 1945 (photographer unknown)
              Courtesy of the Erich Neumann Estate

PREFACE

This preface should have been written by Dr. Erel Shalit, but, after struggling with cancer for a number of years, he did not live to see the completion and publication of this book. Yet I know he would have been delighted with the outcome. In his stead he encouraged me to write this preface and to continue our joint work.

My interest in Erich Neumann's work goes back to the early days in my Jungian analytical training, when I was introduced to the writings of Erich Neumann. I immediately recognized not only his brilliance and clarity of thought but also his unique ability to relate through feeling to feminine nature, an experience of being in the presence of *eros*. This was so different from reading C. G Jung's writings. As a thinking type, Neumann easily moves into abstraction, but his writings soon enough return to a more feeling/sensation ground. Reading Neumann is an interplay between these two opposites. What I later discovered was that in the watercolor paintings (not yet published), which correspond to his active imagination, one can immediately recognize this related quality. They are thoughtful yet unrestrained images, with a colorful, flowing quality that depicts his journey of individuation while also imparting his lived, personal, feeling experience of them. The images are both collective and personal, reflecting the archetypes as well as their worldly equivalent, complexes. Throughout *The Roots of Jewish Consciousness*, Neumann gracefully moves into and out of this more feeling territory, especially in the second part, where the feminine is prominent in his discussion of Jewish mysticism.

Appreciating Erich Neumann's profound contribution to analytical psychology, I became focused around 2006 on publishing *The Correspondence between C. G. Jung and Erich Neumann*, which was finally published in 2015. That same year I formed a company called Recollections, the purpose of which is to edit and publish first-generation Jungian analysts' unpublished writings. Partnering with Erel Shalit, our initial focus was on the unpublished material of Erich Neumann, to create a revival of interest in this brilliant man's writings. Our first project was *Jacob and Esau*, published in 2015, edited by Erel Shalit and translated by Mark Kyburz. Our second project was this two-volume manuscript, now published as *The Roots of Jewish Consciousness*, edited by the Jungian scholar Ann Conrad Lammers, and translated by Mark Kyburz and Ann Lammers. Erel Shalit, as general editor of Recollections, oversaw the project and contributed his valuable guidance and understanding of ancient and contemporary Hebrew, the complex etymology of words and their underlying symbolism, his understanding of the sacred Jewish texts, general mythology, folklore, philosophy, and especially his own innate wisdom. He, like Erich Neumann, died prematurely. Erel Shalit and I have remained most appreciative of Neumann's children, Professor Micha Neumann and Rali Neumann-Loewenthal for their on-going support and encouragement with these publications. Special gratitude goes to the hardworking team that brought these projects to publication.

Erich Neumann began working on the *Roots* manuscript after he emigrated from Berlin in 1933, stopping off in Zurich for eight months to analyze with C. G. Jung. He began planning the manuscript while in Zurich. He sent his family on ahead to Palestine, and then continued on himself to join his family and settle in his new homeland, where he kept working on *Roots* all the way through World War II. In other words, through the whole Hitler era! It was no easy task to leave one's land of birth, one's family and friends, while recognizing the shadow of evil that was noticeably permeating the collective and emerging into the reality of everyday life. At the same time, life in Palestine/Israel was precarious. War and death were all around him. Rommel was moving closer from the south. Such a chaotic, destructive world of reality presents us with the question of how to make sense of the senseless.

For Neumann, after leaving Germany where he and many Jews were non-observant, moving to Palestine was a return to his roots, to his identity as a Jew, with the desire to establish his connection to the soil of his new land and all it represented to him—the ground of his very being. Descending into a study of Judaism was a way to do that. He was re-claiming himself. Neumann focused his attention on humanity's relation to God, revelation, consciousness, and the nature of good and evil. He did this in a way that made sense to him as a Jew and as a Jungian analyst, exploring the development of the Jewish religion from the early sacred texts through Hasidism and Jewish mysticism, and finally using the lens of psychological understanding that pointed to a human–God reciprocal interdependence, an inner being.

The descent into introversion for Neumann at 28 was not a dissimilar reaction to that of C. G. Jung before World War I. How do creative, brilliant, introverted human beings deal with the onslaught of horror? One way is to embark on an inner journey that tries to make sense of it, to try to understand why God would allow this to happen. Each was led by a different *daimon* and expressed his descent in a different way, but each came to a mystical understanding of the human–God relationship: Jung through Christianity, eastern religions, Gnosticism, and alchemy,

FIGURE P.1 Erich Neumann at home in Tel Aviv: on his balcony, overlooking the Mediterranean, circa 1945.

Photographer unknown. Courtesy of the Erich Neumann Estate.

and Neumann through Judaism, Hasidism and Kabbalah—and both from the perspective of Jungian theory. Towards the end of Jung's life his dreams pointed to the knowledge and experience of Jewish mysticism. Both men, a Christian and a Jew, found their way to a deep understanding of the nature of the psyche and humanity's relationship and responsibility to the essence of what we are able to understand of God, as the archetype of meaning and wholeness. In Neumann's 1948 paper, "Mystical Man," he sums up his understanding, when he says:

> . . . now man and the godhead meet one another in the open. The world takes form around a united personality . . . . The inexplicable fact that man's very center is an unknown creative force which lives within him and molds him in ever-new forms and transformations, this mystery which accompanies him throughout his life, follows him even into death and beyond. So the circle closes, and man ends as he began, a *homo mysticus*.[1]

The Roots of Jewish Consciousness was the result of Neumann's descent. Although Neumann referred to this two-part manuscript, with a possible third part, in his correspondence with C. G. Jung, after the war he put it away with no intention to publish it. He did, however, publish *Depth Psychology and a New Ethic* in German in 1949. Much of the material in that book derives from his work on the *Roots* manuscript. In *Roots* it is easy to see the development of his thoughts that led to his formulation of the new ethic, in which humans are shown to be responsible for their own unconscious shadow and expressions of evil, rather than scapegoating or projecting them onto the "other." This new ethic requires a shift from a collective morality, or the old ethic, to now each having individual responsibility for one's actions. This shift impacts not only the individual but the totality of humankind, as well. Making this process conscious ultimately affects the very relationship between humans and God, as delineated in Neumann's discussion of Jewish mysticism.

Neumann's *New Ethic*, however, was not received well by the Jungians in Zurich. It was thought to overstep Jung, to be too intellectual, introducing new concepts and terminology, and to be a dangerous new idea, attempting to destroy cultural stability. Undoubtedly there were many other reasons, such as personal dislike for Neumann, perhaps out of jealousy of his very close relationship with Jung. Whatever it was, the experience was not pleasant for Neumann, and he pulled back from the Zurich group. His most prominent book, *The Origins and History of Consciousness*, was published in the same year and was better received. This one discussed themes that were less threatening and more universal. With this reality of the shadow in the background of the Jungian community, it is no wonder that he decided against publishing *Roots*. As a Jewish manuscript, its reception might have been less than welcome and quite vulnerable to attack. Other factors also, no doubt, played a role in this decision. Jung also decided not to publish his *Red Book*, worrying that it might be seen as the "rantings of a crazy man." Yet, for both men, these precious works served as the *prima materia* for their future understandings of the nature of the psyche.

It is striking to see the introduction of new Jungian concepts that emerged from Neumann's understanding of the psyche, as discussed in *Roots*. Neumann was the first to describe and use the term "ego–Self axis," for example. In addition, his work, presented in *Depth Psychology and a New Ethic*, on the nature of good and evil and humanity's relationship to God, preceded Jung's *Answer to Job*, which struggles with similar material. Neumann's work on the feminine and the soul was seminal. He later published *The Great Mother*, which examines the archetype of the feminine, and the uniquely thoughtful compilation, *The Fear of the Feminine*. His focus on creativity, art, and mythology is extensive. His final book, *The Child*, was to be added to *The Origins and History of Consciousness* as a section on child psychology. Unfortunately, it was left partially unfinished when he died in 1960, but his wife, Julia, completed it and published it as a separate book. It remains an important contribution to child development.

Other concepts emerged in his thinking that have only recently become topical, such as living in the moment, or what is popularly described as mindfulness, and the shift towards identifying as a single sex, a "transindividual being, which still consists of two persons" rather than one side of a polar opposite (*Roots II*, p. 97). This was to be a major topic in Part Three, which was unfortunately never completed.

It is easy to see why Neumann was described as Jung's most brilliant disciple and close friend. He always remained his own person, standing on his own ground of being, challenging thought and theory with experience and plowing new pathways for all of us to follow as we strive to understand the reality, soul, and spirit of our own primal psychic ground—to make sense of what is true for us.

Nancy Swift Furlotti, 2018

Note

1 Erich Neumann (1948). "Mystical Man," in *The Mystic Vision: Papers from the Eranos Yearbooks*, Joseph Campbell, ed., Princeton, NJ: Princeton University Press, 1968, pp. 414f.

ACKNOWLEDGMENTS

Permission to publish text and illustrations was kindly given by the Neumann Estate: Micha Neumann and Rali Neumann-Loewenthal. Primary documents for Volumes One and Two of this work are found in the Neumann family archive at the home of Rali Loewenthal-Neumann, Jerusalem. Additional documents, including Erich Neumann's April 1940 lecture and his four-lecture series between 1942 and 1943, are also found in this collection. Access to Erich Neumann's documents, consultation about his life and work and his relationships with Buber & Scholem, and history of his papers and library were all kindly given by Rali Neumann-Loewenthal.

Warmest thanks are also due to the following individuals. First, to Erel Shalit, for planning and overseeing this project, to which he gave caring attention until his untimely death in January 2018. His expertise in Neumann's writings, especially the recently published *Jacob and Esau*, were necessary resources for me in editing this book. His introduction to *Jacob and Esau* is an ongoing source of inspiration. During the editorial process, he organized two conferences and a webinar on Neumann's work. In 2017 he approved and signed the publication contract with Routledge for this two-volume edition. He studied Neumann's lectures of the 1940s and confirmed their publishability. As his final act in support of the present work, Erel shared his electronic files of Neumann's "Torah" paintings, from which the two volume covers were chosen.

Erel Shalit also wisely invited Dr. Moshe Idel to write the Foreword to *Hasidism*. Professor Idel generously accepted the invitation and, after Erel's death, prepared the brilliant writing that opens Volume Two.

Nancy Furlotti, in her deep commitment to Erich Neumann's work, has supported the entire project from first to last. I am grateful for her advice about archetypal symbolism and her illuminating consultation about Neumann's art and writings. In addition to working closely with Erel until his death, she kept in touch with Micha Neumann and Rali Neumann Loewenthal, especially regarding essential copyright permissions. After Erel's death, Nancy gave careful oversight to the final stages of editorial preparation. As a contributing editor, she provided the graceful Preface to Volume One, wrote the caption for "The Transformative Serpent" in Volume Two, and finally, crafted fully half of our online chapter abstracts.

Tamar Kron, who is expert in Buber, Kabbalah, and Hasidism, gave me invaluable help on issues of translation and annotation, especially involving the Hebrew language. She located many sources underlying Neumann's writing, advised me on Neumann's relationship with Buber, and elucidated important points in Jewish mystical tradition. She and David Wieler, who have been preparing the Hebrew translation of *Roots*, kindly read and critiqued our English translations.

Mark Kyburz, whose specialty is translation from German to English, had worked previously with Erel Shalit in translating Neumann's *Jacob and Esau*. From the beginning of this project, he has been a member of the editorial team, and I thank him for his professional translation work, faithful collaboration, independent research, linguistic advice, and attention to countless details in the text. Mark and I gradually evolved a collaborative translation process, in which each of us corrected the other's blind spots. The book ventures into such a broad range of fields, including biblical hermeneutics, philosophy, Jewish history, theology, and mysticism, that it might have been impossible for anyone to translate it alone. I am very grateful to Mark for his systematic approach to Neumann's terminology. I've continually relied on the skills and resources that are at his command as a seasoned translator.

Before Mark and I could begin translating, however, we needed faithful transcriptions. For these, I trusted Ursula Egli's patient and exacting reading. We puzzled together over the author's textual obscurities and proofread each other's work. Apart from the third chapter of *Hasidism*, which I reconstructed and transcribed, Ursula wrestled first and hardest with Neumann's faded typescripts and difficult handwriting. Her work is the textual foundation for this edition.

In his wide-ranging thought, Neumann draws on areas of study well beyond those that this editor can claim. I have therefore been fortunate that I could turn to a circle of scholars who helped me to understand the implications of the text, refine parts of the translations, and write many of the annotations. In what follows, I try to remember every one of these generous people. If I have nevertheless omitted someone, I ask to be reminded, so that I can amend this list at the first opportunity.

When the project began, I had just a few official consultants. In addition to those already named, I am especially thankful to Richard Corney for his consultation on questions about the Hebrew language, ancient Jewish writings, and a vast number of linguistic and historical issues.

Everett Fox, whose extraordinary biblical translations are quoted in this work, generously advised me at an early stage about Buber's work and thought and the history of Jewish biblical scholarship. In Neumann's *Revelation and Apocalypse*, readers will see many passages quoted from Fox's work, *The Schocken Bible*, Volume I: *The Five Books of Moses*. For these numerous excerpts, copyright permission was sought and received from the publisher:

Excerpt(s) from *Genesis and Exodus: A New English Rendition with Commentary & Notes* by Dr. Everett Fox, copyright © 1983, 1986, 1990 by Penguin Random House LLC. Used by permission of Schocken Books, an imprint of the Knopf Doubleday Publishing Group, a division of Penguin Random House LLC. All rights reserved. Any third party use of this material, outside of this publication, is prohibited. Interested parties must apply directly to Penguin Random House LLC for permission.

Fewer excerpts are quoted from Fox's *The Schocken Bible*, Volume II: *The Early Prophets*. These, falling under "fair use," are also very gratefully acknowledged.

At an early point in the project, due to the arduous treatment he was undergoing, Erel Shalit realized that I needed auxiliary consultants in some of the areas where he had hoped to guide my work. With his support, in 2016 I turned to Steven Joseph for advice about a challenging theme in Neumann's *Hasidism*. I was also grateful, later on, for Steve's reading of my two introductions. Murray Stein helped with several fine points in Jungian diction. Thomas Kirsch, while he lived, advised me about Neumann's relationship with James Kirsch. Andreas Jung helped me to locate an obscure reference in Jung's *Über die Energetik der Seele*. Sanford Drob advised me on Kabbalah and Jewish tradition, shedding light on several passages in *Hasidism*. Nomi Kluger-Nash wrote to me about the symbolism of Jonah and the meanings of *t'shuvah*. Lance Owens opened my thinking about Neumann's Eranos lectures and his concept of the "great individual." Robert Segal gave much learned advice about the writings of Lucien Lévy-Bruhl; he also kindly referred me to his student, Nico Fehlbaum, whose doctoral work at the University of Aberdeen is on Cassirer and myth, and who gave expert consultation on the writings of Ernst Cassirer in relation to Lucien Lévy-Bruhl. Peter Kingsley kindly advised me about Neoplatonism. Steve Zemmelman referred me to Rabbi Jonathan Omer-Man and also to Rabbi Dr. Zvi Leshem, and later he devoted deep and critical reading to my two introductions. Jonathan Omer-Man gently advised me on the unwisdom of publishing Neumann's unfinished short story, "David and Saul." Zvi Leshem read an early draft of my introduction to Volume One and led me to essential readings on the history of the Buber–Scholem debate.

For this project, I have had the pleasure of doing research at several libraries, including: St. Mark's Library, The General Theological Seminary, New York, NY; the library of the Graduate Theological Union, Berkeley, CA; the ETH-Bibliothek, Zurich, with assistance from Yvonne Voegeli at the C. G. Jung-Arbeitsarchiv; the Zentralbibliothek, Zurich; the New York Public Library, with assistance from Eleanor Yadin at the Dorot Reading Room; the library of the Jewish Theological Seminary, New York, NY; the Lillian Goldman Reading

Room at the Leo Baeck Institute, New York, NY, overseen by Renate Evers. Finally, I've spent many hours at the Brandeis Library, Waltham, MA. I owe special thanks to the Judaica Librarian at Brandeis, Jim Rosenbloom, for his patient support and guidance.

Funding for this edition has come from Recollections, LLC: Nancy Furlotti, President, and Erel Shalit, CEO.

I would also like to thank the excellent team at Routledge, especially Susannah Frearson, who shepherded this work through its editorial process and Heather Evans, who, with Susannah, oversaw its production stage. It was also a pleasure to work with Ellie Jarvis at Swales & Willis, under whose supervision Jane Sugarman did the expert copy-editing, and Vanessa Tamplin created both the general and the scriptural index.

ABBREVIATIONS

Abriss	Julius Wellhausen, *Abriss der Geschichte Israels und Juda's* (1884).
Ancient Judaism	Max Weber, *Gesammelte Aufsätze zur Religionssoziologie*. Vol. 3: *Das antike Judentum* (1923). English edn, *Ancient Judaism* (1952).
Apok & Pseudep	Emil Kautzsch, ed., *Apokryphen und Pseudepigraphen des Alten Testaments*; v. 2: *Die Pseudepigraphen des Alten Testaments* (1900).
Bab Tlm	*Babylonian Talmud;* also *The Hebrew–English Edition of the Babylonian Talmud*. London: Soncino Press (1967–88).
Baudissin	Wolf Wilhelm Friedrich von Baudissin, *Kyrios als Gottesname im Judentum und seine Stelle in der Religionsgeschichte* (1929). Four volumes.
Beziehungen	C. G. Jung, *Die Beziehungen zwischen dem Bewusstsein und dem Unbewussten* (1921). (CW 7,2)
Bischoff	Erich Bischoff, *Die Elemente der Kabbalah, Erster Teil: Theoretische Kabbalah* (1913).
B&R	Martin Buber and Franz Rosenzweig. German translations of the Five Books of Moses (Pentateuch), six books of history, and the major and minor prophets (1930/1934).
Charlesworth	James H. Charlesworth, ed., *Old Testament Pseudepigrapha* (1983). Two volumes.
Chassid Büch	Martin Buber, *Die chassidischen Bücher* (1928).
CW	The Collected Works of C. G. Jung. Bollingen Series XX. Princeton, NJ: Princeton University Press (1956–79). Twenty volumes.
EJ	*Eranos-Jahrbuch, -bücher* (annual collections of Eranos lectures). O. Fröbe-Kapteyn, ed. (1933–).

Enc Jud	*Encyclopaedia Judaica (Jüdische Enzyklopädie)*. Ten volumes, A–Lyra (1928–34).
Energetik	C. G. Jung, *Über die Energetik der Seele* (1928).
Geheimnis	C. G. Jung and Richard Wilhelm, *Geheimnis der goldenen Blüte* (1929).
Glatzer	Nahum N. Glatzer, *Untersuchung zur Geschichtslehre der Tannaiten* (1933).
Gnosis	Hans Jonas, *Gnosis und spätantiker Geist: Teil I, Die mythologische Gnosis* (1934).
Integration	C. G. Jung, *The Integration of the Personality* (1939).
IV Ezra	The Fourth Book of Ezra (late first century CE). German edn: Kautzsch, ed., *Apok & Pseudep*, v. 2; English edn: Charlesworth, ed., *Old Testament Pseudepigrapha*, v. 1.
Jacob & Esau	Erich Neumann, "Jakob und Esau" (unpublished typescript, 1934); *Jacob and Esau: On the Collective Symbolism of the Brother Motif*. Erel Shalit, ed., Mark Kyburz, trans. (2015).
Jer Tlm	*Jerusalem Talmud*. In English: *The Talmud of the Land of Israel: A Preliminary Translation and Explanation*. Jacob Neusner, ed. and trans. Chicago, IL: Chicago University Press (1984/1990).
J-K Letters	*The Jung–Kirsch Letters: The Correspondence of C. G. Jung and James Kirsch*. Ann Conrad Lammers, ed. Ursula Egli and Ann Conrad Lammers, trans. (2011/2016).
J-N Corresp	*Analytical Psychology in Exile: The Correspondence of C. G. Jung and Erich Neumann*. Martin Liebscher, ed., Heather McCartney, trans. (2015).
Jonas	Hans Jonas, *Gnosis und spätantiker Geist: Teil I, Die mythologische Gnosis (*1934).
Königtum Gottes	Martin Buber, *Königtum Gottes,* v. 1: *Das Kommende* (1932/1936).
Kyrios	Wolf Wilhelm Friedrich von Baudissin, *Kyrios als Gottesname im Judentum und seine Stelle in der Religionsgeschichte* (1929). Four volumes.
Löwe	Angelica Löwe, *"Auf Seiten der inneren Stimme . . ." Erich Neumann—Leben und Werk (*2014).
Major Trends	Gershom Scholem, *Major Trends in Jewish Mysticism* (English edn 1941; German edn 1957).
New Ethic	Erich Neumann, *Depth Psychology and a New Ethic* (German edn 1949; English edn 1969/1990).
Origins and History	Erich Neumann, *The Origins and History of Consciousness.* (German edn 1949; English edn 1954).
Psych & Rel	C. G. Jung, *Psychology and Religion* (1938) (CW 11,1)

Roots I, II	Erich Neumann, *The Roots of Jewish Consciousness*, Ann Conrad Lammers, ed. Mark Kyburz and Ann Conrad Lammers, trans. (2019). Two volumes.
Seelenprobleme	C. G. Jung, *Seelenprobleme der Gegenwart* (1931).
Sinai & Garizim	M. Bin Gorion, *Sinai und Garizim: Über den Ursprung der israelitischen Religion* (1926).
Soncino	*The Zohar, Soncino Edition*, J. Abelson, ed., H. Sperling and M. Simon, trans. (1933). Five volumes.
Tales I, II	Martin Buber, *Tales of the Hasidim*. Olga Marx, trans. Vol. I: *The Early Masters* (1947). Vol. II: *The Later Masters* (1948).
Tannaiten	Nahum N. Glatzer, *Untersuchungen zur Geschichtslehre der Tannaiten* (1933).
Typen, Types	C. G. Jung, *Psychologische Typen* (1921) [*Psychological Types*]. (CW 6)
Volz	Paul Volz, *Die Eschatologie der jüdischen Gemeinde im neutestamentlichen Zeitalter* (1934).
Wandlungen	C. G. Jung, *Wandlungen und Symbole der Libido: Beiträge zur Entwicklungsgeschichte des Denkens* (1912/1925). Revised and expanded: *Symbols of Transformation*. (CW 5)
Wirklichkeit	C. G. Jung et al., *Wirklichkeit der Seele* (1934).

INTRODUCTION TO VOLUME ONE

About the work

The present two-volume book is Neumann's only full-length work devoted to Jewish psychology and spirituality. Conceived when he fled Nazi Germany in 1933 and written in stages over more than a decade, *The Roots of Jewish Consciousness*[1] reveals the young author's acute intellect and wide range of learning. It also shows his deep affinity with Jewish mysticism, his early commitment to Jung's analytical psychology, and—perhaps most important—his fiercely independent spirit.

While Neumann was training with Jung in 1933–34, he conceived the plan for a major work, in three parts, on the psychological history and present situation of the Jews. He completed the first part, on the problem of revelation in Jewish antiquity, in 1940, and the second part, on the psychological meaning of Hasidism, early in 1945. But he never wrote his third part, on the psychological experience of modern Jews. Instead, for reasons explored below, he put the entire book aside.

Part One launches into an interpretation of biblical texts, using a combination of nineteenth- and early twentieth-century biblical criticism, Buberian hermeneutics, and archetypal symbology. Part Two explores the Jewish mystical tradition of Hasidism, in Kabbalah, and particularly the *Zohar*. Here Neumann leans heavily on writings by Martin Buber, while making far less reference to the many studies of Hasidism by Gershom Scholem that were available at the time of writing.[2]

Although Neumann chose not to publish either of the completed volumes of this work, he never lost interest in them. He kept typescripts of the two parts and occasionally shared them with colleagues. In a paper published in 1980, the Jungian analyst Dr. Gustav Dreifuss describes the impact of reading Neumann's unpublished work in the 1950s, and the important dialogue with Neumann that ensued.[3]

About the author

Erich Neumann (1905–60) was born in Berlin, the third child of a successful grain merchant, and raised in a well-to-do, assimilated Jewish family. He received a first-rate German education at the height of the Weimar Republic, graduating from his *Gymnasium*[4] in 1923 and entering the university of Erlangen. As a student he tended to skip classes and devote himself to Jewish discussion groups,[5] and at nineteen he joined the Berlin Zionist Union. Once at university, he completed his doctorate in six semesters, studying philosophy, psychology, pedagogy, literature, art history, and Semitic studies. In these years he developed a keen interest in Freudian theory and Jung's psychology of the collective unconscious. His dissertation, on Johann Arnold Kanne, a philosopher–poet of the Romantic period, was accepted in March 1927. The following year he married Julie Blumenfeld, whom he had met in Berlin when they were both fifteen.

After university, the young Neumann began to study medicine in Berlin, intending to become a psychoanalyst. He completed his medical degree in 1933 but was prevented by anti-Jewish laws from entering a medical internship. In late summer of 1933, recognizing the disaster that had overtaken the nation, Erich and Julie Neumann, with their one-year-old son, Micha, left Berlin to settle in Palestine/Israel.

FIGURE I.1 Erich and Julie Neumann, Berlin: taken before Micha's birth and their departure for Tel Aviv.

Photograph: © 1931, Tim Gidal. Courtesy of the Erich Neumann Estate.

On the way, they stopped in Switzerland to attend the first Eranos *Tagung*,[6] which took place that August in Ascona, and spent several months in Zurich, where both received analytic training (Löwe, 2014, p. 364). Until February 1934, Julie trained with Toni Wolff; then she and Micha moved to Tel Aviv. Erich stayed behind for a total of eight months, continuing his training with Jung, during which he began to plan the present work. He rejoined his family in Tel Aviv in May of 1934.

Neumann's plan for this book

Erich Neumann produced major works during his lifetime. Some, like *The Origins and History of Consciousness* and *The Great Mother*, have never been out of print. He is also known for significant monographs, including *Depth Psychology and a New Ethic* and *Amor and Psyche*. Another important title, *Jacob and Esau*,[7] written in 1934 but not published until 2015, provides a first glimpse of the young Neumann's interpretation of Jewish biblical themes, seen through the lens of Jung's psychology. In that sense, it is a forerunner of *The Roots of Jewish Consciousness*.

In a letter to Jung dated 5 December 1938, Neumann described the contents of a three-part work, the first two parts of which he had already begun to draft:

> In the first part, I want to present how in Jewish antiquity the principle of direct revelation was valued, and how it stood in productive dialogue with the strong dependence of the people on earth and reality. The Law as a secularization of the traumatic experience of exile, whereby, in the seeming acceptance of theocratic prophetism, the earth-principle asserted itself to the exclusion of direct revelation. Apocalypse, eschatological messianism (primitive Christianity). Gnosticism, as the emergence of the direct inner revelation that had been suppressed into a sideline. This is as far as I have got in the first draft.

Then follows his sketch of Part Two:

> After a short chapter on the repression of direct revelation in the Talmud and the counter-movement in Kabbalah, there follows, as a comprehensive chapter, Hasidism. Religious renaissance of Judaism with the individual as central phenomenon, but in collective constraint, through the enduring acceptance of the Law as a confining cage for direct revelation. (A course on this is already prepared in note form.) Assimilation and emancipation as a necessary de-collectivization of Jewish consciousness. Uprooting and the loss of memory.

This letter suggests that he had already drafted a significant part of the work,[8] for his list of contents, so far, closely resembles the work we have today.

Finally, he shares his plan for the never-completed third part, the projected table of contents for which makes one wish he had gone on to write this part, as well:

> On the problem of the modern Jew. Using dream and fantasy material to illustrate the historic–collective connections. Reemergence of direct revelation, but now in the individual, in direct connection first with individuation and second with the collective problem of revelation in Judaism. Emergence of the earthly dimension as the location of revelation today—the converse of where the problem was located in Jewish antiquity—in a tension of opposites with the "spirit" principle that seems to hinder revelation. That is, while the revelation-principle used to stand opposed to the pagan earth-principle, now it arises positively paired with a strong Near Eastern Gnostic and pagan symbolism, in a strong tension of opposites with the Law.
>
> (J-N Corresp, *pp. 141f; alt. trans from* Briefe J-N, *pp. 189f)*[9]

This book bears witness to the author's resilient spirit. In the shadow of the Hitler era, to write about the psychological and religious roots of Jewish self-awareness was implicitly an act of existential resistance. Nevertheless, Neumann's approach is almost never polemical. Rather, it reflects the close study and integrative thought of a disciplined and often masterful young writer.

Steps in the work's creation

Erich and Julie Neumann had been Zionists since their teens. They had long imagined life in *Eretz Israel* and were mentally prepared to emigrate. Nevertheless, the shock of Hitler's rise and the violence and destruction that quickly followed caused them to experience personal loss, separation from family and community, and cultural disruption in abandoning the country where they had grown up and received their educations. It therefore may be that writing a book about Jewish psychological identity and spiritual heritage was partly a form of self-healing for the author.

Neumann's most significant motivation for the project, however, was his conviction, shared by Jung, that psychological and spiritual renewal was urgently needed by modern Jews. He wrote that he wanted to contribute to a "self-meditation from a new angle" ("Introduction to the work," *Roots I*, p. 9) for individual Jews, whom he saw at risk of spiritual as well as physical annihilation.

In preparing to write, Neumann studied sources in German, including Martin Buber's and Franz Rosenzweig's recently published translations of scripture;[10] Buber's *Die chassidischen Bücher* (English edition: *Tales of the Hasidim*);[11] works on Kabbalah and the *Zohar*, including Bin Gorion's *Sagen der Juden (Jewish legends)*, and a few of Scholem's writings.[12] He studied all the works of Jung that had been published up to that point, and those of contemporary Jungians. He read sources in Hebrew, including Samuel Horodezky's works on the great Hasidic teachers.[13] He also lectured and gave seminars on this material.

Starting in early 1935, Neumann drafted several versions of Part One, to which he gave the title, "Beiträge zur Tiefenpsychologie des jüdischen Menschen und zum Problem der Offenbarung" ("On the depth psychology of the Jewish person and the problem of revelation"). His final revision of this part was written between December 1938 and May 1940. Meanwhile, in mid-1935, he began to draft Part Two, which he called "Der Chassidismus und seine psychologische Bedeutung für das Judentum" ("Hasidism and its psychological meaning for Judaism"). The final draft of this part appears to have been written between May 1940 and the spring of 1945.[14] Although we do not have his planned Part Three, his lecture of April 1940, "Die religiöse Erfahrung in der Tiefenanalyse" ("Religious experience in depth analysis"),[15] and his four-lecture series of 1942–43,[16] provide glimpses of what he intended for that final part.

On 5 December 1938, he writes to Jung that he is finally about to revise the Jewish work that he had conceived in 1933. Two events seem to have moved him to pick up his early drafts at this time and revise them for publication. The violence in Germany had escalated, which affected Neumann both personally and at the collective level. On 25 March 1937, Neumann's father had died after a Gestapo interrogation. And the pogrom of *Kristallnacht*, on 9–10 November 1938, launched a new, overt phase of anti-Semitic violence. Neumann's statement to Jung suggests that this confluence of events was part of what drove him back to his Jewish work:

> Alongside this, against this, and to some extent also because of this, I am now trying to write the work that I took on while I was with you in 1933–34, and that I have been working on ever since.
>
> (J-N Corresp, p. 140; alt. trans. from Briefe J-N, p. 189)[17]

Eighteen months later, Neumann writes that Part One is essentially finished. He is about to send Jung a lecture that belongs to the third part.[18] And he is now writing Part Two, on Hasidism:

> The lecture belongs to some extent in the third section of my book, *On the Depth Psychology of the Modern Jew*, whose second section, 'The Psychological Meaning of Hasidism', I am now writing, and whose first section, 'The Problem of Revelation in Jewish Antiquity', happily now only needs, in part—after the umpteenth reworking—to be typed up.
>
> (Ibid., p. 156, alt. trans. from Briefe J-N, p. 203)

His revision of Part Two occupied him for the remainder of the war (ibid., pp. 159f). Based on a key statement in his letter to Jung on 1 October 1945, he probably completed his work on Hasidism just as the war ended in Europe:

> But then . . . the Jewish problem and my work on it ended for me precisely at a time when it became conspicuous in the world in an indescribably ghastly way.[19]
>
> (Ibid., p. 160, alt. trans. from Briefe J-N, p. 206)

I am struck by two words in this sentence: *genau* ("precisely") and *augenfällig* (conspicuous; literally "falling on the eyes").[20] While Neumann wrote his work on Hasidism, the plight of the European Jews was growing steadily more appalling. Finally, the true situation became clearly visible—*augenfällig*—to the whole world. I interpret Neumann's statement to mean that he finished his work on "the Jewish problem" just as the German death camps were liberated and their photographic evidence published.

The book's themes

In Neumann's introduction, he uses grand strokes to describe world history and the history of ideas. He begins with psychological anthropology, reviewing the history of ideas since the Enlightenment and the French Revolution, and showing how scientific advances have led to a shift in human consciousness. On the basis of evidence from myths, rituals, symbols, and evolutionary science, he argues that the concept of humanity has become universal, embracing every period of history and every cultural, religious and national group.

Once having established the universal category, "human," he proceeds to differentiate. He does so by drawing on the neo-Kantian epistemology that was Jung's philosophical starting point: "The past 150 years have taught . . . that any standpoint is relative, and that knowledge is contingent upon the personal equation of each group" ("Introduction to the work," *Roots I*, p. 3). He is then ready to introduce his primary topic, the inner and outer problems facing modern Judaism:

> Historically, we have reached a stage that represents a reversal of what happened when the Second Temple was destroyed. At the time, there was a saying: the Jewish people may suffer, but Judaism must survive. Now the opposite saying is true: Judaism may suffer, but the Jewish people, the Jewish person, must live and survive. . . . Today it is not about Judaism, but about the individual Jew.
>
> *(Ibid., p. 6)*

For Neumann, Jewish survival must be understood in psychological and spiritual terms, as much as physical. It entails an individual reconnection with the inner world of the divine—a fundamental reality that he says was understood by the ancient Jews but was largely lost during the Babylonian Exile and the Second Temple period. So he writes, "The problem of inner experience is a central problem of the modern Jew and of Jews in general" (*Roots I*, p. 7). "Inner experience" means, for Neumann, the capacity to encounter the sacred directly, to receive revelation as an individual, and thus to regain the capacity for charismatic prophecy.[21]

Part Two is devoted to the psychological and spiritual symbology of Hasidic tradition. In addition to occasionally citing Scholem and Horodezky, Neumann quotes at length from Buber's *Tales of the Hasidim* and *Des Baal-Schem-Tow*

Unterweisung im Umgang mit Gott (*Teaching of the Baal Shem Tov in conversation with God*). He uses tools derived from Jung's psychology to present Hasidism as the healing compensation for the legalism and anti-feminine bias that he sees dominating collective Judaism since the Babylonian Exile. Modern Jews, he suggests, may rediscover their psychological wholeness by reconnecting with the archetypal power in Hasidic teachings, Talmudic texts, Kabbalah, and in particular the *Zohar*.

Neumann shows a strong preference for individual, charismatic revelation, with a corresponding denigration of rabbinism and priestly legalistic "prophetism." This Romantic view, privileging prophecy over priesthood, is a perspective he shares with both Buber and Jung. In the first chapter of his Part One, we read:

> This failure of the people as a collective must be compensated for by prophecy, as represented by Moses. Contrary to the later Levitical and priestly Aaronite–Zadokite tendencies, prophecy remains connected with the people and the collective. Indeed, it represents the potential of each member of the people to receive the gift of prophecy, i.e., to enter into immediate, direct contact with YHWH.
>
> *(Roots I, p. 33)*

The decision not to publish

Neumann's decision not to publish his major work on Judaism, which originally mattered so much to him, was made in stages. He seems to have had different sets of reasons for withholding Part One and Part Two. When he completed Part One, in May 1940, he still intended to publish it. But during the next few years, he apparently decided that this first part was unpublishable. On 1 October 1945, he wrote to Jung:

> After I had completed a rather large work on Jewish antiquity—On the Psychological History of the Jewish Person—(it is now out of date and only useable as source material), I wrote a book on the psychological meaning of Hasidism for the modern Jew, by which I still stand.
>
> *(J-N Corresp, p. 160; alt. trans. from Briefe J-N, p. 206)*

What made him call Part One out of date? A partial answer, offered by Angelica Löwe, is based on well-founded factual observations. but her analysis is overlaid, regrettably, by an interpretation that is unnecessarily reductive, damning toward Jung, and not well supported. Based on passages in the Jung–Neumann correspondence, particularly of December 1938, she argues (Löwe, 2014, pp. 146ff, 370ff) that the intellectual ground shifted under Neumann's feet when Jung abandoned his early teaching about the racial and ethnic collective unconscious. This teaching had provided Neumann with part of the theoretical scaffolding for his Part One. But now, because it was no longer supported by Jung, the foundation of Part One was shaken. Even more upsetting, Löwe believes, was that, in the wake of Neumann's father's death and *Kristallnacht*, Jung, whom Neumann had once honored as his righteous teacher, his *tzaddik*,[22] suddenly became aloof and inaccessible.

There are good grounds for saying that, by abandoning his long-held theory of ethnic differentiation in the collective unconscious, Jung had inadvertently undermined the theoretical structure of Neumann's writing. Jung's change of mind on this point—Löwe calls it his "self-correction"—forced Neumann to reevaluate the idea of a Jewish collective unconscious. But Löwe makes a mistake when she implies that, in changing course so fundamentally, the teacher betrayed his disciple. She seems to miss the fact that, with independent reflection, Neumann, too, revised his thinking about the collective unconscious.

Jung wrote in 1938 that, in the light of current events, the collective unconscious of Jews must be viewed as essentially the same as that of other groups:

> To be sure, there are specific Jewish traits in this development; but it is also a general one, which is happening equally for Christians. It is a question of a general and identical revolution of minds. The specifically Christian or Jewish traits have only secondary meaning. . . . The whole problem in itself is of paramount importance for humanity; for that reason, individual and racial differences play an insignificant part.
>
> (J-N Corresp, *p. 146, alt. trans. from* Briefe J-N, *p. 193*)

Neumann wrestled for a year with the inconvenient implications of this theoretical revision. Then he admitted that his own conclusions were consistent with Jung's. In November 1939 he wrote:

> In the meantime, I have also recognized that Jewish symbolism . . . is consistent with that of European people, that here something secular is taking place. Of course, I knew this before, but the problem of the singularity of the Jews would have been so much simpler if a specific symbolism could have been demonstrated.
>
> (Ibid., *p. 196*)

Neumann accordingly revised his Part One, "On the Depth Psychology of the Jewish Person," to reflect the universality of the collective unconscious. But now he faced a deeper, more personal dilemma. His letter continues:

> I have got rid of all that and stand without preconceptions before something that is incomprehensible to me. . . . My slogan—it is no longer about Judaism but about the Jewish person, about the individual as revelation-center and realization-center of the Self—seems to require and to signify, along with the abolition of the old Judaism, something like a new Jewish beginning. And how should I believe in that, why must I believe in it?
>
> (J-N Corresp, *p. 149; alt. trans. from* Briefe J-N, *pp. 196f*)

This internal dilemma surely set Neumann's project back. Löwe is mistaken, however, to argue that he therefore abandoned the work. In 1939, when the outbreak of war kept him from sending Part One to Jung, he launched into Part Two. Six months later, he offered to send Jung the first part, said he was busy with the second, and enclosed a lecture belonging to the third.

Then their correspondence underwent a five-year break. This silence, Löwe argues, reinforced Jung's emotional distance and undermined Neumann's self-confidence so deeply that he lost all faith in his Jewish work.[23] Löwe's view of Neumann's inner struggle may be right, but she applies her insight too broadly, glossing over the reality of Neumann's inner resilience and discounting other factors whose influence on his decisions can be documented. Neumann may indeed have felt abandoned by Jung for a time, but this disappointment did not stop him from writing. Between 1940 and 1945, he completed his work on Hasidism. When he wrote to Jung in October 1945, he declared himself satisfied with it.

Löwe further implies that anti-Semitic feeling was an underlying motive for Jung's badly timed emotional distance from his young follower.[24] Given Neumann's circumstances in 1938, such a withdrawal was shockingly cold, but it may have revealed a detachment that belonged, in a general way, to Jung's personal psychology. As various members of his family attest,[25] he tended to respond to others' dependence and neediness, even with friends and family, not by showing greater warmth but with cautious silence.[26]

It was typical of Neumann's intellectual agility that, once he had accepted the universality of the collective unconscious, he immediately found a place to apply the concept in his writing. During the war years, when he and Jung were out of touch, he wrote most of *Depth Psychology and a New Ethic*.[27] In this context he deliberately built upon Jung's revised theory of the collective unconscious. For instance, in his first passage about "recollectivization," he states: "We are only just beginning to understand that this identity of human nature at the deepest level has to do with the collective unconscious" (*New Ethic*, pp. 71f). He then goes on to define the collective unconscious as "the precipitate of all identical and original reactions of the species *homo sapiens*" (ibid., p. 72). Likewise, when he revised Part One of the present work, he wove a universalist definition of the collective unconscious into his introduction:

> C.G. Jung's discovery of the collective unconscious provides the *unifying aspect* under which all these detailed researches have become essential components of the history of humanity and of the individual.
> ("*Introduction to the work,*" Roots I, p. 3, emphasis added)

Neumann's appropriation of Jung's psychology

In addition to being faithful to Jung's theory of the collective unconscious in its changing interpretations, Neumann shares Jung's leaning toward the subjectivism of the Romantics. Like Jung, he emphasizes the individual quality of spirituality and the profoundly ambiguous nature of all religious experience. Neumann also frequently refers to central Jungian concepts in the symbolic and archetypal realm, including the Self, the anima, and the shadow.

In this regard, a point that Neumann and Jung share is the complexity of the Self. For Jung, the inner God-image has a shadow. The numinous (the holy) is by its nature a source of fear; thus any direct encounter with the God-image can be terrifying. In Part One of *The Roots of Jewish Consciousness*, Neumann cites Jung's writing on *deus absconditus*, the unknown and unknowable God, who appears to the soul in strange and fearful forms.[28]

When writing this work, he had not yet encountered Jung's piercing saying, "God has a terrible double aspect."[29] Neumann's and Jung's perspectives regarding the divine paradox overlap here, but Neumann's insight does not depend on Jung's in that regard. The unity of good and evil in God is a recurring theme in Hebrew scripture and Jewish tradition. The biblical *locus classicus* for this insight is Isaiah 45:7, a passage that Jung also knew and quoted: "I form the light, and create darkness; I make peace, and create evil; I am the LORD, that does all these things." For Neumann, God's terrifying side is vividly reflected in the story of the Israelites at Mount Sinai, a central theme in his first chapter.

Neumann carries this paradoxical perspective into his discussion of the unitive Hasidic vision of good and evil, a theme on which he touches in the fifth chapter of *New Ethic*, and develops more fully in Volume Two of the present work. This theme, fraught with contradiction and made even more complex by historical associations, will be explored in the editor's introduction to Volume Two.

Another concept of Jung's, the teleological quality of the unconscious, was important to Neumann. In Jung's 1937 Terry Lectures, delivered originally in English (*Psychology and Religion*, 1938), the first lecture is titled, "The Autonomy of the Unconscious Mind." A phrase in Neumann's text, *Tendenzen des Unbewussten* (tendencies of the unconscious),[30] echoes Jung's theory that the unconscious drives toward its own goals. Like Jung, Neumann warns that the unconscious, as a force of nature, is neither good nor bad. Thus its "goals" are not necessarily positive from the ego's point of view.

Neumann highly respects the ethical role of the conscious ego, and emphasizes that the moral canon must be protected by a stable ego-consciousness against the unbridled power of the unconscious. The unconscious may achieve a sublimely positive purpose, as for example in "the appearance of the transcendent function, that is, the revelation of YHWH" (*Roots I*, p. 50). But this also implies, for Neumann, that ego-consciousness has a responsibility to discern the tendency of the unconscious and to respond to it with conscious moral judgment.[31]

Themes particular to Neumann

The centrality of Neumann's concept of ego-consciousness becomes clear in his exchange with Jung over precisely this issue, where both must confront the fact that ego-consciousness carries greater moral weight for Neumann than for Jung. In 1949, at Neumann's request, Jung had written a foreword for the expected English edition of *Depth Psychology and a New Ethic*.[32] In sending his foreword to Neumann, however, he set a condition: Neumann might publish it, but only if he made "a few more changes to the current text" (ibid., p. 246, alt. trans.).

Jung's "few changes" were contained in several pages of typewritten comments, affecting fifty passages in Neumann's book.[33] Neumann adopted about two-thirds of Jung's comments without protest. Those that he declined to change, in almost every instance, concerned the autonomy and moral responsibility of the conscious ego, even in the face of evil. On this subject, Jung and Neumann carried on a vigorous debate in their letters.

Jung's perspective was summed up in a general admonition:

> I do not wish to discourage activity, but only to emphasize that the shadow or the unconscious absolutely cannot be eliminated from the world and made subject to consciousness. We can only learn how a grain of corn must behave between hammer and anvil.
>
> *(J-N Corresp, p. 361, alt. trans.)*

Neumann promptly protested: "The ethical behavior of the personality cannot *only* experience itself as the grain of corn between hammer and anvil" (ibid., p. 254). Soon thereafter, in his 1950 appendix on the shadow, Neumann invoked Jung's writings on alchemy to support his own position:

> As Jung has shown, the real, secret, heretical aim of alchemy is not simply to "endure" the shadow and accept him in a passive way, but actively to seek him out and to redeem him in the *opus magnum*.
>
> *(New Ethic, p. 145)*

The theme of ego-stability is repeatedly sounded in *The Roots of Jewish Consciousness*, where it is a stepping-stone to Neumann's signature contribution, the "ego–Self axis."[34] In this book he begins to explore that breakthrough concept within a biblical and Jewish frame of reference.[35] Volume One examines the concept under the category of "YHWH–earth tension," i.e., the challenging but essential relationship between the infinite and the finite. Volume Two approaches the ego–Self axis more directly, both in the context of spiritual maturation (*Roots II*, p. 106; pp. 151ff), and in describing the "Copernican revolution" of individuation (ibid., pp. 136f), where the Self displaces the ego-complex, yet is united with it. And now, Neumann writes, joining the language of Jewish mysticism to that of depth psychology, the ego-complex may offer itself to the Self:

> This offering of the "I" differs not only from the ego's identification with the Self in the ancient mysteries, but also from its dissolving in a state of ecstasy. The essence of this offering is that ego and Self, I and God, are joined, thereby removing the wall that separates the system of consciousness from the one outside this working center.
>
> *(Ibid., p. 137)*

Neumann's use of Buber's writings

Alongside Neumann's deep commitment to a psychological form of Zionism and his wish to master Hebrew,[36] his deep and lifelong German acculturation formed his cultural–linguistic frame of reference. He could read and translate Hebrew, but he always wrote in German. Consistent with this cultural orientation, it would seem that a large part of his education in Jewish mystical tradition came from Martin Buber's influential works on the subject.[37]

Neumann was not an intellectual clone of Buber, however. When he discusses the hypothetical influence of the biblical "redactor," borrowing the term from Buber and Rosenzweig and their contemporaries, he employs the concept in a way Buber would not have done.[38] Neumann is prepared to bracket out great quantities of the canonical text, viewing them as later priestly redactions (*Roots I*, pp. 32ff) to be removed, in the same way as "repaintings" are removed from an artwork to recover the artist's original intention.

From 1938 on, Martin Buber lived and taught in Jerusalem, only an hour's drive from Neumann in Tel Aviv, yet there is no evidence of their ever meeting in person.[39] A limited correspondence is documented, however. On 13 November 1935, Buber sent Neumann a letter expressing judicious criticism[40] of the latter's unpublished Kafka commentaries, which Neumann had sent him for comment. He wrote that he was willing to talk further with Neumann about his valuable work, but there is no record of further correspondence between them.

Be that as it may, from beginning to end of *The Roots of Jewish Consciousness*, we see that Neumann's reading of Jewish tradition is profoundly influenced by Buber. He mentions Buber's early classic, *Ich und Du* (*I and Thou*) only occasionally, but Buber's theme of the dyadic relationship is like background music in Neumann's discussions of biblical and mystical theology.

Other scholars of Jewish mystical tradition, including Samuel Horodezky and Gershom Scholem, play a lesser role for Neumann in this book. Horodezky, a generation older than Buber, is represented through references to his encyclopedia articles on the Baal Shem-Tov and Lilith. Two of his books in Hebrew, one on Dov Baer, the Great Maggid, and the other on Rabbi Nachman,[41] are also frequently quoted, in German translations that may have been written by Neumann himself.

When it comes to Scholem's writings, a more complicated story needs to be told. Buber and Scholem, two eminent teachers of Jewish mystical tradition, both German educated, both Zionists, were separated by a generation and occupied distinct scholarly territories. Whereas Buber found the core of Jewish mysticism in the lives and legends of the great Hasidic teachers, Scholem and his students explored the theoretical and historical character of Hasidism "by using classical tools of textual analysis, by relating ideas to their background, and above all by attempting to locate Hasidism within the larger scheme of Jewish mystical and messianic trends" (Idel 1995, p. 2).[42] A major theoretical debate broke out between Scholem and Buber in the 1960s,[43] since when, according to Moshe Idel, "the Scholemian approach has been accepted as the standard method by modern scholars" (ibid., p. 3). The decades that concern us here, however, are the 1940s and 1950s, the last twenty years of Neumann's life, when the public relationship between Buber and Scholem was generally positive, even if their diverging philosophical orientations were already discernible.

In the first edition of *Major Trends of Jewish Mysticism* (1941), Scholem named Buber as the first among the twentieth century's "thoughtful and scholarly writers on the subject" of Hasidism (*Major Trends*, p. 325). His own focus, however, was on philological, historical, and theoretical aspects; he cared less about the Hasidic legends and personalities that were Buber's stock in trade.[44] It also may be telling that, up to the end of the 1920s, Scholem's study of Jewish religious tradition included many works written in German,[45] but after settling in *Eretz Israel,* he published the major part of his work in Hebrew.[46] In contrast, Buber continued to write and publish for a German-speaking audience.

As a beginning writer, Neumann's relationship with Scholem and his work seems to have been ambivalent, perhaps partly for linguistic reasons. He clearly respected Scholem's stature as a scholar; but in the two volumes of *Roots*—aside from his frequent references to Scholem's 1932 article on Kabbalah in the *Encyclopedia Judaica*, and his essay on Jewish mysticism in the 1936 *Schocken Almanach* (both in German)—Neumann barely refers to Scholem's huge number of relevant publications already available at the time of writing.

We have only slight evidence of Neumann's contacts with Scholem before the war, but they may have met once. Citing correspondence between Scholem and Gustav Dreifuss, Angelica Löwe notes that Neumann approached Scholem in 1934, soon after reaching Tel Aviv, and tried unsuccessfully to persuade him to apply Jung's archetypal theory to his interpretation of the Kabbalah (Löwe, 2014, p. 130, n. 21). After the war, from 1949 until 1960, they met repeatedly at Eranos,[47] where both lectured regularly, so each was exposed to the other's developing thought.

Neumann's daughter, Rali Neumann-Loewenthal, recalls that Gershom Scholem was critical toward scholars who relied on German, rather than Hebrew, for their sources. She also recalls that his distrust of Jung partly reflected a general distrust of psychology. She remembers no meetings in Israel between Scholem and her father, but only their yearly encounters at Eranos.[48] No firm evidence has come to light that Neumann showed Scholem the present work, nor that Scholem counseled him against publishing it. Still, it seems clear that, if Scholem had expressed an opinion about these two volumes, he might have voiced misgivings about both Buber and Jung. Neumann himself could not have failed to notice that Scholem's writings on Hasidism went in a different direction from Buber's and, consequently, his own. In his independence of spirit, Neumann would not have bowed automatically to the opinion of a colleague, but as time went by, he may have internalized aspects of these implicit critiques.

Neumann's conversation with Dreifuss

In about 1950, Neumann lent the typescripts of his unpublished work to Gustav Dreifuss, an analysand and friend. According to the first-person account that Dreifuss later published, in 1959 he tried to persuade Neumann to publish the book. This passage from Dreifuss's long paper is worth review, because it provides our only documentation of Neumann's mature assessment of this work. In brief, Neumann said that publication was forbidden by "his 'scholarly conscience'."[49]

To publish, Neumann explained, he would first have to be "completely certain of the Jewish sources," and he believed that such certainty:

> . . . would require not only a complete mastery of the language of the origi-
> nal text, but also a greater closeness to the form of life of the Jewish ancestors
> than was possible for him, since he had grown up in the German cultural
> milieu. He lacked the strength and freedom to immerse himself for years in
> the Jewish material and the Hebrew language.

By Dreifuss's account, Neumann described Buber's contribution in critical terms:

> [I]n these manuscripts he had relied primarily on Buber, specifically on
> Buber's interpretation of Hasidic material. It now seemed to him, however,
> that this material was inadequate; for Buber had very much shaped his selec-
> tion and translations to fit the general heritage of European thought.

Then, humbly admitting his own limitations, Neumann concluded by stating that "an understanding of the archetypal images in Judaism must grow from a full knowledge of its authentic writings and the history of Jewish people—a knowl-edge that he just did not possess."[50]

Although he respects Neumann's reasoning, Dreifuss offers a contrary argu-ment. Depth psychology and Hasidism, he writes, are such highly developed and specialized fields that almost no one can claim mastery in both. Neumann's interdisciplinary study is extraordinary, Dreifuss says, in its rich, psychologi-cal interpretation of archetypal Jewish images. And when one remembers the outer circumstances of its writing, during a time of immense collective stress and upheaval, one sees even more clearly the author's exceptional creativity.

The decision to publish

Writing nearly forty years after Dreifuss, I will employ the liberty of the editor and go further than he did. I will say, first, that Neumann himself held conflicting opinions of this major work of his youth. He did not publish it. but he preserved it in several versions and duplicate typescripts, including a hand-bound lending copy.[51] I would point out that the voice we hear in these pages is neither Buber's nor Scholem's, but Neumann's. It is the voice of a passionate and brilliant young writer, who dares to embrace and interpret the entire history of his people, invoking the prophetic spirit of Moses in confrontation with the Divine Presence on Sinai. This is Neumann's own voice, and we are privileged to hear it.

Neumann's great psychological works have become justly famous in the decades since he laid this early work aside. But all this time, there was a gap in the record, for *The Roots of Jewish Consciousness* is the only full-length writing of his that can properly be called his Jewish work. Now that it has been released for publication, thanks to the wisdom and dedication of Erel Shalit and Nancy Furlotti and the generous permission of Micha Neumann and Rali Neumann-Loewenthal, that gap can be filled.

If I may be allowed a personal comment, I occupy a position outside of, but also—by personal inclination, ongoing study, and several important relationships—increasingly connected with aspects of Jewish tradition. In the process of preparing the present project for publication, I have been and remain only a journeyman student, constantly learning. But from what I know, I believe this book will be an enormous gift to Neumann's present-day audience, including Jungians, anyone interested in mythology and comparative religion, and especially, but not only, modern Jewish readers.

Thus, we are daring to publish a work that Neumann valued but about which he expressed misgivings. Knowing the scope of his misgivings, readers will be able to make their own judgment. We are releasing this work in the midst of a historical era that in some ways bears little resemblance to Neumann's, yet one with alarmingly similar political and psychological shadows. Individuals and communities today have no less need than those in Neumann's time to rediscover their heritage of symbolic understanding, psychological maturity, the feminine values of relationship, and a conscious connection with the holy.

Ann Conrad Lammers
June 2018

Notes

1 The title of the present two-volume work, *The Roots of Jewish Consciousness* (hereafter: *Roots I, II*), emerged for me early in the editorial process and gained approval from Erel Shalit, Nancy Furlotti, Mark Kyburz, and Tamar Kron in January 2016. Neumann's own suggested titles for the book included, at various times, the following: "Ursprungsgeschichte des jüdischen Bewusstseins" ("The origins and history of Jewish consciousness"); "Zur Wiederentdeckung des Judentums" ("The rediscovery of Judaism"); "Zur Tiefenpsychologie des modernen Juden" ("The depth psychology of the modern Jew"); and "Zur Seelengeschichte des jüdischen Menschen" ("The psychological history of the Jewish person"). We chose *The Roots of Jewish Consciousness* because it echoes, without repeating verbatim, Neumann's word *Ursprungsgeschichte* (origins and history). That word—or phrase, in English—is now firmly associated with his title, *Ursprungsgeschichte des Bewusstseins* (*Origins and History of Consciousness*) (1949) (hereafter: *Origins and History*), which properly stands as an independent volume.

2 When Neumann was writing *Hasidism*, numerous related writings by Scholem were published and available, as shown in the *Bibliography of the Writings of Gershom G. Scholem* (1977), pp. 7–25. Most of these were in Hebrew, making them less accessible to Neumann.

Scholem's groundbreaking work, *Major Trends in Jewish Mysticism* (English edn, 1941; German edn, 1957), came out after Neumann finished most of his research for this work. It is barely acknowledged in *The Roots of Jewish Consciousness*, but it is cited in Neumann's lectures of the early 1940s (cf. Appendix B, *Roots II*, p. 247, n. 21; p. 269, n. 17).

3 Gustav Dreifuss, "Erich Neumanns jüdisches Bewusstsein" (Erich Neumann's Jewish consciousness), *Kreativität des Unbewussten* (*Creativity of the unconscious*). *Analytische Psychologie*, Vol. 11, 1980 (in honor of Neumann's 75th birthday).

4 German: academic preparatory school.

5 For many details of Neumann's life, I am grateful to Angelica Löwe's (2014) biography of Erich Neumann, "*Auf Seiten der inneren Stimme . . .*": *Erich Neumann—Leben und Werk* ("*On the side of the inner voice . . .*": *Erich Neumann, life and work*) (hereafter: Löwe). Cf. especially significant dates in Neumann's life, pp. 353ff.

6 Eranos, an annual symposium held in Ascona, Switzerland, from 1933 on, involves scholars and clinicians from many parts of the world, who attend by invitation and lecture on topics related to Jung's archetypal psychology. Even during World War II, these sessions (*Tagungen*) continued. Neumann returned to Eranos in 1947. He lectured there in 1948 and every year until his death in 1960.

7 Erich Neumann, *Jacob and Esau: On the Collective Symbolism of the Brother Motif* (hereafter: *Jacob & Esau*), Erel Shalit, ed., Mark Kyburz, trans., 2015. Neumann wrote most of this essay in 1934 (ibid., pp. xix *et passim*).

8 Typescripts of Neumann's early drafts of Parts One and Two still exist among his unpublished papers.

9 C. G. Jung and Erich Neumann, *Analytical Psychology in Exile: The Correspondence of C. G. Jung & Erich Neumann* (hereafter: *J-N Corresp*), M. Liebscher, ed., H. McCartney, trans., 2015. As the McCartney translation sometimes lacks accuracy, alternate translations, as noted, are based on the Patmos edition: *C. G. Jung und Erich Neumann: Die Briefe, 1933–1959: Analytische Psychologie im Exil* (hereafter: *Briefe J-N*), M. Liebscher, ed., 2015.

10 With few exceptions, Neumann quotes the Buber and Rosenzweig translations of the Pentateuch, the historical books, and the Prophets (hereafter: B&R). Rosenzweig, who died in December 1929, collaborated with Buber on the Pentateuch and five other books, through Isaiah. Buber alone then translated Jeremiah. (He finished translating the Scripture in 1962.) With few exceptions, Neumann quotes the B&R version of the first three portions of *Tanakh*, newly available at the time of writing. These volumes included the 11-volume 1929 Lambert Schneider edition, the textually identical 1931 Schocken edition, a 20-volume Schocken set which followed, and a 3-volume set, comprising the same 20 books, published by Schocken in 1934.

11 As far as possible, excerpts from Buber's *Die chassidischen Bücher* are rendered in the translations of Olga Marx, in her two-volume *Tales of the Hasidim* (Schocken, 1947, 1948, 1991) (hereafter: *Tales I, II*).

12 In *Hasidism*, Neumann cites some of Scholem's early writings in German, including his major article "Kabbala" in the *Enc Jud* (1932), an essay, "Die Geheimnisse der Schöpfung: Ein Kapitel aus dem Sohar" ("The Mysteries of Creation: A Chapter from the Zohar") (1935), and "Zum Verständnis des Sabbatianismus: Zugleich ein Beitrag zur Geschichte der Aufklärung" ("Understanding Sabbatianism: Also on the History of the Enlightenment"), *Almanach des Schocken Verlags 5697* (1936).

13 Two books by Samuel Horodezky, available to Neumann only in Hebrew, are cited in his footnotes as "The Great Maggid" and "Rabbi Nachman of Bretzlav." Passages from these works, in German translations by Neumann (perhaps with help from colleagues), appear in Volume Two, *Hasidism*. Neumann also quotes Horodezky's doctoral dissertation, *Mystisch-religiöse Strömungen unter den Juden in Polen im 16.–18. Jahrhundert* (*Mystical and religious trends among the Jews of Poland in the 16th to 18th centuries*).

14 My timeline of the work's composition differs from that of Löwe and Liebscher, both of whom state that Neumann wrote the work between 1934 and 1940 (Löwe, 2014, pp. 153, 386 *et passim*; *J-N Corresp*, pp. xxxv *et passim*).

15 Neumann, "Religious Experience in Depth Analysis" (lecture, April 1940). Cf. introductory comment, Appendix B.IV, *Roots II*, p. 256.

16 Neumann, "The Importance of Consciousness in the Experience of Depth Psychology" (four-lecture series, 1942–43), published here as Appendix B, *Roots II*, pp. 190–274.

17 In the McCartney translation, Neumann refers to "the work I planned with you" (*J-N Corresp*, p. 140), which invites misreading. Neumann's phrase is "die Arbeit, die ich mir bei Ihnen . . . vorgenommen habe" (*Briefe J-N*, p. 189). That is, during his time with Jung, Neumann himself resolved to undertake this work.

18 This lecture, "Religious Experience in Depth Analysis," was later incorporated into an expanded, revised version, "The Religious Meaning of the Path of Depth Psychology."

19 "Dann aber, ... war für mich das jüdische Problem und die Arbeit an ihm gerade in einer Zeit beendet, in der es in der Welt in unbeschreiblich grauenhafter Art augenfällig wurde" (*Briefe J-N*, p. 206).

20 In the English-language edition of the correspondence, *augenfällig* is rendered "palpable," a rough equivalent, omitting Neumann's reference to the sense of sight.

21 The publication of the present work coincides with a current Jewish resurgence, in some quarters, of vivid interest in charismatic prophecy. Dr. Zvi Leshem kindly directed me to a collection of passages on this topic, published in 1990 by Bezazel Naor. The following comment, cited by Naor, describes a modern source, but it applies equally well to Neumann's position in *Roots*: "The author treats prophecy, not as a concrete corpus of literature, but rather as a general phenomenon. Prophecy is viewed as typical and central in Judaism. The Holy Scriptures are viewed almost as an expression of a spirit which pervades all paths of Judaism, rather than a one-time happening . . . . Bible, Halakha, Kabbala, Hassidism, even (granting several reservations) Medieval Philosophy, all merge into one: Prophecy" (Naor, 1990, p. 34; citing A. Lichtenstein, *Shivhey Qol ha-Nevuah*, p. 42, commenting on D. Cohen, *Qol ha-Nevuah/ The Voice of Prophecy*, Jerusalem, 5739/1979).

22 Hebrew: lit., righteous one. [As with many words in Hebrew, transliterations may vary: *tzaddik*, *tsaddik*, *Zaddik*, etc.] On 19 July 1934 Neumann had written to Jung that he found in him what Jewish tradition calls a "*tzaddik* of the nations": "Before I came to you, I was rather sad that I was not able to go to a Jewish authority, because I wanted to go to a 'teacher'. . . . According to Jewish tradition, there are *Zaddikim* of the nations . . ." (*J-N Corresp*, pp. 35f).

23 Löwe's argument, that Neumann abandoned his Jewish work on account of Jung's betrayal, is based on a psychodynamic reading of their letters of 1938, together with an interpretation of Neumann's early writings (Löwe, 2014, pp. 146ff). She makes the same argument in her 2007 lecture, "Neumann, Jung, and the Jungians," which she includes in her book as an appendix (ibid., pp. 361–72). Her lecture ends with a pair of sentences implying causality and imputing blame: "Jung konnte Neumanns Dialogangebot nicht erwidern. Neumann stellte das Projekt, an dem er seit seiner Ankunft in Israel gearbeitet hatte, ein" ("Jung could not respond to Neumann's offer of dialogue. Neumann put away the project on which he had worked since his arrival in Israel") (ibid., p. 372).

24 This implication is clear in Löwe's comparison of Jung and Buber (ibid., pp. 100f), and her allusion to Jung's "pejorative-distorting external attributions and anti-Semitic stereotyping" (ibid., p. 116).

25 Franz Jung, interview, 16 August 1991; Andreas Jung, personal communication, 26 April 2016. Cf. also Lammers, 2012, p. 23 and p. 31n5.

26 James Kirsch was upset by Jung's distancing reaction when he and his family were fleeing Germany in 1933. Later he wrote to Jung of his distress and asked him to justify his behavior. Jung replied that he had offered only limited support because he had felt that Kirsch needed to rely on his own libido when making such a momentous move (Jung, 20 February 1934, *J-K Letters*, p. 39). The next year, Jung apologized for another long delay in writing to Kirsch, who was then in the process of divorcing his wife and moving to England: "It's atrocious how I neglect you, but the things I perceived via your wife were so wide-ranging and made everything about your future seem so uncertain to me

that I instinctively shrank from them. Somehow I wanted to be 'not involved'" (Jung, 17 February 1935, *J-K Letters*, p. 67).

27 In a footnote to his first edition of *New Ethic*, Neumann notes that he completed most of the book in 1943 (*Neue Ethik*, 1949, p. l22n; *New Ethic*, 1990, p. 130n). In his letter to Jung on 9 April 1949, he calls that book a "by-product" and "a chapter from a bigger conceptual framework" (*J-N Corresp*, p. 254). By "a bigger conceptual framework," he can only have meant the present work.

28 Cf. *Roots I*, p. 38, n. 86. Neumann cites Jung's 1933 article on Bruder Klaus (Saint Niklaus von Flüe) ["Bruder Klaus," *Neue Schweizer Rundschau*, August 1933, pp. 223–9]. A passage in Jung's article reads, in Hull's translation: "There are many indubitable lunatics who have experiences of God, and here too I do not contest the genuineness of the experience, for I know that it takes a complete and a brave man to stand up to it. Therefore I feel sorry for those who go under. . ." (CW 11, ¶482).

29 When Neumann was writing, this passage had not yet been written: "God has a terrible double aspect: a sea of grace is met by a seething lake of fire, and the light of love glows with a fierce dark heat of which it is said '*ardet non lucet*'—it burns but gives no light. That is the eternal gospel: *one can love God but must fear him*" (C. G. Jung, *Answer to Job*, CW 11, ¶733).

30 In *Roots I*, cf. p. 49, n. 131. In *New Ethic* (1990), cf. Jung's Foreword, p. 17, and Chapter IV, p. 98. One might also cite passages from Neumann's lectures of 1942–3 (e.g., Appendix B-I, *Roots II*, p. 202.).

31 Neumann's criticism of James Kirsch, in a letter to Jung on 9 February 1935, illustrates his awareness that negative consequences result when the unconscious is recklessly given too much authority (*J-N Corresp*, p. 87).

32 Although in 1949 Neumann probably expected his *New Ethic* to be published promptly in English, in fact the English edition appeared only two decades later. In 1959, Neumann wrote a preface, but the English edition was still delayed. In 1969, it was finally published, in Eugene Rolfe's fine translation, by Putnam. This edition was reprinted in 1973 by Harper & Row, with an added foreword by Gerhard Adler. A later reprinting (Harper Torchbooks, 1990) includes a third foreword, by James Yandell.

33 In his page numbers and brief quotations, Jung's critical comments correspond to the first edition of *Neue Ethik* (Rascher, 1949). There one may locate all the passages he asked Neumann to revise. Because McCartney's renderings of Jung's comments (*J-N Corresp*, pp. 361–9) seldom correspond to Rolfe's translation in *New Ethic*, Jung's critical comments (*Briefe J-N*, pp. 370–8) are best read in German, if possible, side by side with the first edition of *Neue Ethik*.

34 Neumann's concept of "the ego–Self axis" was first fully articulated in his 1952 Eranos lecture, published in *Spring 1956* (English trans. by H. Nagel), as "The Psyche and the Transformation of the Reality Planes: A Metapsychological Essay." Cf. *The Place of Creation*, W. McGuire, ed., 1989, pp. 3–62 (cf. esp. p. 20).

35 Neumann had approached this concept even earlier in his 1934 essay, *Jacob and Esau*. Steve Zemmelman writes, "Taken together, secondary mythologizing and objectification of the archetypes constitute the germ of the concept for which Neumann would eventually become most well-known, namely the ego–self axis" ("C.G. Jung and Erich Neumann: Conflict, Philia, and Finding the Other in Oneself," *Jung Journal: Culture and Psyche*, 2016, vol. 10.3, p. 82.)

36 Neumann's daughter recalls that her father faithfully practiced his Hebrew, for example by reading the daily newspaper; but she adds that his scholarly reading was almost always in German (Rali Neumann-Loewenthal, telephone conversation, 3 June 2018).

37 Because Buber wrote in German, Neumann's knowledge of Hasidism came mainly from his work. In this respect, Neumann was not alone. As noted by Moshe Idel (1995), Buber's early work had been uniquely influential for European Jews in the first half of the twentieth century (*Hasidism: Between Ecstasy and Magic*, p. 2).

38 The concept of the unity of Scripture, central for both Buber and Rosenzweig, is discussed in their essays on biblical translation. Cf. Franz Rosenzweig's essay, "The Unity of the Bible," in *Scripture and Translation*, pp. 22ff.

39 Tamar Kron, interview, Jerusalem, 29 April 2015.

40 Buber's previously unpublished letter is printed in Löwe's biography of Neumann. In his letter, Buber ventures the opinion that Kafka's meaning, insofar as it can be conceptualized at all, might be better grasped by a theological concept than by the metaphysical one that Neumann favors. ("Auch scheint es mir, daß mitunter ein theologischer Begriff, den Sie aus einer mir wohl verständlichen Scheu meiden, das Gemeinte, so weit es überhaupt begrifflich zu erreichen ist, eher treffen würde, als der von Ihnen verwendete metaphysische"—Löwe, 2014, p. 84.)

41 "Rebbe Nachman" could be the preferable title, as designating the spiritual leader of a Hasidic community. The generic title is used here because, when referring in his text to this important figure, Neumann habitually writes "Rabbi" (cf. *Roots* II, pp. 14, 22, 27, *et passim*).

42 Moshe Idel's (1995) introduction to *Hasidism: Between Ecstasy and Magic* (pp. 6ff.) gives a balanced overview of Buber's and Scholem's contrasting treatments of Hasidic tradition, which he analyzes partly in terms of "proximism," i.e., the continuity or discontinuity that each writer ascribes to Hasidism, against preceding religious movements.

43 For a polemical but informative overview of their debate, cf. Jerome Gellman's article, "Buber's Blunder: Buber's Replies to Scholem and Schatz-Uffenheimer" (*Modern Judaism*, 2000, Vol. 20, No. 1, pp. 20–40).

44 After signaling his own direction in the comment, "[T]here is still room for further attempts to interpret Hasidism, particularly in relation to the whole of Jewish mysticism," Scholem adds pointedly: "You will not expect me to add anything to the wealth of Hasidic tales and teachings contained for instance in the writings of Martin Buber . . ." (*Major Trends*, p. 327).

45 Scholem's *Bibliographia Kabbalistica* (Leipzig, 1927) lists German-language works by Jewish writers since the fifteenth century. The subtitle reads, in translation: "List of printed books and essays on Jewish mysticism (Gnosticism, Kabbalah, Sabbatianism, Frankism, Hasidism), from Reuchlin to the present."

46 Cf. M. Catane, ed., *Bibliography of the Writings of Gershom G. Scholem* (Jerusalem, 1977), pp. 9ff.

47 Scholem always maintained his opinion that in the 1930s Jung had had "links" to Nazism and had done real harm by some of his statements at that time (G. Scholem to J. Kirsch, 3 November 1973, unpublished correspondence, the James Kirsch archive). In addition, according to Rali Neumann-Loewenthal, he disliked psychological hermeneutics in general. Nevertheless, after learning in 1947 about Jung's post-war apology to Rabbi Leo Baeck (Jaffé, 1989, p. 100), he decided to accept the invitation to return to Eranos, where he lectured frequently from 1949 on. According to the librarian overseeing the Scholem Collection at the National Library of Israel, many works by Jung are found in Scholem's library, including some dedicated to him by the author (Zvi Leshem, private correspondence, 24 April 2018).

48 Rali Neumann-Loewenthal generously shared recollections about her father's relationships with Buber and Scholem, in personal conversation (Jerusalem, 29 April 2015) and by telephone (3 June 2018).

49 Dreifuss, 1980, op. cit., p. 240. (Trans. by ACL. Unless otherwise noted, works previously unpublished in English are translated by Mark Kyburz and Ann Lammers in collaboration. Cf. "Editorial Note," *Roots I*, p. 174.)

50 Ibid.

51 Hand-bound typescripts of the work were sold at auction in 2006. The auction catalogue describes "2 volumes . . . some typed and manuscript corrections on strips of paper affixed to the typescript, cloth-backed card wrappers, repairs to a few pages with translucent adhesive tape, some small tears, browning, creasing to second title, small tears to wrappers" (Sotheby's, London, 2006). Nearly identical carbon copies of Neumann's typescripts were available to the editorial team while we prepared this edition for publication. None of them, however, is hand bound. The two typescripts in "cloth-backed card wrappers" were, I surmise, Neumann's lending copies.

INTRODUCTION TO THE WORK

Erich Neumann

The discovery of mythical prehistory

The revolution that has transformed the mental situation of the western world in the past 150 years[1] has assigned to human beings a surprising new position in the cosmos, utterly unlike any they have occupied so far.

What we are talking about can be summed up as the emergence, in all areas of life, of a tremendous prehistoric and primordial world, which places the individual within an infinitely ramified context. In this context, human history represents only one part of the evolution of living beings, this evolution is only one part of the history of the earth, and the earth itself represents only one part of the history of the cosmos.

This process signifies much more than a development in natural science, although science has played a considerable role in remaking the world edifice. We must remember that the past 150 years have bestowed on human beings a biological relationship with the animal kingdom, thus restoring humanity to the lineage of natural creatures. By contrast, medieval people, as lonely sons and daughters of God, were cast out into an alien and hostile world of temptation.

But also, during these last 150 years, a human consciousness, as the self-consciousness of the human species, has actually begun to form for the first time. Earlier human groups, unlike modern ones, were isolated and unaware of each other's existence. Based on their unconscious assumptions, they each considered themselves the center of the world.

The first Indian text came to the western world at the end of the eighteenth century; and Japan emerged into world history at the end of the nineteenth. By now, we've surely reached a point in the history of ideas where humanity as a subject[2] encompasses western people and Asians, primitive people[3] and primordial humans, as branches of one large tribe. In the various cultural orientations of all these groups, the expression of a great development may be seen: the developing consciousness of the human species. The positive meaning of this fact remains unaffected by the political landslides engulfing peoples and nations. These upheavals are ephemeral symptoms of a major historical transformation, in which for the first time the subject of humanity is starting to emerge as a reality. This was the unrecognized meaning signaled by the French Revolution. Nations, as specific configurations of the human race, can now claim for themselves only relative importance. The nationalist obsessions of our time are, in part, an understandable reaction to this relentless development.

The justification for this temporary nationalization, or renationalization, is that, with the emergence of the perspective of humanity, every people must reflect upon its own voice, which it is destined to play in the human orchestra.

The western world, having been determined essentially by Christianity and antiquity, is just now beginning to relativize its own standpoint by learning about the rest of the world—for instance, Asia. Quite independent of this development, the emergence of classical studies means that the prehistory of the western world is now also starting to be discovered. This involves, first, the study of pre-Hellenic antiquity, which teaches one to recognize and understand the rise of Greece as the end point of both a larger context and a longer historical process, and, second, the discovery of pre-Christian and pre-Jewish antiquity.

Knowledge of the ancient Orient, biblical criticism, and comparative religious studies, taken together, undermine the singular, pivotal status held by Christianity during the Middle Ages. Christianity now coexists with Asian religions, and also with Islam and other world religions, past and present, all of which have their particular strengths and weaknesses.

The history of religion provides evidence for the close interrelationships of various religions, where one developed in the seedbed of another. Also increasingly obvious, as an eye-opening phenomenon, is the way that seemingly theoretical scientific discoveries in linguistics and classics are awakening previously unknown connections. For instance, the Indo-Aryan Renaissance suddenly establishes completely different interrelationships than those previously at work in history. Christianity, as a transnational religious entity, is undermined by nationalist[4] connections, which are thought to link the Germanic-Christian peoples to Indo-Brahman and Buddhist ones.[5]

All these developments are contingent on contemporary history, and so far no homogeneous lines of spiritual reorientation have emerged. Nevertheless, the rediscovery of the mythical world is crucially important for the history of ideas, from Romanticism through to the present.

The discovery of the mythical and later of the primitive world provided material for a fundamental adjustment in human consciousness, creating a new familiarity with the preconscious world, that is, the world of the unconscious, which precedes that of consciousness.

The history of human evolution, as a sequence of developmental stages, does not necessarily result in greater consciousness. Only by considering all cultures and all peoples can we gain an overall view. Such a perspective enables us to recognize what human consciousness has achieved for itself so far. Over time, individual groups of the human species have specialized, so that each group attained particular achievements. Western humanity, for instance, turned its consciousness more toward the outer world, whereas eastern humanity turned more toward the inner world. Taken together, they reveal the actual scope already attained by human consciousness. Neither group, however, can claim the entire scope of the conscious world as its own.

In cultures shaped by specific human groups, we find extremely diverse stages of consciousness and varied forms of unconscious reality, such that the history of humanity could be said to constitute the development of human consciousness. In Asia or Europe, America or Africa, a particular group unknowingly took the lead, only to relinquish its leadership, still unknowingly. Then this hidden leadership passed to another group, again without its knowledge.

The past 150 years have taught western humanity and western Christian culture that any standpoint is relative, and that knowledge is contingent on the personal equation of each group. This insight also underlies, as effect or cause, the fact that today there is *one* world, with one monetary policy, one world economy, and one world war.[6]

The new orientation given by depth psychology

The relativizing integration of these developments into a larger human context reaches its peak in two discoveries: the discovery of prehistory, which everywhere conditions human consciousness, and the discovery of the world of the unconscious. From a perspective that regards human history as the history of human consciousness, the manifold paths that the past 150 years have blazed into unexplored terrain are unified, in a highly characteristic fashion. Evolutionary history and geology, the history of antiquity and ethnology, the study of language and religious studies, anthropology, and psychology are all merely different methods, perspectives, and materials enabling an understanding of the prehistory of human consciousness.

C. G. Jung's discovery of the collective unconscious provides the unifying aspect under which all these detailed researches have become essential components of the history of humanity and of the individual. The many-layered complexity of the unconscious structure of the psyche, together with its symbolism, reveals traces of the development of consciousness from our animal ancestry through the psychology of the primitive, all the way to the modern individual. The archetypal symbolism of the unconscious is the mother of all mythical, cultic, and religious concepts and images discovered and compared by the history of religion, classical studies, and ethnology.

Therapeutic work done with the modern individual provides evidence for the existence and effects of the collective unconscious, that is, a human unconscious the images of which precede the formative influences on individual peoples and their conscious attitudes. This therapeutic work has liberated the scientific research of the past 150 years, which is otherwise of merely antiquarian interest, and given it vital importance.

Gnostic symbolism,[7] for instance, becomes highly relevant if it proves to be at work in the modern unconscious. The study of primitive psychology also loses its specialized character if this psychology still largely determines the behavior of groups and of the so-called modern person.

The existence of a universal human psychic structure, viewed in terms of evolutionary history, manifests itself in the identical symbolism and fundamental notions that we find among all peoples and at all times.[8]

It is deeply moving to investigate the collective unconscious, because such research reveals how far even the contents of human consciousness are archetypal. It also becomes self-evident to what extent the universal structure of the human nervous system, as the embodiment of ancestral experience, expresses itself in the experiences made and formulated everywhere by the human species. Races, peoples, and groups are distinguished by the constellations of archetypal contents that have assumed importance for them, rather than by different contents of the collective unconscious.

A time of self-reflection will be needed by the peoples, in order to work out how these constellations act in history. We must not forget, though, that these constellations are merely variations in how the universal human heritage is assimilated.

Essentially, this development amounts to a change in consciousness. It also reveals not only how, but also how far, consciousness works through unconscious contents. These unconscious contents remain unchanged as elements, as archetypes, over great expanses of time. For instance, the "sun's phallus" appears as the origin of the wind on an Egyptian magical papyrus, just as it does in medieval art and in the unconscious production of a schizophrenic patient living in twentieth-century western Europe.[9] This suggests the permanent nature of these elements. Even if the approach seems unhistorical at first, this fact is important because it allows us to assemble texts from different times and different peoples, in which the same images occur.

Unquestionably, the conscious working-through of an archetype may be entirely different from one people or epoch to another. Thus, for instance, medieval Christianity condemns as a witch the same feminine aspect of the magically powerful woman that India worships as a dangerous aspect of female magical power. And yet the archetypal image of the woman capable of magic appears both in India and in Europe. Astonishingly, as already noted, the modern unconscious also conveys these images in unaltered form, thus permitting them to ascend through consciousness largely undisturbed.

Ultimately, however, the identical functioning of the psychic structure is just as extraordinary, and just as ordinary, as the fact that today the autonomous nervous system governs human breathing and digestion exactly as it did 5,000 years ago, whether in southern Africa or in northern India. And yet human bodily identity strikes us as unproblematic and self-evident, whereas psychic identity does not.

The Jewish situation

In the present phase of the history of ideas, the western world is revolutionizing itself "from below"[10] and appears to be establishing a new foundation for itself, which will no longer be shaped by antiquity and Christianity, or at least not wholly. Amid these developments, the Jewish situation has become particularly confused and catastrophic.

The previous phase of western Jewish intellectual history involved a strong and largely successful assimilation into the western world, as well as the separation from the primordial religious and collective situation of Judaism.[11] The revolution of the western world has been characterized by a fierce aversion to Christianity, or at least to a form of it that was associated with early Christianity, including the Old Testament. So whereas the ecclesial development of Christianity made room for a growing number of pagan elements, a strong bias[12] against the Old Testament emerged in the last century.

Biblical criticism and research into the ancient Near East climaxed in a deliberately disillusioning and often highly anti-Semitic aggression against the Old Testament. The Indo-Aryan Renaissance, and the discovery of Persian influences, competed with the Panbabylonists to demonstrate the Old Testament's secondary importance. For obvious reasons, some theologians were forced to exercise greater caution. Ultimately, however, neither was this process arbitrary nor did it amount to a conspiracy of evil-minded anti-Semites. Rather, these traits are integrated into the intellectual revolution of the western world, which is now overcoming its Christian and classical assumptions.

Highly interesting in this respect is the new discovery[13] of heresy, from mysticism to alchemy and Gnosticism. Particularly the rediscovery of Gnosticism,[14] with its strong rejection of the Old Testament, is immensely significant, because its reemergence brings forth exactly those problems that were contested during the rise of Christianity and finished with the victory of the Church. It almost seems as if this ancient process were being revived. Just as the motifs of Hellenism, Judaism, the Near-Eastern religions, Gnosticism, and Zoroastrianism collided at the beginning of Christianity, so the subcurrents and secondary currents ousted by the dominance of Christianity are now resurfacing, because Christianity appears to have lost its power to shape human life and history.

Without even the slightest idea about the future direction of this process, in which new Indo-Aryan groups and their worldviews may stake out an utterly new intellectual continent against the peoples of Asia, and indeed without even knowing whether such groups represent only temporary worldviews, one fact remains unalterable amid these developments: the reality of the Jewish problem.

The revolution of the western world excludes Judaism precisely because it has assimilated itself to *that* form of the western world that is currently undergoing total and relentless transformation. The western world, for the assimilating Jew, meant humanism in the sense of a universal human consciousness. It meant transnationalism and internationalism. Indeed, in part, it also meant what the intellectual revolution now unfolding will bring at some stage: the self-consciousness of the human species.

Tragically, however, the process in which the western world finds itself presupposes a reconnection with the pre-Christian, that is, the pagan collective unconscious. The self-examination engaged in by peoples and by individuals must include the unconscious worlds that preceded, indeed opposed, the conscious orientation at the time. The western world must become conscious of its pre-Christianized layers, precisely because its consciousness was Christianized. Likewise, the individual must become conscious of the unconscious layers excluded from conscious orientation.

Economic developments that run parallel to these intellectual processes, having been directed by them, lead likewise to an elimination of the Jewish element. The frivolous bestiality with which this process is sometimes carried out cannot blind us to its apparent necessity.[15]

Judaism, then, is facing a crisis that threatens its very existence. Not because economic or political expulsion is at stake—this, of course, is the Jewish fate, although previously it never spelled an existential crisis—but because Jewish religion is no longer an effective force in the world, just as little as, or even less than, Protestantism. This situation affects modern Jews and modern western Christians alike, because currently emerging developments in their unconscious will prompt new philosophical and religious influences.

Whereas all other peoples continue to exist, and have time to undergo such developments, the rootless and homeless Jew faces the danger of not surviving this age. And there is a danger that Judaism will perish as a result.

Today, however, it is not about Judaism, but about the Jew as a person.

Historically, we have reached a stage that represents a reversal of what happened when the Second Temple was destroyed. At the time, there was a saying: the Jewish people may suffer, but Judaism must survive. Now the opposite saying is true: Judaism may suffer, but the Jewish people, the Jewish person, must live and survive. Whereas the beacon of an abstract Judaism shone above the martyred Jewish destinies burned, broken on the wheel, lynched, and impaled, now what proclaims itself is the right of the Jew as an individual, who must realize that what is at stake is his life, his blood. Today, it not about Judaism, but about the individual Jew.

If, as Jung writes, "Religions are therapies for the sorrows and disorders of the soul,"[16] the plight of the modern Jew is that the ancient sufferings are not today's. Therefore, the therapies for ancient sufferings are ineffective for the sufferings of the modern Jew. Alongside the famous affirmation of Judaism, a productive negation of Judaism is needed as well, by those who assume that the individual's plight is inextricably bound up with the community's. Beyond the paralysis of dogmatic Judaism, innumerable hidden creative tensions exist within the Jew. These tensions must be identified and kindled, so that the old sources of living water will once again flow from the seemingly lifeless stone.

Contrary to what one might think, however, the argument that it comes down to the individual Jew, rather than Judaism, does not follow simply from the fact that individual psychotherapy stands at the beginning and the end of the problems observed here. As this work attempts to show, the Jewish histori-cal process inexorably moves in this direction. This, in turn, explains why only the individual can rescue and regenerate Judaism. Later we discuss the fact that individuals, as members of their people, must exist under natural living condi-tions, that is, under conditions that also permit their unconscious to live, and not merely their stomach and their business.

Our present attempt starts from the unconscious problem of the modern Jew. This set of problems, as far as it is rooted in the Jewish collective unconscious, requires an in-depth study of the basic problems and contents affecting Jewish existence and its history. We shall understand the difficulty at the depths of the modern Jew only if we fathom those problems and contents.

The theme

Our central theme, of course, is the relationship between consciousness and the unconscious. This problem is closely entwined with the problem of revelation theologically defined, that is, with the rise of new and normative contents from the unconscious into consciousness. Our endeavor, it should be noted, is psycho-logical. Thus, we need to review the great problem of the ancient Jew, solely to establish how it persists as the inner problem for the modern Jew. The problem of inner experience is a central problem of the modern Jew and of the Jewish person in general. For this reason, our recourse to history is anything but antiquarian.

Given our particular starting point, we are aware that our thematic emphasis is somewhat one-sided and idiosyncratic. Nevertheless, we believe that we have not violated historical truth in this book. We must remember that everything confronting us as biblical criticism, for instance, is contingent upon history. The contrast between Buber's often-cited research and the findings of conventional biblical criticism rests not on his less critical or less scientific perspective, but on the fact that Buber, unlike non-Jewish biblical researchers, starts with the text and its intention. By no means do we mean to detract anything from the enormous achievements of biblical research. We are still following in its footsteps, because at a time of Jewish disintegration and Jewish self-neglect, generations of biblical researchers[17] undertook in all earnestness those tasks that we left unattended, being fully occupied with our assimilation into the western world.

No depth psychology of the modern Jew can ignore the historical antecedents that have determined the structure of the Jewish person[18] to this day. This explains why our inquiry into the structure of the ancient Jew is so intensely topical. The end point of our study, whose primary concern is the modern Jew, will reveal just how topical this inquiry really is.

We shall consider two great historical epochs and their offshoots, in order to trace the development of this problem, at least as far as it is relevant to understand-ing the psychic background of the modern Jew.

The first epoch is Jewish antiquity, where we focus on prophetism[19] and the opposition between YHWH and the powers of nature. Subsequently, we discuss the psychology of the apocalyptic writers and the psychic transformation that occurred at the time of the destruction of the Second Temple.[20] This is the period spanning the last pre-Christian century and the first Christian century, during which Gnosticism flowered.

The second epoch of concern to us is Hasidism, the late eighteenth-century religious movement that established, it seems to us, a new basis for resolving the essential problems of the Jewish person.

We shall also discuss emancipation and assimilation, as constituting the Jewish psychology of the nineteenth century. These themes lead to the third part of this study,[21] which attempts to describe the existential problem of modern Judaism directly, on the basis of the unconscious material of the modern Jewish person, that is, of his dreams, fantasies, and images. This part also attempts to trace the lines of development arising from this unconscious material.

It is widely known that Jewish existence exhibits a crucial break, but the actual meaning of this event and its full implications have not become clear, either in the non-Jewish world or in Jewish self-consciousness. The inner trans-formation of the ancient Jew into a galut Jew[22] is not bound to the historical date of the destruction of the Temple. It corresponds instead to a process that had essentially already taken place between the destruction of the First and Second Temples, and that merely reached its most obvious climax after the destruction of the Second Temple.

The psychology of Jewish antiquity and the psychology of the galut are incom-mensurable. In falsely claiming continuity, Jewish self-interpretation has been self-deceiving, obsessed with the dogma of a stable Judaism. For too long, this self-deception has prevented, indeed thwarted, Jews from understanding their own fate. Up to now, this dogma has formed the basis of Jewish existence. For ortho-doxy, as the existential attitude of the Jews, insisted until about 100 years ago that the revelation on Sinai was identical with the entire oral doctrine that emerged from the process of historical change. Thus, ultimately, it insisted on the artificial exclusion of historical reality in its endeavor to create, through the Law and its ful-fillment, a level of existence possessing absolute validity. This permitted the Jewish people, despite the vicissitudes of world events, to persist in claiming exceptional status, as originally guaranteed by revelation. The Jewish people simply had to sur-vive the triviality of historical events in order to be restored, on the arrival of the messianic era, to its original, central, never-relinquished place in the world, which it has maintained through its insistence on continuity.

It is striking, of course, that the destruction of the Temple and the beginning of the galut represent a decisive turning point in the self-consciousness of the Jew, leaving its mark on Jews down to the smallest minutiae and symptomatizing itself in a total adaptation of life and also of the Law. Despite this, however, that is, despite all consciousness of the galut, there was a refusal to see that continuity with the pre-exilic state was illusionary. On the contrary, every effort was made to strengthen the consciousness of continuity and to consolidate it through the establishment of traditions.

Whereas the real character of the mid-eighteenth-century Jew differed, crucially and catastrophically, from that of the ancient Jew, Judaism remained almost unchanged.

> Essentially, this Judaism remained as it had been two thousand years before, or at least, if it had developed, it had developed only in nuances. It still upheld the same eschatological concepts of history, with the chosen people at its center.[23]

This discrepancy, between an unchanged Judaism and a changed Jewish person, then leads to a conflict within Judaism and subsequently to its inner catastrophe, whose shock waves, underground and on the surface, surge around every modern Jew's existence, knowingly or unknowingly.

To establish a genuine sense of the actual psychic situation of the ancient Jew, that is, the Jew living before the destruction of the First Temple,[24] we must depart from the notion commonly held by theology, to a degree not attempted hitherto. Indeed, the reality of the Jewish person has—more or less understandably—never been a focus of research, except insofar as Judaism provided material for the theological concerns of a particular age, from the Church Fathers to the German Faith Movement.[25] But, also, Jewish apologists have carefully steered clear of the reality of the ancient Jew, because they were solely concerned with morality, social sensibility, and the prophets' elevated conception of God. The apologists also shunned this reality because, at least in the past 150 years,[26] the Jew has lacked the self-understanding to utter his "*Ecce homo.*"[27]

The constant fear that evidence of the negative aspects of the Jews could be abused by the enemies of Judaism has influenced and prevented the Jew from any movement toward consciousness. Today, however, matters are different. The surging hatred of the Jews is a powerful driver of history, isolating the Jewish people. It is eliminating them from western communal life, to the point where Balaam's long-forgotten sentence is once again true: "Here, a people, alone-in-security it dwells, among the nations it does not need to come-to-reckoning" (Num 23:9).[28] For this very reason, however, coming to reckoning cannot mean answering to other peoples.

Unquestionably, the entanglement of Judaism with the "peoples of the earth" determines its fate. And yet the poisonous wave of these other peoples' hatred of the Jews, which threatens to corrode the psychic structure of the Jew, can be averted only if Judaism places itself on maximum alert, and only if it establishes, through radical self-contemplation, a meaningful connection with its deepest levels. Our present attempt, including all the back roads and detours that seem necessary, is intended to approach this self-meditation from a new angle.

The plight of modern Jews—who like all modern humans lack direction, yet find themselves caught up in an age shaken to its foundations by catastrophes, lacking historical continuity, and plunged into a bottomless sociological pit—compels us to try to reconnect with the past in our own way. By assembling a wide-ranging collection of texts and interpretations, diverse conceptions of history, and individual studies, we attempt here to reveal basic psychological attitudes and work out forms of psychic behavior and outlooks on life, which, related to the unconscious problem of the modern Jew, can perhaps illumine his dark path.

Notes

1 "The past 150 years" refers roughly to the time since the French Revolution or the Enlightenment.
2 *das Subjekt Menschheit*: Alternatively, "the concept of humanity."
3 *Primitivmenschen*: Neumann's use of "primitive" reflects late nineteenth- and early twentieth-century thinking. His frame of reference includes the anthropological and ethnological works of Max Weber and Lucien Lévy-Bruhl, as well as Jung's early writings. (Cf., for example, Jung, "Archaic Man" in The Collected Works of C. G. Jung (hereafter: CW), v. 10, ¶105).
4 *völkisch*: In the 1930s, this term meant both "national" (pertaining to a people) and "nationalist" (Nazi jargon for "racially German"). Here, used ironically, the second meaning applies.
5 The German racialist concept of Aryanism, with its reference to eastern religions, had recently found expression in Jacob Hauer's German Faith Movement. Cf. below, note 25.
6 Written before World War II.
7 Scattered references to Gnostic symbology appear in Jung's early works. Here, Neumann is likely referring to Jung's then-unpublished *Septem Sermones ad Mortuos* (1916), which Jung had given him as a gift in 1934. Cf. *Analytical Psychology in Exile: The Correspondence of C. G. Jung and Erich Neumann*, 2015 (hereafter: *J-N Corresp*), p. 22.
8 *EN*: Despite its misinterpretations, psychoanalysis has compared vast amounts of material to establish common symbolism among the nations and peoples of the world. Such comparisons are evident also in specialized research, including the Thematic Index in Alfred Jeremias's *Das Alte Testament im Lichte des alten Orients* (*The Old Testament in the context of the ancient Near East*). See also the historical references in C.G. Jung's "Psychologischer Aspekt des Mutterarchetyps" ("Psychological Aspects of the Mother Archetype"), *Eranos-Jahrbuch 1938*. [(Cf. CW 9.i, ¶148–98.) The *Eranos-Jahrbuch* (hereafter: *EJ*) is the annual volume of papers from the interdisciplinary Eranos symposium, started by Jung, which has been held every August since 1933 in Ascona, Switzerland.]
9 *EN*: C.G. Jung, *Seelenprobleme der Gegenwart* (*Current psychological problems*) (hereafter: *Seelenprobleme*), "Die Struktur der Seele" ("The structure of the psyche"). [Cf. CW 8,7, ¶317ff, where Jung discusses the case of the "sun's phallus," in relation to wind and *pneuma* (spirit).]
10 Neumann's reference is evidently to nineteenth- and early twentieth-century science, philosophy of religion, etc.
11 Neumann sees the post-Enlightenment period as crucial to the experience of Jews in western Europe. In 1934 he wrote to Jung that, although the Enlightenment meant emancipation for European Jews, it also led to their decline, because "the collective bond disintegrates" in a wave of assimilation (*J-N Corresp*, p. 47).
12 *Tendenz*: lit. "tendency." In both English and German, when applied to written or spoken words, the term may connote "purpose," "intention," even "bias." (Cf. *Roots I*, p. 72, n. 131.)
13 *Neuentdeckung*: not a literal "new discovery" but a scholarly re-evaluation of the meaning of heresies.
14 This remark predates the historic discovery at Nag Hammadi, in 1945, of ancient papyrus scrolls containing Gnostic texts. One scroll, Codex I, bought in 1951 by the C. G. Jung Institute in Zurich as a birthday present for Jung, is now known as the Jung Codex.
15 Neumann alludes to contemporary events, in Germany and elsewhere, expressing neopaganism. His references to "frivolous bestiality" and "apparent necessity" are heavily ironic.

16 *EN*: R. Wilhelm and C. G. Jung, *Das Geheimnis der Goldenen Blüte* (hereafter: *Geheimnis*), p. 64. [Cf. English edition, *The Secret of the Golden Flower*, p. 126.]

17 In addition to citing Jewish biblical scholars, such as Buber, Rosenzweig, Auerbach, Baer, etc., Neumann also cites the work of Protestant scholars of the Old Testament, such as Baudissin, Gunkel, Kautzsch, and Wellhausen.

18 *die Struktur des jüdischen Menschen*: i.e., the *psychological* structure of the Jewish person. When using the term *Struktur* (structure), Neumann sometimes adds a modifier, such as *die Struktur der Psyche* (the structure of the psyche). When he leaves the term unmodified, as here, it may generally be read as a synonym for psyche.

19 *Prophetismus*: the practice or system of biblical prophecy, as distinct from particular prophetic sayings or actions. The corresponding English term is partly defined by the *Oxford English Dictionary* as "the system or principle of the Hebrew prophets." As "prophetism" is now a rare term, even in biblical studies, we have rendered many of Neumann's uses of *Prophetismus* as "Hebrew prophecy," "the practice of prophecy," etc.

20 For Neumann, the destruction of the Second Temple by the Romans, in the year 70 CE, marks the point at which "ancient" Judaism may truly be said to end.

21 "Part Three" is anticipated by Neumann several times in the existing two parts of this work. He did not complete his planned third part, but its themes are sketched out in his letter to Jung on 5 December 1938 (cf. *J-N Corresp*, pp. 141f.). His lecture of April 1940, which he sent to Jung (ibid., p. 156), anticipated this third part, as did his four-lecture series of 1942–43. (Cf. *Roots II*, Appendix B.)

22 *zum Galuthjuden*: *Galuth* (galut), a Hebrew borrowing, meaning "exile," has been adopted into both German and English. A "galut Jew," in Neumann's context, is one whose psychology has been shaped by the experience of living in exile from the Holy Land, i.e., the Land of Israel. The collective exilic experience began, he explains, with the destruction of the Solomonic Temple, 586 BCE, marking the beginning of the Babylonian Exile, and it culminated with the destruction of the Second Temple, 70 CE.

23 *EN*: Baer, *Galuth*, p. 93. [First page of ch. 16 in Baer's *Galuth*. (In the 1988 English edition, cf. p. 109.)]

24 Neumann's definition of "ancient Judaism" appears here for the first time. The destruction of the First Temple, with the exile of Israelites and Judahites into Babylon, occurred in 586 BCE.

25 German Faith Movement: a racialist–nationalist religious system, founded in 1933 by Jakob Wilhelm Hauer (1881–1962). Hauer, a German Indologist and professor of religious studies, had taught a weeklong seminar on yoga at the Psychological Club in Zurich in 1932. A year later, he began reshaping his professional life consistent with the direction set by National Socialism.

26 Again, Neumann sees the post-Enlightenment period as having special application to the experience of the Jews.

27 Latin: "Behold the man." From the Vulgate Latin translation of Pilate's statement in showing Jesus to the crowd (John 19:5).

28 When citing Scripture, Neumann usually quotes the German translations of Buber and Rosenzweig (B&R) (cf. above, "Introduction to Volume One," p. xxxviii, n. 10.) In preparing this edition, we were fortunate to be able to use Everett Fox's recently published translations, because his work is the nearest available equivalent, in English, of the distinctive translation philosophy of B&R (cf. "Editorial Note," *Roots I*, p. 174). Unless otherwise noted, the five Books of Moses (Genesis, Exodus, Leviticus, Numbers, Deuteronomy) and the early prophets (Joshua, Judges, 1 and 2 Samuel, 1 and 2 Kings) are cited according to the translations of Everett Fox. Other biblical books, including the major prophets, are generally cited according to the New Revised Standard Version of the Bible (NRSV).

The problem of revelation in Jewish antiquity

1

THE YHWH–EARTH RELATION AND PROPHECY

1. Moses and the revelation on Sinai

The Near East and the significance of the Mother Goddess

The transformation of the psychology of the Jewish people by the men who wrote and redacted the Bible should not cause us to forget that they stood *against* what the Jewish person actually was. We shall need to discuss not only the fact that, but also how and why, these men went on to shape history. First, however, we must attempt to deduce the psychology of the ancient Jew from the negative of the picture created by—to put it briefly—the prophets. If the history of the Jewish people is that of its "apostasies,"[1] then the stage to which it "regressed"[2]—as seen from the perspective of prophetic historiography—indicates the people's natural psychic situation, above which it only seldom rises or is able to rise.

Greatly simplified, this psychology reveals a highly belligerent, cruel, and primitive group, whose defining characteristic is that it is powerfully possessed by the earth. Quite possibly, this hunger for land corresponds to the transition from nomadic life to a settled, agricultural life. Here, however, we come up against unresolved problems, because nomadic peoples loathe settled forms of life. Thus, we would need to assume that, in their hunger for land, the psychology of the nomadic Hebrew tribes differed from that of other nomadic Semitic peoples. This assumption coincides with the fact that the tension of opposites with regard to the earth also remained a central problem for the Jewish people in later stages of its history. This exceptionally strong tension of opposites characterizes the Jews still to this day.

A fanatical attachment to the land is evident in all ancient accounts, a determination to claw oneself into the earth and cling to its fertility. Several fundamental motifs emerge repeatedly in these narratives: fertility of the soil, the land of milk and honey, fertility of the herds, fertility of the tribes, becoming like the dust of the earth, like the stars of heaven, like the ocean sand. A great and powerful sensuality, desiring "that it may go well,"[3] is everywhere manifest in the genuine, ancient affirmation of existence. These elements surely correspond to what is usually called paganism. At this point we must point out that, in its depths, the psychology of the still largely unconscious Hebrew tribes strongly resembled, and had to resemble, the psychology of the related Semitic tribes and their surrounding world.

It is beyond our present scope to consider the surrounding pagan religions. Nevertheless, we must emphasize the significant role played by the cult of female deities among the Canaanite and Syrian peoples and those of Asia Minor.

Paganism, in its Near-Eastern form, is characterized by the predominance of nature, of earthy femininity, and the orgiastic sexuality that accompanies it. One outstanding feature of the peoples surrounding early Judaism is the grandiose dominance of nature's power over humankind and of the Mother Goddess over the depotentiated male. The omnipotent goddess and ruler, celebrated in orgiastic intoxication, governs all creatures through the fecundity of earth and womb, and in the overwhelming power of sexuality. This powerful sensuality and primitive attachment to the forces of nature continue to this day to be one of the dangers for the Jew. Although Jewish development has taken a different course over the past 2,000 years, a curious Dionysian tendency remains evident, as manifest in Near-Eastern festivals, Hasidic circle dances, and the night-long Hora dancing of the modern Jew of *Eretz Israel*.[4] Israelite–Canaanite folk religion certainly bears strong characteristics of nature, as reflected by the shape in which the God of the patriarchs reveals himself.[5] The worship of tree and water-source, mountain, and idol is related closely to the cult of natural powers and its life-giving, generative aspects. Until late antiquity, the Baal–Astarte side of Canaanite religion was an essential part of folk religion. Here, we also find the cult of the chthonic deity, of the earth and its central symbol, vegetation, plant and tree. Ubiquitously associated with this symbol of vegetation are the cult of the son of the earth, as the Earth Mother's son-lover, and the mysteries of the god who dies and rises again.

Behind all these forms of religion, however, stands always the image of the Great Mother, beside whom the brother–son–husband is merely secondary. He may occupy an important role as the darling and object of the mysteries, because he kindles the hope of rebirth and immortality, yet he remains surrounded by the powerful and superior figure of the Great Mother, who embodies nature and the soul, whether as Ishtar or Isis, Anat or Artemis. Her overwhelming powerfulness encompasses death and life, fertility and dying.

Even later stages of development—in which the male side, initially inferior, places itself alongside the great female ruler and ultimately above her, a development in which the "prince consort dethrones the queen"[6]—are unable to change the opposition between YHWH and these pagan deities. The Baal religions, too, remained religions of merely cosmic forces. Whether the power of the womb and the earth prevails, or the power of the phallus and heaven, this opposition is maintained. What is celebrated is the dominance of these only-natural forces, to which humans subordinate themselves.

These forces of natural existence give life to the pagan pantheon. Prophetistic and yahwistic religion must grapple with the celebration and worship of these powerful, life-determining forces, in whose midst the Hebrew people is situated.

The prophetic conception rests on the tension of YHWH and earth, the opposition between these polarities, and their close association. We can only fully grasp the significance of Hebrew prophecy if we understand the contrast between Canaan and Israel, through prophecy, as a conflict situated within Israel itself. In this internal conflict, the universal and fundamental tension between YHWH and earth has attained its specific and historical effectiveness, particularly if the early soothsayers must be assumed to have been influenced by the forces of nature. As much is suggested by their appearance under sacred trees (Judg 9:37; Gen 12:6; 2 Kings 5:24)[7] and at cultural sites characterized by natural phenomena, as was common throughout antiquity. One distinctive feature of early *navitum*,[8] widespread also in Israel, is the ubiquitously chthonic character of such ecstasy. This earthy character is associated with a certain layer of the unconscious, which comes out in ecstatic states and governs consciousness. This layer is known to us from the psychology of the modern individual and from comparative folk psychology, where it plays a particular role, for instance, in Kundalini yoga in India. One part of this layer is fertility symbolism; another part, directly linked with it, are orgiastic sexual cults, at whose center stand fertility symbols.[9] Both mass ecstasy and the intoxication procedures employed in divination are largely meant to exclude consciousness and to actualize the deep layers, which are believed to have magical effects and are central to every fertility spell. This explains why, for a land-cultivating, agricultural population, these cults worshiping the forces of the earth are not only understandable but also characteristic.[10]

As is well known, opposition to orgiastic excesses brought forth the rigorous sexual ethics of Judaism, prohibitions of nudity, and so on. These phenomena were symptomatic both of a conflict that needed to be overcome and of the struggle against the dangerous power of the sexual earth-sphere, which was manifest in the infectiousness of the cults of the surrounding Canaanite peoples. We must re-emphasize, once again, that the strong energy of the instinctual sphere meets its correlative in the compensatory opposition of what we are calling, in brief, prophetism.[11]

The revelation on Sinai and the people's failure

Moses and this event (Figure 1.1) stand at the center of the processes that are fundamental to the essence and history of the *Bnei Israel*.[12] The person of Moses, if we go back and remove the later alterations and repaintings,[13] is the central figure of Hebrew prophecy. And the events on Sinai, as we shall see, are prototypical of Judaism's past and future, in terms of what they tell us about the people's capacity or incapacity to receive revelation. This is the essential aspect of these basic texts: in them we can discern the structure of the Jewish people and its possibilities. Not only the past and the history of the Jews, but also their present and future, or lack

FIGURE 1.1 Moses and the revelation on Sinai: the divine presence burns above the mountain, in a red and orange cloud. After Moses has received the Law, YHWH threatens to consume the people with fire for their apostasy. Here, lightning falls on the tents at the foot of the mountain, while Moses is shown arguing with YHWH in the people's defense (Ex 32:7–14).

Watercolor: © Erich Neumann (date unknown). Courtesy of the Erich Neumann Estate.

Note: This figure is shown in color on the front cover of the paperback edition and can also be found in the eResources for this book: www.routledge.com/9781138556201.

of it, are still being decided on Mount Sinai, as the living revelation still meets with acceptance or nonacceptance.

The revelation on Sinai, like all forms of revelation, must be seen as an irruption of the collective unconscious. On the primitive level, this phenomenon is always experienced as a real event that is projected onto the outer world. Such mass visions are known to have occurred as recently as the World War,[14] when whole military units experienced the same vision. The more collective, that is, the more deeply unconscious, the irruptive contents are, the more strongly they appear as an "external" phenomenon. The contents of the collective unconscious which appear to ego-consciousness as "not-I," as coming from the "inside–outside," that is, as a psychic event occurring outside the personal sphere, are projected, as "outside–outside," as a manifestation of the external object-world. This phenomenon—the projection of the unconscious, which is the fundamental psychic fact underlying manifestations of ghosts, visions, etc.—is also an essential phenomenon at the heart of the Sinai event.

Strikingly, however, the danger posed by these invasions of the numinous is familiar to all primitive peoples and forms an essential part of ritual.[15] All mana, taboo, and *kadosh*[16] phenomena are centered on the danger of irruptions from the unconscious, for failure to observe appropriate behavior toward them leads to the death of the transgressor. Cases of such deaths are well transmitted from primitive psychology. Today, it is necessary to support and substantiate the messages of the Bible with the findings of "scientific" research into the psychology of early peoples, because the biblical accounts, which are highly accurate in part, have been discredited as theology. These accidents, which happen when taboo-laden contents are not properly handled,[17] found their strongest representation in the revelation on Sinai: a fence was erected around the mountain of revelation, because setting foot where divinity revealed itself would have fatal consequences for creatures who were not equal to the revelation (Ex 19:10–12).

Here, a whole people prepared itself for the inner dimension[18] of the collective unconscious to burst through, in exactly the same way as has been done since the existence of humanity, that is, at all times, among all peoples in all parts of the world: namely, through asceticism, "purity," sexual abstinence, refusal to sleep, and often also bloodletting. This is the somewhat violent procedure with whose help humanity has brought about the introversion of libido and an awakening of the unconscious. Withdrawing libido from the outer world compensatorily awakens the collective unconscious. This method is therefore used everywhere, whenever a revelation from within is necessary.

All these measures, familiar to us from magic, the mystery cults, initiation rites, ecstasy, and so forth, involve two seemingly opposing tendencies. On the one side, we have the awakening of the unconscious, which occurs through introversion or through stimulating the unconscious with music, for instance. On the other side, we have an increase in ego-stability. Ego-stability, with the capacity for concentration and the exertion of willpower, is increased by all measures that are ascetic or aimed at overcoming pain. The practice of simultaneously increasing ego-stability and awakening the unconscious produces a heightened psychic tension, which is then released by a vision or revelation. Another, somewhat inferior measure simply aims to awaken the unconscious while diminishing, altering, and shutting out consciousness. These measures include the widespread use of narcotics and mass ecstasy. At the higher range of these cultic practices, aimed at achieving ego-stability, measures like the magical circle are often added. The manifestations of the unconscious are viewed from the center of the circle, where one is protected against being torn apart and flooded by the unconscious.

But such preparations, which enable the awakening of the collective unconscious and thus also theophany, release forces that can cause the average person, coming into contact with these phenomena, to perish from the psychic blow. The effect of these irruptive phenomena evidently depends on the strength of consciousness. An adequate consciousness experiences such phenomena as revelatory; one that is too small bursts (madness, schizophrenia, *Pardes*[19]); and one that is even smaller dies from the psychic blow, either quickly or after lengthy suffering.[20]

All these preparatory measures can also be found at the revelation on Sinai. But although they are observed, and although the distance from the site of the theophany becomes greater and greater, the psychic shock of the people is tremendous. Those who are waiting are gripped by such fear, lest the theophany address them directly, that they ask Moses to block its path to them. They want to receive the revelation from him as a report and no longer to experience it directly (Ex 20).

At first it was still believed that the people could enter the place of theophany at a certain point in time, that the priests should later be involved in the revelation (Ex 19:21), and finally Aaron as well (Ex 19:23). In the end, however, Moses went alone. The people "trembled with fear," just as the mountain "trembled with fear"[21] (Ex 19:16, 18); they "faltered" and "stood far off" (Ex 20:15).

These stages of the text are not different sources, but all represent points on the scale of resistance to revelation. Or, alternatively, the sources are composed so that they produce such a scale.

It is decisive for the history of Judaism that the whole people could not be involved in the smelting furnace at Sinai (Ex 20:19). Though one midrash[22] reports that, when the revelation occurred, Sinai was placed over the people like a pot, precisely this did not happen. Instead, direct theophany revealed its meaning and revelatory character only to Moses. The people, who could not cope with the tremendous collective force of this irruption, were seized, trembling, only by the external phenomenon. "Now all of the people were seeing the thunder-sounds, the flashing-torches, the *shofar* sound, and the mountain smoking; when the people saw, they faltered, and stood far off. They said to Moshe: You speak with us, and we will hearken, but let not God speak with us, lest we die!" (Ex 20:15–16).[23]

Thus, the people's basic shock is only the overwhelming uncanniness of the numinous. Moses said to the people, "Do not be afraid! For it is to test you that God has come, to have awe of him be upon you, and so you do not sin" (Ex 20:17), but the fateful outcome is that "the people stood far off, and Moshe approached the fog where God was" (Ex 20:18).

This rejection of direct revelation by the people, who were unable to cope with it, is a central phenomenon of Jewish existence, irrespective of whether we regard the text as a core account, which its psychological consequence suggests, or whether we assume that its writers were aware of this central phenomenon and, guided by it, redacted the report. In his essay "*Leitwort* Style in Pentateuch Narrative"[24] and elsewhere, Buber has provided the most astonishing evidence that the writers of these texts knew perfectly well what they were doing.[25] But that the people's rejection of direct revelation was also understood as such follows from the fact that the institution of prophecy is closely associated with this rejection and ensues as its compensation.

> A prophet from your midst, from your brothers, like myself will YHWH your God raise up for you, to him you are to hearken, according to all that you sought from YHWH your God at Horev on the day of the Assembly, saying: I cannot continue hearing the voice of YHWH my God, and this great fire I cannot (bear to) see anymore, so that I do not die! And YHWH said to me: They have done-well in their speaking; a prophet I will raise up for them from among their brothers, like you; I will put my words in his mouth, and he will speak to them whatever I command him.
>
> *(Deut 18:15–18)*[26]

Moses, at least, representing prophethood—in contrast to priesthood—did not agree with this fact,[27] a point that emerges mostly clearly from the account of the two men in the camp who are seized by the spirit (Num 11:27). When Joshua demands that Moses put an end to this business, Moses replies: "Are you jealous for me? O who would give that all the people of YHWH were prophets, that YHWH would put the rush-of-his-spirit[28] upon them!" (Num 11:29).

The extraordinary, revelatory invasions of the collective unconscious are so forceful that the individual can often barely endure the whirlwind of experience (Is 21:2), not to mention that delivering the message involves the greatest, life-threatening risk. If even the great prophets, from Moses to Isaiah, were afraid to accept the numinous irruption, then the people's collective fear of the irruptive events on Sinai is most understandable. This is the danger that the midrash means when it says: "At that time the earth shook and its chasms yawned."[29] It is the impending danger of flooding, the chaotic invasion of the unconscious.

But despite everything, this flooding almost destroyed the entire people, a fact demonstrated by the remarkable episode of the "Golden Calf," which is even more striking coming just here in the text.

The phenomenology of YHWH's irruption

The divine descent to the mountain is the image under which the people's Sinai experience stands. This connection between the two polarities—YHWH and the mountain—takes place amid the thunder, lightning, and fire of the revelatory explosion. When Buber writes, "Israel observes that its folk-God also rules the earth-powers,"[30] he touches on this same tension of opposites. But as the leader-God of the Semitic peoples, this folk-God is characterized by his primary alienation from nature. Baudissin has observed that the tribal god, as the direct ruler of the tribe, is a phenomenon whose power operates within the specific community he leads, that is, within a human group and its psychic foundation. "Since time immemorial, the Semitic peoples have apparently treated the relationship of nature to religion as secondary."[31] This alienation from nature also expresses itself insofar as the Semitic gods are not "identical with natural things," but instead "possess something else, which belongs specifically to them."[32] Or as Baudissin adds, in a passage of great significance for us: "For the Semites, the religious life of the person relates to the naturalistic substance of the gods, almost as if it were something else, something independent. For them, the natural powers are gods only as they exist for the human being, not insofar as they belong to nature."[33]

Later in this work, we shall closely examine this phenomenon, that the Semitic gods are related essentially to human beings, that is, that they are considered and perceived in terms of their effects on and for people. Here, in regard to the Sinai experience, we must consider to what extent the character of the theophany is natural, or how we should otherwise understand the transmitted experience of revelation, in the divine descent to the mountain, as a volcanic manifestation. YHWH's character is still represented far too often as that of a "volcanic god," although his hostility toward nature, to use this ambiguous expression for once, should have warned against equating him with a natural phenomenon. But along with this hostility toward nature and earth, and in fact because of it, fire and storm belong to the dominant symbolism of YHWH's theophany and way of acting (Gen 19:24; Lev 9:24, 10:2; Num 11:1; Deut 32:22; Amos 5:6, 7:4; Is 30:34, 34:9, 43:2, 65:5; Judg 6:21, 13:20; 1 Kings 18:24, 38; Job 1:16; Dan 7:10; 2 Chr 7:1; Jer 5:14, 17:4; Ps 18:9; 104:4).[34]

As we shall see, it is precisely YHWH's psychically invasive character, his catastrophically moving presence, that suggests this symbolism, together with the powerful affectivity induced by and accompanying this state of possession. Fire-symbolism has the character of spirit and light, and also of affective kindling. Thus it corresponds to the typical form of prophetic possession, which is a state of being emotionally seized and consumed by a prevailing, spiritual, inner force. In contrast, what belongs to an outbreak of YHWH's wrath is its character as an attack, and the impact of this devouring intrusion on the psychic system of the one seized by it. We shall later discuss what makes this phenomenon both characteristic and highly significant. For the moment, this brief comment may illustrate the explosive character of the revelation on Sinai, in its symbolic and structural meaning. For the symbolism in which a phenomenon manifests itself, whether conditioned individually or collectively, expresses the corresponding process within the psychic structure of the one having the experience. Only by its universal, identical appearance in the human structure does each symbolism and each symbolic experience become readable, understandable, and universally effective. Thus, for anyone, the experience of a divinity surrounded by fire has a specific meaning and impact, which is different from the meaning of, for instance, the experience of a tree-divinity.

The model for the collective Sinai experience is Moses' individual experience of the thorn bush.[35] For that reason, these two experiences are juxtaposed, whereas the difference of location, which matters not in the least, is preserved. The Sinai experience is so overwhelmingly powerful because, unlike the experience of the thorn bush, it is not constellated by the psychological structure of a single individual, but by the seizure of a whole people.

Two levels of the Sinai event must be distinguished. Although connected, these levels have completely different effects. The revelation on Sinai, as a vision, is the projection of the people's state of emotional possession. There, a process with immense consequences erupts outward from the people's unconscious. It is irrelevant whether and how far this collective vision is supported, brought about, accompanied by, or occurs independent of a real volcanic eruption.

YHWH's invasive revelation through or out of the primordial depths of the people can only take place amid fire and lightning, because these are the corresponding psychic symbols that would appear even if the Sinai were a dead volcano. Whereas the people cannot cope with this overpowering psychic irruption, Moses is able to enter into the explosive, life-threatening event. The blending of outer and inner experience characterizes every psychic projection, and the individual's containment in a projection of the collective unconscious is even now a common feature of collective phenomena. In earlier, that is, more unconscious stages of humanity, however, the more or less optical reality of a vision is absolutely everywhere in evidence. Thus, the account of YHWH's fiery descent to the mountain relies on the eyewitness of both the people and Moses.

The Tablets of the Law

Moses is capable of bearing and enacting the YHWH–earth tension, which is concretized here on the mountain. In him, the actual phenomenon of revelation now constellates itself, in what depth psychology calls the unifying symbol. The unifying symbol appears here in the Tablets of the Law. These tablets, the stones inscribed by YHWH's fiery finger, the Law, are the fruits of the opposition constellated in Moses and the people between spirit and matter, YHWH, and earth. Pervading the reality of the world, YHWH's Law, the Torah in the form of the Tablets of the Law, is the fruit of the revelation on Sinai. This symbolic vision is the actual core of the Sinai event, which was later blurred by falsely attributed empirical laws, whatever their origin. But in contrast to priestly law, or any other forms of law, these tablets, as we shall see, symbolize what we shall call the prophetic law.

The Golden Calf

While Moses experiences this on the mountain, the Golden Calf event erupts among the people. The Golden Calf, worshiped in orgiastic dancing and screaming celebration, is without doubt the symbol of the earth-polarity. How is this possible, and how should it be understood?

The Golden Calf is—it seems to us— the fateful outcome of the split between Moses and the people caused by the people's exclusion from direct revelation. The Sinai experience corresponded to a tremendous awakening of the unconscious, which was originally meant to lead the people in the planned progression to the mountain and the explosive event of theophany.[36] One possibility was that this progression would have occurred, and that part of the people would have perished. The other possibility is what actually, fatefully, took place. The people were protected by their exclusion from the inner experience of the YHWH-polarity—the outer experience proves to be devastating enough—and so were forced, in line with a familiar psychological law, toward the opposite polarity, that of the earth. This earth-polarity, which is obviously very strong in a people belonging to the family of Semitic peoples, is now activated by the powerful awakening of the unconscious and leads, in a splitting-off, to the celebration of the Golden Calf, that is, the hostile counter-principle to YHWH. This magnificent and tragic myth of the founding act of Jewish religion contains one of the basic problems, if not *the* central problem, of Jewish existence and history.

The decisive misconstellation causes YHWH's wrath to erupt. The constellation of forces, corresponding to the people's YHWH-polarity, had just taken effect in YHWH's theophany. But now, having been repressed by the people's turning to the Golden Calf, these forces turn violently against them. The disastrous consequences of such manifestations of wrath, which correspond energetically to very strongly repressed contents, are familiar to us from other situations (e.g., Ex 4:14, 24). Only Moses' intervention prevents a disaster, the total annihilation of the people. He thwarts (Ex 32:14) or at least appeases YHWH's wrath by venting his own anger instead (Ex 32:19). By placing himself at the center of events, and by becoming conscious of the catastrophic conflict and responding to it as the leader of the people, he prevents the catastrophe in the people's unconscious from further consuming them.

Moses as rescuer from the danger of the unconscious

Plague, ordeal, murder by the Levites

Tradition distinguishes the three levels of death sentence that are here imposed on the people.[37] The first is the outburst of YHWH's wrath, followed immediately by a plague (Ex 32:35), corresponding to the people's unconscious regression and taboo violation. The danger of being flooded by the unconscious, which could have occurred progressively by setting foot on Sinai, now occurred anyway through the regression to the Golden Calf. Whereas the progression of the whole people, which was initially contemplated and intended, failed because of their fear, that is, their psychic inadequacy, Moses in their place nevertheless accomplished this progression when the Tablets of the Law were revealed to him as the unifying symbol. This outcome remained fruitful for the people, and also resolved the conflict within their unconscious, as long as their contact with Moses was preserved, and as long as he received the revelation for them. But at the moment when the people regressed, as the text clearly shows (Ex 32:1), this contact, the people's *participation mystique*[38] with Moses, broke off, due to his long absence.

We believe—at least by way of illustration—that the midrash about the foundation stone[39] ought to be mentioned in this context, because the clay shard bearing YHWH's seal, which is said to be the lock on the abyss and counts as the foundation of the world and the Temple, seems perfectly analogous to the stone tablets (clay shards) inscribed by God's finger (YHWH's seal). Both instances are modeled, of course, on the cylinder seals of Babylon, which were imprinted on clay.

The unifying symbol of revelation achieved by Moses, in which the great tension of opposites powering the Sinai event is productively bound together, is destroyed the very moment the regressing people relinquish their contact with Moses. When he sees the people's regression to the Golden Calf, Moses erupts with YHWH's wrath and smashes the stone tablets, and thus this first synthesizing event of covenant-creation fails and falls back into what has not come to be. This, however, corresponds to a smashing of the foundation stone that had locked the abyss of the unconscious conflict.[40]

The chaotic abyss of the unconscious breaks open, causing a negative, ruinous irruption and, through the plague, the death of the people. This death is indicated in the text, but it is also known to us from other events where YHWH's wrath causes the death of the afflicted; it corresponds to the taboo-death of the primitive.[41]

The reaction to these events is the ordeal, a divine trial, in which Moses gives the people water to drink, mixed with the pulverized golden coating of the calf. This ritual ordeal is familiar to us from the ordeal of the woman suspected of adultery (Num 5:12–31). She must drink holy water mixed with the dust of the temple floor, here represented by the crushed parts of the earth-calf symbol. If found guilty, the woman perishes from drinking the cursed water. The Old Testament frequently conceives idolatry as fornication and as adultery toward YHWH, so that the analogy to the ordeal is obvious.[42] The consequence of drinking this administered water is, as shown above, perceived by tradition as a second kind of death sentence.

If the plague represents a direct, destructive effect of the regressive unconscious, and if the ordeal is a trial initiated by Moses, that is, an ethically oriented trial whose executor is YHWH himself—a divine trial—then the third kind of death sentence imposed on the people is the killing of the three thousand. This marks an entirely new level, namely, the active and conscious intervention by a part of the people. Later this group, which killed the three thousand, is seen as embodied by the Levites.

Thus, in the response to the people's regression to the Golden Calf, three levels and stages must be distinguished: plague, ordeal, trial. These stages also represent various levels of consciousness. The plague, as a direct reaction of the collective unconscious, requires the strongest containment in the unconscious. It corresponds to what we called, above, a "psychic blow," the catastrophic reaction of the unconscious when the individual or the group becomes half-conscious or is made fully conscious of violating a taboo.

The ordeal already represents a higher level. In it, YHWH is the god, the one who acts and judges, who intervenes through institutional action, and no longer in the form of a biologically effective fate. The ordeal has a judicial, that is, an ethical, character, and is conducted by an institutionally appointed figure, a medicine man, or a priest, as a conscious representative of the divinity. In the trial of the slaying of three thousand, carried out by the Levites, YHWH's magical and ritual power, which transcends the unconscious of those concerned, is replaced by the ethical, conscious responsibility of those who are "with YHWH."

Quite possibly, these three reactions correspond to three layers interwoven in the text, because the levels of consciousness also represent distinct historical layers. These structural and psychological levels provide adequate criteria for distinguishing textual layers, but without tearing them apart. Here, even if three texts and layers could be differentiated, they are intentionally woven into a unity.[43] Instead of dissecting the text analytically, it is a matter of understanding the synthesizing redaction that weaves these distinct texts into one.[44]

The nature of the countermeasure is not only highly characteristic but also deeply revealing of the problem of the conflict between YHWH and nature, as manifest in the regression to the Golden Calf.

> Moshe took-up-a stand at the gate of the camp, and said:
> Whoever is for YHWH—to me!
> And there gathered to him all the Sons of Levi.
> He said to them:
> Thus says YHWH, the God of Israel:
> Put every-man his sword on his thigh,
> proceed and go back-and-forth from gate to gate in the camp,
> and kill every-man his brother, every-man his neighbor, every-man his
>   relative!
> The Sons of Levi did according to Moshe's words.
> And there fell of the people on that day some three thousand men.
> Moshe said:
> Be-mandated to YHWH today,
> even though it be every-man at the cost of his son, at the cost of his brother,
> to bestow blessing upon you today.
>
> *(Ex 32:26–29)*

What shines through the unnatural act of the Levites is the great vision of immediate loyalty to YHWH. This is a vision of the absolute and exclusive obedience to the inner voice, an obedience that severs all natural ties. An unbroken chain stretches from the sacrifice of Isaac, through this deed of the Levites, to the prophets, who at God's command hasten away from their plowshares for the sake of those who follow, and all the way to Jesus, who "does not know his mother" (John 2:4). We shall discuss this problem in detail later. What matters here is how one part of the people sides unconditionally with YHWH's irruptive power. The reaction of those gathered around Moses dissolves the bond with the earth, compensates for the regression to earth by the rest of the people, and thus saves them.

This text was certainly written by men for whom prophetic experience, the direct revelation of the divinity, was the decisive phenomenon for both inner and outer history. Indeed, much suggests that, historically, this prophetic class was opposed to the priesthood, the guardian of what later became of the Law. Aaron's calamitous role, as opposed to that of Moses, is clearly emphasized here, especially when their stances are compared. Despite all his punitive power, Moses wants to take the entire blame upon himself (Ex 32:10–14; esp. 32:32). He defends the people until the very end, whereas Aaron lies and directs all guilt away from himself onto the people (32:2–6 versus 32:20–24). Identifying those who crowded around Moses with Levi is doubtless meant to contrast with Aaron and the Aaronites.[45,46]

Thus, ultimately, the great revelation on Sinai failed in a central respect, perhaps the most crucial of all, and the text was clearly composed in this knowledge. The people did not participate in direct revelation. Not only could they not cope with this event, but they could be rescued from their fall into regression only at the cost of great effort and loss. They could not bear the incredibly strong psychic tension ensuing from their Sinai experience, which signified a tremendous invasion into their structure. This insight into the people's incapacity was accompanied by profound resignation, and this incapacity later led to the institution of prophetism, as discussed above. Here it finds its peculiar expression, which can be understood only from this particular perspective.

Most characteristically, the Jewish genius allows its foundational story—the basic revelation, the Sinai event, which turned the people into a people—to begin with its own catastrophic failure. This recurrent trait—the ability not only to look one's own shadow in the eye, but also to see the dynamics of life playing out in the conflict with that shadow—characterizes Hebrew prophecy, the authority of which rests on prophesying disaster. This tension, between a clear vision of failure and an obdurate "nevertheless," is one of the driving forces of all Jewish existence. It is associated deeply both with the paradoxical nature of YHWH and with the way his people takes upon itself the paradox of life.

The elevation of Moses and the introduction of prophecy

It seems to us, however, that the people's failure at Sinai forever destroyed the possibility of revelation realized in the first tablets, which were smashed. Only a highly important and fateful event makes it possible for the second tablets to be revealed all the same: the transformation and elevation of the figure of Moses.[47]

The latent prophetic capacity of the individual

The original purpose of the transformation of the entire people through its possession by the revelation on Sinai, this alchemical transformation of its structure in the smelting furnace of revelation, did not occur. Instead, only one figure, Moses,[48] survived the fire of this irruption. On account of the people's failure, an extraordinary chasm now opened between Moses and the people. Already at the beginning, when the people trembled with fear, Moses became the intercessor between them and YHWH. But in this role, he was still human. He was a pre-eminent part of the people, so to speak, its representative. Now, however, after the Golden Calf, the distance between Moses and the people has become extraordinary. His identification with YHWH's wrath, as whose executor he appears, together with the theophany of grace, has turned Moses' YHWH-likeness into an experience for the people. Moses, as YHWH's representative, now becomes himself the *numinosum et tremendum*.[49] The people are afraid to approach him, just as previously they were afraid to approach the mountain of revelation. The skin on his face is radiant (Ex 34:30), to such a degree that he must cover it with a veil. Moses has become what we call a "mana-personality."[50] This transformation at first causes the loss of something irretrievable—the people's autonomy with regard to revelation. The people now have a "leader," a central, law-giving figure, whose essence is numinous, and whose messages have the character of revelation. This representation of YHWH by Moses is most decisively manifest in the second Tablets of the Law, which, unlike the first, are written by Moses himself.

Our preoccupation with the biblical text may seem completely unrelated, at first, to the psychological purpose of our project. But in that respect it is appropriate, even when it can provide only a starting point or an initial perspective, because the real wellsprings of Judaism, constrained and buried, have become so inaccessible that we must venture an attempt to remove these secondary changes,[51] even if that venture opposes not only Jewish tradition but also what has become authoritative in the scholarly treatment of the Old Testament. We must really attempt to rediscover the figure of Moses, because he represents one, if not *the*, decisive habitus of the religious Jewish person, and precisely as a prophet. But Moses' prophetic nature has been almost concealed by secondary priestly revisions, which have turned him into the "Father of the Law," trying to support their anti-prophetic concept of existence with Moses' own authority. The same process occurred in the political sphere at the time, when Moses' followers were systematically oppressed and excluded in favor of the Zadokites.

It is important to realize that the text was composed from a prophetic point of view, that is, from a perspective representing the importance of direct revelation. Moses, in this view, is the prototype of prophecy, in clear contrast to the priest, and represents the necessity of direct revelation. For this reason, too, the people's failure is used to justify the institution of prophecy:

> A prophet from your midst, from your brothers, like myself will YHWH your God raise up for you, to him you are to hearken, according to all that you sought from YHWH your God at Horev on the day of the Assembly, saying: I cannot continue hearing the voice of YHWH my God, and this great fire I cannot (bear to) see anymore, so that I do not die! And YHWH said to me: They have done-well in their speaking; a prophet I will raise up

for them from among their brothers, like you; I will put my words in his mouth, and he will speak to them whatever I command him.

(Deut 18:15–18)[52]

The connection between the Sinai account and this passage in Deuteronomy is crucial. Equally important, however, is the wholly unpriestly and anti-cultic character of this passage, which places the prophet in the midst of the people and thus simply shifts onto him, in some sense, the people's own capacity to receive direct revelation. The people's prophetic function, their potential capacity to receive direct revelation, is dynamically embodied in the prophets. But only a few of the prophets are of priestly descent, and for them the question of descent has no meaning whatever.

The traditional, central figure of Moses unites the law-giver and the prophet. But whereas the biblical account—especially if we exclude the priestly code as its most recent part—represents Moses time and again, over his entire lifetime, as a prophet, a man of direct revelation and direct relationship with God, the priestly reworking has managed to turn Moses into a figure who shapes history, precisely in his capacity as law-giver, cult-founder, God's seal on the dogma.

If we consider the Moses narrative, excluding all the passages about the Law and concentrating on the actual account of events, then his prophetic traits are depicted as immeasurably strong, whereas his organizational, law-giving traits are strikingly weak. He is described as an extremely passionate and extraordinarily large-souled man, whose inner span extends from his deadly blow (Ex 2:12) to his vision of grace (Ex 33:12–23), from his shyness at being unable to speak (Ex 4:10) to his claim to out-argue God (Ex 32:10f.). Most strikingly, his attitude toward the outer world is always awkward, from his difficulty in dealing with the people (Ex 4:28, where he hands his assignment over to Aaron) to his inability to devise a simple and straightforward organization for delivering judgments (Ex 18:14ff.).

Moses is obviously a man of introspection. This trait, as we know, is thoroughly compatible with his role as a leader, indeed as *the* leader of the people. It does not at all suit the law-giver, however, in the sense that the people later received him under the influence of the priesthood.

This brings us to an important distinction: namely, between the law arising from direct, prophetic revelation, as a solution to a present conflict, and the law as a statutory power.

We have seen that the unifying symbol of divine law, the stone tablets inscribed by God, emerged from the principle of opposites, the YHWH–earth tension, and this is how we should imagine all prophetic law-giving. It is born from the urgency of a situation, in an introspective moment, in which the numinous appears and conveys the law in a spontaneously occurring word or image.[53] Such a situational law will later become permanent law often enough, just as prophetic covenants will often be associated with conditional laws that continue to exist as permanent laws. But in that case, the prophetic origin, that is, the relation of the required behavior to the inner revelation, is always crucially important. The origin of the law in YHWH's contact with the prophets, and that alone, is the living warrant of a law that changes in the course of history, and of a leadership of the people that stands in living contact with God through continuing direct revelations to the prophets. This is primitive theocracy,[54] and this is the political and religious meaning of prophecy, from consulting the divine oracle, the *Urim* and *Thummim*, to the "word of YHWH" to the prophets.

Unquestionably, the law-giving component also plays a decisive role for the real figure of Moses. But even today the text shows that this law-giving was purely prophetic. It involved "inquiring" of the divine in cases of dispute (Ex 18:13) and probably also in cases of illness, where the institution of *Urim* and *Thummim*, as oracles to be consulted, and also of the *Ohel Moed*,[55] the tent of direct divine revelation (Ex 33:7), plays a role.

Prophetic law-giving and the healing function

The connection between law-giving and healing the sick is most illuminating in this context. The crucial verse, Exodus 18:15, in which Moses sums up his actions, says: "The people comes to me to inquire of God." Toward the people, Moses calls this action to "make known God's laws and his instructions" (Ex 18:16). Nachmanides remarks on this passage: "When the people now come to me, to inquire of *Elohim*—that is, that I pray to him about their sicknesses, or tell them what he is saying to them."[56] This was called inquiring of God. The same was done with the prophets: "Formerly in Israel, thus would a man say when he went to inquire of God: Go, let us go to the seer" (1 Sam 9:9). Further: "Inquire of God through him, saying: Will I live through this sickness?" (2 Kings 8:8). The man of God was supposed to pray for King Ben-Hadad and to let him know whether his prayer would have been heard. This is also meant by the verse, "And she went to inquire of YHWH" (Gen 25:22). This Nachmanides citation needs to be compared with the passage in which YHWH describes himself as a doctor (Ex 15:26), and with the passage about the bronze serpent (Num 21:9), the healing symbol of YHWH that continued to be worshiped into historical times and was removed only by Hezekiah (2 Kings 18:4).

Prophetic law-giving, which from time to time subjects the people to God's direct volition, is the original theocracy, in which the leader-God actually decides the problems of the tribe or people belonging to him. He, YHWH, has the function of judge, whereas Moses is merely the divine executor. This basic conception, which was doubtless universal in human antiquity, emerges from the consultation of oracles such as the *Urim* and *Thummim*, just as it does from the ordeal, which we saw in use with the Golden Calf. Characteristically enough, in the text Moses can be felt to be "merely a prophet." In every life-situation where the divinity, who is the people's leader, needs to be consulted, or where there is a summons to speak, that is, to "go with God" or to be "a man of God," the prophet necessarily becomes God's mouthpiece. The more unstable the times and the people's fate, the more necessary is the prophet as mouthpiece of the guiding leader-God.

Moses finds this function so natural that he needs Jethro to suggest to him the institution of the elders as assistant judges (Ex 18:13–23), because Moses can no longer cope with the burden. Most tellingly, the transition from prophetic law (inquiry, oracles) to statutory law is encouraged by Jethro, a non-Jew. Assistant judges, of course, need a codified law. The transition from prophetic to secularized law—this, too, can be deduced from the text—is necessary with a growing population, in which the charismatic personality of the leader or prophet can no longer penetrate the tribe or group, nor maintain a living contact with God.

Also part of this context, historically, are the oasis at Kadesh[57] and the consolidation of separate tribes to form a people, at the center of which probably stands this oasis and a years-long sojourn there. But this problem can be mentioned only in passing. The name of the main source of the oasis, Sources of Judgment,[58] and also the power there of Jethro the Midianite, as far as this is indicated in the text, suggest the foreign influence and the adoption of a codified law, which may definitely be assumed to have existed in this ancient place of judgment. If Kadesh is seen as a way-station between the exodus from Egypt and the conquest of Canaan, then such an exodus—as far as we are familiar with the psychology of ancient groups and Semitic religious movements, for instance, Islam—takes place under the leadership of a prophetic figure, in this case Moses. The revelatory and visionary character belongs to this process, as well as the present-oriented, prophetic giving of the law. In contrast, the great oasis at Kadesh, as an ancient historical place of judgment and a central gathering point for the surrounding nomadic tribes, probably needs to be thought of as possessing a complicated law and judicial institutions.

Here, as always, we are dealing with fluid transitions. The oracle,[59] as a technique of divine inquiry, already stands—and this is important—halfway between prophetic law and codified law. Whereas original prophetic inquiry presupposes the charismatic gift of the prophet, who, in direct contact, takes up and passes on the hint breaking forth from the unconscious, oracular prophecy has already developed a major technical aspect. The focus lies no longer on the charismatic person, but on the institution being served, which explains why oracles, for instance, can also be inherited. Moreover, it is already crucial how the question is asked, especially in the case of a "Yes–No" oracle, which the *Urim* and *Thummim* are assumed to be, that is, the inquirer's conscious attitude plays a role. From oracular to codified law is an easy step, because recording the results of the oracles inevitably leads, and always has led,[60] to collections of divine judgments. But this presupposes that the people have a stable sociological structure, making it possible, even probable, that they will keep a more or less statistical record of the oracular sayings and a codifiable problematic of the questions. But in times of upheaval, human migration, and unprecedented life situations[61]—and this is true for a wandering people—the questions that are asked are unique and unrepeatable. For this reason, they cannot be answered by codified law, but only through direct contact with God.

The elevation of the figure of Moses after the event of the Golden Calf was the necessary process by which the people's failure was made up for by the mana-personality of Moses, who as a prophet, healer, and leader assumed the great mediatory function between YHWH and the people.[62]

But a later priestly redaction had elevated Moses' authority to divine heights, in order to support priestly and legal interests. The insertion of lengthy passages referring to the law should be understood in this sense. The passages were now all covered by Moses' authority, even if they directly contradicted the original depiction of Moses in terms of prophecy. The original concept of the text was based on other statements of these problems, which, although blurred at a later stage, are still evident today.

Prophecy, false prophecy, pagan prophecy

It is not our task to perform exacting biblical scholarship with a view to unraveling the finely enmeshed prophetic, Levitical, and priestly texts, redactions, and intentions in the text before us. Nevertheless, we must provide some general clues to how, behind the problems of biblical scholarship and textual criticism, the *problem of direct revelation* and the attitude toward it amount to the basic problem of the text and its revisions.

If one omits the lengthy insertions dealing with the law (Exodus, Chapters 20–23, 25–31, 35–40; Leviticus through Chapter 10; Numbers, Chapters 1–8, 15, 18, 19, 26–30, 32-35), and then considers the now-continuous account of the events in the wilderness, the interconnections that matter in the text become obvious.

Two kinds of basic facts become apparent: first, that the wandering in the wilderness is a continuous chain of failure by the people and, second, that the internal struggle with the people concerns the assertion of prophetic authority, as represented by Moses. This basic prophetic orientation clashes with priestly and Levitical counter-tendencies. In this regard, we must leave open the question whether, as we believe, a basic text, redacted by priestly writers, pre-existed the prophetic redaction, or whether we are instead looking at the priestly redaction of a prophetically revised basic text. One thing is certain, however: whichever way the basic text was worked on, the prophetic orientation, centered on the figure of the prophetically accentuated Moses, was very strong.

Elias Auerbach's[63] plausible and important thesis is hugely important for understanding these matters.[64] Auerbach argues that the writings of the fathers (Genesis, the Moses cycle, Judges, the two books of Samuel) all belong to a great, unified work of history written by a single author, Abiathar of the house of Eli,[65] a direct descendant of Moses.

To reconstruct a continuous sequence of the people's failure, one needs to place the numbers of the chapters dealing with failure beside the shorter version of the text that remains after the chapters about the law have been omitted:

Before the revelation on Sinai: Marah, Massah, Meribah (Ex 15–17)[66]

then: Failure in the face of the revelation[67]

then: The Golden Calf[68]

After the so-called setting forth from Sinai:

Tabera and YHWH's plague (Num 11)

The graves of craving and YHWH's plague (Num 11)

Aaron's and Miriam's complaints and punishment (Num 12)

Failure after the return of the spies and the curse of wandering in the wilderness (Num 13,14)

Disobedience and defeat by Amalekites and Canaanites (Num 40f)

Dathan's and Abiram's revolt, Korah's rebellion, and punishment (Num 16)

The people's complaint and YHWH's plague (Num 17)

The waters of strife and plague (Num 20)

The people's complaint, plague of poisonous serpents, the bronze serpent (Num 21)

The sinning at Shittim with the Baal of Peor and YHWH's wrath (Num 25)

This failure of the people as a collective must be compensated for by prophecy, as represented by Moses. Contrary to the later Levitical and priestly Aaronite–Zadokite tendencies, prophecy remains connected with the people and the collective. Indeed, it represents the potential of each member of the people to receive the gift of prophecy, that is, to enter into immediate, direct contact with YHWH.

The basic concept of latent folk-prophecy[69] becomes clearest, as we have seen, in the seventy men possessed by the *ruach* that rested upon Moses, and also in his reply: "O who would give that all the people of YHWH were prophets, that YHWH would put the rush-of-his-spirit upon them!" (Num 11:29). This possession of the seventy by prophecy, which follows YHWH's proposal, stands in emphatic contrast to the appointment of the assistant judges at Jethro's suggestion.

The fundamental conception of the latent prophetic character of the people's psychological structure necessarily leads to manifold conflicts about authority, in fact to all kinds of conflicts. First, the people face opposition from parties pursuing utterly different orientations, including the bearers of the cult, the priests, then the "false prophets," that is, other prophets making their claim, the bearers of hereditary prophecy, if any exists, and finally the pagan prophets.

The text before us engages with all these positions, all of which contradict the basic conception of prophecy, which demands the anonymity of prophetic authority, that is, that it not be defined by any institution, group, or caste.

But the various textual revisions have layered themselves upon the original picture, and must be removed again to make it clear. The prophetic orientation[70] which, as we have mentioned, emphasizes the general capacity of all parts of the people to be possessed by YHWH, first becomes evident after the Golden Calf, where the men who are "with YHWH" slay their neighbors and avert disaster.[71] The fact that these men are attributed to the tribe of Levi, from whom its *priestly* right "to fill its hands" is derived, belongs to the Levitical layer of the text, which will concern us later.

Next follows the outpouring of the *ruach* on the seventy men, and on Eldad and Medad, and Moses' previously mentioned cry. Included in the people's failure and its complaint, and now also in Aaron's and Miriam's complaint, is the excelling of Joshua and Caleb (Num 14).[72] At first, Caleb is an anonymous character, like Pinchas, who is called to the priesthood on account of his deed (Num 25). His attribution to the house of Aaron is secondary.

The struggle between the prophetic conception of Moses and the rivaling opposition parties becomes evident—despite the repaintings still to be discussed—on the one hand in Aaron and Miriam's complaints against him, and on the other in Korah's rebellion. Korah invokes, just as Aaron and Miriam do, the sacred character of the *whole* community, and that YHWH is in their midst, and thus endangers Moses' prophetic leadership. These claims, which are based on the false application of a correct prophetic conception, are joined by Dathan's and Abiram's uncomprehending opposition (Num 16). Far removed from any religious notion, they misconstrue Moses as the power-usurping, "power-political" leader. (Characteristically, this typical allegation is made by people with a materialistic outlook. Their motto is "the land flowing with milk and honey," and their attack on Moses is accordingly pointed: "Egypt is in reality the land flowing with milk and honey, but you have seduced us into the wilderness, which is your land flowing with milk and honey.")

Once again, we are not talking about two confused texts, as biblical criticism assumes, but about two different, opposing parties. Appropriately, the party of "false prophecy" is annihilated by fire, whereas the party that misunderstands in terms of earthly power-politics is devoured by the earth. These differing kinds of annihilation correspond symbolically, in precise ways, to the two false standpoints. Korah and his group, who are consumed by fire outside the Tent of Meeting,[73] are clearly distinguished from Dathan and Abiram, who stand in the entrance to their tents.[74] The text emphasizes precisely the opposition between the two parties and the different forms of their downfalls.

The original topic—Korah's rebellion against Moses, which is juxtaposed with Dathan's and Abiram's on the one hand, and Aaron's and Miriam's on the other— was only later inflected into a rebellion against Aaron, in the context of the major priestly, Aaronite–Zadokite falsification of the text.

This direction continues when Aaron's and Miriam's death follows Korah's, and when immediately afterwards Moses proves to be a prophetic-priestly "healer" in the context of the bronze serpent. Quite independent of this serpent's symbolic, cultic, and historical meanings, the text evidently intends to demonstrate the supremacy of the figure of Moses, immediately after all oppositions from within have definitely been overcome. In a consistent enforcement of the primacy of prophecy over all other currents, the struggle with "false prophecy" is followed by that with pagan prophecy, as we see in the great Balaam episode.[75]

This original line, which is still evident in the text, is blurred by the battle between the Levites and the Aaronite–Zadokite priests, who both oppose the prophetic conception of YHWH's direct charismatic choice.[76]

This prophetic conception distinguishes the primacy of the prophets' charismatic calling from false prophecy, which appears here in the claims of laymen (Dathan and Abiram), Levites (Korah), Aaronites (Aaron), and the family of Moses (Aaron and Miriam). All these rival claims are rejected in favor of the man Moses, who is the genuine and sole bearer of the commanding power of the leader-God, YHWH.

A good example of this folk-prophetic tendency to emphasize YHWH's charismatic independence occurs, it seems to us, in the account of Moses' sin (Num 20:12), which is garbled to the point of incomprehensibility, and his sentencing to death in the wilderness. In this account's extraordinary elevation of the prophetic figure of Moses, its evident intention is to reduce even *his* absolute authority to a human scale, and so to ensure the dominance of the leader-God over every one of his executors.

The inclusion of Aaron at this point merely blurs the original fact, namely, his death and Miriam's after their complaint. For this reason, evidently, the sin of Moses has been brought forward to this place in the text. Primarily, the narration of Moses' trespass was linked directly to his punishment, namely, his death on Mount Nebo. This corresponds to the schema used to teach this entire series of "trespasses and punishments," which extends from the exodus from Egypt through Sinai to the wandering in the wilderness and the conquest of Canaan.

The inclusion of the great Balaam episode (Num 22–24) in this context completes the explication of Hebrew prophecy, the basic intention of which we have discussed. The Balaam episode concerns the confrontation of prophecy with *pagan prophecy*, insofar as this cannot be dismissed as chthonic divination. There are true prophets among the peoples. But as all genuine prophecy comes from YHWH, and only from YHWH, these prophets pose no threat for Israel, because their prophesying must necessarily coincide with YHWH's basic intentions. (The later negation of Balaam in Jewish tradition misses the inner meaning of this episode, for which it was important to show Balaam as a *true* enemy prophet. He is harmless and must bless Israel rather than curse it, precisely and only because he is a *true* prophet.)

Very much later, in Deuteronomy, the confrontation with pagan prophecy—as well as the fundamental significance of folk-prophecy—reaches conscious formulation (Deut 18:15). Also evident here is the connection between prophecy and the people's failure on Sinai, as well as that sentence that, as we have seen, practically serves as a title for the narrative about the people's failure from Exodus to Numbers: "Rebellious have you been against YHWH from the (first) day that I knew you!" (Deut 9:24).

The link between these passages and the folk-prophetic depictions and redactions of the other books is evident, although it remains to be seen, for this reason, whether these passages in Deuteronomy are not considerably older than is generally assumed.[77]

But, whereas in Deuteronomy these problems have reached conscious formulation and institutionalization, in the accounts we have discussed they live as a living process and a destiny-shaping event. We are talking here about the basic problematic of the Jewish people, the question of the revelatory connection between YHWH and Israel, the fundamental question of what prophecy means for the collective.

The role of prophecy is the key to understanding the people's suspension between YHWH, on the one hand, and its natural involvement with the earth, on the other. This tension has its magnificent projection in the revelation on Sinai, in the regression to the Golden Calf, and the prophetic function of Moses. But the basis of this tension can be understood only by elucidating the relationship between JHWH and the earth-principle.

In its affinity with pagan–Semitic psychology, however, this people—"seduced by Canaan," as it were—is not only attached to the earth, as its own written record of the perpetual "falling away from YHWH" would have one believe. It is also given an essential part of its structure, attached to the here and now, oriented toward life, and allied with the world.

2. YHWH and the earth-principle

It is no coincidence that the Hebrews lack any notion whatsoever of the hereafter, nor that it is the world, as "this world," with all its various colors and nuances, that matters to them. For the Hebrews, no realm of death nor any hereafter frames earthly existence, the good and evil of which they live with the great naivety of a strong and primitive people. It has always been the incomparable charm and awe-inspiring greatness of the Bible—disregarding its determinative religious content for a moment—that it is governed by a powerful closeness to the earth, an undistorted view of good and evil, which no other people or time in the world knows. This ultimately quite untheological stance has always aroused the resentment of Christian and Jewish moralizers. Entangled with the here and now, this unconcern and piety are great enough to permit the tribal father, who wrestles with and defeats the angel,[78] nevertheless to skillfully increase his property, just as they allow the law-giver of Sinai to be a man slaughterer and at the same time a timid person.[79]

It is a powerful vitality that lets the God-filled Samson, a Nazarite, be killed by a foreign prostitute, while still holding him to be filled with God, and that almost grants permission to King David, the people's and God's favorite, to commit adultery, to murder, and to be a coward. If one compares this with the heroic endeavors of other peoples, for instance, the Neo-Germanics, one understands a point that is striking but otherwise not immediately obvious: namely, how passionately a mistaken theology bestowed its poison upon the Jewish people of the Old Testament, whose lack of feigning evoked its disapproval and misjudgment. Here, too, Nietzsche saw both sides correctly: the greatness and autochthony of the Old Testament on the one hand, and the clericalizing of its critics on the other.

The affirmation of nature and nature's purity

Even after the priestly guild had divided the world into "pure" and "impure,"[80] the principle of nature's purity persisted. Primarily, uncleanness concerns humanity, and only secondarily nature, because the basic law is that things can become unclean only in and through their relation with human beings.[81] Central to the principle of impurity is the corpse, death, in stark contrast to YHWH, who, as we shall see, represents the living and the enlivening. Only from the perspective of this tension can we understand early Jewish psychology, for which everything earthy and watery stands in critical opposition to the principle of air and fire. The impurity of the fruits of the tree in the first three years, the so-called "foreskin" (Lev 19:23) of the tree,[82] which leads to proscription of the fruits in this time, is related to the prevalence of the aspect of earth and water, which has not yet been fully formed by the principle of light and sun.

Molitor (1839) rightly connects this with the fact that only a seven-day-old animal may be sacrificed. Only the reshaping force of the cosmic sevenfold, which ensures that a holy seventh-day Sabbath has contributed to developing the living being, makes that creature "ready," that is, mature. Naturally, circumcision on the eighth day also belongs in this context, as we shall see.

The cosmic process first establishes a balance of forces for the living creature, which, as a natural being, stands primarily under the dominant of the unconscious, under the predominant aspect of earth and water. But whereas all these distinctions about the human being are of the greatest importance for the ancient Jew, because the balance of their life system is threatened to the utmost by flooding with the forces of the unconscious, nature as such lacks the capacity to absorb physical impurity. Thus, neither animals and plants in their living state, nor water, as long as it flows, nor air, as long as it is not trapped, nor inorganic substances, as long as they are neither closely nor vitally connected with the soil, can be made impure from the outside.[83] Only those bodies can become impure that human beings draw out of general natural life into their own sphere, and which therefore, being governed by human beings, enter into an intimate relationship with them and participate in their essence. It is of great, and specifically psychological, importance that nature as such is not impure, but is drawn into the sphere of purity and impurity only because it represents a danger for the ancient Jews, who were so close to nature. The anthropocentric worldview that is evident in this stance, and also characteristic of the Semitic idea of God, is actually a psychological view, except that here it is projected in naive concretizing. But it is only possible to understand the relativity, that is, the relatedness of this view, if one refers it to the psychic structure of the people, whose "earthiness" comes with the constant threat of being devoured by unconscious forces, and who therefore—differentiating—are forced to distance themselves from these forces again and again.

For the Jew, attached to the earth and to the here and now, a steadying counterweight is formed by the prophets, who, in their primordial experience of YHWH as the irruptive God, are seized by the numinous supremacy of his ambivalent spirit-nature.

YHWH's invasive character is plainly obvious, and the force of the irruptive numinous, the overwhelming character of which we know from experiencing the collective unconscious, characterizes what is often said to be specific to the Old Testament. The "terrifying" nature of the living God, into whose hands one has fallen, can be deduced not only from the symbolism accompanying these theophanies,[84] in which the preferred symbolism is that of the elements, natural disaster,[85] and the animal kingdom, but also from the reactions of the afflicted, the shock and rapture of those seized by the supreme power. However, as Jung has again recently pointed out,[86] this side of the divinity, as *deus absconditus*,[87] is an inescapably real experience for the religious person, who does not have idyllic religious experiences, but has been beheld and called from the abyss within. Demonizing this aspect of YHWH, however, as frequently happens, merely represents the tendency, well known from history, to subordinate "old gods" to the victorious god as demons.

All prophetic experience is based on this primary experience of the numinous. In it is embedded each dealing with YHWH, time and again, as a harrowing and world-shattering irruption. The power of this numinous manifestation grows from the patriarchs, who are "mere" individuals, to the folk-God, the leader-God who determines the people and the history of humanity. From individual experience, we are very familiar with the invasive power of the numinous. Today, we still witness the traumatic reaction of the individual afflicted by the irruption of the unconscious, not only when a person is seized by a mental illness, but also when the integrity of the personality is maintained. This is true of every serious engagement with the deep level of the psyche, the incredible dynamics and universal expanse of which we customarily label the collective unconscious.

YHWH's irruptive character, as an invasion into a psychic system, is necessarily accompanied by a certain symbolism, and the confusion of this symbolism with the one whose irruption brings up the symbolism, as it were, has caused many misunderstandings. Insofar as YHWH's irruption is clad in nature-symbolism, his characteristic symbolic manifestations are fire, light, storm, wind, and cloud. A psychological knowledge of the reality of these phenomena allows one to recognize the inner content of this fire-and-air symbolism without concretizing it, and thus not to confuse the symbol with what is expressed through it. YHWH's spirit-character, the preferred form of his manifestations, contrasts starkly with the earth–water character of the unconscious. It corresponds to one side of the unconscious, the spirit- and meaning-giving side, which breaks into the psychic system of the possessed and expresses itself with the tremendous dynamics of the depths. We cannot discuss the phenomenology of the spirit-experience in any detail here.[88] Nevertheless, a few references may help to outline these phenomena, insofar as they occur in the Old Testament.

Behind the prophet's state of possession, as behind anything possessed by the spirit, stands that which wants to become loud, which wants to express itself, which is destined to intervene in life as word or saying. This aspect of wind and spirit[89] is still widely known in the phenomenon of in-spiration, of breathing in, although the dynamics of the one who in-spires stretches from the storm that shatters normal existence to the barely perceptible breath of the spirit. The relationship of this *ruach* aspect with fire has two prominent causes. What primarily corresponds to the irruptive character is an ecstatic and affective state of possession, which ranges from the heated, fiery, affective obsession of the possessed in all degrees of ecstasy to the passionate willingness to fight for YHWH. Moreover, the light-filled character of illumination also shimmers through, although here it changes in a highly characteristic way into militant affectivity. It is not—or only very seldom—the quiet light of illumination, but almost always the consuming fire of a spiritual content, which, violently taking possession, wants to break into the world, fervent and blazing.

The theological concept of the "Holy Spirit"[90] makes it appear highly desirable to eliminate the principle of the "spirit of God," the *ruach* of YHWH, from the Old Testament, although many passages still reveal the primitive notion of being possessed by the *ruach* of God.[91] Baudissin also takes the view that the idea of a "breath of life" in the human being is probably neither ancient Hebrew nor ancient Semitic,[92] although Hebrew, Babylonian, and Phoenician evidence suggests otherwise.[93] The fact that this *ruach* occupies a central, indeed *the* central, position in the first chapter of the Bible is conjured away as supposedly being "a foreign element that does not fit the whole," or even better by simply turning רוח אלהים [*Ruach Elohim*] into "a strong wind."[94] Nor does the allegedly later emergence of this chapter constitute an essential objection, because its central position suggests that the concept of the *Ruach Elohim* had a long history, or else was so commonly held, based on a corresponding primitive notion, that this chapter not only became capable of acceptance but also exercised its decisive influence on the Jewish and Christian history of ideas.

Standing in emphatic opposition to this view is Rudolf Otto, whose basic idea of the numinous is the final word on the matter in all religious scholarship.[95] After emphasizing the numinous character of the *ruach,* Otto agrees entirely with our view when he writes:

> The intuition of the contrast between *ruach* and *bassar, pneuma* and *sarx*— "spirit and flesh"— is the basic intuition. It underlies the entire biblical world of feeling and is its universal condition, its primary *a priori.*[96]

He describes the *ruach* in exactly these terms:

> In itself, however, inducing burning and striving, it blazes restlessly, urges and drives, comes and goes, grants and retreats. It is not static, but wholly dynamic and energetic.[97]

The unity of soul, spirit, breath, and wind is archetypal, that is, part of the common heritage of humanity, making it irrelevant to discuss whether this notion belongs primarily or secondarily to Judaism. Its historical effects are far more important.[98]

Although he refutes the idea that the *ruach* of God expresses a basic Semitic concept, Baudissin, of all people, has assembled important material to substantiate this fact.

The concept of "vitality" is of central importance to the Semitic concept of divinity. As we have seen, the corpse is said to be the incarnation of impurity. Although generally understood as a protest against Egypt and its death cult, this explanation does not go into matters in depth. Baudissin writes:

> In Semitism, "life" and "alive" in the absolute sense are the property and characteristic that distinguish the gods from human beings, thus a qualifier of the gods in general. This seems to have been the ancient Semitic idea.[99]

But this association of vitality with YHWH as the "living God" also forms the background to the Genesis narrative, in which the earth-*adam*,[100] through the breathing-in of the *nishmat-hayim*, the breath of life, becomes a *nefesh-hayah*, a living being. "What is communicated to him is breath, and from it comes life."[101]

In the creation of the human being, the contradiction between the principle of *pneuma*-breath and the system of body-blood is virtually skipped by the life-creating, in-breathing, divine force. Precisely this characterizes the special status of the human being in relation to nature. But the tension between YHWH and earth still continues to exist in the relationship between the human being and the divine. Baudissin writes:

> Unmistakably, however, a greater distance somehow exists between the divine and the human for the Semites than for the Greeks and especially for the Hindus. For the Semites, in contrast to the Indo-Germans, human nature does not include an element of divinity which needs only to be freed from the bounds of the strictly human in order to appear as fully divine. In Semitism, if one tries to define the contrast between God and man, one can only express it as the contrast between power and powerlessness, or, as the Old Testament puts it, in a form that can only be spoken and thought in Hebrew, as the contrast between *ruach* and *bassar* (Is 31:3), in which *ruach*-breath is designated as effective and lasting, and *bassar*-flesh as ineffective and transitory.[102]

This passage, it seems to us, expresses what is disputed elsewhere: namely, that the dimension of breath, wind, and spirit is specific to the divine and is what is actually alive, whereas the dimension of earth, flesh, and nature rises to its own dignity only in relation to the divine. Although this aspect of nature is not associated with the pervasive divine spirit, that does not prevent it from exercising a strong influence of its own on the human being, but its influence is then considered demonic.

Modern research has already established that "for all Semites, with the sole exception of the Hebrews, male and female deities appear next to each other."[103] The exclusion of the female deity doubtless favored regressions, instances of falling back into pagan cults.

Regardless of whether this absence of the feminine principle is primary or secondary, the unconscious component corresponding to this absent projection had to be strongly over-emphasized. Aside from the regressive transgressions into the cults of pagan mother goddesses, this led to the over-emphasizing of the earth factor that we mentioned before. This transference onto the soil is archetypally predetermined by the Mother Goddess, who, in the collective unconscious, is always simultaneously an earth goddess and an earth mother.[104]

The exclusion of the feminine principle from the cult, that is, the absence of a female deity, led to its unconscious projection onto the earth. The earth thus becomes the Holy Land, as *Eretz Israel* now assumes the role of the Jewish soul, which is occupied for other peoples by the projected Mother Goddess. The tremendous significance that the Holy Land and Zion, its incarnation, have had in Jewish history and its history of ideas, is well known, but what it means for the psychology of this people to have created the concept of the Holy Land has never been sufficiently understood.

Unquestionably, we are dealing with a concept familiar from the history of religion, that of the holy precinct. But its extension to the entire land, which parallels the extension of priestly holiness to the entire people, is more than a quantitative expansion. For better or worse, the earth and the Holy Land become a highly active and destiny-determining partner of the Jew, who owes his vitality to the projection of the archetypal mother-image onto the earth.

This projection of the mother-image onto the earth establishes the *participation mystique* with earth which is characteristic of the primitive person, and against which it is a major task of the prophets to struggle. We shall show elsewhere[105] that it is precisely imagelessness, as a principle of Hebraism, and its hostility toward all idolatry, which prevents the projection of images and excludes the usual path to consciousness. The other Semitic peoples, like all early peoples, experience their attachment to and dependence on the earth unconsciously and extremely powerfully at first, and they project this attachment onto an image of the mother-earth deity. Through engaging with her and practicing her cult, they gradually become conscious of this content, as the Mother Goddess becomes part of their conscious idea of the world. Or else the content remains semi-conscious but loses its negative, explosive effect, because it has a path toward people's consciousness via the cult.

For the Hebrews it is different. Because for them the content remains unprojected and animates the unconscious, it constellates there a typically negative situation: "the earth as threat."

Earth as threat

The earth only becomes threatening, however, when the Hebrews become unconscious, that is, when they lose their conscious orientation toward YHWH.

The endeavor of prophecy to liberate the people from this *participation mystique* with the earth follows another path than projection onto the image. It is an attempt to subordinate the earth-principle to YHWH and to consciousness, that is, to emphasize YHWH's cooperation with the earth, and to "sanctify" the earth to YHWH's more encompassing spirit-principle.

This basic fact, however, that the principle of earth is secondary also stirs up prophetic protest wherever the earthly world claims pride of place. The propensity to rein in the dominance of the earth, which we attribute for simplicity's sake to prophecy, can also be observed in crucial passages of the Old Testament.[106] This is not, however, an "anti-biological" tendency, as Goldberg suggests, but corresponds to what Buber calls "hallowing,"[107] a notion that should be understood not in theological, but in metaphysical, or better still psychological, terms. It means classifying and subordinating the simply natural under YHWH's order, that is, under prophetic law, the law that arises, in contact with the inner dimension, as the revelation of YHWH.

This prophetic law-giving begins with circumcision, as the symbol of the sacred transformation from purely natural procreation into a generational system of family (patriarchs) and people (Egypt), that is, into a system oriented toward the inner voice of YHWH, not toward the natural voice of worldly, practical–political, or economic circumstances.

Along the same lines, with the purpose of being freed from determination by the natural givens, lies the basic idea of the earth's dependence on the human being.[108] This reversal of the pagan principle of nature, according to which human beings rely on the earth and the Mother Goddess, does not correspond to a primary hostility toward the earth, but rather to the prophetic endeavor to compensate for the Jewish people's existing *participation mystique* with the earth.[109]

The tension between the natural–animal–pagan part, which obviously predominates in the early human, and the spiritually meaningful part, which appears projected in the YHWH–earth opposition—this tension is the energetic background for the historical events of chosenness and apostasy. Canaan, and the pagan surroundings, thereby represent the Semitic-primitive part of Hebraism, that is, the influences of this aspect resonate in the pagan layer of the people's unconscious and its needs, whereas the aspect of YHWH and spirit resonates only in prophecy, thus in individuals, or at most in prophetic circles.

We have already observed how even the revelation on Sinai was not received by the people, because their Semitic–pagan element was too strong (the Golden Calf). Later, however, Hebrew prophecy was based directly on this experience and created a metaphor for the phenomenon of chosenness, clearly formulating the structural particularity of the situation: chosenness and the threat of falling away.

For us, the essential aspect of this formulation is that the wording chosen was not moral but more or less biological, which does the best possible justice to the psychological facts and circumstances.

Characteristically, Jeremiah formulates this in YHWH's complaint about Israel:

> Yet I planted you as a choice vine,
> from the purest stock.
> How then did you turn degenerate
> and become a wild vine?.
> *(Jer 2:21)*[110,111]

The same image occurs in Isaiah, in the song of the vineyard planted by YHWH:

> He expected it to yield grapes,
> but it yielded wild grapes.
>
> (Is 5:2)

Expressed here is a degeneration, a genuine regression to the ignoble, pagan foundation of nature. YHWH's power represents a grafting, a transformation of substance, and its refinement through the intervening act of his prophetic revelation. Simultaneously, however, this inoculation is an act of begetting and corresponds to YHWH's marriage with Israel, which is why this falling away is both regarded and represented not only as a regression to the natural state, but also as adultery.

YHWH's substance-transforming intervention, which we have described with the symbol of grafting, this chosenness as YHWH's nature-transforming entrance into corporeality, as his marriage with Israel, is fulfilled in the individual in the *milah*, the circumcision, and in the collective in the Passover ritual, which bears obvious traits of a marriage rite.[112]

The fact that the covenant with YHWH, as a substantial transformation, represents not only an ethos, but also another hierarchy of the unconscious constellations of drives and powers, also explains the emphasis with which lordship is ascribed again and again to YHWH himself, even over the earth, fertility, and well-being.

Only the contrast with the universally worshiped cosmic powers of earth, heaven, or both makes it necessary to show the Hebrews that, despite his essential otherness, YHWH was, fundamentally and always, lord over these cosmic powers, as well.

YHWH as lord of fertility

Characteristically enough, however, as the lord of fertility he is always shown in relation to a certain meaning—indeed, if you will, as acting in a particular direction, in starkest contrast to the fertility principle of the great mother-goddesses, with their arbitrary and directionless spilling-out of abundance.

This is most typically seen in the cases of barren women, where YHWH proves that he is not only the lord of fertility, but also the lord of paradox and miracle. Whether he gives the son to elderly Sarah or to barren Hannah, it is precisely the special destiny of the childless (and at the time this meant accursed) woman that is transformed, as she becomes the mother of a special son—not just any son, and not just a nameless horde of children. Becoming the mother of Isaac, the son of promise, or the mother of Samuel, the prophet: this is the actual meaning of the fertility conferred on these women by YHWH. Thus, Rachel, as mother of Joseph and Benjamin, is superior to Leah with her many sons.

Shown here is one of the meanings of fertility, which is merely a vehicle for the voice of YHWH. Indeed, one could almost think that it is precisely through being alienated from her natural destiny that the barren woman is initiated by this destiny into a more intimate contact with YHWH, and is thus formed beforehand as the mother of the special son.

The awakening of this instinct for what is uniquely and meaningfully willed by YHWH contrasts with the anonymous birth-giving principle represented by the Great Mother as the mistress of the womb. Only a familiarity with this principle of fertility, recast into something meaningful and associated with YHWH, enables the mother who understands this principle—"against nature," and against the intentions of the "blind" husband and father—to secure the blessing for her real son, Jacob, ahead of Esau. For in Esau, her own, older son, YHWH's willed intention, the source of the woman's fertility, has proven incapable of fulfillment.

Also, as the lord of the fertility of the earth and the womb, YHWH does not deny his unclassifiable essence: he does not become "earthy." Even as lord of the earth, he still remains a wind-spirit, a charging and demanding principle of meaning, wanting to realize itself in and on the earth, which he places under his command.

Despite YHWH's providence, which already determines and chooses the prophet in the mother's womb, his appearance is experienced as sudden and overwhelming. YHWH's irruptive character, which represents a state of spiritual possession, has the fulminant character of suddenness, because the possessing force has not grown from the earth; it has not developed through slow, continuous growth, that is, in an earthy, vegetative way. Rather, what characterizes this level of experience is that something suddenly appears and violently takes possession. But this possessing force has a demanding, commanding, and directing character.

YHWH is always the God of distance. He can make himself present, to be sure, and the endeavor to maintain permanent contact defines the cult; yet he remains the remote one, regardless of how direct the relationship and regardless how much the answering one is a "Thou."[113] In this, YHWH is unlike the spirits of divination, which come from "nearby"[114] (Deut 32:17).[115] The experience that the provider of guidance emerges from the depths of the unconscious—always new, always different, but always overwhelming and meaningful—still today possesses this character of a "spirit," as it has since time immemorial: "yet you know not whence it comes or whither it goes" (John 3:8). But this invasive force—and exactly this characterizes its "distance"—is always infinitely superior to the particular formation of the here and now, the historical situation of the collective and the individual. Exactly the same is true when, as in late prophecy, the spirit becomes political and intervenes in the situation.

3. YHWH and prophecy

The nature of YHWH

Distance, paradox, unconditionality

The paradox of numinous experience consists in the fact that the unexpected and the impossible are always demanded, and do in fact occur. For it is the character of the compensatory phenomenon of the unconscious that it moves and occurs in opposition to the world's situation of consciousness and the horizon of knowability. Ever again, and always in new ways, the numinous, and the meaning it gives, refutes conscious knowledge and its orientation toward the world, for, in ways that are always new and overwhelming, the numinous rests on factors that are unconsidered, overlooked, repressed, and despised. Herein lies the eternal and eternally mysterious reality of the figure of God's servant: that the actual power of the numinous prevails through the one who is despised and supposed to be powerless. It is also clear that, and to what extent, the men of prophetic experience were destined to compensate for the Jewish people's attachment to this world and their addiction to the earth. It is just as obvious, however, that again and again the prophets were heard—if they were heard at all—only in times of great need and historical change. The people's habitus, though, which emphasized the here and now, their basic habitus of falling back, always sought to exclude the experience of the numinous and to keep it at arm's length.

The so-called nomadic ideal, the ideal of the desert, is actually the prophetic demand to be ready for and to follow YHWH's call, for YHWH, as leader, is never in principle "settled." Rather, he is the one who leads, breaks in, and summons the one who is constantly "here" in new ways in the prophet, and whose tie to cult and temple can be understood and conceded only under particular conditions. In the principle of YHWH's earthly attachment to the temple, the inner conflict between prophet and priest became evident and ultimately disastrous.

The unconditional willingness to follow the call of God's inner voice always includes the willingness to abandon all natural, worldly, earthly ties. We have already indicated this line. It extends from Abraham's summons, "Go-you-forth from your land, from your kindred, from your father's house" (Gen 12:1), through his sacrifice of his son Isaac, and from there to the Levites, about whom is written: "Who said of his father and his mother: I do not know him, his brother he did not acknowledge, his children he did not recognize!"[116] (Deut 33:9). It leads from the prophets to Jesus of Nazareth and his "cruel" saying: "Woman, I know you not."[117]

If the Rekabites' law of life—"You shall never drink wine, nor shall you ever build a house, or sow seed; nor shall you plant a vineyard; but you shall live in tents all your days" (Jer 35:6f)[118]—is placed beside that of the Nabataeans and of Islam,[119] then this is undoubtedly correct.[120] But behind this explanation stands not only an ethnological contrast (nomad versus farmer), or a merely social one (sheer poverty versus a life of opulence).

All the above oppositions are just implicit in those that exist between earthly nature and YHWH's transcendence. Later, these oppositions break apart, in a way that shapes history, in early Christianity and Gnosticism. Bread and wine and the fruits of the earth are prohibited—precisely the things that play such an important role in ancient Greek mystery cults, in Mithraism, and (in a transformed way) in Christianity. Becoming settled means attachment to the earth, whereas the provisionality of dwelling in tents is the existential form of an eschatology that is ready for the call.

By no means does this imply that the prophetic concept of being is identical with the nomadicized one. This extreme case simply highlights what existential conflict is alive behind the YHWH–earth tension, and what the desert ideal basically intends, in relation to the people's rootedness in nature. And the sacrifice of blood, of offering to YHWH the body that belongs to the earth, ultimately also has this character of placing oneself at the disposal of the in-breathing spirit, whether this takes effect by leading and seizing, by urging, or by cleansing through the medium of blood.

The nature of prophecy

Prophecy, mysticism, divination

This phenomenon of being possessed by something that "speaks out" also characterizes the crucial difference between prophecy and every form of mysticism.[121] The one who breaks in always remains the lord, expressing his will, which is thoroughly irrational even in giving meaning. What determines the attitude of the human being, as God's servant who must fulfill his will, is just the sublimity of the divine, his powerfulness, over anything human. This sublimity is experienced not simply "in the tribe's (and the people's) sense of dependence upon a force presiding over it,"[122] but also, in particular, in the helplessness of the individual toward the numinous power of the force seizing him, the יד יהוה,[123] the hand of YHWH.

The mysticism of escapism originates—greatly simplified and stripped of all historical determinacy—either in neuroticized introversion, which turns its entire intensity inward, out of a fear of life, or else in an extraversion that has satiated itself on the world, that has had enough of this world, and now legitimately transcends it to turn inward. This explains mysticism's anti-communal rejection of culture and the world, its ethical indifference and its propensity, assisted by various techniques, to achieve an emptying, a withering-away of the leaning toward life. It also explains the attitude of mysticism, which is self-reflecting, on the one hand, and consciousness-dissolving, on the other.

Prophecy, by contrast, stems from a primary introversion—this much can be said quite generally, without dwelling here on the particular psychology of the prophets—and from a state of possession from the inside, which, expressing itself, wants to *enter the world*. This explains the militant character of all prophecy, from emissary prophecy to actual mission. This state of possession is reflected in its activity, affectivity, and dynamics, the relentless one-sidedness of which, bordering on monomaniacal obsession, arises from the person's being filled completely by the possessing content. The greater the difference between the consciousness that is seized and the seizing content, the greater the intolerance. The absolute and unshakable faith of this type, due to the paradox of what is believed, rests upon the dominance of the seizing content, which takes such fierce possession of the entire structure of the possessed that the ensuing flooding of consciousness leaves no room for any doubt whatsoever, that is, for any autonomous activity of consciousness.

This incongruence, between the seizing content and the seized consciousness, is the central problem of all prophecy, as we have already seen in our discussion of pagan prophecy and the false prophets.

Only in this context do we understand a phenomenon that at first seems to conflict with the prophetic demand for direct inner experience: namely, the strict and harsh rejection of all soothsaying, divination, etc., which is demanded time and again in an exceptionally large number of passages. It would surely be mistaken to regard this as an expression of the priestly inclination against the appearance of direct revelation, because the problem of the false prophet is a central and genuine problem of Hebrew prophecy.

The depth of the revelatory layer and the conscious attitude

The rejection of divination, to summarize in this word the entire sphere of unconscious revelatory forces known to paganism, stems not from rationalism, as late Judaism often interpreted this phenomenon, but from an essentially different attitude. The phenomenon needing explanation is the strange fusion of inner revelation, as the revelation of YHWH, and the simultaneous emphasis on consciousness.

This phenomenon becomes understandable and highly illuminating if it is translated into the language of modern depth psychology. Prophecy excludes the entire layer at work in divination, namely, the personal unconscious and the deeper-lying complex nature of the psyche, insofar as it is more or less closely associated with the personal sphere. This explains the peculiar criterion for the prophet, that "if he prophesies peace, he is a false prophet,"[124] and thus also the crucially mistaken identity of prophets and prophets of doom in the Old Testament. All levels of the unconscious that are pregnant with wishful images, etc., belong to divination, to the sphere of false revelation deemed worthy of banishing. So what actually characterizes true prophecy? When we referred to it above as the primal depth of the unconscious, from which true prophecy proceeds, this was not by accident. It is the level that arises in a form utterly alien to the ego and to consciousness, which not only possesses no personal connections with consciousness or to the personal sphere, but also the contents of which are rejected outright by consciousness as alien and unacceptable.[125] This is demonstrated clearly by the behavior of the prophets, who struggle against revelation as against a burden, a threat, and a violation, and want to flee from it, all clear symptoms that the contents of the arising revelation are ego-alien.

These contents originate from a level that the ego rightly experiences as not its own, but as stemming from the "wholly other," which is to say as coming from YHWH. But primary ego-alienness, that is, the origin in the collective unconscious, is just one criterion. Beyond this, the fact that the revelation compensates for the prophet's conscious situation, and especially for the people's, is a criterion that is frequently derided or misunderstood. The proof of a true prophet is that his prophecy actually occurs. It has been repeatedly pointed out that some of the prophecies of the great prophets verifiably failed to materialize, but this criterion nevertheless has a decisive meaning, which is entirely unrelated to the rate of success.

The fact that crucial historical events occur more or less completely independent of what human consciousness wants and plans led early humans to hold the gods responsible. Although we are using different terminology, we mean a corresponding phenomenon when we speak of the inherent activity of the collective unconscious. A true prophet is only someone to whom are whispered[126] the contents of the collective unconscious, the inherent activity of which determines the historical process. This is the deepest foundation for the idea of YHWH as the God who determines history.

For ego-consciousness, the layer of revelation appears, and must appear, as wholly other. This fundamental criterion fits perfectly with the criterion of the prophet whose highest level, which Moses reaches, is to receive the revelation while fully conscious and by day. In this state, the content projected in the revelation is undoubtedly most intense. Precisely this, however, characterizes the true prophet. The other forms of true prophecy, those that occur in visions and dreams, are less elevated, emerging in altered or limited states of consciousness, because the content asserting itself under such conditions requires just this change in consciousness, *l'abaissement du niveau mental*,[127] to make itself understood. The "manifestation without mystery," as in Moses' form of revelation, accessible only to Moses, sees YHWH face to face in fully maintained consciousness, whereby Moses engages directly in a dialogue with YHWH's theophany (Num 12:6–7).

The emergence of an unconscious content in projected form requires that this content bear no association with the ego-complex, namely that it be experienced by the ego as alien, as external, as wholly other, because this lack of ego-ownership is identical with the unconsciousness of the content.

Now, such a content may nevertheless break into consciousness if for any reason an *abaissement du niveau mental* has occurred, whether in sleep, in a dream, or in pathological changes of consciousness, or also if any artificial interventions have diminished normal consciousness, as in mass ecstasies, intoxication, etc.[128]

When a projected unconscious content appears in a state of fully maintained consciousness, this can happen only if that content possesses a particularly strong energetic charge, that is, one that exceeds the energetic charge of consciousness. In such a case, this content breaks into maintained consciousness as an ego-alien projection. The closer to the ego the emerging content is, the more clearly transparent is its subjective character. And the more ego-alien it is, the more objective it appears.

Now, the contents of the collective unconscious become so energized that they are able to influence consciousness on their own, "when far-reaching political, social, or religious changes occur in the life of a people."[129] The ego-alienness of the emerging content, as a divine saying or theophany, is precisely what enables the integrity of consciousness. Even among true prophets, consciousness very frequently changes and becomes impaired during YHWH's pronouncement. But what counts as the highest category of prophecy is received with fully maintained consciousness.

This marks the essential difference between divine prophecy and any kind of divination. But, in turn, it guarantees the prophet's partnership with YHWH, his active and responsible cooperation with him. From this basic phenomenon derives the ethical power of the prophet, which emphasizes the central position of responsible consciousness. At the same time, however, the deepest root of the dialogic relationship between human beings and God is located here, and corresponds to the basic structure of prophetic Judaism.

This connection between direct revelation and the maintenance of responsible consciousness is a fundamentally Jewish phenomenon. But also, only this cooperation enables the recurring absorption and responsible processing of the thrusts of revelation from the primordial depths, as these arise through the psychic structure of the prophet.

Ego-stability and its religious significance: Partnership with YHWH and morality

The problem of ego-stability emerges here as the greatest challenge to the prophet, and we recognize it as an essential feature of Jewish prophecy. Ego-stability is the capacity of the ego and its associated system of consciousness not to surrender to the contents and dynamics of the unconscious, but to be resistant toward them. Ego-stability is a characteristic that underlies the structural formation of consciousness, insofar as contents align themselves with the ego–complex and form with it a more or less unified structure, which differentiates itself from the unconscious. This structural wholeness of consciousness is never perfect, that is, there are always fluid transitions and connections between consciousness and the unconscious. But the history of human evolution is characterized precisely by the fact that the consciousness-ego system becomes progressively more able to safeguard its inherent structure against the influences of the unconscious. A primitive consciousness, equally a childlike or pathological one, distinguishes itself from that of the modern adult by succumbing easily and unresistingly to unconscious influences. The fact that developed consciousness has at its disposal a greater amount of psychic energy than undeveloped consciousness, for instance in terms of will-power, is due to the greater structural wholeness of consciousness, the strengthened ego-dominant and ego-stability, meaning its power to resist the dissolving or leveling influences of the unconscious. Secondary personalization,[130] as well as resistance against the unconscious, thus renders meaningful service to ego-stability, which in turn serves to establish the unity of consciousness against the unconscious.

In this sense, morality is also symptomatic of ego-stability, in that it is meant to protect the canon of conscious and cultural contents, which are affirmed by the ego, against the different and opposing tendencies of the unconscious.[131] This connection of morality with ego-stability is hugely significant for Jewish psychology up to modern times. All mass-psychological phenomena, and all those that diminish the level of consciousness, such as divination, must reckon with the resistance of ego-stability.

In early cultural periods, in which the stability of consciousness, and also its differentiation from the unconscious, are still relatively insignificant, the preservation of ego-stability is consequently very much in the interest of consciousness and cultural progress. Judaism especially has always emphasized this primacy of consciousness. But this orientation works—however improbable this may seem at first—in the same direction as YHWH's stand against the dimension of earth and nature, without, however, giving up the principle of inner revelation. On the contrary, the character of what reveals itself is determined in a certain way by adherence to consciousness and ego-stability. Through ego-stability, and by rejecting the earthly and natural side of the unconscious while still holding on to the principle of revelation, an energetic tension is produced between consciousness and the unconscious. This tension limits the phenomenon of revelation to the emergence of the transcendent function, which alone constitutes revelation, but which corresponds to YHWH's specific spiritual nature.

The spirit phenomenon is distinguished by the ambush-like invasion of a "higher consciousness" from the deep layer.[132] Due to its contrast with consciousness, we call this layer the unconscious, without, however, meaning to say that its contents are necessarily inferior to consciousness. In the unconscious, some contents are inferior to consciousness and "primitive," whereas others are superior to consciousness and "yet to come." The invasion of such a superior content, which, when assimilated by consciousness, promotes its expansion and further development, is characteristic of the spirit phenomenon. Spirit revelation among the early peoples is characterized by contents from the unconscious breaking into consciousness, increasing differentiation from the unconscious and enhancing ego-stability. Thus, for instance, the revelation of prophetic–moral law-giving serves to strengthen consciousness, while also suppressing unconscious tendencies that had been allowed to influence consciousness up to then. Through ego-stability, and the resulting confinement of revelation to the transcendent function, all the layers of the unconscious that merely oppose the conscious system are excluded from revelation. But a symptom of all ancient cults is the compensation provided by admitting unconscious tendencies that run counter to the canon of consciousness. These cults' orgiastic and mass-ecstatic festivals served to eliminate, at least temporarily, the tension of opposites between consciousness and the unconscious, providing the charged libido with a release valve. Judaism and prophetism, however, relentlessly tended to heighten the tension of opposites, increasing the distance between consciousness and the unconscious. The aversion to symbols also stems from this tendency. Thus they established the precondition for the appearance of the transcendent function, that is, the revelation of YHWH.

At the same time, however, ego-stability, and the emphasis on consciousness identical with it, enables a religious phenomenon highly characteristic of the basic prophetic stance of Judaism. This is the awareness of a partnership with YHWH, as the ultimate expression of the covenantal relationship between YHWH and Israel.[133] Only through ego-stability, and precisely because of it, does the human being encounter the self-revealing YHWH, and at the same time is also able to negotiate with him, influence him, in short adopt a definitive stance toward him. Nothing less than this basic character defines the nature of prophecy, as is clearly shown by Abraham's bargaining with God to save Sodom and Gomorrah and his designation as a *navi*[134] (Gen 18:25; 20:7). Only Moses' intervention on behalf of the people (Ex 32:32) will be additionally referred to here, but this orientation within the nature of Jewish prophecy could be pursued much further.

The basic fact of the partnership with YHWH, based on ego-stability, is profoundly related to the significance of the human being for the world at large. This anthropocentric emphasis, which already begins in Genesis with the creation of human beings in God's image and their dominant position in the world, continues in the prophetic partnership with YHWH and eventually reaches its peak in Hasidism with the importance of the *tzaddik*.[135] In ancient Hasidism, as we shall see, the nature of the *tzaddik* is still latent in every Jew. In this very concept—which was later lost—lies not only an essential continuation of the ancient Jewish partnership with YHWH, but also a promising new approach, precisely because, through Christianity and Gnostic–Kabbalistic speculation, this quality of being in God's image had been withdrawn from the individual and projected onto *Adam Kadmon*,[136] the redeemer.

Connected with the principle that ego-stability must be preserved, another phenomenon of fundamental importance is the emphasis on the individual. Prophecy presupposes that the one charismatically possessed is the individual as an individual; indeed, his essential isolation as an individual is to some extent a basic phenomenon of this kind of prophecy. Being set apart like this makes him an individual and affects him as an individual, because YHWH's hand, which chose him, and now weighs upon him, summons the individual to be a partner who embraces the challenge, who is not only a mouth for the call but also answers it. The dialogue between the prophet and YHWH, as well as the prophet's compensatory otherness toward the people, are marks of his uniqueness and individuality. His particular function as a mediator between YHWH and the people requires consciousness and ego-stability, for he must, if necessary, be able to withstand not only YHWH but also the people, and be able to represent each side reciprocally toward the other.

The content of revelation originates in the history-shaping layer of the collective unconscious. This is what leads to the isolation of the prophet and his prophecies of doom, or, one might better say, it leads to the compensatory character of prophecy, with its rejection of divination, mass ecstasy, and individualistic mysticism.

The compensatory character of the unconscious, as it reveals itself, necessarily isolates the one who pronounces it, because—apart from rare instances of consoling prophecy amid deep misfortune—he always points, correctively, toward the negative. As the prophet of disaster, he is YHWH's instrument for correcting the people, and thus a stumbling block for those who are corrected. Baudissin writes:

> It is characteristic of Semitic religion, however, that the individual fully possesses religion only through the mediation of the community, and that the collectivistic religious relationship still remains evident as a basic form among the most developed individualistic forms.[137]

Likewise, even in developed religious individualism,

> [there] remains the underlying idea that what the individual possesses of YHWH, indeed possesses most directly, has been handed down historically through his membership in the people Israel.[138]

Moreover,

> [I]n ancient tribal religions, God and the tribe stood side by side since time immemorial, although no one knew how they had come together. Israel, on the other hand, had experienced the emergence of its connection with YHWH. Thus, all individuals must have been especially strongly aware that this God belonged to the whole community.[139]

This fact lies at the deepest heart of Hebrew prophecy, the mission of which is YHWH's decree to this people, a decree that arises from the people's collective layer, even though the people want nothing to do with it. Therefore, nothing is further from the prophet than an individualistic "enjoyment" of the divine. To him, the mystical "having" of the deity is as alien as any self-deification or any quiet submersion in the dissolving essence of divinity. The relationship of faith and loyalty, indeed of deepest friendship with the divine, which has grown from dealing with YHWH and from the familiar partnership of dialogue, from the formulaic and yet thoroughly characteristic "my" God to the personal declaration of love for the divine, always remains overshadowed by the infinity and intangibility of the numinous mystery. Even God's reaching out, as father and friend, which fills the human being to the brim with the miracle of encounter, is no more than a flickering facet in the immense, brilliant diamond of the hidden light of the divine.

But the paradox of this relationship with YHWH also manifests itself in the fact that, although he remains the God of distance, nevertheless the covenant of the chosen people[140] is based on a relationship freely taken up between him and Israel, as it is between him and the prophet. For this very reason, what is crucial is not the descent from him as father or creator of the world, or ruler over the natural forces of life, but rather the free choice, the acceptance of mission, which, precisely due to this act of decision, is characterized by chosenness and at the same time by obligation.

Beyond the most personal relationship with God, what always prevails in the missionary character of prophecy is the collective nature of the covenant, both in the God who reveals himself to the people and in the prophet who is destined to deliver the message to them. Thus, audition, hearing, also corresponds to the imagelessness of YHWH, who is infinitely superior to any concretizing, even in symbolic form. Hearing, moreover, is more adequate than any vision[141] would be to the introvert's intimate contact with and obedience[142] to the depth of the divinity that speaks to him. Only the interpretation of the vision, but this means first its transformation into sense and saying, is appropriate to YHWH, which is why speaking directly with the divine represents a higher level of revelation than the vision and the dream. Word, saying, and sense, that is, the Logos, are the revelation, which breaks in from the depth and seeks, directively, to determine the fate of the peoples.

And just here, the overall Semitic conception of the divine, and also of YHWH, once again proves characteristic, namely, that he seems to relate only to the human being. Baudissin writes:

> It is as if these gods existed only for the sake of human beings, as if they had no existence for their own sake or on account of anything external to humanity. Also in the background of the Babylonian myths, which seemingly narrate nothing but a . . . history of the gods, stands the influence that this history exerts on human beings, on their dependence upon the earthly world. In a completely different way, the Greek gods act in a world of their own, in which they live their own lives, often unconcerned about the human being.[143]

This more or less anthropocentric idea of God, which, paradoxically, can coexist with the infinite superiority of the numinous, is the basis for the reality and the truth of all psychic religious experience.

But because the validity of the revelation depends upon the deep level of its origin, the rejection of divination and mass ecstasy is as understandable as it is justified. Regardless of how far, and how long, divinatory and mass-ecstatic elements have influenced prophecy, their rejection is necessary. The key factor distinguishing prophecy from divination is the confinement of revelation to the deepest layer of that which we call the unconscious, which addresses and challenges few individuals, and only seldom, but then with compelling necessity.

The individual as a bearer of revelation

Jewish prophecy insists that *individuals* are charismatically seized by YHWH. The outpouring of the "*Ruach ha-Kodesh*"[144] over a mass of people is a phenomenon that was crucial for early Christianity. The fact that pagan converts were seized by the same mass ecstasy as the Jewish Christians was used as an opportunity to erase the original distinction between these two groups, with which began the universalizing of Christianity over the pagans.[145] Hebrew prophecy rejected mass ecstasy as a divinatory phenomenon belonging to a pre-messianic era, even though this prophecy also originated partly in a *navitum*[146] in which divinatory and mass-ecstatic phenomena are quite at home. From a psychological perspective, this rejection was right, because every mass ecstasy means an *abaissement du niveau mental* and abandons the primacy of consciousness in favor of unconscious forces, the observance of which is extremely dubious. This is confirmed not only by the ecstatic states of sects, which strive to attain such ecstatic phenomena and mostly lapse into the sexual–orgiastic (as the layer of the unconscious closest to consciousness), but also by the futility and meaninglessness of the glossolalic phenomena frequently accompanying outpourings of the allegedly "holy" spirit.

Confirmation comes likewise from spiritualistic manifestations, the analysis of which reveals at best the effect of animus- or anima-figures,[147] if not of even "lower" complexes, that is, autonomous complexes[148] from the personal unconscious of persons involved in such phenomena. Divinatory phenomena have surely existed all over the world, also ones that stem from the depths through which YHWH speaks (as discussed above, concerning the Balaam episode). But these always seem to entail merely the self-expression of partial divinities, i.e., archetypes, or else to be rare phenomena. They do not involve a relationship of choice, a covenant, between tribe or people and the one presenting himself as YHWH, on which was formed the basic constitution of existence and behavior, enabling a lasting contact. YHWH's supremacy over the other gods, whose existence and way of acting are not disputed in the Old Testament, consists, to highlight *one* aspect, in YHWH's associating the deep layer with himself from the beginning, in its character as meaning and speech. In contrast, every god-archetype only represents a certain content- or meaning-related dimension of the unconscious.

This definition of the individual's charismatic state of possession does not contradict the declared possibility that *each* individual may attain this state, which, if collectively achieved, would mean the messianic state of the world. Both biblical prophecy and Judaism are characterized by skepticism, however, corresponding to an emphasis on responsibility and an insistence on preserving the dignity of consciousness. This skepticism is prepared to argue tenaciously against every insinuation of a supposedly attained and fulfilled end-time, based on observation of a world that is not pervaded by YHWH.

The resistance of prophetism must therefore begin most emphatically at the point where divinatory prophecy—which, as we have seen, merely represented subservience to the earth-archetype—threatens to steal its way in. Precisely because Hebrew prophecy partially emerged from and was originally entangled with these phenomena, the compulsion to differentiate itself became especially strong.[149] This also explains its extremely cautious approach to the earth.[150]

Above, we discussed the unconscious projection of the image of the Mother Goddess onto the earth, which led to a particularly strong attachment to the earth among the Israelites. It was particularly strong because there existed no image of the Mother Goddess, whose cult always signifies a preliminary stage in the conscious realization of this attachment.

At first, the projection in an image does not lead to a genuine acquisition of consciousness. It does, however, relieve the unconscious through concretizing, by which the unconscious content is brought closer to the consciousness of the cult worshipper. This relieving effect is well known to us from modern psychotherapy, where we directly strive to concretize unconscious contents for this very reason. Concretizing does not yet represent a conscious realization, of course, but it has an extraordinarily relieving effect on the unconscious, in that the libido concretized in the image no longer awakens the unconscious anonymously. Rather, having taken shape, having become an object, it *can* at least become the subject of conscious realization.

Now, the path of Judaism does not proceed via projection and concretizing. Time and again, prophecy appears as the decisive factor. The imagelessness of the prophetic YHWH, who reacts to ever-new constellations with ever-new revelation, rules out any fixation in concretizing, which is most fiercely rejected as idolatry. YHWH's word and the prophetic law given by him are aimed at the acquisition of consciousness. From Adam and Cain, through the age before the patriarchs, and up to the founding of the kingdom, the earth's dependence on humankind is repeatedly emphasized and demonstrated. If it is polluted by a mistaken reaction,[151] and if it actively spews out the human being as a counter-reaction to humanly caused pollution, this means that the pivotal point of the human–earth relationship is shifted onto responsible human consciousness. The *participation mystique* with the earth is replaced by responsibility for the earth. This anthropocentric emphasis stands at the heart of the ethical development initiated by Hebrew prophecy.

The concretizing of unconscious contents in images, myths, rituals, and cults represents the direct expression of the unconscious and its interpretation. Later this may be followed, but need not be, by an inquiry into meaning and thus by conscious understanding. Even without this subsequent act of consciousness, people who live with image and myth, in cult and ritual, are connected with the meaningfulness of the unconscious, which acts upon them without passing through consciousness.

Matters are different with the almost sacral emphasis on consciousness that is fulfilled in Jewish prophecy. As a partner of the deep layer through which YHWH speaks, prophetic consciousness more or less strongly excludes all the intermediate stages of mythological concretizing. This phenomenon represents what we can call an anthropocentric emphasis, as we noted earlier in connection with the notion of deity as such.[152] Phenomena characteristic of YHWH—the spoken proclamation and the inquiry directed to him in times of distress—lead to prophetic law-giving, which appears as divine utterance, appealing directly to consciousness and issuing demands, that is, possessing a strong ethical emphasis. Here, an unconscious situation in the prophet's consciousness becomes a question answered by God's spoken command, which both shapes and challenges consciousness.

All moral and social law-giving gains its meaning from this perspective. Its meaning is therefore a genuine product of direct inner revelation in prophetic law, because YHWH's irruptive decree, bestowing spirit and meaning, and, emerging from the depth of the collective unconscious, leads to the acquisition of consciousness in a people still rooted in the natural unconsciousness of early humanity. As we shall see, this genuine prophetic gift of moral law is infinitely different from what a later era understood as morality and claimed as the "dignity of Judaism."

Early prophetic law-giving, arising in the act of revelation, is characterized by coming to consciousness and thereafter remains open to ever-new irruptions of the self-revealing God. Later priestly morality and statutory law-giving, in contrast, exist to rule out any new revelation—which always proceeds from the primal depth of the unconscious, breaking open and transforming consciousness—and thus to prevent any real conscious expansion. But an attitude that reckons with the constantly renewed readiness of consciousness, one that takes a provisional standpoint, always open to renewal through inner revelation, obviously contradicts any development aimed at constancy, security, property, regularity, and balance.

Prophecy, cult, and law

The threat of a prophetic life, or of a life directed by biblical prophecy, is so great, and so powerfully contradicts any naturalistic and reasonable worldview, that all the people's forces aiming in the latter direction were forced to search for a corresponding counter-expression, which indeed they found. This expression is the cult, particularly the sacrificial cult and the priestly law. Here we must emphasize yet again that this is not a temporal sequence, nor does it need to be. Even if, historically, the cult existed prior to a developed or systematized prophetism—which is possible, but by no means certain—the central position of the cult must nevertheless be understood as a counter-movement to the prophetism that undoubtedly already existed very early in ancient Hebraism, partly in rudimentary form, partly as a real force shaping history.

The line of development, from the magical–sacrificial ritual of the cult to the sacrificial mechanism of the Temple Period, extends over a very long time, of course, and the contrasts between these two developmental poles are extraordinarily great. And yet, despite their contrasts, both stand on the same side in their opposition to the basic vision of Hebrew prophecy. Common to both is the potential elimination of responsibility through the figure of a mediator, whose effectiveness is partly magical and partly institutional. The purpose of this elimination, always and everywhere, is the disconnection from primary inner experience, even though this experience is precisely what constitutes religious reality.

The subject in the magical ritual is still the whole people, which, in its primitive state of *participation mystique*, participates to a greater or lesser degree in the process of sacrifice, that is, the reality of the cultic encounter. The more the people develop into a total community of consciousness-bearers, the less effective, and the less real, the magical cult ritual becomes.[153]

At this point, the line of development bifurcates into the practice of prophecy and the institutionalization of the cult. In this connection, we need to stress that the central phenomenon of prophecy—the acceptance of direct inner revelation—has essentially nothing to do with religious individualism, for the prophetic person's entanglement with the people as a collective forms the basic constellation of his calling.[154] His compensatory effect on the people, which, as we have seen, belongs to the basic institution of prophetism, guarantees the exclusion of religious individualism, which would be irrelevant in any case. At issue here is not individual salvation, but the collective salvation of the *Bnei Israel* summoned by YHWH. Note, however, that, in Hebrew prophecy, the individual's latent capacity for contact with YHWH becomes the starting point for outer and inner movement. Through the priesthood, on the other hand, the very capacity of the individual to be represented is accomplished by the priestly mediator, and the direct contact with YHWH is eliminated by fulfillment of the law.

That this representation before YHWH is concealed by the law and its fulfillment does not change the fact that primary revelation is systematically excluded in favor of a codified law.

In cult and law we have the necessary dogmatic hardening that safeguards the individual and the community against the invasion, the assault, the unexpected appearance of the new. The entire conservative attitude of the human being— and, as we know, the more conservative and more fearful of novelty humanity is, the more primitive it is—can be lived out in the law as the apodictically guaranteed knowledge of what should and should not be done. The authority of the priesthood and its work rests upon this human need, which is obviously also very great in the Jewish person. That is, while being prepared to bear great, indeed the greatest, sacrifices, restrictions, and yokes, the Jewish person also needs absolute, guaranteed certainty of possessing salvation in return. Standing behind every dogma, the existential uncertainty of human beings, their need for guaranteed certainty, contrasts starkly with the uncertainty of prophecy, which must always prove itself anew, and the unconditional willingness of which cannot be captured in an eternally valid law. Instead, prophecy, forever transforming itself and risking itself in new ways, is in danger of losing its own continuity. But the chain of revelations, of the self-manifesting divine sayings and theophanies, bears within itself an unfolding continuity, which corresponds to some extent to the self-unfolding of the divinity, in cooperation with prophetic consciousness.

Priestly law, particularly in its amalgamation with pieces of prophetic law-giving, doubtless also had the function, which it partly fulfilled, to compensate for and balance out the earthiness and pagan unrestraint of primitive Jewish nature. The hardening of the law and the immutability brought about by its secondary establishment in the revelation on Sinai, together with the equally secondary transformation of the prophet and leader Moses into the law-giver, now created a solid and unshatterable foundation, upon which the people could stand and live. But the people's actual productivity consisted in their vibrant inner tension and the tension of opposites within the unconscious. This tension of opposites became productively generative in the YHWH–earth opposition on Sinai. It becomes generative in all prophetic revelation, because it builds on the conflict between the people, obsessed with the earth and clinging to nature, and the prophet, clinging to YHWH in compensation. This tension of opposites is concealed by the law, when the law becomes statutory and dogmatic. True, the "mouth of the abyss" is now shut, but, at the same time, the creative possibility of fertilization by the deep waters has been lost. The certainty of knowing what to do is dearly paid for with the barrenness of a constant stance in life, which can no longer be melted and recast.

Prophecy as protection against the unconscious

If original Hebrew prophecy has the assignment of giving to the in-breaking YHWH a voice and a place to act, then by doing so not only does it fulfill the highly productive task of fertilizing reality, but also—and this is not to be forgotten—it performs the additional task of protecting the people. For if the powers of the deep and YHWH's call remain unheard and unchanneled for too long, they gather themselves for a forceful and annihilating invasion, the paradigm of which is the Flood, the eruption of the waters of the abyss. This phenomenon is repeated with the Golden Calf, where it is prevented only by Moses' and the Levites' intervention.[155]

The same patterns are familiar to us from the psychology of the unconscious, which is the same in the individual as in the collective. So with the individual, even today, when the unconscious communicates in either symbolic or spoken form, the compensatory intervention of the unconscious must be guided toward an acquisition of consciousness. Likewise, if this communication is not received and accepted, what follows even today is regression and neuroticization, or flooding by the unconscious, the Deluge.

The protective aspect of prophecy then naturally leads to prophetic law-giving, which attempts to formulate and create a form of existence structured to enable continuity of life for the people, while at the same time establishing the pre-condition for new revelation to appear. Balancing these two tendencies, which are equally necessary and yet not necessarily aligned, constitutes the political difficulty of prophecy, where the priesthood then lodged itself. By weakening the dynamics of the problem, it succeeded in creating an allegedly irrefutable law of revelation, which no longer needs any new revelation, at the same time providing the people with a continuity of life. Gradually, however, and of necessity, this continuity followed the gravitational pull of natural political and social conditions. Under the seal of theocracy, the priesthood secularized prophetic Judaism, which had come to expression historically in the prophets, who took up the primordial prophetic tradition. These prophets also elevated the conflict between these two schools of thought, which secretly pervades the entire history, to make it the central problem of consciousness.

Until the destruction of the Temple,[156] i.e., for as long as ancient Judaism existed, it was alive in this tension between prophetic and priestly intentions. The conflict between these opposing positions, both aspiring to lead the people, surfaces time and again in the Bible, and this very conflict was the expression of a lively social organism.

Both positions, the prophetic and the priestly, applied to a people that was strongly rooted in the earth and closely related to Semitic paganism. But whereas the priesthood sought to create separation only institutionally, through external law-giving and a life-determining sacral law—following the same intention and conception as every priesthood—the practice of prophecy starts from an entirely different and incommensurable conception.

Secularizing, which was really implemented under priestly rule, would have been a necessary process of development, even in the normative sense, if prophetism had persisted in its old stance, exclusively oriented toward prophetic law-giving. Obviously, a developing social and national structure requires a different form of law-giving, not one that may be prophetically inspired at any moment.

Earlier, in relation to Moses' transferring the power of judgment to the elders,[157] we saw a reference to this *de facto* legislative development, from a prophetic–dynamic law into one that is codifiable and static.

The law, as that which restrains, which curbs the earth-principle, at first stands in the closest possible contact with prophecy, for, ultimately, the moral postulate, assisted by consciousness, emerges once again from a form of interpretation agreeable to YHWH, in order to shape the natural person. This fact clearly underlies all law-giving and all morality. It would need to be examined to what extent, and also where in allegedly Mosaic law-giving, those parts can be found that correspond to the practice of prophecy, that is, to the form of action and demand that is specific to YHWH.

Such contents cannot always be found in general, social law-giving, but rather at points that are considered impracticable and therefore secondary.

The sheer paradox of the crop failure in the seventh year, when the field should remain uncultivated, and when YHWH himself must provide for the people (Num 25:20), or the requirement that the whole people go on pilgrimage to Jerusalem at the time of the festivals, when YHWH must guarantee protection against their enemies, are all traits of such a primary prophetic attitude toward the power of YHWH.

These demands are based on the relationship of alliance and marriage between YHWH and Israel, a genuine togetherness, which was real and therefore was thought to be effective, as originally guaranteed by cult, circumcision, Passover, and so forth.

The magical effectiveness of these rituals, as we know, represents a certain reality of primitive, that is, original–primitive psychology, in which the observance of ritual conditions and the powers of the unconscious set in motion the direction intended by the ritual.

The prophetic interpretation of the covenant between YHWH and Israel as a "grafting"[158] has moved very far from this basic primitive–magical notion, without affecting the covenant as such.

Already evident here is a decided introversion of the relationship between the people and God; one is almost inclined to speak of a psychological understanding of this relationship. Now, this introversion of the earlier ritual is specific to Hebrew prophecy. Nevertheless, it should by no means be identified with simple moralizing, even if a strong moralizing tendency is in fact connected with the reintroduction of the individual ego as a figure bearing responsibility for the covenant.

At this exact point, a new conflict begins between prophetism and priestly legalism. As is generally the case, however, this conflict cannot be reduced to the opposition between faith and the fulfillment of the law; rather, a much deeper problem lies behind it. In actual fact, what this problem always concerns, and concerns still today, is the adequate behavior toward YHWH, behavior that enables his covenant partnership. Prophetism represents the reality of this covenant relationship, just as the ancient ritual did, save that in its view the changed psychology of the people is met by a changed reaction by YHWH. Only an introversion of the originally magical relationship can guarantee YHWH's partnership. Prophetism therefore rejects both the cult and the "magical" effect of circumcision.

In earlier times, when the collective lived in total *participation mystique*, cult, circumcision, and the Passover ritual were all effective in any case. The passage about the bridegroom of blood[159] demonstrated the real effectiveness of circumcision by halting YHWH's attack. In just the same way, the narrative of the tenth plague is intended to prove the effectiveness of the Passover ritual by sparing the Jewish first-born. At the time of late Hebrew prophecy, neither is effective anymore, because the people are no longer a primitive collective upon which ritual can exercise such a powerful effect. Therefore—thus, not for idealistic–ethical reasons—biblical prophecy turns against the cult and external circumcision.

Because these men assume that YHWH's power is effective, they demand a behavior that is adequate to YHWH's way of working. YHWH's theophany changes, however, with the people's conscious attitude; therefore any adherence to the old theophany fails to recognize how YHWH actually works. But this means that, by clinging to ritual and to a belief in the magical protection provided by circumcision, the people become defenseless against YHWH's new way of working and fall victim to the invasive YHWH. The struggle against an inferior morality is secondary. Primarily, these men possess direct experience of God, and so they know and declare that the people can remain the people and partner of YHWH only by accepting the changing theophany. If they regress, however, or adhere to their old behavior, which was once adequate and effectively true to an earlier theophany and earlier states of being, then—and this is the actual fear of the prophetic writers—they will be unequal to YHWH's new theophany and will perish. Whereas all other peoples grow from below, and have the earth beneath them, from which they come and upon which they can lean while growing, the Jews have YHWH above them, lying upon them, besetting, assailing, and enspiriting them. From him comes, irruptively, the impetus of their development, and the earthly dimension must follow, adjust, and integrate. This fact, which corresponds to the psychic structure of prophetism and the prophets, is the great uniqueness of Jewish antiquity and the enormous danger facing Judaism after the ancient period.[160]

Law and cult as protection against the unconscious

This danger is complicated by the conflict already evident in the opposition between prophecy and the priestly cult. The primacy of consciousness, and its tendency to distance itself from the unconscious, can have an impact in two entirely opposite directions. So long as the orientation toward YHWH is maintained, as the one who reveals himself in the transcendent function—that is, so long as the orientation toward the creative primal ground of the unconscious is preserved—so long will the living connection be kept open, despite the tension between the systems of consciousness and the unconscious. Indeed, ultimately, the conscious system will be prepared for YHWH's transforming intervention. The ego-stability of consciousness does not lead to a state of identification between consciousness and YHWH; the phenomenon of spirit, YHWH's irruptive revelation, remains always and unconditionally dominant over the system of consciousness and ego. Ego and YHWH are partners. This configuration, however, includes in itself the living polarity of the relationship between YHWH and earth, and the polarity of consciousness and the unconscious. This is both the assertion and the attitude of prophecy.

The primacy of consciousness and its dangers

In the law of the priestly cult, the primacy of consciousness has hardened to such an extent that consciousness has been strangulated from the unconscious. In an exaggeration of the primacy of consciousness, the unconscious is identified entirely with the earth-polarity, as if it contained only earth elements, and the polarity of YHWH and earth withers away to the polarity of consciousness and the unconscious. Eventually, this leads to an identification of spirit and consciousness, of YHWH and the conscious system, as can be found in later Judaism. The revealed Torah and the interpreting consciousness form a unity that prevents and systematically excludes new revelation, that is, the irruption of YHWH. For, once YHWH's revelation has become conscious; he is identified with it and pinned down by it. The tension between consciousness and the unconscious, which was originally so consciously heightened, now leads to the isolation of consciousness from the unconscious. This disastrous shift in Jewish psychology determines far-reaching problems connected with the Jewish condition.

The basic notion of Hebrew prophecy, which sees Israel's relationship with YHWH in the covenant and in the obedience shown toward the incomparable majesty of the Lord, and in following what he commands, is not related to a world of order directed by unshakeable laws. This perspective knows no *moira*,[161] no worldly dependence upon the law of the stars, but instead an incessant, dynamic change of events initiated by God. Wellhausen writes:

> YHWH had unpredictable moods. He let his face shine and concealed it,[162] one did not know why. He created good and evil, punished sin and enticed to sin—at that time Satan had not yet relieved him of any part of his nature,[163]

Here Wellhausen has unquestionably touched upon a very essential aspect, although he demonizes it; it is an aspect that might hold true even for an early stage of this concept of God. In biblical prophecy, however, the idea of the paradoxical nature of God is immensely deepened. Contrary to every static notion of God and the world, the prophetic perspective (to put it strongly) places the catastrophic and unpredictable nature of events at the center of the world. In Israel's special case, the human being's creaturely inferiority in relation to the numinous can enter into a covenant. But it can never, if it has any insight, close its eyes to the primordial fact that the paths of the numinosum, in their incommensurability, are never rationally comprehensible or transparent to human ego-consciousness. This basic fact guarantees the pre-eminent importance of divine revelation, in which the divinity emerges from its hiddenness, laying bare and disclosing its secret. The covenant consists precisely in guaranteeing, among other things, this community of revelation and its continuity.

This incommensurability of the human being with the divine corresponds perfectly to what Jung formulates, although on a different level, when he says, "The individuated ego senses itself as the object of an unknown and superordinate subject."[164] In no way, however, does this prevent a functional mutuality in the relationship between God and the human being. On the contrary, existing alongside this inequality of the partners is their interdependence. God's standing above the law, which looks like "capriciousness,"[165] corresponds to the fact that he voluntarily places himself in the hands of humankind, becoming dependent upon it, so to speak. His "varying decisions" correspond to his ability to be influenced by antecedent human action, which causes him (YHWH) to "repent."[166] For, unlike a *moira*,[167] YHWH does not stand above human beings, but changes direction when they do. The mutual dependence characterizing the God–human structure goes so far that he even disavows his own prophet (Jonah), in order to make a fitting response after humankind (pagan Nineveh) repents.[168] The basic prophetic principle—"the prophet prophesies for repentance"—seems to be prophecy's paradoxical self-disavowal, in that its aim and purpose are to belie itself. For indeed, if it is successful, what is prophesied will not happen. But even this fact is a symptom of the dynamic view of reciprocity in the God–human interaction. God's absolute dominion over existence is precisely what establishes the non-determinability[169] of the God–human interaction, as it manifests itself negatively in the incalculable, catastrophic nature of worldly events, and positively in the eternal reality of the seemingly impossible.

The paradox of the miracle is to some extent the natural expression of YHWH's existential dominion over the constant level of being. No situation is so forlorn that YHWH, given this incalculable dominion, could not intervene and change it, because he is the Lord. But likewise, no situation is so secure that it could not be fundamentally overturned in an instant by his catastrophic irruption.

YHWH and the Mother Goddess

Just here, the fundamental contrast between YHWH and the principle of the Earth Mother becomes obvious once again. This contrast alone explains why the Hebrews, surrounded by mother-cults, remained the only tribe, among the Semitic tribes, that possessed no female deity.

The principle of the great Mother Goddess, even when pushed into the background by the later male deities, always includes the determinacy of fate. Therefore, when a male-patriarchal pantheon governs the image of the world, the restrained Mother Goddess mostly continues to exist as a goddess of fate, whether as the Moira of the Greeks or the Norns of Germanic mythology.[170]

Beside the symbolism of fertility and life, the symbolism of the Great Mother always includes that of fate: that which is fixed, the structure, the cosmic law, the unalterable necessity—this is the Mother. The weaving and spinning female forces of nature, rulers over vegetative life and over the life of source and tree, are also the great custodians of the natural basis of life, which holds tight and entangles both the individual and the collective, as structural conditionality in the web of fate.

It is irrelevant whether this fate is formulated in astrological terms, as suggested by antiquity, or whether the modern person prefers the corresponding notion of constitution. In both cases, what is meant is the supremacy of what is given by nature over creative spontaneity. But YHWH, as an in-breaking and overwhelming principle, represents precisely this spontaneity.

This perspective helps us understand the Jewish rejection not only of astrology but also of the prophesying of fate, and it explains, as well, the assertion that the Jews, as the chosen people, YHWH's partner, stand outside the compulsion of the stars. This "being above the stars," which distinguishes the Jewish people, corresponds to YHWH's own "being above the stars." As the one who breaks in, YHWH is an enemy of every kind of cosmic determinacy. When it is written that YHWH "allotted" the power of the stars to the peoples, while claiming Israel as his own possession (Deut 4:19–20), this is consistent, psychologically speaking, with YHWH's representing a reality beyond the archetypes, the constellation of which forms the structure and particularity of every normal people.

The power of this principle of affiliation is also portrayed in the typical individuals who violate their own belonging to YHWH.

One striking example is Samson, who loses his role as a Nazirite to the principle of sexuality, represented by the Philistine Delilah, and pays dearly for it. The berserker-like frenzy,[171] evident throughout the description of Samson's actions, already indicates a great threat of flooding by the unconscious. He is enticed into danger by his seducibility and over-emphasized sexuality, so that his Nazirite status perishes, succumbing to the principle of the hostile feminine.

The tragedy of Saul unfolds similarly, although on an entirely different level. He also reveals the primitive traits of a berserker-like obsession (1 Sam 10:10; 11:6; 19:23ff.). When he emancipates himself from Samuel's superior prophetic authority, he succumbs when, in a highly characteristic manner, depressions appear—an evil spirit-visitation from YHWH (1 Sam 16:15; 19:10)[172]—as the negative flooding by the unconscious when consciousness is inadequate. In the end, he encounters the Witch of Endor (1 Sam 28:7), that is, he succumbs to the negative female power of fate, representing YHWH's antipode, and thus perishes with and through her prophesying of destiny.

It is only half-correct to try to deduce this basic conception of Hebrew prophecy either from the political uncertainty and endangerment of the time or from the psychological structure of the prophet. Although both conclusions are possible, they are only of limited interest. For beyond this reduction, an aspect of the world is formulated, the validity of which has determined, and still determines, the entire history of humanity and of Israel in particular. This is the paradox of an experience of history that does not refer to the earthly law of historical development. Its incalculable, catastrophic, and revolutionary nature, being determined by the wind of the spirit, cannot be refuted by any reality, because it reshapes every reality in the strength of its connection with YHWH's irruptive force. The same prophetic authority, which is animated, amid the ominous prophecy of the destruction of Jerusalem, by the deepest faith in the possibility of repentance and salvation, and every fiber of which hopes for its own refutation, comes to terms with the resulting downfall with indescribable detachment from its own involvement. Supported by its own downfall, it changes this very downfall into a pillar of faith, by glorifying in it the absolute dominion of the numinous. The same basic conception that adorns YHWH's altar with the firepans of Nadab and Abihu, who were consumed by YHWH's fire, glorifies the righteous and superior power of YHWH, who has destroyed Jerusalem and smashed Israel to pieces. The same numinous dominion that penetrates transformatively into the world through the faith and obedience of Israel, its covenant partner, also enters the world through this partner's infidelity and disobedience, by glorifying itself, calamitously, amid ruin and terror.

The people's covenant is indissoluble, whether it glorifies YHWH as proof of its chosenness, serving as an example to the world, or whether, having become the abomination of the nations, it proves its chosenness when it fails, by demonstrating the power of this God through the putrefaction of its own body.

Author's note

It should be emphasized that we have often deliberately preserved theological formulations, because they are appropriate to the times studied here.

Only in that part of this work dealing with the psychology and problems of the modern Jew[173] will we offer a psychological analysis of the processes and relations confronting us here in theological guise.

The problem of consciousness for even the modern Jew is largely determined by the constellations of his collective unconscious. For this reason we were forced to draw on historical material to demonstrate this collective problem.

The largely collective nature of this historical material means that it is only partly possible to offer a full psychological analysis of the phenomena. Only in the last part, where we will consider not only the collective material, but also the conscious position of the individual, are these phenomena accessible to an exhaustive psychological analysis.

Notes

1 "*Rückfälle*": lit. fallings-back, relapses ("backslidings").
2 "*regrediert*": a clinical term, "regressed" here connects with the biblical idea of apostasy, or falling away, viewed from the perspective of depth psychology. Neumann's use of quotation marks around the two terms ("regressed," "apostasies") has the effect of emphasizing them, while alerting the reader to this meaningful connection.
3 "*dass es ihr gut gehe*": the phrase echoes God's repeated promise in Deuteronomy (Deut 4:40, 5:16, etc.).

4 Hebrew: the Land of Israel. In Neumann's text, written before Israel became a nation, the phrase reads: "des modernen palästinischen Juden," literally, "of the modern Palestinian Jew."

5 *EN*: Baudissin, *Kyrios*, v. 3, p. 148. [Wolf Wilhelm Friedrich von Baudissin (1847–1926): German Protestant theologian, professor of Old Testament in Marburg and Berlin. A historian of religion, he studied the Old Testament in relation to other ancient Semitic faiths. His four-volume work, *Kyrios als Gottesname im Judentum und seine Stelle in der Religionsgeschichte* (*Kyrios* as the name of God in Judaism and its place in religious history) (hereafter: *Kyrios*), the third volume of which Neumann frequently cites, was published posthumously.]

6 *EN*: Jean Przyluski, "Ursprünge und Entwicklung des Kults der Muttergöttin" ("Origins and development of the Mother Goddess cult"), *EJ 1938*. [The cited passage has not been found, but a related passage occurs in *EJ 1938, p. 43.*]

7 Two of Neumann's biblical references mention sacred trees: the Oak of Moreh (Gen 12:6) and the Soothsayers' Oak (Judg 9:37). The other reference, 2 Kings 5:24, seems to be an error.

8 Compound word, combining *navi* (Hebrew, "prophet") and -*tum* (German nominal ending): "practice of prophecy."

9 *EN*: See the universal occurrence of the phallus and the Yoni cult from India to Egypt.

10 *EN*: Cf. Max Weber, *Gesammelte Aufsätze zur Religionssoziologie*. v. 3: *Das antike Judaism* (Collected essays on the sociology of religion. v. 3: *Ancient Judaism*) (hereafter: *Ancient Judaism*), pp. 202ff. [The passage occurs in a section titled "Der Kampf des Jahwismus gegen die Orgiastik" ("The fight of Yahwism against orgiasticism"), pp. 200–7. In the 1952 English edition, the passage begins on p. 189.]

11 *EN*: Cf. Appendix I. ["On Methodology," *Roots I*, pp. 138ff.]

12 Hebrew: children (lit. sons) of Israel, i.e., the Jewish people.

13 The image is of added layers of paint, obscuring the original picture. Elsewhere Neumann refers to "textual revisions [that] have layered themselves upon the original picture and must be removed again, to make it clear" (*Roots I*, p. 33; cf. also p. 17).

14 That is, World War I.

15 *EN*: Cf. Goldberg. Like the primitives themselves, Goldberg interprets these phenomena in concretistic terms, instead of fully acknowledging their reality in relation to the structure of the psyche. [The citation is to Oskar Goldberg, *Wirklichkeit der Hebräer: Einleitung in das System des Pentateuch* (*Reality of the Hebrews: Introduction to the System of the Pentateuch*). Goldberg was a physician and philosopher of religion, whose chief work, *Wirklichkeit der Hebräer*, Neumann cites twice, somewhat critically. Here the reference may be to Chapter 10, "Der Hintergrund des Rituals" ("The background of the ritual") (pp. 203–300). In "Die Nachtseite des Elohim" ("The night-aspect of *Elohim*") (pp. 216–34), Goldberg cites Exodus 4:24–26, where YHWH—but Goldberg speculates that it is one of the dark gods, whose power emerges at night—threatens to kill Moses, a threat averted by Zipporah's immediate circumcision of their son (pp. 222ff.).]

16 Hebrew: "holy," i.e., involving an encounter with the numinous.

17 *EN*: E.g., the Ark of the Covenant: 1 Sam 6.

18 *Innenseite*, lit. "inside" or "inner aspect." Neumann's use of "Innenseite," referring to the realm of interior psychic reality, appears frequently in his writings of the 1930s, including *Jacob & Esau* and the present work. It is rendered here in various ways depending on context.

19 *EN*: *Pardes*. [The classic Kabbalistic work by Moshe Cordovero, *Pardes Rimmonim* (*Orchard of Pomegranates*) (1548), tells of four individuals who enter paradise, one of whom goes mad.]

20 *EN*: Lévy-Bruhl. [No related passage has been found in the books of Lévy-Bruhl mentioned by Neumann in the present work. Robert Segal advises that, as a Durkheimian, Lévy-Bruhl discusses primitives in sociological rather than psychological terms, focusing more on beliefs than states of mind.]

21 *"angstbebte,"* a word coined by B&R in their translation of Genesis.

22 A Hebrew word, "midrash" (plural, "midrashim") has passed into English usage. The appendix to an English translation of *Sendung und Schicksal* (*Mission and destiny*), a collection of Jewish readings compiled by N. Glatzer and L. Strauss, defines midrash as "investigation, exposition ... the exegesis of scriptures, especially of nonlegal portions (*Midrash Haggadah*), compiled in the Talmudic period and in following centuries. Midrashic collections [are] very often in the form of commentary on Scriptures or on single books of the Bible" (Olga Marx, trans., *In Time and Eternity*, p. 251).

23 *EN*: Exodus 20:18f. [B&R use the traditional verse numbers in Exodus 20, the chapter concerning the Ten Commandments. These numbers differ slightly from those used in many modern translations. The translation quoted above, by Fox, likewise uses traditional Hebrew numbering. Neumann, perhaps mindful that many readers lacked access to the B&R translation, assigned "modern" numbers to these verses.]

24 An essay by Martin Buber in his collection, with Franz Rosenzweig, *Die Schrift und ihre Verdeutschung* (*Scripture and its translation into German*), pp. 211–38. In the 1994 English edition, pp. 114ff., Buber explains *"Leitwort"* (lit: guiding word) as a word or root in Hebrew, the repetition of which in a text adds meaning or emphasis. Neumann himself sometimes uses this device in German, cf. his appendix, "On Methodology" (*Roots I*, p. 128, n. 2).

25 *EN*: Also in Buber, *Königtum Gottes*, v. 1, pp. 15ff. [Neumann regularly cites *Das Kommende* (*That which is coming*), the first volume of Buber's 1932 work (hereafter: *Königtum Gottes*). In the 1967 English edition, cf. pp. 66ff.]

26 Passage from Deuteronomy also quoted below, *Roots I*, pp. 28f.

27 "this fact": the institution of prophecy.

28 The phrase is Fox's rendering of *ruach* (which means both "spirit" and "wind"). In their translation of this verse, B&R also invented a word, *Geistbraus* (spirit-uproar).

29 *EN*: Midrash to Samuel 26:2; cited in Bin Gorion, *Sagen der Juden*, v. 5, p. 133. [(Cf. *Roots I*, p. 141, n. 12.]

30 *EN*: Buber, *Königtum Gottes*, Second Introduction, p. xliv. [In English edition, p. 35.]

31 *EN*: Baudissin, *Kyrios*, v. 3, op. cit., p. 515.

32 Ibid., p. 520.

33 Ibid.

34 *EN*: Cf. Kautzsch, p. 756, for references to storm-phenomena, fire, and smoke. [No reference to storm-phenomena occurs on p. 756 in any volume by Kautzsch cited in this work. A reference to fire, signifying God's presence, occurs in Kautzsch's translation of the Old Testament: "the Glory of YHWH took up dwelling on Mount Sinai. The cloud covered it for six days ... And the sight of the Glory of YHWH (was) like a consuming fire in the eyes of the Children of Israel." (Ex 24:16f; cf. also Lev 9:6, 23f., Num 14:10, 16:19, 20:6) (Kautzsch, *Biblische Theologie des Alten Testaments*, p. 90). (Ex 24:16f., trans. by Fox.)]

35 *Dornbusch*. This version of the story, specifying that the burning bush in which Moses meets God is a thorny bush, is supported by the Hebrew text (Ex 3:2ff.) and plays a role in Hasidic tradition. Cf. *Roots II*, Chapter 3: "Life in this world," p. 106.

36 *EN*: Bin Gorion, *Sinai und Garizim*, p. 251. [M. J. Bin Gorion, 1926, *Sinai und Garizim: Über den Ursprung der israelitischen Religion. Forschung zum Hexateuch auf Grund rabbinischer Quellen* (*Sinai and Garizim: The origins of the Jewish religion. A study of the Hexateuch based on rabbinic sources*). (Hereafter: *Sinai & Garizim*).]

37 *EN*: Jerusalem Talmud (hereafter: *Jer Tlm*): *Sota* 3:19a; Babylonian Talmud (hereafter: *Bab Tlm*): *Sotah* 6b. [These passages, cited in Bin Gorion, concern trial by ordeal for a woman accused of sexual misconduct in the Temple, and for a woman accused of adultery (*Sinai & Garizim*, p. 279). The passage in Bin Gorion reads, in translation: "*Rashi*: Why were there different death sentences if the sin of the Golden Calf was the same for everyone, and if by the same token everyone was forbidden to worship? For there are three kinds of death: death by the sword ...; death by the plague ...;

death by edema . . ." (ibid., p. 280). *Bab Tlm: Sotah* 6b concerns the trial by water of a woman accused of misbehavior in the Temple-precincts (*The Hebrew-English Edition of the Babylonian Talmud: Sotah*, trans. by A. Cohen. Soncino, 1985) (hereafter: Soncino).

38 French: mystic participation. The term is used frequently by both Neumann and Jung (cf., for example, CW 6, ¶12, ¶781). It is derived from the writing of Lucien Lévy-Bruhl, in his book *Les fonctions mentales dans les sociétés inférieures* (1910) (*How natives think*), which Neumann cites as *Das Denken der Naturvölker*. In *How Natives Think* (trans. by Lilian Ada Clare), Chapter 2 is titled "The Law of Participation." Robert Segal advises that "mystic relationship" occurs on p. 61, and "mystic participation" on p. 82. In his first lecture in a four-lecture series of 1942–43, Neumann writes: "As the experiences of primitive peoples teach us, the early state of humanity is characterized by the ego's lack of psychic detachment from the powers and contents of the unconscious and of the world, a state called *participation mystique*" (cf. *Roots II*, Appendix B.I, p. 191, n. 6).

39 Cf. Neumann's appendix to this chapter, "The foundation stone and the waters of the deep," *Roots I*, pp. 140f.

40 Cf. *Roots I*, p. 141.

41 Cf. above, *Roots I*, p. 20, n. 20.

42 *EN*: In the Talmud, these passages run parallel to both ordeals.

43 *intentionell einheitlich verarbeitet*. The verb *verarbeiten*, rendered here and in the next sentence as "weave (woven)," may also be translated as "assimilate(d)" or "work(ed) through." (Cf. Neumann's appendix, "On methodology," *Roots I*, p. 138, n. 2.) The reference to a redactor, who deliberately works several versions into a unified text, shows Neumann's reliance on the redaction theory elaborated by some contemporary scholars, including Buber.

44 *EN*: Cf. also Numbers 25:1, where the falling away at Shittim to the Baal of Peor is punished by a plague caused by YHWH's wrath and by the slaying of the people by the leaders. The most recent layer is probably the deed of Pinchas, an Aaronite, which is supposed to support the Aaronite tradition, as the story of the Calf supports the "Levites."

45 *EN*: Highly characteristic of the late victory of the Aaronites over prophecy is the fact that the narrative of the Golden Calf, with its strong anti-Aaronite tendency, was withheld from the people by not being translated into Aramaic in the reading of the word. (*Tosefta Megilla* 4:36, as cited in *Sinai & Garizim*, op. cit.) [Tamar Kron advises that the correct citation is *Tosefta Megilla* 4:19. Bin Gorion writes: "The second story about the Golden Calf is only read aloud, not translated. But this is the second tale about the calf: 'And Moses said to Aaron: What did the people do unto thee, etc.; when Moses saw that the people were unruly, etc., for Aaron had made it unruly.' And at the end it is said: 'The calf that Aaron made'" (*Sinai & Garizim*, p. 279).]

46 Aaronites: the family and descendants of Moses' brother, Aaron, who became the first High Priest (*ha-Cohen ha-Gadol*). Erel Shalit further advises: the line of priests (*cohanim*, from the Hebrew root meaning "to stand," "to serve," "to officiate") was supposedly made up of descendants of Aaron. Aaronites are thus distinguished from the other Levites (descendants of Levi), who served as assistants to the priests.

47 *EN*: There is an intrinsic link between Moses' transformation, in which YHWH's wrath plays a decisive role, and the transformation of the theophanies, in which his grace is crucial.

48 Describing Moses as a charismatic mana-personality, Neumann begins to develop a theme that he further elaborates in the first chapter of *Roots II, Hasidism,* where the characteristics and gifts of the *tzaddik* are explored. In later writings, including his 1948 Eranos lecture, "Mystical Man," and his books published in 1949, *Depth Psychology and a New Ethic* (hereafter *New Ethic*) and *The Origins and History of Consciousness* (hereafter *Origins*)—this concept is designated "the Great Individual."

49 Latin: numinous and terrible one.

50 *EN*: C. G. Jung, *Beziehungen zwischen dem Ich und dem Unbewussten* (*The relations between the ego and the unconscious*) (hereafter: *Beziehungen*), p. 184. [In the 1928 German edition, Part Two, Chapter 4 is titled, "Die Mana-Persönlichkeit" ("The mana personality"). Cf. CW 7, ¶374–406.]

51 Neumann's metaphorical reference is to layers of paint ("repaintings"), which must be removed. (Cf. above, *Roots I*, p. 17.)

52 Same passage quoted above, p. 21.

53 *EN*: On this process, which is also evident today, see C. G. Jung, "Traumsymbole des Individuationsprozesses" ("Dream symbols of the individuation process") and *Psychologie und Religion* (*Psychology and religion*) (hereafter: *Psych & Rel*). [The latter was first published in English (1938), then in German (1940). Cf. CW 11.1, ¶56–107. "Dream Symbols of the Individuation Process," Jung's 1935 Eranos lecture, was first published in English (1939) in *The Integration of the Personality* (hereafter: *Integration*). Cf. CW 12, Part II.]

54 *EN*: Buber, *Königtum Gottes*, p. 143. [Cf. *Kingship of God*, p. 161.] Also Buber, "Die Sprache der Botschaft" ("The language of *Botschaft*"), *Die Schrift und ihre Verdeutschung*, op. cit., p. 55. [In the English edition, translators Rosenwald and Fox explain that, for Buber, *Botschaft* "reveals divine instruction" and so goes beyond the usual meaning of "message." (*Scripture and Translation*, p. 27, n. 1.)]

55 Hebrew: Tent of Meeting

56 *EN*: *Sinai & Garizim*, p. 225.

57 *EN*: Among others, see Auerbach, *Wüste und Gelobtes Land* (*Wilderness and paradise*), v. 1, pp. 66ff. [Cf. also note 63, below.]

58 "*En-mishpat*" was an alternate name for Kadesh-barnea (Gen 14:7). *Mishpat* means "judgment."

59 *EN*: The oracle of *Urim* und *Thummim* is often traced to the sojourn at Kadesh and possibly also involves taking over an institution that existed there.

60 Neumann's statement is supported by a passage in *Ancient Judaism*, "Sacrifice and Expiation" (pp. 162–8), where Weber mentions the *Urim* and *Thummim* and points to the shift from oracular to codified law.

61 *Seinslage*: a term possibly borrowed from Karl Mannheim, a Hungarian-born Jewish sociologist.

62 *EN*: See above, pp. 43ff. [*Roots I*, p. 27, "The elevation of Moses."]

63 Elias Auerbach (1882–1971): German Jewish physician, biblical scholar and historian. In addition to practicing medicine, Auerbach taught and wrote as a biblical historian. His major work, *Wüste und Gelobtes Land* (*Wilderness and paradise*) was published in two volumes, 1932 and 1936.

64 *EN*: Auerbach, *Wüste und Gelobtes Land*, v. 1, pp. 22ff.

65 Abiathar, a priest of the house of Eli, was banished by Solomon (cf. 1 Kings 2:26f and 1 Sam. 2:27–36). "Some have theorized that the banished priest composed what we now call the Early Source of Samuel" (*Oxford Annotated RSV*, p. 417, note).

66 Marah, etc., are place names, serving as summary references to key events that reportedly occurred there.

67 *EN*: See above, pp. 28e and following. [*Roots I*, p. 20, paragraph beginning: "At first it was still believed . . .".]

68 *EN*: See above, pp. 33ff. [*Roots I*, pp. 23f., "The Golden Calf."]

69 *Volksprophetie*: lit. "folk-prophecy" or "popular prophecy." The term has special meaning in relation to Neumann's thesis, spelled out in the previous paragraph, that the Jewish people collectively have a prophetic capacity and calling, which, though often unrealized, is part of their identity.

70 *die prophetische Tendenz*: lit. "the prophetic tendency." Neumann ascribes a socio-religious purpose to early passages of scripture. Cf. *Roots I*, p. 5, n. 12 and p. 49, n. 131.

71 *EN*: See above, p. 40 [*Roots I*, p. 27.]

72 Cf. especially Numbers 14:6–10, 24, and 36–38.

73 *"Zelt der Gegenwärtigkeit"*: lit. "Tent of Presence." Referring to the *Ohel Moed*, the Tent of Meeting.

74 *EN*: Korah is mistakenly inserted into verses 24, 27, and 32. [Erel Shalit advises that Neumann's perception of a textual mistake seems to be driven by his symbolic reading of the death penalty imposed on Dathan and Abiram, as distinct from that imposed on Korah.]

75 Numbers 22–24. A key moment in the story arrives when Balaam, a Midianite prophet, is converted to belief in the God of Israel by the miraculous intervention of his donkey (Num 22:21ff.).

76 *EN*: See Appendix III. [*Roots I*, p. 146. In an early version of Neumann's typescript, the material of Appendix III ("Methodological comments on the form of the Pentateuch") followed here.]

77 *EN*: See, for instance, the anti-Aaronite tendency in Deuteronomy 9:20 and the pro-Levitical tendency in Deuteronomy 10:8.

78 The patriarch Jacob wrestles with "a man," later revealed as an angel (Gen 32).

79 In his youth, Moses slays an Egyptian slavemaster (Ex 2:11f.) but is too insecure to speak as God directs (Ex 4:10–17).

80 " *'rein' und 'unrein'"*: familiar English terms for these concepts (e.g., in Leviticus) are "clean and unclean." Concerning the concept of "impurity," Everett Fox explains the inadequacy of all the English equivalents for the Hebrew term, *tamei*: "[T]he term is not well served by negative translations such as 'impure' or 'unclean'; the Hebrew signifies that something is in a charged state and must not come in contact with the sanctuary" (Fox, *Five Books of Moses*, p. 525, n. 2).

81 *EN*: Cf. Molitor, *Philosophie der Geschichte* (Philosophy of history), v. 3, pp. 172ff. Cf. also Buber, "Die Sprache der Botschaft" ("The language of *Botschaft*"), in *Die Schrift und ihre Verdeutschung*, p. 62. [The Molitor passage is mistakenly cited as p. 109. Franz Joseph Molitor (1779–1860), a German Christian philosopher and Kabbalist, taught at an institute in Dalberg, the mission of which was the uplifting of Judaism. His 1839 work is subtitled, in translation: "On tradition in the Old Covenant and its relationship with the Church of the New Covenant. With special attention to the Kabbalah." According to Buber's statement, "The 'blemish' of the human race … blemishes the earth itself" (*Scripture and Translation*, p. 31).]

82 *EN*: Leviticus 19:23. [In Fox's translation: "Now when you enter the land, and plant any-kind of tree for eating, / you are to regard its fruit (like) a foreskin, a foreskin. / For three years it is to be considered-foreskinned for you, / you are not to eat (it)."]

83 *EN*: Molitor, op. cit., pp. 172ff. [Mistakenly cited as p. 109.]

84 *EN*: Häussermann [1932], "Wortempfang und Symbol in der alttestamentlichen Prophetie: Eine Untersuchung zur Psychologie des prophetischen Erlebnisses" ("Reception of Word and Symbol in Old Testament Prophecy: The psychology of the prophetic experience"), pp. 22, 31, 39. ["In a certain sense, receiving the word involves suffering" (*Wortempfang und Symbol*, p. 22). In translation: "Among the *natural phenomena*, fire, tempests, dark clouds, darkness, downpours, and earthquakes especially come to symbolize Yahwe's essence and work. As the fire devours the stubble, Yahwe destroys those who reject his instruction and who despise his word (Is 5:24)" (ibid., p. 31). "What we know about Amos, Isaiah, or Jeremiah is enough to demonstrate the groundlessness of pathological interpretation. Their experiences could have burst a consciousness with a weaker foundation. Isaiah's 'Woe is me, I am lost' speaks volumes" (ibid., p. 39).]

85 *EN*: Weber, v. 3, op. cit., p. 138. [In the 1952 English edition, the passage reads: "In pre-prophetic times, the 'spirit,' the *ruach* of Yahwe, is neither an ethical power nor a religious state of habitation, but an acute demonic-superhuman power of varying, most frequently frightful, character. … Yahwe, like Indra, is fit to be god of war because, like Indra, he was originally a god of the great catastrophes of nature" (*Ancient Judaism*, p. 128).]

86   *EN*: Jung, "Brother Claus." ["Bruder Klaus," *Neue Schweizer Rundschau*, August 1933, I. Jg, Heft 4, pp. 223–9.) On p. 226, the relevant passage reads, in Hull's translation: "Using a very cautious formulation, we could say that the underlying factor here is a considerable tension of psychic energy, evidently corresponding to some very important unconscious content . . . . The tremendous power of the 'objective' 'psychic' has been named 'demon' or 'God' in all epochs with the sole exception of the recent present. We have become so bashful in matters of religion that we correctly say 'unconscious,' because God has in fact become unconscious to us" (CW 11, ¶479).]

87   Latin: lit. the hidden (departed) God.

88   *EN*: See Jung, "*Geist-Leben*" (Spirit-Life), in *Wirklichkeit der Seele* (*The reality of the psyche*; hereafter: *Wirklichkeit*); Zarathustra Seminars; "Wotan." ["*Geist-Leben*" is apparently Neumann's shorthand reference to Jung's idea of the reality and autonomy of the spirit. Relevant passages may include the following: In *Wirklichkeit* (1934), the chapter titled "Das Grundproblem der gegenwärtigen Psychologie," contains a passage found in Hull's translation, "The Basic Postulates of Analytical Psychology," CW 8.13, ¶¶679–88. A relevant passage in "Paracelsus" may be found in CW 15.1, ¶11f. In the "Zarathustra Seminars" (unpublished, multigraphed typescript, 1934–39), Jung quotes Nietzsche's description of his state of inspiration: "'[O]ne is the mere incarnation, mouthpiece or medium of an almighty power. . . . [A] thought suddenly flashes up like lightning, it comes with necessity . . . I have never had any choice in the matter'" (typescript, v. 1, p. 27). In the 1936 article "Wotan," Jung writes: " Not that 'psychic forces' have anything to do with the conscious mind . . . 'Psychic forces' have far more to do with the realm of the unconscious" (CW 10, ¶387).]

89   *EN*: On the ideology of the spirit–*ruach–pneuma/anima–animus–spiritus*, cf. Jung's Eranos lectures. [At the time of writing, Neumann had access to the Eranos lectures through *EJ 1939*. Passages relating spirit/wind to anima/animus are found in three of Jung's lectures up to 1939: "Über die Archetypen des kollektiven Unbewußten," *EJ 1934* ("Archetypes of the Collective Unconscious," CW 9.i, 1) "Traumsymbole des Individuationsprozesses," *EJ 1935* ("Dream Symbols of the Process of Individuation," CW 12.3, Part II), and "Die Erlösungsvorstellungen in der Alchemie," *EJ 1936* ("The Idea of Redemption in Alchemy," CW 12,3, Part III).]

90   A reference to the Christian concept of the Holy Spirit. Neumann goes on to argue, against Baudissin, that the spirit of God, or Holy Spirit, is an essential concept in the Hebrew Bible.

91   *EN*: Cf. Kautzsch, v. 2. His index to *Geist Gottes* (*Spirit of God*) contains these passages in full. [No such entry is found in the index in any of Kautzsch's works. However, in his *Biblische Theologie des Alten Testaments* (1911), the subject index has an entry for *Geist Gottes*, listing ten passages. A relevant passage, in translation: "In all these passages, 'the hand' designates divine influence, which seizes the prophet, irresistibly, almost tantamount to the 'spirit of YHWH,' who also 'falls' upon the prophet (Ezek 11:5) and conveys God's particular revelations to him" (pp. 194f.).]

92   *EN*: Baudissin, v. 3, n. 5, pp. 486ff.

93   *EN*:Virolleaud, "Anat-Astarte," *EJ 1938*. [Cf. Part Two of lecture by Charles Virolleaud, pp. 141–60.]

94   *EN*: Baudissin, v. 4, p. 54.

95   *EN*: Rudolf Otto, "Prophetische Gotteserfahrung" ("Prophetic Experience of God") in *Sünde und Urschuld* (*Sin and primal guilt*). [The reference is to Chapter 6.]

96   Ibid., p. 64, slightly paraphrased.

97   Ibid., p. 66, slightly paraphrased.

98   *EN*: Cf. Appendix IVa. [*Roots I*, pp. 148ff.] So as not to clutter the main text, various details have been included in the appendix. Appendix IV discusses related matters. The references to the various sections of the appendix are meant to provide readers with orientation, without interrupting the reading of this chapter.

99   *EN*: Baudissin, v. 3, p. 486.

100 The Hebrew word, *adam* (human being), is also the name of the first human being, Adam. The noun and the name are related to Hebrew *adama* ("earth, soil").

101 *EN*: Cf. Appendix IVb. [*Roots I*, p. 152, n. 71; citation to Zohar II 142a, Bischoff, v. 1, p. 111. Cf. Appendix A, *Roots II*, p. 186.]

102 *EN*: Baudissin, v. 3, p. 633, slightly paraphrased.

103 *EN*: ibid., p. 481.

104 *EN*: Jung, *Wandlungen und Symbole der Libido* (*Transformations and Symbols of the Libido*) (1912/1925) (hereafter: *Wandlungen*). [This pioneering work, which led to the end of the Jung–Freud collaboration, was available to Neumann in its original version. Later extensively revised and retitled, it was republished in 1952 as CW 5, *Symbole der Wandlung* (*Symbols of transformation*). In early editions, Chapter VII, "Das Opfer" ("The Sacrifice") (pp. 294–413) discusses the duality of the mother-figure in terms of the nourishing and destroying aspects of the mother-archetype and the double births of heroes. Jung here distinguishes the personal mother from the mother-imago (identical with the unconscious). In CW 5, this material is expanded into two chapters: "The Dual Mother" and "The Sacrifice."]

105 *EN*: See below, pp. 88f. [*Roots I*, pp. 54f.]

106 *EN*: See Goldberg, *Wirklichkeit der Hebräer* (*Reality of the Hebrews*), op. cit. When translated critically from their atavistic–primitive concretizing, his findings often prove highly illuminating. His "reality" is to some extent that of a physician. It does approach the reality of the Hebrews, but only where that reality exists on a primitive level.

107 "*Einheiligung*": Buber's term, for a conscious, religious act of making holy. He writes, for example about *Einheiligung der Geschlechtlichkeit* (*Die Schrift und ihre Verdeutschung*, op. cit., p. 62): "To hallow sexuality in protest against its being proclaimed intrinsically holy is the deep goal of *Botschaft*, which in the Genesis story has found narrative expression" (*Scripture and Translation*, 1994, p. 31).

108 *EN*: Cf. Buber, "Die Sprache der Botschaft" ("The Language of *Botschaft*"), *Die Schrift und ihre Verdeutschung*, op. cit., in "Schicksalsverbundenheit von Volk und Land" ("The joined destiny of people and land"), pp. 62–6. [Cf. *Scripture and Translation*, pp. 31ff.]

109 *EN*: Cf. Appendix IVc. [*Roots I*, pp. 153f.: "Earth and bull."]

110 Biblical books untranslated by Fox, including the major prophets, are generally cited by the New Revised Standard Version of the Bible (NRSV).

111 Buber's translation of *Jirmejahu* (Jeremiah) originally appeared in the 1930 Lambert & Schneider edition, along with the ten volumes that he and Rosenzweig had completed before the latter's death. It was reprinted unchanged in the 1934 Schocken edition.

112 *EN*: See Appendix IVd. [*Roots I*, pp. 155ff., "Circumcision and Passover."]

113 *Du*: alternate translation: "You." A reference to Martin Buber's central concept in *Ich und Du* [*I and Thou*] (1923). Buber writes, in Kaufmann's translation: "The basic word I–You can only be spoken with one's whole being. . . . The You encounters me by grace – it cannot be found by seeking" (*I and Thou*, pp. 54, 62).

114 *EN*: Besides the "earthly" opposition, a principal one is heard here, referring, in our terms, to the layers of the unconscious in their varying proximity to the center.

115 Neumann's note is based on the association of "neu" and "nah" in Deuteronomy 32:17, as translated by B&R: "Göttern davon sie nicht wußten, / neuen, von nah gekommen . . . ." (Fox's version includes a similar alliteration: "gods they had not known, new-ones from nearby came.")

116 "*Der von seinem Vater und seiner Mutter sprach: ich kenne ihn nicht, seinen Bruder nicht ansah, seine Kinder nicht kannte!*" In this case, unusually, Neumann does not quote the B&R translation. We have translated the verse as it stands in Neumann's typescript.

117 *EN*: Eisler, "Das Rätsel des Johannisevangeliums," *EJ 1935*. [The verse cited here (John 2:4), Jesus' saying to his mother, may also be rendered, "Woman, what have you to do with me?" (NRSV). The adjective *roh* ("Jesus von Nazareth und seinem 'rohen' Wort") does not occur in Eisler's paper but is consistent with his discussion of this passage in the story of the Marriage at Cana (cf. Eisler, 1936, pp. 486ff.).]

118 Neumann's quotation of these verses is accurate to the Hebrew, but slightly abbreviated. Buber's *Jirmejahu* was available to Neumann at the time of writing, but this wording does not follow Buber's.

119 *EN*: Auerbach, v. 2, op. cit., p. 114.

120 Apparently referring to a passage in Auerbach's *Wüste und gelobtes Land*, comparing the Rekabites' rule of life with that of their neighbors. For Neumann, Auerbach's ethnological observations are true as far as they go, but they fail to acknowledge the prophets' rejection of the people's over-attachment to the land.

121 *EN*: See Heiler [1920], *Das Gebet: Eine religionsgeschichtliche und religionspsychologische Untersuchung* (*Prayer: A study in the history of religion and of psychology*). [Perhaps referring to the sixth part of Heiler's book: "Das Gebet in der individuellen Frömmigkeit der großen religiösen Persönlichkeiten" ("Prayer in the individual piety of great religious personalities").]

122 *EN*: Baudissin, v. 3, p. 632. [This page falls in a section called "Die Art der Größe des Gottes in seiner Auffassung als des Herrn" ("The kind of greatness belonging to the god who is apprehended as Lord." The quoted text is apparently Neumann's own; it does not appear on the page cited or adjacent pages.]

123 *yad YHWH* (Hebrew): hand of YHWH.

124 This phrase is not a verbatim biblical quotation. It combines texts found in Jeremiah 23 and 28. (Cf. Jer 23:16f and 28:9ff.)

125 *EN*: For an analysis, see Friedrich Häussermann, 1932, *Wortempfang und Symbol in der alttestamentlichen Prophetie*, op. cit., especially pp. 41 ff. [Häussermann's approach to biblical imagery resembles Jung's treatment of inner psychological experience. His chapter titled "Die Deutung des Symbols" ("The interpretation of the symbol") (pp. 41–102) reviews biblical and extrabiblical accounts of numinous experiences, which are found to be overwhelming. For example, regarding Amos 3:8, he writes: "The prophet is assailed by knowledge and, like the unsuspecting wanderer, is frightened by the roaring lion" (p. 51).]

126 *soufliert*: lit. "prompted"

127 French: "lowered mental level"

128 *EN*: See above. [*Roots I*, p. 17, referring to "mass ecstasy and intoxication" in divinatory procedures.]

129 *EN*: Jung, "Die psychologischen Grundlagen des Geisterglaubens" ("The psychological foundations of belief in spirits"), pp. 200–24 in *Über die Energetik der Seele* (*On psychic energy*), 1928 (hereafter: *Energetik*). [Cf. CW 8,11, ¶594.]

130 *EN*: Cf. "Jakob und Esau," Chapter 3. [Neumann's early monograph, unpublished at time of writing. In the 2015 English edition, *Jacob & Esau*, cf. pp. 84–98. "Secondary personalization" is further developed in the lectures of 1942–43, especially "Symbols and Stages of Conscious Development" (cf. Appendix B.I, *Roots II*, pp. 205f.). It is also thoroughly explored in *Origins and History.*]

131 *Tendenzen des Unbewussten*: Neumann's use of "*Tendenz*" echoes Jung's concept of the autonomy of the unconscious. In Jung's *Psych & Rel* (1938), the first lecture is titled, "The Autonomy of the Unconscious Mind" (CW 11.1, ¶1–55). With its implied intentionality, "*Tendenz*" here approaches "aim" or "movement toward a purpose." An example of a positive purpose in the unconscious is found in Neumann's observation that an unconscious goal was achieved in "the appearance of the transcendent function, that is, the revelation of YHWH" (*Roots I*, p. 50). In contrast, Neumann's criticism of James Kirsch, in a letter to Jung dated 9 February 1935, points to the negative consequences that may result when the unconscious is uncritically given too much authority (*J-N Corresp*, p. 87).

132 *EN*: Jung, *Energetik*, op. cit. [No exact source has been found for the quoted phrase. Neumann may be referring to Jung's previously cited chapter, "The psychological foundations of belief in spirits" (cf. CW 8,11, ¶580–90).]

133 In this context, Neumann's word "partnership" refers to the biblical theme of a covenant of betrothal or marriage between God and Israel. (Cf., for example., Hosea 2:18ff.).

134 Hebrew: prophet

135 On the character and importance of the *tzaddik*, cf. *Roots II*, especially pp. 120ff.

136 Hebrew: the primordial human being. In the Lurianic Kabbalah, Adam is said to be the microcosm of the entire creation. Cf. *Roots I*, p. 162 and *Roots II*, pp. 69ff.

137 *EN*: Baudissin, v. 3, p. 609.

138 Ibid., p. 606. [Neumann omits this reference.]

139 *EN*: Ibid., p. 604.

140 *Wahl-Bund*: covenant with YHWH, marking the people of Israel as chosen.

141 *Gesicht*: lit. "sight" or "face." The word, which contains a form of the verb *sehen* ("see"), can also mean a "vision." In this passage, which contrasts hearing and seeing, "*Gesicht*" has the latter sense.

142 Hyphenated by Neumann, as *Ge-horsam* (lit. "obedience"). The added hyphen may be meant to emphasize the root, *hören* ("hear").

143 *EN*: Baudissin, v. 3, p. 629.

144 Hebrew: Holy Spirit

145 *EN*: Cf. Weber, v. 3, pp. 429f. [In this passage, a relevant sentence reads: "The revival of the holy spirit in all men accordingly would be a sign of the advent of the Messiah and of the kingdom of God at hand" (*Ancient Judaism*, p. 412).]

146 Compound word, consisting of *navi* (Hebrew, "prophet") and *-tum* (German nominal ending): "practice of prophecy."

147 Animus and anima are key terms in Jung's psychology, designating complexes of the collective unconscious. Cf. CW 9.ii, *Aion*, ¶20–42.

148 Jung's observation that unconscious contents function autonomously is significant to Neumann. Cf. above, p. 49, n. 131. Also, in *New Ethic* (the 1990 English edition), cf. Jung's "Foreword," p. 17, and Chapter IV, p. 98.

149 In Neumann's typescript, this sentence reads: "Gerade ihre teilweise Herkunft aus und urspruengliche Verwobenheit mit diesen Phaenomenen musste den Zwang zum Sichunterscheiden besonders verstaerken." The pronoun (*ihre*) is apparently an error. Its only possible antecedent is "divinatory prophecy" (*mantische Prophetie*). That reference, however, reverses Neumann's logic, by saying that divinatory prophecy was once "entangled with these phenomena." In translating, we have taken the liberty of supplying the subject, "Hebrew prophecy," to produce the sense we believe was intended.

150 Cf. Neumann's discussion of the "earth polarity" above, in relation to the Golden Calf, *Roots I*, p. 24.

151 Cf. *Roots I*, p. 37, under "The Affirmation of Nature and Nature's Purity."

152 Cf. *Roots I*, p. 49, p. 53.

153 *EN*: See above. [The reference is to the previous paragraph.]

154 *Bewirktwerden*: lit. "being brought about." Biblical prophets are closely involved with the people to whom they are sent. In the powerful narrative of Isaiah's vision, the prophet originally shrinks back: "I am a man of unclean lips, and I dwell in the midst of a people of unclean lips" (Is 6:5, RSV). Having accepted his calling, he is immediately sent to speak to the people (Is 6:9ff.). The collective role of the prophet also means, not infrequently, that obedience to God's call puts one's life at risk (e.g. Jer 26:7–11).

155 *EN*: See above. [*Roots I*, pp. 24f., on the Golden Calf and the Levites.]

156 In one passage Neumann describes the ancient period of Judaism as ending with the destruction of the Solomonic Temple (cf. "Introduction to the work," *Roots I*, p. 9, n. 24). Elsewhere, he describes a change that began in the Babylonian Exile, reaching full expression when the Second Temple was destroyed (ibid., p. 8).

157 *EN*: See above. [*Roots I*, pp. 31f., on Moses and Jethro.]

158 *EN*: See above. [*Roots I*, p. 59, on grafting.]

159 The passage is biblical: Exodus 5:24–26.

160 *des nachantiken Judentums*: lit. "of post-ancient Judaism."

161 Greek: fate. In ancient Greece, the Fates were worshiped as three sisters, the *Moirai*, with power to spin, weave, and cut off the thread of life.

162 Slightly paraphrasing Wellhausen: "liess sein Antlitz leuchten und zürnte" ("let his face shine and was angry") (*Abriss der Geschichte Israels und Juda's* (*Outline of the history of Israel and Judah*) (hereafter: *Abriss*), p. 46.

163 Ibid., p. 46. Also cf. Wellhausen's *Israelitische und Jüdische Geschichte*, p. 108.

164 *EN*: Jung, *Beziehungen*, p. 207. [The passage occurs near the end of Jung's final chapter, "The Mana Personality." (Cf. CW 7, ¶405.)]

165 *EN*: Wellhausen, *Abriss*, p. 46.

166 "*die ihn (JHWH) zur 'Umkehr' bringt*": lit. "which brings him (YHWH) to 'turning back'." Neumann's use of *Umkehr* echoes the Hebrew root *shuv* ("turn, turn again, turn back, return"). Like *Umkehr*, the Hebrew term *tshuva*, usually translated as "repentance," lacks the connotation of being sorry and emphasizes a change of direction. (With thanks to Erel Shalit and Richard Corney.)

167 Greek: fate (personified as a woman)

168 "And when God saw what they did, how they turned from their evil ways, God changed his mind about the calamity he had said he would bring upon them, and he did not do it" (Jonah 3:10, NRSV). Nineveh, capital of Assyria, represents all that is foreign to the worship of God. Jonah at first resists God's command to preach to the people there. Then he grows angry when, in response to their thorough-going penitence, God spares the city from destruction.

169 *Un-festlegbarkeit*: Neumann's hyphen emphasizes the negative prefix.

170 *EN*: See Martin Ninck, *Götter- und Jenseitsglauben der Germanen* (*Belief in gods and the other world*). [Ninck discusses the Norns in his eighth chapter: "The Powers of Fate: the Origin and Final Destiny of the World" (pp. 144–58): "The spinning, weaving fates survive in fairy tales to this day" (pp. 145f.).]

171 *EN*: Ninck, *Wodan und germanischer Schicksalsglaube* (*Wotan and the Germanic belief in fate*). [In Ninck's third chapter, "The Lord of the Berserkers" (pp. 34–67), he writes (in translation): "Odin had such power that he could make his enemies blind or deaf in battle, or as if paralyzed with terror. . . . But his own men went [into battle] without mail-coats, and they were wild like dogs or wolves. . . . They battered people to death, and neither fire nor steel could harm them. This was called 'going berserk'" (p. 34).]

172 "Now here, an evil spirit of God is tormenting you" (1 Sam 16:15); "But an evil spirit of YHWH [came] upon Sha'ul" (1 Sam 19:9). (Fox's edition numbers the second verse differently.)

173 Neumann anticipates writing Part Three of the present work. For a summary of the uncompleted third part, see Introduction to Volume One, *Roots I*, p. xxvi. Cf. also Neumann's four-lecture series of 1942–43 "The importance of consciousness in the experience of depth analysis," Appendix B, *Roots II*, pp. 190–274.

2

THE APOCALYPSE

Heightening the YHWH–earth tension

1. The new worldview and alienation from salvation

Israel gradually became a historical people, and in the process it came to occupy a certain status within the system of Near Eastern cultures. In other words, as the extra-historical or pre-historical[1] confederation of tribes became historicized, it also grew to be secularized, with an ever greater focus on the here and now.

The original concept of prophecy had brought theocracy back into prominence as a goal, and in doing so had most likely revived an ancient theocratic tribal tradition. But with Israel's entrance into the historical world, the tension between YHWH and earth was immensely heightened and energized. Being entangled in the political and economic reality of a world system, one that had extraordinary powers of domination and an increasingly palpable influence on all areas of life, inevitably led to a progressive politicization and the need to "be like the other peoples."[2] This conflict, which was closely related historically to the acceptance of the kingdom,[3] intensified more and more as the order of everyday life became consolidated—both externally, due to historical and political circumstances, and internally, due to the resistance arising from the people's orientation toward earth and Canaan. So a theocracy, understood as the rule of YHWH, became increasingly remote and improbable.

As it became ever more evident that Israel could not assert itself as a historical factor on the political stage, what emerged was not only political messianism but also the projection of a theocratic ideal into the future, the end of days. In the messianic ideal, two forces come together that, in reality, never had anything in common: the power-political ideal of a secularized Israel as a historic force, and the theocratic ideal, according to which reality only makes sense, that is, has a right to exist, insofar as YHWH forms and has power in it.

The Exile and the end of the primitive collective

The downfall of the kingdom and the Babylonian Exile fatefully deepened the previously fruitful tension between YHWH and earth, even if outwardly it could appear that this was exactly where the prophetic tendency achieved complete success, in Ezekiel's theocratic construction and its attempted realization at the time of the Second Temple.[4]

The fulfillment of the disaster prophecies[5] boosted the prestige of Hebrew prophecy enormously. Indeed, one may say that it was not until the destruction of Jerusalem that prophecy became historically powerful for Judaism, because the catastrophic shattering of all worldly and political claims and ties with the earth seemed to provide irrefutable evidence of the power of prophecy, and particularly of YHWH's ascendency over existence.

But the shock of the Temple's destruction and the exile calamitously altered the theocratic and prophetic direction. As we see in the highs and lows of the biblical account, original prophecy conflicted with an overly strong earthly attachment and affirmation, and confronted the natural force of a strong people. In contrast, by its overwhelming, catastrophic nature, the great upheaval created a changed Jewish person.

After the exile, the Judah-ism[6] that emerged no longer knew the opposition of the ancient, pagan principle of nature as an effective power of the unconscious, but it also no longer knew the meaning given by YHWH, which erupted in theophany and decree. The original, primitive community of the people had dissolved, the religious relevance of which had consisted in its being a subject, as a people, that bore certain attitudes and realizations directed by YHWH. The people's partnership, in covenant with YHWH, was lost.

Within the tribal confederacy, the individual lived in such *participation mystique* with the community that no individual guilt existed, but the totality always appeared as the guarantor and the subject of guilt. Now this tribal confederacy had declined, and the emergence of religious individualism, evident in Ezekiel,[7] was the necessary consequence of a fate that wrenched the human being out of his collective shelteredness and into an individual destiny.

In later cultural eras, an overwhelming event throws human beings, who until then had been conscious only of their individuality, back into the collective and melts down the individual in the cauldron of the collective event. The power of collective forces threatens the integrity of the individual with annihilation. In earlier times, however, when the individual exists only in rudimentary form, because the focus of existence is on collective events and with the collective, the opposite reaction occurs. Here, the twilight of containment in the collective is violently interrupted. The sense of oneness with the people, the land, and events, the subject of which is the people, is destroyed by the shattering of this people and its being led out of the land. Now personal suffering becomes prominent, behind which the collective disappears.

These two opposing developments may be observed time and again. On the one hand, in the midst of collective catastrophes, a highly differentiated individual finds his way back to the collective. On the other hand, a less differentiated, less conscious individual, experiencing suffering, begins for the first time to think or feel, in short, to differentiate himself.

However, the reversal of this development, from individual to collective and from collective to individual, takes place only when the irrupting collective event is consciously realized. Otherwise, it leads to a radicalizing of the original development: one who is individualized becomes even more individualized and perishes, and one who is collective becomes even more collective and disintegrates as an atom in the mass.

When the original primitive entity, the people, falls apart, this leads not only to religious individualism, which generalizes the contact between God and humans—a contact previously reserved for the tribal fathers, the prophets, and the chosen—but also to collective tendencies on another level, namely, the theocracy of legal Judah-ism, on the one hand, and secularized politics, on the other.

The construction of the Second Temple, Ezra's and Nehemiah's foundation of Judah-ism on the basis of priestly law, the violent introduction of the cult, and the fundamental establishment of Judaism's isolationalist tendencies are well-known historical factors. Their inner meaning was that a consciousness of collective guilt, received[8] through the historical shock, would create for itself, in the shape of external, almost obsessively neurotic institutions, a collectively binding security system. The constitution of the kingdom of God was anticipated and violently installed in a world unpervaded by theocracy, whether from without or from within. This externalization of the original, prophetic intentions was historically understandable and, in a certain sense, even necessary. The construction of a kingdom of God, instituted by the law, helped to create a new collective basis for the people, whose natural development had been interrupted by the catastrophe of exile.

Judah-ism and subjective religiosity

Beside this collective religion, which now assumed a denominational character, genuine religiosity also developed within the individual. This happened precisely because the God–human relationship no longer existed in the original, naive form of a covenant, but nor could it achieve fulfillment through the externalized priestly form of the cult.

In contrast to the diversity of the earlier mountain cults in Deuteronomy, the centralizing principle led to the monopoly of the Temple in Jerusalem and intensified considerably after the exile. Apart from the threat of Canaanite influences, the earlier decentralizing of the cult had also had an individualizing effect, in that the many cultic sites and places offered scope for individual development in the life of the single person, of small groups, and of their Levites. Through the centralizing effect of the Temple, individual religious activity had been decisively driven back. Alongside the collective festivities in Jerusalem, individual religious life—unless it went over, in apostasy, to the local Canaanite deities—expressed itself in two ways: first, by fulfilling the law and collectively prescribed religious behavior, and, second, in the introversion of prayer. This doubleness, pervading daily life, once again corresponds to the prophetic leaning toward direct revelation, which exists in a weakened form in prayers, above all in the psalms. And, on the other hand, it corresponds to the legal–priestly tradition, which increasingly affected national policy and thus determined the *form* of life.

The heightened centralization within Judah-ism had an underground compensation in religious individualism, which was decentralizing. This individualism had to shift the emphasis of religious life more and more toward the inside, demanding a life pregnant with conviction.

By renouncing a new and vibrant revelation, the externalized priestly theocracy forsakes YHWH's true penetration of the world, which prophetic theocracy had intended. And the more it does so, the more the individual becomes the new bearer of the theocratic principle. Apart from every cult form, but through his attitude toward life and his particular experience, that is, through his interpretation of the world, the individual now had to intend and try to fulfill the penetration of *his* world by YHWH.

The principle of internalizing, which had reached its peak in Jeremiah in the conception of the "new covenant and the new heart"[9] (Jer 31:31, Is 66:1; but see also Jer 7, Hos 6 and 8, Amos 5, Mic 6), extends to the figure of YHWH's servant in Second Isaiah[10] and to the protest of the so-called Third Isaiah[11] against the Temple and the priesthood.[12] This inner line manifests itself not only in the creation of the psalter, as a typical expression of individual religiosity, but also in the formation of smaller sectarian groups, from the "pious" and the "humble" to the Therapeutae[13] and the Essenes.[14]

Without overestimating the practical effectiveness of these groups, they are a clear symptom of how ordinary religious life was increasingly forced away from the official line of priestly theocracy and toward the individual. But, in addition, these small groups, as we know, were the seedbed of the new religious movements that found their visible expression in apocalypticism and early Christianity.

The founding of the Second Temple and Judah-ism led to the ultimate decline of actual prophecy,[15] which reached its high point, effectively its canonization, with the determination that, after the deaths of the three post-exilic prophets, Haggai, Zechariah, and Malachi, direct intercourse was ended between God and human beings.[16] After that, revelation occurs only from time to time, through the "heavenly voice," a residual form of revelation, the fate of which we shall consider later on.[17]

Despite all inward attempts at regeneration and compensation, a growing awareness of historical decline was set in motion by the fall of the Temple and the kingdom, and by the exile. This awareness was mirrored by the historical idea of a lost connection to revelation. The predominance of this negative historical development never permitted the feeling to arise that the second temple wholly replaced the first. In one passage, the Talmud says: "Five things were missing from the Second Temple: the heavenly fire, the Ark of the Covenant, *Urim* and *Thummim*, anointing oil, and the Holy Spirit."[18] This means, however, that it lacked every-thing essential; it was no longer "God's dwelling" and the center of revelation.

The ending of the direct connection to revelation, brought about by Judah-ism, the theocracy of priesthood and law, meant that all revelation was now pushed into a sideline. Correspondingly, the next experiences of revelation within Judaism, those of the apocalypticists, were all disguised and hid themselves behind pseu-donymity. This was necessary, because true prophecy would supposedly not be renewed until the end of days; so the apocalyptic writers had to ascribe their visions and revelations to earlier times: Moses, Ezra, Enoch, Baruch, etc.

At the same time, however, this basic conception brought the idea of the last days into current reality, because, wherever genuine experiences of revelation occurred, the conviction *had* to arise that now, as proclaimed, with the re-awakening of prophecy, the end of time had begun.

The naive position of the individual in the midst of his people, in direct prox-imity to God, and at the center of the world, that is, the primary attitude of the pre-exilic Jew, was destroyed, but it was replaced among the apocalyptic writers by a new worldview.

It is only in apocalyptic literature that the unmistakable foreignness of the world as a whole begins to be seen by the Jews. The many-sidedness of the world had certainly been experienced long before, even in the Old Testament. This was especially true in Palestine, which was illuminated by all kinds of cultural centers. And yet the universe that was now depicted, in the complexity of its hierarchies of spheres, heavens, and hells, is fundamentally different from the anthropocentric conception of the world in Genesis. As a basic approach to historical events, the dialogic experience of God, for the human being created in his image, stands in stark contrast to the form of world history now outlined.

The end of direct revelation

An interest in cosmology, as a need to learn about the laws of nature and thus to expe-rience the external structure of the world, is based on a consciousness that distances itself from the world, being no longer naively or primitively bound to it. This distance, however, not only expresses a "scientific" worldview, as against an anthropocentric–magical one, but also represents an enormous deflation of self-consciousness. This self-consciousness, which once named and gathered the world around itself as the center, was now, in the time of the apocalypse, in danger of being crushed by it.

The apocalyptic perspective on world history needs to be understood in the same way. It summarized the succession of the world's empires as a single instance of the principle of the world, which is hostile to God. And it depicted a process of historical decadence, progressively declining under the rule of evil.

This philosophy of history also springs from the fact that individual conscious-ness, having lost its connection to revelation and being left entirely isolated, was increasingly unable to work through its ever more overwhelming experiences of the world in a meaningful way.

The tremendous widening of the horizon, which Judaism so pleasingly calls a "universalistic worldview," disintegrated the state of unconscious security within the religion and the people. This disintegration was conditioned by the devouring world powers that appeared on the horizon, and by the reality of a people that was extremely small in terms of power politics. The drawback of this universalism was the forlornness of the individual in the world, given the smallness of the people and its limited sphere of influence. Fearful images, in which the world empires appeared as gigantic animals pregnant with doom,[19] were the reflection of this existential situation, in which everything was darkened by the overwhelming shadow of world events, before which individual existence trembled.

From within, however, religious individualization urged in the same direction, as it moved the focus of events away from the people as a subject, and shifted it onto the individual.

The final result of the strong emphasis on ethics and consciousness was that the individual himself, as a responsible being, became the object of the historical process. The historical process was decided within himself, as it were, because the course of the world depended on his right or wrong doing. This overburdening of the system of ego-consciousness,[20] to which was given a seemingly unbearable responsibility, led to a strong coercion of conviction and, as a partial consequence, a rigid legal stance. Over-responsibility, with its guilt feelings and heightened need for repression, is immediately compensated for by a tremendous activation of the unconscious. Collectively, this demonization of the world corresponds in every respect to what we repeatedly see in the saints and their "temptation": the negative activation of the unconscious, in compensation for an overly radical, ethicized, conscious attitude.

Earlier we saw that the dominance of ethical consciousness was also indispensable for the Jew in every revelatory situation. The autonomy of ethical consciousness was actually the measure of the depth of revelation. Characteristically, this measure is also preserved in the conception of the Last Judgment. This becomes clear, for instance, if one considers the opposing attitude of the Egyptians to the judgment of the dead. There, religion essentially endeavors to influence the act of judgment through magical initiation, through magical formulae, i.e., magical sayings, and thus leads it *ad absurdum*.[21] This guarantee of salvation still also survives in the later religions of redemption, in the magical efficacy of the sacraments. To some extent, among the apocalypticists, the law still possesses a corresponding sacramental character for the righteous, but on the whole any guaranteed certainty has been abandoned, apart from the fact that the fulfillment of the law presupposes a certain ethical stance and conscious orientation, in contrast to a magical knowledge of the names of the gods and magical formulae. In the face of YHWH's irruption as judge, "everyone shall bear his righteousness or unrighteousness alone" (IV Ezra 7:105).[22]

The oppressive weight of this darkened present, along with religious individualism, urged toward the prophetic apocalypse, by projecting the positive state of salvation into the future. It also made for an extraordinary introversion, turning the libido inward. In the pictorial apocalypse, this activation of the unconscious leads to a representation of the inner world in projected form, which involved description of heavens and hells and their inhabitants, hierarchies of angels and demons, intermediaries, hypostases, etc. Although Babylonian, Iranian, and Hellenistic influences are certainly present, they are secondary. What is primary is the attitude toward existence, together with the activation of the collective unconscious, which led to experiences corresponding to those that brought forth the demons and angels of the surrounding Babylonian–Iranian–Hellenistic world. But this only set the pre-condition for letting in such previously rejected influences.

The end of the original collective closeness to God, which had marked the former covenant relationship, occurred parallel with the end of the original primitive community. This community was replaced by a more universal image of the world, in which Judah and Israel[23] had lower status than the large dominions of successive world rulers. In the same way, amid the introversion of that time, an interior universalism emerged, with a lofty divinity, existing immeasurably far from the individual ego, separated from it by many worlds.

The introduction of intermediaries, ranks of angels, and central hypostatic figures like Sophia, Logos, Metatron, or the *Shekhinah*,[24] is merely one symptom of the divinity's retreat into the heights, into unfathomable transcendence, into sublime mystery.

As the closeness of the divinity once manifested itself in YHWH's visit to Abraham and again in his speaking to Moses face to face, so the overwhelming and fear-inspiring magnificence of the heavenly palace and the blinding radiance of images of the throne (Dan 7:9; IV Ezra 8:2;[25] Enoch 14:9, 71:5;[26] Baruch 21:6, 46:4;[27] etc.) are symptomatic of YHWH's remoteness and the ego's smallness, facing the overpowering numinosities that rule the outer and inner worlds. An era that still had an extremely strong sense of protection, in both the dimension of life and the unconscious, did not yet feel lonely or forlorn in the fear-inspiring worlds that now confront us, from the discrepancy between the experiencing ego and the transcendent sphere of magnificence and power.

The prophetic idea of the messiah,[28] this worldly, emphatically national expectation that God himself would bring redemption, had still been at least partly associated with the idea of a direct, collective theocracy. But now, corresponding to an altered mode of existence, the idea of theocracy shifted toward a universal, cosmically expanded hope for salvation, in which the mediating messiah-figure gained increasing importance as savior. Activation of interior and exterior dimensions intruded more and more strongly between God and humanity. Viewed from this perspective, the doctrine that revelation had ended, after Haggai, Zechariah, and Malachi, was the authentic recognition of fundamental changes in the psychic structure.

The original YHWH–earth tension is, and should be, overcome in the direct fulfillment of YHWH's words by the people bound to him in the covenant. Yet early experience had taught that this accomplishment was exceptionally difficult, and the messianic conception rested on that recognition. The orientation toward earth so strongly resisted being penetrated, outwardly and inwardly, that the fulfillment of YHWH's words was projected to the future, in the idea of the "end of time."[29]

The genuineness of messianic expectation is guaranteed as long as the arrival of the last days is considered possible and can be expected at any moment. Over the history of the Jews, in the emergence of messianic movements, believed to fulfill the end of time, we see how intensely and how long this expectation could be genuinely maintained. Nevertheless, the messianic conception involves a shift, in that the theocratic fulfillment is no longer left to the people, but rather YHWH's irruptive power now takes charge of the final realization, whether directly or through the mediation of the messiah. This shift undoubtedly entails a weakening of the original conception, in which the people, as a holy people, executed YHWH's fulfillment and the world's salvation. Only when weariness sets in, under pressure of the obstructive dimension of world and earth, and as a projection of its impermeability and heaviness, is the realization deferred to an image of the end of time.

This process of alienation from salvation, in contrast with the original realization in the here and now, persists and gains ground through what is called the "retreat of divinity," or the "movement upward."[30] The projection of divinity into the remotest heaven poses a contrast with the Tent of Meeting, where in early days the deity had settled in the midst of the people's impurity. An identical contrast is posed by the projection of salvation to the end of days, as compared with the original idea of a salvation, the fulfillment of which was ensured through the covenant partners' direct contact in revelation.

The cosmic expansion of apocalyptic messianism worked in the same direction. Instead of YHWH's wars, which the covenant people had to wage, and with an end signifying something like a process of salvation fulfillable on earth, now there were cosmic wars against the principle of evil and its epitome, Satan. These wars reached as high as the heavenly host of angels (Dan 10:13, see above; Enoch 10:6, 13, etc.; Assumption of Moses 10:1; IV Ezra 5:6[31]), and thus drove the YHWH–earth tension almost to the point of breaking the polarities apart, which actually happened later in Gnostic dualism.

The cosmic expansion of the universe therefore denotes an extraordinary alienation from salvation, because it demonstrates that the overpowering tension of opposites, which tears existence apart, can no longer be synthesized by the individual. The tension between spirit and life, which underlies the tension of YHWH and earth, can no longer be worked through[32] by the individual. When there is no longer any possibility of working through, the world-historical process descends into meaninglessness. In this realm, salvation is also impossible, or, at least, it is the realm of alienation from salvation.

2. The psychological meaning of eschatology

The Last Judgment is the concept of compensation, which has the task of balancing out the apparent meaninglessness of world events and the cruelly evident prevalence of the negative side, in its aspect of earth, power, and Satan. The essential function of the Last Judgment is not only to restore the balance—so completely distorted by reality and the process of human history running through it—between

YHWH and earth, inside and outside, good and evil, Israel and the nations, moon and sun. Beyond that, it must also decide in favor of the inner aspect of YHWH, which in practice is valued too little .

Apocalypticism regards history as universal history and the course of history as the fulfillment of a plan, which ultimately turns out to be a plan for salvation. At first, though, this seems only a magnificent attempt to subordinate the over-whelming reality of the power of evil, finally, forcibly, and constructively, to the theocratic intervention of the deity.

But the divine victory is not only guaranteed by the state of things at the end. Rather, the plan is conceived in such a way that every developmental point— even low points in this historical process, where evil increases—has its God-given importance, and thus its secret, not-yet-revealed, but still powerful, saving inten-tion. The hypothesis of the "history-rejecting apocalyptic doctrine"[33] is therefore only superficially correct.[34] Insofar as the consciousness of the apocalypticist suffers under the weight of history, it surely does reject history. But to the extent that it is a bearer of revelation, that is, insofar as it is initiated into the great, overriding divine plan for history and salvation, it affirms history. For, in this revelatory con-sciousness, every historical low point is only ever temporary. Indeed, if one looks closely, the nadir in the course of history is precisely what guarantees final salvation and shows its closeness.

The historical form of the certainty of salvation

Embedded within the seemingly static schema of the plan of salvation, which ends with divine revelation, the ancient fundamental idea is still at work, that history unfolds as humanity's active struggle between YHWH and the dimension of earth and world. This may be illustrated most clearly by the way the original experience of being rescued from evil through YHWH's intervention has become a pattern, just as the primal historical experience of liberation from Egypt has become the prototype and archetype of historical experience as such.[35]

The question to what degree the exodus from Egypt is a real historical experi-ence is irrelevant to the problem. As we shall see, the account in the Old Testament is probably also shaped by the universal archetype of being rescued from the depths by God's intervention. For the Jew, however, this rescue from Egypt is a constitu-tive historical experience, an irrefutable reality and a historical certainty—indeed, in a way, the substantial guarantee of rescue. It is a historical form of the certainty of salvation, in the image of which the Jews experienced and still experience their entire history, namely, as the realization of the miracle, the paradox, as a certainty of the sudden turn toward salvation at the point of despair. This very specific history was then generalized by the apocalypticists and became the history of humanity, in the sense that, at the lowest point, when evil rules the whole world, in the "fullness of time," the turning point comes and the messiah appears.

To begin with, this historical form of the certainty of salvation is no valid guar-antee for the individual, but rather a living experience of the collective, which has made this experience conscious and gives ever new reality to the consciousness of this experience in historiography, prophecy, cult, and prayer. Knowledge of YHWH's paradoxical nature here becomes the knowledge of a law by which this paradox is overcome, a law by which the possibility of miracle and liberation is always greatest just at the moment when all rational orientation fails, and consciousness no longer sees any escape but doom.

Here again, human partnership is not uninvolved in the arrival of the new fate and the overthrow of the old one, but its part is irrational. What reverses the movement is the depth of suffering and despair itself, or, as the Old Testament says, "The Children of Israel cried out, and their cry came to God."[36] Thus, the history-shaping power of despair triggers the avalanche that leads from the call of Moses to the annihilation of the Egyptians and the exodus. Events surrounding the exodus from Egypt are prototypical for the events of the end of time and of salvation, and this "prototypicality" is so illuminating, because the exodus account seems to have been constructed so that all the typical elements that later proved crucial for the apocalyptic vision of the last days and of freedom are already developed in it.

Already in Egypt, and subsequently in the Last Judgment, a law came into clear effect, which might be described thus: justice is an equal and opposite reaction to YHWH's irruption in various structures. For YHWH's judgment rests on the fact that, as an invasive God, he acts differently on different structures, destroying one while expanding the other. The exodus from Egypt makes it very clear—this is verifiably depicted in the plague text in its various stages—that, among the Jews who receive him openly and positively, YHWH's irruption leads to selection, chosenness, and the emergence of a people, indeed to the elevation of the whole people, so that the miracle-working capacity of every individual Jew surpasses that of the Egyptian magicians—the most powerful and renowned magicians in the ancient world. This same irruption, however, acts on the Egyptians, who have turned away from YHWH, as plague, disaster, and ruin. It is the same "power of *kadosh*,"[37] which carries off the priest who offers false sacrifice (Nadab and Abihu; see above) or the unpriest-like Jew,[38] and which here, in a nature-like irruption, leads to the judgment of the Egyptians and the election of the *Bnei Israel*,[39] making them God's people.

YHWH's self-glorification always takes the form of a sudden, ambush-like intrusion. And just as the catastrophe of Egypt in the plagues is the divine manifestation, leading to the exodus of the Jews, so the Last Judgment, the end of the world, is the actual manifestation of the hitherto concealed divinity, leading those who survive YHWH's invasion on an exodus into the new world.

YHWH's approach, his emergence from hiddenness into visibility, is the cause for nothing less than the catastrophe of judgment. Just as the approach of an exceptionally large heavenly body leads to unforeseeable physical revolutions and catastrophes on earth, so YHWH's drawing closer, his descent or irruption, leads to corresponding psychic catastrophes.

Rabbi Simeon ben Lakish said:[40]

> There is no *Gehenna* in the Future World, but the Holy One, blessed be He,
> brings the sun out of its sheath, so that it is fierce:[41] the wicked are punished
> by it, the righteous are healed by it. The wicked are punished by it, as it is
> said: "For behold, the day cometh, it burneth as a furnace; and all the proud
> and all that work wickedness shall be stubble" (Mal 4:1).[42] The righteous,
> however, will be healed, as it is written, "But for you who revere my name,
> the sun of righteousness shall rise with healing in its wings."
>
> *(Mal 4:2; Deut 20)*[43]

When such an event occurs, as seen in this text and in countless others from all
peoples and times, partly in theological form and partly in older, magical concre-
tizations, it has a reality that is not unknown to modern depth psychology. The
constellation of an archetypal content in the unconscious of either an individual
or a group may lead, today as always, to two possible reactions, depending on the
capacity, receptiveness, and transformative ability of consciousness. If the conscious
attitude is positive, such a constellation leads to the transformation and renewal of
consciousness, even when preceded by catastrophes and shockwaves. But if the
conscious attitude is blocking, or inelastic and rigid, this leads either to a bursting
or shattering of consciousness, as in a genuinely psychotic condition, or else to
an escape into a state of neurotic contraction. It would therefore be utterly mis-
guided to consider the narrative of the Exodus in "symbolic" terms. The situation
is entirely different. The Exodus text represents this sort of irruption experience
as a historical event, along with all the consequences and attendant phenomena
belonging to such an event.

As with all corresponding experiences, the historical reality of the exodus from
Egypt is irrelevant, because the fact of any such experience is a reality only for the
group experiencing it. For this group, however, it represents a valid and powerful
reality, which is verifiable only through the historical impact of the experience, but
not, however, through historical and "scientific" research. By no means does the
relative reality of the experience apply only to individual psychology; it also applies
to the psychology of groups and peoples, and thus also to history.

With regard to the early history of peoples, where collective–unconscious
components play an obvious role—whether as magical, religious–cultic, or mythological ideas—the validity of this category[44] will be readily acknowledged. But
a glance at the historical power of modern peoples' ideas soon instructs us that
relative reality still applies today, as it always has. And it always will, as long as
mass psychology exists, which is to say, a psychology dominated by the collective
unconscious.

Whether the exodus from Egypt was experienced in this form, or whether the
undefined memory of this historically decisive event was shaped by the historian or
the history-writing people using these categories, in any event, after withstanding

God's irruption, the experience of renewal is at the center. Here, renewal stands under the sign of becoming a people, and for the apocalypticist it stands under the sign of the new eon. Both here and there, what happens is drawn as a historical event. In the exodus from Egypt, it is attached to an actual historical memory. In the Last Judgment, by analogy with such historical experiences, it is drawn as a historical image of the future.

In the depiction of the exodus from Egypt and of the miraculous events preceding and determining it, the magical character of YHWH's irruption still resonates powerfully. Of course, the contrast between the magic-entangled Egyptians and the *Bnei Israel* gathered around Moses is already shaped in this text in such a way that YHWH represents a principle of revelation superior to magic. And YHWH's power over nature and over the forces of nature, which he commands with increasing might in the plagues, is an unmistakable content of these events. For all that, when YHWH acts through natural forces, his way of working is represented in strongly magical and materialistic terms, and this is also how Moses and Aaron use YHWH's power. What happens is an event in the outer world; it has no contact with the psychic system of those who act. That is, YHWH's way of working appears on the level of an objective projection of psychic contents. We find the same thing in the rituals of early cultures, where events that we would call psychic today are concretized in an objective projection.

Nevertheless, what is given here is the fundamental overthrow of magic, which would then develop into the crucial factor in the apocalypse. In the plagues, to be sure, YHWH places some of his irruptive power into Moses' hands, who can then magically execute it. Indeed, the plagues are conceived and presented as a series of direct instructions for Moses to practice his miracle working in cooperation with YHWH. But this partial sphere of magical execution is incorporated completely into a series of revelations. It is these self-revelations of YHWH that bring about the expansion of consciousness for Moses and the people (Ex 3:15, 6:12, 12:1).

Eschatological psychic space[45]

The projection of YHWH's way of working into natural events accords with the naive structure of the early Jewish person, who was unindividualized, like all ancient people, and who experienced the intrapsychic only outside himself. Corresponding to the nature of the apocalyptic person, YHWH's way of working takes hold of his whole, complex psychic structure, projected into psychic space as heavens and hells and their inhabitants. To be sure, as we shall see, this state of possession still has the character of a projection, that is, it is not consciously experienced as an intrapsychic event, but, for instance, as cosmic, with images of nature symbolism still generally playing a large role. But in all of this, the psychic character of these ideas, not to mention their psychological reality, is strongly evident. This becomes apparent if we consider only the fact that apocalypticism is about *visions* of the future, in contrast to the writing of *history*, where internal factors, co-determining the interpretation, must achieve at least a possible unity with the objectively contributing factors of the external world.

Messianism and apocalypse

In light of the above, the fact that final catastrophes are frequently represented by the apocalypticists in images of nature symbolism does not contradict our point of view. But it is highly illuminating that, as we have seen, YHWH's preferred attributes, fire and storm, now also appear correspondingly as the preferred symbols of the Last Judgment and the end of the world.

Within the now-familiar context of storm, wind, spirit, breath, and breathing stands also the word. One side of the word is its creative potential, but its annihilating side appears in the Last Judgment, like the lethal breath, the deadly storm, or the consuming fire, as the "the killing word of God."[46] This juxtaposition of the killing word as an abstraction, and the tempest or fire as a concrete natural symbol, the spiritual meaning of which barely glimmers through, is highly characteristic of the apocalyptic vision, which swings back and forth between the ancient projection of natural symbols and their inner, psychic–spiritual meaning.

In the Book of Daniel, to take one of countless examples, when a stream of fire pours forth from God's seat of judgment,[47] what matters is the symbolic unity, which is welded together from the concrete cleansing and annihilation by fire and the spiritual meaning of the judgment that is carried out. YHWH's manner of working expresses itself in its twofold effect, physical and psychic. So, in a primitive theophany, judgment is executed more by the natural dimension, whereas in later theophanies—corresponding to a humanity that has become more complicated—more by the psychic.

It is a law that the kind of theophany depends on the structure of the experiencing subject. Thus, the mode of revelation shifts more and more from the plague as an outer event to judgment as an inner event. This category of judgment[48] is experienced by the apocalypticist as projected, as if it were occurring on the objective level. Only 2,000 years later, with the Jew Franz Kafka,[49] is it wholly introjected and taken to a purely subjective level. And yet, even for the apocalyptic writer, the "Egyptian experience,"[50] as a category of judgment, has already shifted decisively from the external and magical to the internal and psychic.

The experiences of the apocalypticists were genuinely visionary. Of this there can be no doubt, and only the rationalist cluelessness of the research undertaken at the turn of the century[51] could fail to recognize that fact. A certain tradition took shape, within the framework and style of which the apocalypses were composed, but the extraordinary difference between the apocalyptic writers and the ancient prophets, as well as the differences between their individual personalities, causes this traditional schema to disappear entirely behind the new, visionary content. Religious interpretation, both Jewish and Christian, tends to exclude inner revelation, which it calls "pneumatic experience," recognizing the time of revelation on the Jewish side as lasting only up to the prophets, and on the Christian side as covering both this time and that of the New Testament. This interpretation obviously degrades the apocalyptic writers and turns them into epigones and imitators. In reality, all knowledge of inner experiences, their symbolism and the way in which they appear, for which evidence exists from all places and times, teaches us that the apocalypticists, like the prophets before them and the Gnostics of their time and later, were men of genuine inner experience. That they disguised these experiences, adapted to the times, assimilated and revised, changes nothing in the genuine substance of the documents. The particularity and significance of these phenomena and these men must now be rediscovered—as is currently happening with Gnosticism—because the unconscious, pragmatic–rationalist bias of contemporary research is gradually becoming more evident.

The psychic situation at the time of Christ's birth is only now starting to be acknowledged as an integral part of a turning point in world history. This has already happened, for instance, with regard to Gnosticism.[52] But it is not until one learns to see the early Christian movement and the foregoing, closely related eschatological–apocalyptic movement within Judaism as the varied expressions of a historical situation that one will be able to avoid the incorrect assessment made in the last century.

The transformation process extending from national messianism through mixed eschatology to a pure doctrine of the hereafter corresponds to a process of *internalizing*, that is, to a growing dominance of inner, psychic components, while the goals and factors of the outer world recede into the background. The development goes from an envisioned time of national victory and restoration—which, incidentally, was always and consistently conceived theocratically, and thus represented a nationally tinged expression of the kingdom of God—to the idea of a hereafter, the world to come, the new eon, the projection of reality and description of which, however, leave no doubt that this is a new category of reality, which has an inner character, like all hells, heavens, and paradises. The historical process, at the end of which stands the Last Judgment, is unmistakably re-conceived here in terms of the archetype of rebirth, in that the cosmic projection of the Last Judgment signifies the crisis of death necessary for all rebirth. The labor pains of the messianic era lead to the birth of a new eon. This New Eon signifies a rebirth of the whole world, from humans to the animal world, from the cosmic constellation of the heavenly powers to the form of divine revelation.

The original conception of a direct theocracy of YHWH within the historical process, and of the "turning"[53] preceding it, are replaced by YHWH's direct theocracy, which begins after the transforming process of rebirth is executed in the Last Judgment.

The renewal of the world, the slaying of the serpent, the disappearance of the negative, the concluding of the new covenant through the new Temple and the old instruments, the outpouring of the holy prophetic spirit over all humankind, the return of direct divine revelation, the recreation of heaven and earth: these are all messianic motifs. They only become significant, however, through the apocalyptic writers' conception of rebirth. This conception, too, is prophetic, but it could take its plain form only in a time when experience of existence and of the world became so negative that it was no longer possible to believe in direct theocracy as the conclusion of the historical process. Instead, the deepest insight of the time was to know that only a central process of collective transformation could make the negative world and negative humanity at all capable of salvation.

This connection of old prophetic elements with new apocalyptic–eschatological contents is not, however, any kind of syncretism. Beyond all pseudonymity and all belief in the end of revelatory prophecy, what speaks to us in it is a continuity of inner revelation. In a new era and a changed humanity, this is what protects and preserves the prophets' original orientation toward inwardness.

The end of the historical, nationally restricted idea of the messiah, that is, the end of belief in YHWH's direct theocracy, becomes intertwined with a messianic projection of the end of days, to form a hybrid structure, revealing its transitional character. Although seldom expressed fully, this involves the doubling of the final crisis, which is divided into resurrection, on the one hand, and the ". . . kingdom,"[54] on the other. Finally, it also involves a doubling of the messiah figure. In all these manifestations, the original idea, which is closer to salvation, and the apocalyptic one, which is further from it, run parallel or coalesce.

Beside the final, messianic battle with the Messiah from the tribe of David, who wields the sword and brings about a messianic kingdom with strong national features and the resurrection of the righteous, there appears another apocalyptic sequence. Here a messiah, freed of earth and indeed deified, judges with the word, with the breath of his mouth.[55] He does not fight and, after the final judgment over Satan, he ushers in the eon of resurrection.

This dual sequence mirrors the development that interests us here, namely, the growing divergence of the polarities between YHWH and the earthly world, and the increasingly threatening inner tension of opposites within humanity. Clearly apparent in the primary messianic sequence is the original, earth-level, theocratic tendency, which in the final struggle brings about the changing of the world. In the secondary, apocalyptic sequence, the polarities YHWH–earth, God–human have already moved so far apart, and the divinity has moved upward so far— corresponding to humanity's movement downward[56]—that only a transformation process makes YHWH's genuine theocracy possible. This transformation, which appears later as a new creation, signifies the deity's *permanent* dwelling in the world.

In the documents, these lines run parallel, coalesce, and reach a compromise in the divisions and doublings already mentioned.

The messiah's separation from earth can be traced in apocalyptic literature. Corresponding to the divine movement upward, the messiah goes from kingship to judge of the world, and from being named a man of the clouds (Dan 7:13) to possessing a heavenly pre-existence (Enoch 48:37,[57] 62:7). This expanded identity parallels the changing image of the world, for, in order to be a counterforce to the world's overwhelmingly visible Satanic aspect, the messiah had to be, and was, elevated equally in power.

As we have seen, the opposition of *ruach* and *bassar* (spirit and flesh) corresponded to a basic Semitic concept. In this regard, however, the prophetic intention was aimed especially toward penetration of the earthly dimension by YHWH's *ruach*. This intention, which we found expressed in prophetic law, in the symbol of the tablets inscribed by YHWH, pervades the entire achievement of Jewish prophecy, and the prophetic endeavor to permeate reality can be understood on the basis of this very aspect.

In the apocalyptic age, this *ruach–bassar* opposition recurs in heightened form in symbolism, showing the intensified contrast of heaven and earth. The idea of heaven as the seat of divinity and the dwelling place of the righteous (Enoch 71:15),[58] who are the children of heaven (Enoch 101:1),[59] the fortifying of heaven by the ascension of holy men (Enoch, Moses, Isaiah, Baruch, Ezra, etc.), the depiction of the heavenly worlds: all these important precepts, which later became the fundamental idea in Christianity, are already fully developed in the apocalyptic books (Assumption of Moses 10:9,[60] many passages in Enoch). Accordingly, not just in Christianity but already here, the earth is often in the hands of the devil, who is the lord of this world.

The pre-existence of the messiah (Talmudic comment on Psalm 72:17)[61] guarantees YHWH's dominance, by counterbalancing the factual preponderance of earth and world. At the same time, it guarantees not only the possible, but also the certain and ultimate synthesizing of the opposition of YHWH and earth, *ruach* and *bassar*. YHWH himself, the creator of heaven and earth before time began, the creator of the very principle of opposites, guarantees this synthesis and keeps it safe "with him." YHWH, as the earth's opposite polarity, enables to some extent the historical process that is energized by the principle of opposites. He does so by occupying one of the poles, but not by becoming dualistically identical with it, or by being dissolved into the pair of opposites.

The eschaton and the archetype of rebirth

The conception of messianism and the end of time needs to be understood as a compensation that prevents the threatened disintegration of the YHWH–world polarity. No matter whether the end of time is made possible originally by struggle and reversal, or subsequently by a process of rebirth, in either case, peace is the valid symbol of the end, peace in which the opposites have come to rest, in which the beast of prey and the domestic animal can dwell together.

As we have already said, the eschaton formulated by the apocalypse largely corresponds to the archetype of rebirth. If one studies it more closely, certain consecutive stages characteristic of the transformation process can easily be distinguished. At the beginning of the eschaton comes the splitting into opposites, which takes place over the course of world history, and which we have described as the coming apart of the tension between YHWH and earth, or rather between heaven and earth. This condition reaches its peak in the retreat of divinity to the highest heaven, and the rule of evil on earth.

In the fullness of time, that is, with the completion of a process, the rules of which are defined in advance, during which the negativity of the world continuously increases and with it the power of suffering, YHWH breaks in with the Last Judgment. At this point, the messiah figure appears as a unifying symbol, a fundamentally new content in the world, whereas YHWH's irruption standing behind and above these events asserts itself both in the messiah and in the movement within humanity toward annihilation and transfiguration, which is shown in cosmic symbols. This process is an exact analog to the exodus from Egypt, where the messiah figure of Moses stands at the center of both the Egyptians' annihilation and the singling out of the *Bnei Israel*. Moses is explicitly turned into a "god" for Pharaoh (Ex 7:1); that is, YHWH has taken hold in him, just as he does in the messiah at the Last Judgment.

In the Last Judgment, this final confrontation takes place as the beginning of the new creation, before which, however, stands chaos (Ezra 7:30; Baruch 3:7; Sibylline Oracles 5:482),[62,63] as the second chaos before the beginning of the second creation.[64] Creation presupposes chaos, now symbolized in a variety of ways as the end of the world. Among other forms, this annihilation of the world manifests itself as the world on fire, with the oceans burning, the earth devoured by the abyss, and heaven crashing onto earth. The death of the world, also characterized as the world's decaying and dying, means a complete standstill of life. Corresponding to the conception that death by heat is the end of all the energetic tension necessary for life, here, too, all oppositions cease. The mixtures of the godless and the righteous in the world are disentangled (Apocalypse of Abraham 17),[65] and earth and heaven collapse as a pair of opposites. Beyond this, the falling of the stars spells not only the end of day and night, but also the end of time as such, and the laws it constellates. The darkness of the primordial beginning now covers the world—a great antitype of the smaller darkness before the slaying of the first-born in Egypt—and the world has returned to the silence of the primordial beginning (Baruch 3:7).[66]

After chaos, out of the state of death, the new world rises. Now all the differences—transfiguration and transformation of the world, the new creation—are shown to be mere variations and different stages in the one great theme of new birth. The total upheaval that now occurs is of crucial importance. It contradicts the old eschatology, for which the time of salvation was continuous with historical time, in some sense representing its glorious conclusion. The chasm that now opens up between historical time and the time of salvation is even specifically formulated as a cosmic pause,[67] God's day of rest. The "separation of times," the division into this world and the world to come, is now fundamental and irrevocable.

The rebirth, the new world, the time of salvation is represented by such a flood of symbols and shimmers in so many different colors and fields of light that we can mention only the portion here that seems to illuminate our present discussion.

The goal and end of the new state are the new life, which is clearly shown in the symbol of the resurrection to be eternal life. This new world therefore sees itself as the restoration of the situation in paradise, as the state described in Genesis. Time and again, recourse is made to the paradise in Genesis, symbolized as a mandala with four streams and the tree of life in its center (Enoch 48).[68]

Now the forbidden tree of life is permitted, and the condition of the world—that began with the expulsion from paradise and was marked by death and the curse that made the earth negative[69]—is raised. Only the lifting of the curse on the earth (Enoch 10:1; Baruch 29)[70] helps one to understand the otherwise so curiously "materialistic" representation of the earth's fruitfulness, which is often described in all its opulence. Fruitfulness is not a symptom of a Jewish–materialistic fantasy; it is the sign that the curse, which had condemned the earth to infertility and humankind to work, distress, and woe, has been lifted.

Accordingly, the symbol of manna emerges as heavenly food (Baruch 29:8; Jerusalem Targum; Ex 16:15);[71] and here, along with its character as grace, the character of the symbolic communion also shines through clearly. In the heavenly meal are contained all the characteristics of the sacrificial meal, the covenant meal, the wedding banquet, and the sacrament of communion. All of these represent only different stages of the divine community, standing under the sign of the permitted meal, in contrast to the forbidden fruit of paradise (IV Ezra 8:52; 1 Enoch 8:3; Life of Adam and Eve 36).[72] The devouring of Behemoth and Leviathan (Enoch 60:24; IV Esra 6:52; Baruch 29:4),[73] the two primal animals symbolizing female primordial depth and male earthly power, may be understood as reconciling the tension of opposites typical of the old world, where these two polar, primordial powers once dominated,[74] but are now associated with pleasure.

The new era is also often represented as a new mandala, with God or the fountain of life in the center, around which the blessed are dancing (Bab Tlm: Ta'anith 31a; Jer Tlm: Megillah 73a).[75] It is irrelevant whether the place of bliss is represented as earth, paradise, heavenly Jerusalem, divine mountain, or in another way. Each one is merely a variation on the mandala, whose outer shape may change, just as its center does, when it appears as God, fountain, tree of life, temple, radiance, etc.

The attributes of this renewed state are immortality, oil of life, healing, and dew of health (Baruch 29:7; IV Ezra 7:121; Sibylline Oracles 3:369; Enoch 96:3).[76] These are symbols of physical–psychic integrity, in which the perfection of the first creation is restored.

On a different level, and differently defined by its opposition to the old world, the new world is also depicted as a world of light. The illumination and transfiguration of the world's existence come from God, whose character is light, and who shines as the eternal light beyond the light of the stars. The immortal light of God, of Zion, and of the world opposes the darkness of Gehenna[77] as it opposes the darkness of chaos, but, as the symbol of salvation and joy, the light is virtually identical with the new life, as life in the light. Naturally, the symbolic content of light also unites in itself the psychic–spiritual aspect, in which light appears as the outpouring of the holy spirit, the spirit of mercy and sanctity, and as the new revelation.

To this corresponds the luminous nature of the blessed,[78] who have become like angels and are comparable to the stars. The transformation into the divine person, as into the restoration of the human image of God, expresses itself in the bestowal of glory, which initially belongs only to God and the angels. This glorification, as the epitome of physical–psychic–spiritual perfection, shimmers in the manifold meanings of the symbol. Being vested with magnificence or the robe of life, the mantle of imperishability, is an obvious parallel to the glorification and deification of the mystery cults, where transformation is repeatedly symbolized by the new garment.[79] At the same time, however, the light of the *doxa*[80] has the concrete character of the luminous body. The radiance of the blessed, like their starry nature, expresses the transfiguration of the body in its emanation of the luminous inner nature, which has here become substance.

What is perhaps most essential is the symbol of the revelation of the "Hidden Light,"[81] the light of the first day of creation, which was preserved for the world to come,[82] and in which occurs the renewal of being and essence, of hearts, and of the spirit.

This hidden light, which has the character of original knowledge, is knowledge of the unconscious, the primordial wisdom of the collective unconscious:

> Concerning the primordial light, which was created at the beginning of Creation, the Talmud says that in that light the human being had seen from one end of the world to the other; but when the human species became depraved, God removed the light from them and hid it away. For whom did he hide it? For the righteous. And where? In the teaching. But what do they do with the light which they find in the teaching? They bring it out with their life.[83]

Here, original knowledge is described as a knowledge possessed by early humanity, which was later lost. In the same way, we assume today that the life of early humans, whose consciousness had not yet dissociated itself from the unconscious to become its own entity, and who thus still lived in the *Gan Eden*[84] and had not eaten from the tree of the knowledge of good and evil, was characterized by the fact that they lived "in" the collective unconscious and, more than later humans, instinctively followed the guiding light of this original knowledge. The identity of this hidden light with what we must call the collective unconscious, or rather the wisdom of the collective unconscious, is confirmed by the fact that the embryonic state of the human being is characterized by this light shining above the child:

> But above his head rests a burning light, and in his mother's womb the child thus sees from one end of the world to the other.[85]

This foreknowledge, in which the child is shown paradise, hell, and the entire world of its future life, is taken away at birth:

> And when he steps out, the angel strikes him beneath his nose, extinguishes the light that was above his head, leads him out against his will, and he forgets everything that he has seen.[86]

This parallels the insight of depth psychology that the younger the child, the more it still lives in the collective unconscious, and only gradually grows into the conscious world of adult culture, which explains the wisdom of children and the frequently collective character of children's dreams, fantasies, and images.[87]

This original knowledge, which is lost as culture evolves, that is, as consciousness develops, is unveiled in the transformation of the end of time. The great transformation occurs through this original knowledge.

The most crucial symptom of this state of salvation, which begins with the unveiling of the hidden light, is peace. In the nationally tinged eschatology, peace was still conceived as a political situation in the world, but here, taken inward onto the subjective level, it is an expression of successful transformation. This peace, as the property of salvation, is attributed to the messiah as the Prince of Peace, and its extension to the animal world is not only a symptom of peace on earth but also a symbol of inner peace. For now, beside the objective level of interpretation, a subjective level is already taking conscious form.[88] In a way, the connection between wild animals and demons (Testament of Naphtali 8)[89] is the transition to the interpretation of wild animals as the wild instincts in humanity itself. As Sabbath, peace is an inner state, which is a prerequisite for and an expression of the new life.

So the restoration of paradise is expressed by the fundamental transformation of the animal world. The establishment of peace, in which the wild animal grazes beside the tame, and the child and the adder play together, is guaranteed by the promise that God "will make the beasts on earth harmless" (Sibylline Oracles 3:792),[90] that is, by the fundamental transformation of negative animal nature. The equation of wild animals with demons is universal, because all peoples project demonic nature into animal form. In the temptations of the saints, too, it is highly characteristic that animal-shaped demons play a major role, as the negatively valued natural forces of the unconscious. One instance is the temptation of Jesus: "and he was tempted by Satan and was with the wild beasts" (Mark 1:13).

Volz[91] is only partially correct in claiming that:

> according to Jewish sources, however, "eternal life" only ever begins in the future and never means, as in the Johannine (and Pauline) ζωὴ αἰώνιος,[92] an inner, timeless quality, and hence also a quality of being present now.

A projection into the future surely exists, the fundamental meaning of which will occupy us later, but it would be wrong to dispute its inner, timeless character. Our entire study seeks specifically to work out the inward character of these apocalyptic visions, an inward character that is clear despite—indeed, is proven by—their collective relatedness and projection into the future.

The world to come is no longer merely a historical state of the earth, as we have seen, but something *toto genere*[93] different, something incomparable. It is the invisible world, and at the same time it is the revelation of the Hidden Light.[94] Here, eschatology has long become not only a doctrine of blessedness but also a doctrine of the soul,[95] and this not simply because it departs in principle from the reality-level of the old national eschatology, but rather because it is in fact an apocalypse, a revelation of what is hidden. When it is written, "the world beyond is a world in reverse,"[96] this indicates not only the compensatory, balancing character of the world beyond, in which the righteous one is rewarded and the wicked punished; it also points to the hidden background and underground of the world,[97] which is then revealed, which appears, awakens, ascends, or descends. In Faust, a corresponding passage reads: "Then to the deep!—I could as well say height."[98]

The apocalyptic vision is the vision of the manifestation of what is actually at work behind the apparent, visible world. It is the revelation of the hidden divinity, as it takes hold in the visible realm. YHWH's universal theocracy only becomes possible, however, through an upheaval of the world, in which the visible world, the old world, the historical world, has reached its end.

This internalization of the apocalypse is precisely what makes it impossible for YHWH to intervene anywhere in the course of history, or from there to conquer the world in any way. Earlier, the nationally tinged eschatology still leaned in this direction, but the worldly aspect of the apocalypse is already directed at the human being and humanity, and, from this perspective, YHWH—especially after his transformation into the detached divinity—no longer fits into the historical world at any point in time whatsoever.

YHWH's theocracy presupposes the total transformation and recasting of the world and humanity, precisely because the distance between God and humankind has grown so immense that no normal human structure could communicate with it. Correspondingly, the subject of the apocalyptic vision is the invisible world, which powerfully yet invisibly—as we would say, with unconscious power—timelessly determines the times. The total aspect of the apocalypse, which encompasses the whole world and world history, also prevents it from assuming a merely individual, inward character. For as a continuation of Old Testament prophecy, it is based on a conception, the starting point of which is not the human being but the deity, and in it the human being functions only representatively as God's servant. Also, its central and initial concern is YHWH's theocracy, and not human redemption. But precisely for the sake of this total aspect, which incorporates the whole extent of the unconscious world and its concretization into the cosmic upper and lower hierarchies, apocalypticism becomes a doctrine of transpersonal and extra-personal psychic powers.

Apocalypse and alchemy

The apocalypse collectively and cosmically projects the world's redemption into time, just as alchemy individually and cosmically projects individual redemption into matter.[99] In alchemy, in other words, individuation is a redemptive process for the individual. It is projected into matter through a materially bound process, the elements of which have a cosmic character. In the apocalypse, on the other hand, individuation still appears on the collective level. Here, the process of human redemption is projected into time through a historically bound process, the elements of which have a cosmic character.

The three stages of alchemy are contained in this human–historical process of rebirth. The great, common stages are these: the problem of opposites, the death of the world, and rebirth.

If we put the characteristics of the *lapis*,[100] the end-product of the alchemical process, alongside the attributes of the state of salvation, the parallels are obvious. The characteristics of immortality, of light, fruitfulness, health, deathlessness, and those of peace, the reconciliation of opposites, etc., are common to both final processes. The differences and oppositions are, however, at least as important as the similarities and equivalences. One essential difference is the collective character of events in the apocalypse. Here, humanity and the world are seen to some extent as *one* individual, and history as the individuation process of this individual, before whom personal destinies disappear. Although the messiah figure holds the first rudiments of what will emerge in early Christianity as a theme of individualization, nevertheless, the collective still occupies the foreground, first the national collective, and later that of humanity.

In alchemy, it is the individual who performs the *opus*,[101] but in the apocalypse, humanity as a whole is the actor. Freedom from the confined national ideology of the old messianism had led to the worldwide perspective and to YHWH as the lord of humanity and of the world. But if religious individualism and the individual's cosmic fear were an essential part of the apocalyptic movement, it had still not lost its connection with the whole, which was original and central for all of Semitism. The connection with the whole had simply become greater in the apocalyptic movement, expanding into universalism. In overcoming the historical world, this universalism came close to abandoning every kind of individual limitation, as shown by the transition from the devout Jew of the old messianism to the devout person as such.

3. Apocalypse and redemption in time

The history of humanity, as the apocalypse sees it, is therefore collective and cosmic. In comparison with alchemy, this view presupposes greater unconsciousness of the individual as individual, for such a general idea of the whole can never be aware of individual differences within groups. Beyond this, however, the developmental process is not a human work. One may say that the subject of this process is YHWH as lord of time, as lord of the historical process.

In the alchemical process, the element of time has receded into the background; matter and its elements are the agents of the process. The element of time still appears everywhere, without fanfare, in the frequent symbols of growth and duration, as in the "cooking" of one state until it transforms into another. But for the apocalypse, this element of time is really central.

YHWH's working in time[102]

The medium of YHWH's power is time. The plan of salvation is an order of time, for which the sequential process of human history is crucial. The fulfilling of time symbolizes the end, which signifies at once the abolition of time and temporality. Redemptive activity begins with the collective background, and not yet, as in alchemy, with individual consciousness. When Volz remarks[103] that apocalypticism likes to let "things happen" and favors the passive, his observation is far from insignificant. The collective background, which prophecy already considered to be the driving force of history, has YHWH, the lord of events, for its center. This background moves by itself, as it were. that is, it moves according to its own—YHWH's—law. and the world events in the foreground are merely exponents of the real world clock, which rests in YHWH's hand. The plan of history and humanity, as an event in time, arises from this dark underground of the hidden divinity. It moves the peoples and individuals, who, in their own activity, are unconsciously harnessed to this plan, which runs its course through and over them.

This fundamental experience of YHWH's manifestation in time had after all led the Jews to write the historical narrative of the Bible. What we earlier called the "historical form of the certainty of salvation" depends directly upon this experience that events remain effective and exert power in life as a "proto-type,"[104] be it the expulsion from paradise, the exodus from Egypt, or the destruction of the Temple. At Passover, when every Jew ceremoniously confirms that he has been personally liberated from and led out of *Mitzrayim*,[105] this "actualizing of history"[106] gives reality to the power of YHWH, whose regenerative way of being present is precisely what relativizes the past as past.

In Glatzer's opinion, the tannaitic[107] doctrine of history teaches that, contrary to the apocalypse, the activation of history[108] even leads to historicizing the unhistorical, because "the timeless, too, must assume the form of time to become effective."[109] But the characterization of "bright" times in the plan, which must be actualized in order to persevere in the "dark" ones, simply remains stalled in the rational and superficial. Bright and dark times in the plan exist only for an unapocalyptic consciousness, that is, one alienated from revelation, which lacks knowledge of the dual form of divine power. Relativizing the time of misfortune, for instance, as a factor that speeds salvation, and the time of good fortune as a factor that keeps it at a distance, lends to suffering a meaning that is directly associated with the effectiveness of God's plan.[110] This effectiveness is independent both of the actual, external, and superficial situation of the world and of the passive envelopment of the individual and the group in it. YHWH's working in the category of time implies, of course, that every present moment must be relativized, and that the appropriate attitude in a world with a present existence that is forever deceptive is *respice finem*.[111] For the relationship of the bright or gloomy present to the future—that is, the actual meaning of that relationship—is concealed. The same present moment stands at a decisively different point in the plan of history, depending on whether it is located on a falling or a rising curve. This means that the plan reveals its true nature only in the course of the historical process. Only this time determinant, which is not self-evident in every present moment, reveals the true nature of the moment.

Time as the working level of the unconscious

Aware of our lack of conscious orientation in time's passage, we generally try to balance it out by the factor of experience; we try to grasp some regularity within the passage of time. But this experience of regularity is possible only if events are driven by the lawful structures of gods or the stars, that is, by nature. If one is conscious that the motor of events is YHWH's unpredictable power—his structure that evades consciousness, his paradoxical nature that cannot be rationally determined—then this kind of rationalizable experience is unavailable.

The historical form of the certainty of salvation, mentioned above,[112] means something else. It is not an experience of the necessity of a certain course of events. Rather, it is the experience of the way the collective background operates, transcending any apparent regularity. It is the knowledge that every structure that stays open to the working of this collective background remains capable of rescue, against all reason and probability. The category of the miracle implies an experience of YHWH's way of working that breaks through the world's rational lawfulness.[113] Here, most of all, the hidden time factor is crucial. The three-dimensional regularity of the world structure is thwarted, time and again, by the hiddenness of the fourth dimension, the time component, where YHWH's power remains superior to the world. The fact that the *Bnei Israel* were not exterminated in Egypt, against all probability, has to do with the hidden time component. As the narrative puts it, the time of servitude predetermined by YHWH had elapsed.[114] From this moment, the world situation in Egypt became ripe for redemption. But it would be mistaken to believe that a concept of mechanical or fatalistic destiny magically intrudes here.

There is always room for the influence of human attitude and human consciousness, so that YHWH's "plan" always remains open to revision. Besides which, what lies within the hiddenness of the time component, as we have named it, is not a context-alien, arbitrary, and meaningless influence of YHWH. Rather, encapsulated within it is a latent possibility of the world's situation. In retrospect, after it has become a reality in the course of history, this latent possibility of the situation can be consciously discovered and understood. Before its actualization, however, it was visible only to the prophet or apocalypticist, initiated into the background of the situation. But, in looking back, it becomes clear that this hidden possibility, on which YHWH's influence rests, belonged to the situation of the world, and only a consciousness that related purely to the present could not see it. The mythologizing representation now asserts a predetermined, concretized, self-fulfilling "plan," conceived of as the projection of a factual state of affairs. But we would formulate it differently.

Every situation in the world, and every situation affecting the individual, has a three-dimensionality determined by consciously available factors, that is, by whatever is accessible within the current conscious situation. Here, three-dimensionality means simply reality, to the extent that it can be grasped and formulated by the whole scope of consciousness.

The time component, meanwhile, is the factor of *unconscious* reality, mythologically formulated as "that world," the "other" world, etc. For consciousness, within the situation, this unconscious factor is invisible and incomprehensible—in short, it is unconscious. But it may be made partly visible by the passage of time, and thus capable of consciousness. Unconscious factors show their effects over time, during which they gain acceptance. Then in retrospect—or retrogradely—they are assigned as a fourth dimension to the invisible operation, the three-dimensional reality of the past situation. Thus, the time component is nothing mystical. Rather, at any given point it is the reality of unconscious background factors, which move toward actualization over the course of time, revealing themselves as determiners of reality.

Destiny as the possibility of archetypal experience

Depth psychology approaches the meaning of the time factor from another side altogether, namely, the experience of the archetypes. As the archetype represents a psychic content that is always more comprehensive than the capacity of consciousness, it is impossible to assimilate any archetype *uno actu*.[115] It is as if the experiencing eye of consciousness needed to contemplate the shape of the archetype from many different angles to feel out its scope, and could establish an experiential image only through the connections gradually emerging among these particular, separate experiences. In practice, however, every archetypal experience presupposes that consciousness will be overwhelmed—at least temporarily—being devoured or flooded by the archetypal content. Only gradually is the heroic consciousness able to struggle free from the overpowering archetype, like the sun hero in the belly of the whale, distancing itself, making its contents conscious.

So any experience of contents transcending consciousness is possible only within time. Only the sum total of the conscious systems of individual life, which change in the course of time, is capable of having an archetypal experience, because the overly restricted segment of daily consciousness is inadequate. And so it happens that we grasp the transpersonal existence of the collective unconscious only in our destiny, and as a destiny. That is the meaning of historical consciousness for the individual, as it is for a people: experience is made only "as age follows age." The true extent of what confronts the human being as "life" may well seize the individual in a flash, penetrating and transforming, but only gradually, in the course of experience, does it become the real possession of consciousness.

The conception of the "plan" [of YHWH] rests on the fact that, at a time when normal, three-dimensional consciousness perceives nothing, the person intuiting the background, that is, the person oriented toward the factors hidden in the situation, already has the possibility to foresee a future course of events by recognizing latent factors that will become effective over time. Such a person has a fundamental realizationw that the collective background, and not human consciousness, is what determines history. This realization, along with the partial predictability of future

PLATE 2.1 Vision of the Holy Land: before Moses' death, he was led by God to a mountain peak, to see the land that his people would enter (Deut 34:1–4). Aged Moses, anticipating death, is shown partly buried in the mountain. But the land he sees is alive with color, and at the far left, on a hilltop, stands the city of Jerusalem.

PLATE 2.2 Joseph's dream: Joseph, Jacob's beloved son, dreamed that the sun, the moon, and eleven stars bowed before him (Gen 37:9f.). This dream, suggesting dominance over his family, outraged his brothers, who plotted to kill Joseph but instead sold him to traders, who carried him off to slavery in Egypt.

Watercolor: © Erich Neumann (date unknown). Courtesy of the Erich Neumann Estate.

events, leads to the projection of a "plan," which is attributed to YHWH as the lord of the collective background.

From this perspective, the opposition of YHWH and earth transforms an opposition between this world and that, this world and the world to come. But this also means the opposition between present reality and unconscious reality, where unconscious reality is essentially identical with the reality that determines the future.

It would be impossible, of course, to claim that a particular future had been determined exclusively by unconscious factors in the background of the world. In reality, the world is capable of consciousness, and this consciousness also largely determines the course of the future. But history and the destiny of the individual teach us that the course of events is especially directed, always and everywhere, by those factors that have *not* influenced the consciousness of time. Almost all historical turning points arise from an improbable and hitherto overlooked quarter. But this, in turn, means once again that it is precisely the unconscious elements that imperceptibly and surprisingly determine the course of history. At just this point, a prognosis based on "experience" fails again and again, in favor of a perspective that includes the improbable, and, when applied to YHWH, as lord of history, this same perspective determines the apocalypse.

But whereas YHWH's pre-apocalyptic way of working was supra-human, transforming only the chosen person in each irruption,[116] in the apocalypse his way of working is fundamentally different, through the figure of the messiah as a human-divine organ of realization. The fact that the rebirth of the world and of humanity is centered on a human figure has extraordinary implications. Whereas in the national prototype of the exodus from Egypt, Moses was merely YHWH's instrument, the messiah is already something like his human incarnation. The way the messiah appears and is described is highly illuminating, especially in the three characteristic passages (Dan 7:13; Enoch 46; IV Ezra 13:3).[117]

The messiah as a symbol unifying heaven and earth

The messiah, who is also called the Chosen One and the Son of God, is commonly and emphatically identified by the term "son of man" (Dan 7:13).[118] This term is supported by his visionary depiction as "one resembling a man" (Dan 8:15).[119] Whereas one ought to assume that—corresponding to his pre-existence—he is depicted as "coming from heaven," it is highly surprising that in IV Ezra he emerges from the depth of the ocean, then takes up his actual position, hovering between heaven and earth, as a "man of the clouds" (see above: Dan 7:13; IV Ezra 13:3).[120,121]

Only our knowledge of the symbolism of the unconscious allows us to understand the meaning of these images, and wherein exactly the meaning of this messiah figure is found.

This messiah is a typical example of what appears in analytical psychology as a "unifying symbol," a *transcendent function*. In him, the opposition between heaven and earth is resolved. Therefore on one occasion he comes from heaven, on another he rises from the depth of the ocean, which—as we have already seen, and as we know from the symbolism of the collective unconscious—symbolizes the creative ground of the unconscious. A water-and-ocean origin corresponds to his derivation from the earth polarity, as the heavenly origin represents his derivation from the YHWH polarity. This dual origin causes him to hover halfway between heaven and earth as a "man of the clouds." In this double origin we find not only the merging of two messiah images, which we had already encountered in the doubling of the messiah figure; this duality is now also an essential characteristic, which makes the simultaneity of his heavenly presence and his earthly work possible in the first place.

The character of the unifying symbol, which is projected in the messiah figure, and which naturally, like any projection, remained unconscious for the eras when the projection occurred, becomes clearly apparent in the simultaneously emphatic and peculiar term, the "son of man." That the son of God, the messiah, the Chosen One, is specifically a human being, who reconciles and unites the heaven–earth opposition in his dual origin, this is unquestionably the actual background, and his—messianic—significance.

Here, corresponding to the age of religious individualization, a new conception of the human being and of existence also appears *in nuce*.[122] The messiah, as the son of man, is positively the vision and prototype of a humanity changed by the process of messianic rebirth. Adam's earthiness and sinfulness, and that of his human descendants in the old eon, are a well-known apocalyptic theologism (IV Ezra 7:118ff).[123] His antitype is the messianic Son of Man, as the bringer of the new covenant and the new state of being in the new eon. The theology of Paul pursues these contents, which were handed down to him largely by the apocalypticists, and which he develops further and reshapes Christologically.

This new conception was clearly realized in the proclamation of Jesus and early Christianity. It was then lost in the development of Christianity, through the deification of Jesus and the manifold and rich developments associated with that. Just as the Law once appeared as a unifying symbol for the YHWH–earth tension, so the Son of Man, the Messiah, appears here as a unifying symbol for the energetically heightened heaven–earth tension.

Whereas the Law applied at the collective level, on which the people, as a subject, were YHWH's historical partner, the messianic vision applies to the level of religious individualism, on which the individual and at the same time humanity had become YHWH's partner. In the apocalypse, the universal and the national task, depending on the documents, obviously remain at the forefront of consciousness. But the question of the salvation and destiny of the individual, the righteous, in the historical process, energizes the entire apocalyptic movement. When this movement reaches back to the now officially nonexistent direct revelation, it does so, of course, thanks ultimately to its opposition to the collective Law, in which adequate containment is no longer to be found.

The intensity of individual religious emotion, the direct God–human relationship, is strengthened by the now enormously increased distance of the divinity. This heightening in the individual sphere of existence, which circles around the domains of guilt, prayer, faith, and repentance, culminates in the image of the son of man–messiah, who possesses the quality both of an angel and of David's heir, but for whom, as son of man and son of God, the universal human likeness to God has become determining.

This apocalyptic messiah figure is still a vision—indeed, if you wish, a hypostasis, and became human only in early Christianity. Our concern, however, must be to present these essential new traits here, and precisely here, because the development of Christianity largely interrupted this process within Judaism.

The son of man–messiah is absolutely and decisively subordinate, however, to the authority of YHWH and remains so, despite the elevation of the messiah figure necessitated by history. Whereas the original prophetic and theocratic tendency made the human being God's servant, his tool, and Israel his vassal, this direct theocracy is replaced by the indirect theocracy of the messiah, who can, to be sure, always and ultimately be removed by the divinity. Nevertheless, the change in the aspect of expectation remains essential. It is no longer directed toward YHWH, the deity superior to humankind, but toward the son of man–messiah, that is, toward something that is—despite all elevation—human.

Therewith, a decisive step has occurred. Whereas the apocalyptic development absolved itself from the responsibility of realizing theocracy and, as it were, shifted that responsibility onto YHWH, this picture must be filled out. The realization of theocracy—beyond any fulfillment of the Law—is now linked to the emergence of a new idea of the human being, projected as the messiah son of man. This new image of the human being, whose emergence is made possible only by YHWH's intervention, is that of the twice-born messiah, the son of man who comes from sea and sky. Thus a decisive introversion of messianism has occurred, a process that makes the naive historical expectation of the messiah completely obsolete.

Leaving aside the historical catastrophe of the downfall of the empire and the galut, the fact that this unifying symbol of the son of man–messiah long failed to take effect, as the target image of a new religious development within Judaism, is due crucially to a specific danger for the Jewish person, namely, his intuitive stance.

We have already seen that the representatives of Jewish prophecy, whose successors are the apocalyptic writers, compensated as men of introspection for the strong attachment to this world and outwardness that primarily characterizes the Jewish people. This orientation toward inward perception corresponds to what analytical psychology finds characteristic of the intuitive introvert.[124] This type of person had decisive, history-shaping significance for the inner history of Judaism. The great and natural tension that existed between these people and the majority necessarily subsided when, based on their contemplation of the unconscious layer at work in history, all the fateful events prophesied by these men actually occurred.

This tremendous gain in prestige for the intuitives was further enhanced by a historical development, which, because of its real uncertainty and unpredictability, would have urged a stronger orientation toward the introverted intuitives in any case. We see this today in an equally enormous blazing up of all the intuitive arts and sciences, such as astrology, graphology, chirology, and all those sciences and pseudosciences that are adept at dealing with the activation of the unconscious—the demonizing of the age—from spiritualism and sectarianism to depth psychology.[125]

Time and again, the dominance of these intuitive religious persons as representatives of the inner revelation confronts the natural enmity of the representatives of the Law, who want to establish rationalizable and realizable theocracy as an edifice in this world to guarantee salvation. Thus, they stand irreconcilably opposed to the religious intuitives' experience of God, which corresponds to the prophetic experience of God. (It lies outside the scope of the present work to verify this correspondence, as could easily be done, by comparing the dominant features of the prophetic experience of YHWH, as we have posited them, with the psychology of introverted intuitives.)

As Judaism was close to nature and attached to the earth, these religious geniuses succeeded in keeping it alive and fructifying it ever anew with penetrating and erupting religious fertilization. Their achievement becomes an extraordinary threat, however, when this people begins to lose touch with the ground of reality. For at this moment, the collective gains power, which in the psychology of the individual corresponds to the problem of the inferior function.[126] The counterpart to developed intuition is undeveloped sensation, an insufficient *fonction du réel*.[127] Here, guided by religious intuition, a factor that might be called the primacy of the future begins to pose a danger. This primacy of the future comes at the cost of an extremely dangerous negation of the present. For the introverted intuitive, present reality always exists under a negative, dangerous, primitive, overpowering aspect. For him, the dimension of world, body, and earth is a threat; it is prison, seduction and demon. It is the witch that captures, humiliates, and slays the future and its possibility.

This negative aspect, hostile to the world, ascetic, and pessimistic, is familiar to us from all the documents of this turning point in time. Precisely this aspect, however, also bestows on that era its tremendous character of expectation. The pessimism of the apocalyptic writers is not the product of antiquated Oriental peoples, to be contrasted with the New Testament. This pessimistic turning away from the world pervades the apocalypse, just as it does the gospels, Pauline Christology, and Gnosticism, as the inner experience of the turning point in time, which is experienced as the dawn of the new eon and the demise of the old.

This historic upheaval in the history of humanity is experienced by the generation of the upheaval as final, that is, as the end of the world, rather than as a turning point in time. Compassion for sinners, which Gunkel says is "alien to strong ethical religions, and thus also to the Gospel," is not, as he believes it may be interpreted, "a sign of the soft-heartedness of broken Judaism."[128] Instead, it is a powerful symptom of the real uncertainty of salvation during this era, which experienced the last days as burningly, gruesomely close. It is only against the background of the angelic pronouncement, "If you are alive, you will see," for "the age is hastening swiftly to its end" (IV Ezra 4:26f.),[129] which recurs in the gospels and in faith in the Paraclete, that the fears and terrifying visions of the apocalypticists, as well as the era's world-despising, ascetic consciousness of sin, can be understood.

It has been said about the Jews that "this people could not die, because its will to live was always cast forward into the coming centuries and represented all catastrophes merely as temporary obstacles on its path to eventual bliss."[130]

But aside from the question, whether Judaism is still alive due to this primacy of the future, what was said in praise here, and is said again and again, constitutes the most terrible danger, which has threatened to annihilate this people. Discussing the time of the apocalypticists, another scholar writes: "They were no longer or not yet alive; they expected life."[131] This stance has certainly been a crucial basis for all eschatological–messianic movements, but, as a permanent condition, it threatens to hollow out existence. Insofar as it is valid, this basic attitude, which has led to the assertion that even 2,000 years later "the same eschatological idea of history prevails, with the chosen people at its center,"[132] is psychologically a most peculiar phenomenon. At the same time, however, this attitude conceals a devilish threat, because it more or less excludes the life process, the historical epoch spanning the last 2,000 years, thus turning the reality of existence into something merely temporary and leading to a permanently provisional attitude. Unquestionably, this threat was countered at different times within Judaism, but it was not until Hasidism that a truly new existential position asserted itself. One of our tasks at a later stage of this work will be to show to what extent, aside from its fertility, the danger of this intuitive dominant still determines the fate of the modern Jew.

In the genuine practice of prophecy, which essentially compensates for a very different national character, this danger does not exist. It becomes acute only when a people, whose substance has been hollowed out, is carried away from its present-day tasks by the primacy of the future.

Conversely, however, a time like that of Judah-ism, which rejects these intuitives and the possibility of revelation as such, annihilates itself. The prestige gained by prophecy after the downfall of the empire was meant to be restricted, in principle, by honoring the "old" prophecy and excluding its present-day function. This rejection of the possibility of new revelation, however, signified a self-castration, which necessarily also had devastating consequences for the people's self-assurance.

That the bearers of revelation and their writings were pushed aside into a secondary line, leading even to the prohibition of revelation, becomes tragically evident in the consciousness of the Maccabean age that it no longer has a prophet (1 Macc 9:27).[133] This goes so far that, at the dedication of the Temple, no one knows what to do with the deconsecrated altar stones. They are laid aside, "until there should come a prophet in Israel to tell what to do with them" (1 Macc 4:46).

This paralysis of revelation is not only a product of Law-centered theocracy, which is determined to direct every present moment by interpreting a closed-off revelation, but also, in reverse, this Judah-istic legalism, with its notion of the end of revelation, is symptomatic of the alienation from YHWH that has taken hold among great swaths of the people. The apocalypticists' self-assurance, as it speaks to us, for instance, in IV Ezra 14:45,[134] stands in blunt, indeed quite overwhelming, contrast to this attitude. Only a compelling and self-evident revelatory event can lead to such an audacious formulation as the one stating that the twenty-four canonical books should be published and given to the worthy and unworthy to read. The seventy apocalyptic books, "however, you should hold back and only give to the wise among your people. For from them flows the spring of understanding, the fountain of wisdom, the river of knowledge."[135]

The theme of the secret doctrine becomes evident here. It is a historical theme, associated just as much with consciousness of the turning point as with the expectation of salvation that springs from it. The apocalyptic writers shared this theme with early Christianity, with the mystery cults of the period, and with Gnosticism.

Notes

1 *ausserhistorischen und vorhistorischen*: Neumann acknowledges that clear historical evidence is difficult to discover concerning the sociopolitical organization of the Israelites before the time of the monarchy.

2 Not a direct quotation. This theme is explored by Buber in *Königtum Gottes*. In the English edition, a relevant passage reads: "In the covenant of the twelve, whose like we know from Greek and Italian, above all from Etruscan, examples, Joshua has only imported into the primitive system . . . a form corresponding to the living conditions of the settlement of Canaan" (Buber, 1967, *Kingship of God*, p. 147).

3 *EN*: Buber, *Königtum Gottes*. [No page is cited. Possibly a reference to Buber's final paragraph: "The idea of monarchic unification is born and rises against the representatives of the divine kingship. And the crisis between the two grows to one of the theocratic impulse itself, to the crisis out of which there emerges the human king of Israel, the follower of JHWH (I Sam 12:14), as His 'anointed,' *meshiach JHWH*, χριστὸς κυρίου" (ibid., p. 162).]

4 The prophetic ministry of the priest Ezekiel is dated from 593 to 563 BCE. The conquest of the double kingdom of Israel and Judah, the destruction of the Solomonic temple, and the exile of Israelites and Judahites into Babylon occurred in 586 BCE. Beginning seven years before these events, Ezekiel had warned of the approaching catastrophe, God's punishment for apostasy. Once the catastrophe had occurred, his prophecies began to offer hope for the future. To protect the people from ever again betraying God, he prescribed conformity to the Law, overseen by a priestly hierarchy. This prescription, Neumann says, became part of the groundwork for Second Temple theocracy, beginning with the return from Babylon, early fourth century BCE.

5 For instance, Jeremiah's warnings to Israel before the exile.

6 *Judaismus*: usually a synonym for *Judentum* (Judaism). In this section of the book, however, Neumann distinguishes between these terms, using *Judaismus* to refer to postexilic forms of religious life, developed by the Judahites in the Second Temple period. The original kingdom—Judah in the south, Israel in the north—had ended in 586 BCE with the Babylonian Exile. Later, the region of Judah was repopulated and rebuilt (now the province of a Persian satrapy), and a new temple was built in Jerusalem. Here, Neumann begins to describe the religion of the Second Temple period, which he finds psychologically impoverished, marked by a loss of confidence in the original covenant with YHWH. In the following pages, he explores the impact of a legalistic theocracy, defended by a priestly hierarchy, which arose to assure continuity in Jewish religious life. The coined English term, "Judah-ism," here corresponds to Neumann's use of *Judaismus*.

7 Cf. Ezekiel 18, in which this theme is developed. A central verse reads: "The soul that sins shall die. The son shall not suffer for the iniquity of the father, nor the father suffer for the iniquity of the son; the righteousness of the righteous shall be upon himself, and the wickedness of the wicked shall be upon himself" (Ezek 18:20, RSV).

8   *empfangenes*: This adjective is crossed out in the typescript, and an illegible word is hand-written above it. We revert here to Neumann's original word.

9   The quoted phrase conflates Jeremiah 31:31 and 31:33. It also echoes Ezekiel 36:26.

10 In the Book of Isaiah, only chapters 1–39 can be assigned to Isaiah's lifetime (between 742 and 687 BCE). Chapters 40–66 (539 BCE and later) are known as Second, or Second and Third, Isaiah.

11 Chapters 56–66 are sometimes called Third Isaiah.

12 Probably a reference to Isaiah 66, which contains a full attack on temple worship and sacrifice.

13 A Jewish sect, known as the "Healers" or "Attendants," which flourished in the vicinity of Alexandria during the Second Temple period (first century CE).

14 A Jewish sect, consisting of quasi-monastic communities, which flourished between the second century BCE and first century CE. The Essenes lived in many locations, including at Qumran, where the Dead Sea Scrolls were discovered in 1947.

15 Later rabbis taught that direct prophecy had ended at the time of Ezra or of Ahasuerus (cf. Book of Esther), the fictionalized king corresponding to Artaxerxes II of Persia (403–359 BCE). The spirit of prophecy was said to have "ascended" when the Torah, as a code of law, came to serve effectively as the answer to all questions.

16 EN: *Jer Tlm:Yoma* 92.

17 Cf. "heavenly voice" (*bat kol*), below, *Roots I*, p. 125.

18 EN: *Jer Tlm:Ta'anith* 65a. [A mistaken reference. *Jer Tlm:Ta'anith* goes only to page 31a.]

19 An example may be Daniel's vision of four great beasts from the sea (Daniel 7). The Jewish apocalyptic literature cited by Neumann contains many such images.

20 *des Ich-Bewusstseinssystems*: Neumann's description of ego consciousness as a "system" is consistent with the development of his thinking in this period, as seen in his 1942–43 lecture series, "The importance of consciousness in the experience of depth psychology" (cf. *Roots II*, pp. 191, 195, 200, *et passim*.). The same usage is found in Neumann's *Origins*, Part IIB, "The Separation of the Systems," pp. 315ff.

21 Latin: to absurdity

22 In Kautzsch, *Apokryphen und Pseudepigraphen des Alten Testaments*, v. 2: *Die Pseudepigraphen des Alten Testaments* (hereafter: *Apok & Pseudep*), p. 376). Gunkel's wording is slightly different: ". . . trägt ein jeder seine Ungerechtigkeit oder Gerechtigkeit" (p. 376). Phrasing in *The Old Testament Pseudepigrapha*, J. H. Charlesworth, ed. (hereafter: Charlesworth), v. 1, *Apocalyptic Literature and Testaments* (1983), p. 540, is identical with Neumann's. Cf. parallel text, Ezekiel 18:20.

23 The double kingdom of Judah and Israel ended with the destruction of the Solomonic temple and the exile to Babylon (c. 586 BCE).

24 Hebrew: *Shekhinah* is grammatically feminine and is often personified. The basic meaning is "indwelling," referring to the dwelling place of God, as well as the indwelling of God within the world and each soul. By extension, the feminine presence of God.

25 A typing error by Neumann. The text of IV Ezra 8:2 is unrelated. Tamar Kron advises that the intended citation is probably Ezekiel 8:2.

26 Cf. 1 (Ethiopic) Enoch, Charlesworth (1983), v. 1, pp. 20, 49f.

27 Cf. 2 (Syriac Apocalypse of) Baruch, ibid., pp. 628, 635.

28 In this section of the work, Neumann frequently discusses messianic texts, figures, and titles. In translating, we have treated the word "messiah" as a common noun, except when it is clearly meant as a title.

29 No source is cited. In this context, *Endzeit* echoes Hermann Gunkel's saying, "Endzeit gleicht Urzeit" ("the end of time is like the beginning"). Neumann frequently cites Gunkel's translation of IV Ezra and presumably knew his other works. Gunkel wrote, "In der Endzeit wird sich wiederholen, was in der Urzeit gewesen ist." ("At the end of time will be repeated what was in the beginning.") (Gunkel and Zimmern, *Schöpfung und Chaos in Urzeit und Endzeit* (*Creation and chaos at the beginning and end of time*), 1895, p. 370.

30 *"Zug nach oben"*: lit. "upward pull." The term apparently refers to a theological shift in the post-exilic period, early fourth century BCE. At this time, later Jewish tradition taught that the spirit of prophecy "ascended," because the Law, interpreted by rabbinical teaching, had become the all-sufficient source of divine wisdom on earth. As Neumann uses the phrase, here and below, it seems to signify a deep and important shift in Jewish thought, as the Holy One came to be seen more as transcendent and less as an immanent presence.

31 Gunkel's translation of IV Esra 5:6: "und zur Herrschaft kommt, den die Erdbewohner nicht erwarten" ("and one shall reign, whom those who dwell on earth do not expect"). Gunkel reads this verse as foretelling "the dreadful tyrant of the last days, the anti-Christ" (Gunkel, "Das vierte Buch Esra," *Apok & Pseudep*, p. 359; Charlesworth, v. 2, p. 532).

32 *verarbeitet*: this word, whose root means "work," may also be translated as "assimilated." The concept refers to a process of conscious engagement with the psychological and symbolic opposites. (Cf. *Roots I*, p. 138, n. 2.)

33 *EN*: Cf. Glatzer [1933] op. cit. [In fact, Glatzer's 1933 work *Untersuchungen zur Geschichtslehre der Tannaiten* (*Essays on the historical teaching of the tannaim*) (hereafter: *Tannaiten*) is not previously cited. One of its chapters is titled, "Die geschichtsverneinende Lehre der Apokalyptik: Das vierte Buch Esra" ("The history-negating apocalyptic doctrine: The Fourth Book of Ezra") (p. 14). Nahum N. Glatzer (1903–1990) received his doctorate at Goethe University, Frankfurt, in 1931, and was professor there of Jewish religious history and ethics. In 1933 he fled to Palestine, and in 1938 moved to the US, where he taught at Brandeis University and then at Boston University.]

34 Glatzer's thesis, with which Neumann takes issue: "When the apocalypticist considers the history of his people, he does so under the theme of the fall. After wholeness and sin, what follows is not repentance and grace; rather, the world remains condemned in its sin until the time comes for it to end. The judgment of God does not re-establish the order of the fallen world, but founds a new eon" (ibid.).

35 *EN*: Israel was redeemed from Egypt for five reasons, among many others, and future redemption will occur for the same reasons (Deut 4:25). See also passages in Volz, 1934, p. 370. [Paul Volz, *Die Eschatologie der jüdischen Gemeinde im neutestamentlichen Zeitalter nach den Quellen der rabbinischen, apokalyptischen und apokryphen Literatur* (*Jewish eschatology in the New Testament period, following rabbinic, apocalyptic and apocryphal sources*) (hereafter: Volz). In two passages, pp. 346ff. and pp. 370f., Volz draws symbolic parallels between the Exodus and apocalyptic liberation. For example: "Eschatological liberation is the counterpart to liberation from Egyptian servitude at the dawn of Israel's history. . . . To be sure, the new liberation is greater than the one from Egypt" (p. 370).]

36 The reference may be to these verses from Exodus: "The children of Israel groaned from the servitude, and they cried out; and their plea-for-help went up to God" (Ex 2:23); "So now, here, the cry of the children of Israel has come to me" (Ex 3:9).

37 Hebrew: holiness

38 *EN*: 1 Samuel [Probably referring to Eli's two "unpriestlike" sons, who were slain by God (1 Sam 2:12–34).]

39 Hebrew: Israelites (lit. "Children of Israel").

40 *EN*: Bab Tlm: Abodah zarah, 3b, 4a. [*The Hebrew–English Edition of the Babylonian Talmud*, I. Epstein, ed. London: Soncino Press (hereafter: Soncino): *Abodah zarah*, trans. by A. Mishcon.]

41 In Neumann's text: "und macht ein Loch" ("and makes a hole"). The phrase may be a misreading of a Hebrew idiom. In a 1933 German edition of the Babylonian Talmud, this passage reads: "die Sonne aus ihrem Futteral hervorholen und sie glühen lassen" ("brings the sun out of its sheath and causes it to blaze") (trans. by L. Goldschmidt, *Der Babylonische Talmud*, v. 7, p. 803).

42 *EN*: Malachi 3:19 [In the RSV, cf. Mal 4:1. Neumann quotes the Talmud, which differs from Buber's translation of this passage.]

43 *EN*: On this revelation of the "hidden light," see below, p. 133. [*Roots I*, p. 93. Buber's brief volume, *Das verborgene Licht* (*The hidden light*) (1924), became part of *Die chassidischen Bücher* (*The Hasidic books*) (1928) (hereafter: *Chassid Büch*), pp. 559ff.]

44 The reference is to "relative reality."

45 *Der eschatologische Seelenraum*: this heading introduces a concept, "psychic space," which is barely developed here. The concept of psychic space emerges again in the two chapters that follow. Cf. *Roots I*, p. 122.

46 *EN*: Here, as throughout this section, references have been purposely omitted to avoid cluttering the text unnecessarily. Sources may be readily found using the corresponding keyword to search the indexes to the apocalypses; cf. Volz, op. cit. [The reference is to Volz's *Sachregister* (Subject Index), pp. 422ff. Concerning the warfare at the end of time, Volz quotes IV Ezra: "And behold, when he saw the onrush of the approaching multitude, he neither lifted his hand nor held a spear or any weapon of war; but I saw only how he sent forth from his mouth as it were a stream of fire, and from his lips a flaming breath, and from his tongue he shot forth a storm of sparks. All these were mingled together . . . and fell on the onrushing multitude . . . and burned them all up, so that suddenly nothing was seen of the innumerable multitude but only the dust of ashes and the smell of smoke" (ibid., p. 214). (Cf. also IV Ezra 13:9ff., Charlesworth, v. 1, pp. 551f.).]

47 Daniel 7:10.

48 *des Gerichts*: The word means not only "judgment" but also "court of judgment." The association Neumann makes with Kafka's work may have been prompted by several of Kafka's writings, but especially by his novel *Der Prozess* (*The Trial*).

49 As a young man, after finishing his philosophy degree, Neumann wrote commentaries on Franz Kafka's work, which he approached from a Kabbalistic perspective. He finished these commentaries in 1932 and sought Martin Buber's opinion of them. Buber's reply, in late 1935, was positive but gently critical. Neumann's Kafka commentaries remain unpublished. (Cf. above, Introduction, *Roots I*, p. xxxiv).

50 A reference to the events of liberation described in the first fifteen chapters of Exodus, including the experience of slavery, the confrontation with Pharaoh, and the miraculous crossing of the Red Sea.

51 Apparently referring to literary and historical criticism, developed mainly by Protestant Old Testament scholars in the nineteenth and early twentieth centuries.

52 *EN*: Cf. Jonas [1934], *Gnosis und spätantiker Geist*, v. 1: *Die Mythologische Gnosis* (*Mythological Gnosticism*) (hereafter: *Gnosis*). [Neumann may be referring to the whole of Jonas's first volume. In his Foreword, Rudolf Bultmann declares: "Here, for the first time, Gnosticism is fully integrated into the history of late antiquity, and it becomes clear what Gnosticism means for an understanding of the world that was turning from antiquity to Western Christianity" (Bultmann, "Vorwort," *Gnosis*, v. 1, n.p.).]

53 *Umkehr*: lit. turning around (repentance). Cf. *Roots I*, p. 62, n. 166.

54 Neumann's adjective, added by hand in his typescript, is illegible.

55 Cf. above, *Roots I*, note 46 (Volz's quotation from IV Ezra).

56 Cf. above, *Roots I*, pp. 82f.

57 Citation to 1 Enoch 48:37 is incorrect. Neumann may have intended to refer to 1 Enoch 48:6: "For this purpose he became the Chosen One; he was concealed in the presence of (the Lord of Spirits) prior to the creation of the world, and for eternity" (Charlesworth, v. 1, p. 35).

58 1 Enoch 71:15f.: "He . . . said to me, 'He shall proclaim peace to you in the name of the world that is to become. . . . Everyone that will come to exist and walk shall (follow) your path, since righteousness never forsakes you. Together with you shall be their dwelling places; and together with you shall be their portion'" (ibid., p. 50).

59 1 Enoch 101:1: "Examine the heaven, you sons of heaven, and all the works of the Most High" (ibid., p. 82).

60 *Assumptio Mosis*: lit. "Assumption of Moses." Apparently referring to Testament of Moses 10:9: "And God will raise you to the heights. Yea, he will fix you firmly in the heaven of the stars, in the place of their habitations" (ibid., p. 932).

61 "Seven things were created before the world was created . . . for it is written, "His name shall endure forever, and has existed before the sun!" (Ps 72:17) (*Bab Tlm: Pesahim* 54a, trans. by H. Freedman, Soncino).

62 IV Ezra 7:30: "And the world shall be turned back to primeval silence for seven days, as it was at the first beginnings" (Charlesworth, v. 1, p. 537). 2 Baruch 3:7: "Or will the universe return to its nature and the world go back to its original silence?" (ibid., p. 621). Sibylline Oracles 5:480ff.: "There will be moonless night round the great heaven itself. No small mist will cover the folds of the world about a second time" (ibid., p. 404).

63 *EN*: Cf. also Volz, 1934, pp. 335ff. [In this passage, Volz discusses the stars falling; the end of time reckoning; world conflagration and flood; the merger of heaven and earth; the burning of the seas; and the rise of the chaos monster of the deep.]

64 Neumann echoes the theme: the end of time recapitulates the beginning.

65 No verse cited. Possibly a reference to the Apocalypse of Abraham 17:17: "redeemer of those who dwell in the midst of the wicked ones, of those who are dispersed among the just of the world, in the corruptible age" (Charlesworth, v. 1, p. 697).

66 2 Baruch 3:7: "Or will the universe return to its nature and the world go back to its original silence?" (ibid., p. 621).

67 *EN*: Cf. 1 Enoch 33 and *Bab Tlm: Sanhedrin* 97a. [In 1 Enoch (the Ethiopic Apocalypse of Enoch, second century BCE to first century CE), the writer sees the stars leave their places in heaven, while he records "the gates out of which they exit . . . their names, . . . their periods, their months" (1 Enoch 33:3, E. Isaac, trans., Charlesworth, v. 1, pp. 28f.). In *Bab Tlm: Sanhedrin*: "It has been taught in accordance with R. Kattina: Just as the seventh year is one year of release in seven, so is the world: one thousand years out of seven shall be fallow, as it is written, *And the Lord alone shall be exalted in that day*; and it is further said, *A Psalm and song for the Sabbath day*, meaning the day that is altogether Sabbath" (*Bab Tlm: Sanhedrin* 97a, trans. by J. Schachter and H. Freedman, Soncino).]

68 No supporting passage occurs in 1 Enoch 48. The garden of Genesis, with the tree of wisdom at its center, is described in 1 Enoch 32. A description of the mandala-like Garden of Eden also occurs in a later text, 2 Enoch 8:2–6. (2 Enoch is not listed among Neumann's references for this book. Tamar Kron kindly provided this reference.)

69 Cf. Genesis 3:17–15. After Adam and Eve's disobedience, God curses the earth, so that raising food will be a struggle, and imposes mortality on humankind.

70 1 Enoch 10.1ff. describes the promised destruction of the earth. 2 Baruch 29 describes the lifting of the curse and earth's resulting fruitfulness.

71 2 Baruch 29:8: "And it will happen at that time that the treasury of manna will come down again from on high, and they will eat of it in those years because these are they who will have arrived at the consummation of time" (Charlesworth, v. 1, p. 631). Ex 16:15: "When the Children of Israel saw it they said each-man to his brother: "*Mahn hu / what is it?* . . . Moses said to them: It is the bread that YHWH has given you for eating." In one version of the *Jerusalem Targum*: "And Moses said to them, 'It is the bread that was reserved for you from the beginning in the heavens on high, and now the Lord is giving it to you to eat'" (*Targum Pseudo-Jonathan: Exodus*, trans by M. Maher, *The Aramaic Bible*, v. 2, p. 208).]

72 IV Ezra 8:52: "because it is for you that Paradise is opened, the tree of life is planted, the age to come is prepared" (Charlesworth, v. 1, p. 544). Life of Adam and Eve 36: "And Adam said to Eve, 'Rise and go with my son Seth to the regions of Paradise and put dust on your heads and prostrate yourselves to the ground and mourn in the sight of God. Perhaps he will have mercy and send his angel to the tree of his mercy, from which flows the oil of life, and will give you a little of it with which to anoint me, that I might have rest from these pains by which I am wasting away" (Charlesworth, v. 2, p. 272). (Neumann's reference to 1 Enoch 8:3 appears to be an error.)

73 1 Enoch 60:24: "And the angel of peace who was with me said to me, 'These two monsters are prepared for the great day of the Lord (when) they shall turn into food'" (Charlesworth, v. 1, pp. 41f.). IV Ezra 6:40–52: "Then you kept in existence two living creatures; the name of one you called Behemoth and the name of the other Leviathan . . . And you gave Behemoth one of the parts which had been dried up on the third day, to live in it, . . . but to Leviathan you gave the seventh part, the watery part; and you have kept them to be eaten by whom you wish, and when you wish" (Charlesworth, v. 1, p. 536). 2 Baruch 29:4: "And Behemoth will reveal itself from its place, and Leviathan will come from the sea, the two great monsters which I created on the fifth day of creation and which I shall have kept until that time. And they will be nourishment for all who are left" (Charlesworth, v. 1, p. 630).

74 EN: *Jakob und Esau* I. [Reference to Chapter 1 may be an error. In the English edition of *Jacob & Esau*, the feminine and masculine principles are discussed at the beginning of Chapter 2, pp. 51f.]

75 EN: *Bab Tlm: Ta'anith* 31a; *Jer Tlm: Megillah* 73a. ["In the days to come the Holy One, blessed be He, will hold a chorus for the righteous and He will sit in their midst in the Garden of Eden and every one of them will point with his finger towards Him . . ." (*Bab Tlm: Ta'anith*, trans by J. Rabbinowitz, Soncino). Neumann's second reference may be an error. The text in the first column of p. 73, in the Hebrew edition of *Jer Tlm: Megillah*, is unrelated. (Cf. *The Talmud of the Land of Israel*, v. 19, *Megillah*, trans. by J. Neusner, Chicago University Press, pp. 91ff.) With thanks to Jim Rosenbloom.

76 2 Baruch 29:7: "For winds will go out in front of me every morning to bring the fragrance of aromatic fruits and clouds at the end of the day to distill the dew of health" (Charlesworth, v. 1, pp. 630f.). IV Ezra 7:121: ". . . safe and healthful habitations have been reserved for us"; also verse 123: ". . . a paradise shall be revealed, whose fruit remains unspoiled and in which are abundance and healing" (Charlesworth, v. 1, p. 541). Sibylline Oracles 3:369: "The air will be good for pasture for many years, bracing, free from storms and hail, producing everything—including birds and creeping things of the earth" (Charlesworth, v. 1, p. 370). 1 Enoch 96:3: "But you, who have experienced pain, fear not, for there shall be a healing medicine for you" (Charlesworth, v. 1, p. 76).

77 *Gehenom* (for Hebrew: *gehinnom*): hell, place of torment. Originally, the valley of Hinnom, near Jerusalem, where refuse was burned in biblical times.

78 EN: Volz, pp. 396ff. [A section of Volz's chapter on *Seligkeit* (blessedness) is titled, "Die Lichtnatur der Heilsgenossen" ("The luminous nature of the company of the saved"), pp. 396–401.]

79 EN: The symbolic character of the robe reaches from primitive masked dances through all of mythology to the mystery cult and Gnosticism, and to the liturgical vestments of priests, the professional clothing of guilds, and the gowns worn by dignitaries. From time immemorial to the present, the robe is a means of transformation, from the transformation of primitives into their ancestors by virtue of masks to the transformation of the private person into the judge by putting on the gown.

80 Latin: praise.

81 "*Das verborgene Licht*": cf. above, *Roots I*, p. 85, n. 43.

82 EN: *Bab Tlm: Hagigah* 12a. ["For R. Eleazar said: The light which the Holy One, blessed be He, created on the first day, one could see thereby from one end of the world to the other; but as soon as the Holy One, blessed be He, beheld the generation of the Flood and the generation of the Dispersion, and saw that their actions were corrupt, He arose and hid it from them . . . And for whom did he reserve it? For the righteous in the time to come" (*Bab Tlm: Hagigah*, trans by I. Abrahams, Soncino).]

83 EN: *Chassid Büch*, p. 559. [Epigraph to *Das verborgene Licht*.]

84 Hebrew: Garden of Eden.

85 EN: Wünsche [1907], "Von der Bildung des Kindes" ("The Education of a Child"). [*Aus Israels Lehrhallen* (*From Israel's halls of teaching*), v. 3, XIX, Appendix, p. 214. Tamar Kron advises that the original source is *Bab Tlm: Niddah* 30b: "A light burns above

its head and it looks and sees from one end of the world to the other" (trans by Israel W. Slotki, Soncino). Wünsche may also be paraphrasing from *Midrash Tanhuma Yelammedenu*, Chapter 11 (Ex 38:21–40:38), "These Are the Accounts," section 3. In Berman's translation: (The Holy One) "placed a lighted candle at his head, as it is said: *Oh, that I were as in the months of old, as in the days when God watched over me; when His light shined over my head* (Job 29:2). He looked about and peered from one end of the world to the other" (p. 654).]

86 Wünsche, op. cit., p. 216. [Cf. *Midrash Tanhuma Yelammedenu*, Chapter 11 (Ex. 38:21– 40:38), "These Are the Accounts," section 3. In Berman's translation: "Nevertheless, he remained unwilling to leave, and so the angel struck him with the candle that was burning at his head. Thereupon he went out into the light of the world, though against his will. Upon going out the infant forgot everything he had witnessed and everything he knew" (p. 656).]

87 *EN*: Cf. Jung [1936], "Analytical Psychology and Education"; Wickes, 1931, "Analyse der kindlichen Seele"; Geitel, 1937, "Das introvertierte Kind," in Heyer, *Reich der Seele*, v. 2. [These three sources are not uniformly supportive. In his 1924 lecture, originally published in *Energetik*, Jung contradicts Neumann: "The collective unconscious is a problem that seldom enters into practical work with children: their problem lies mainly in adapting themselves to their surroundings" (CW 17.4, ¶211). Elsewhere in Jung's early work, Neumann's thesis is better supported. In "The Psychological Foundations of Belief in Spirits," *Energetik*, he writes: "Although the child possesses no inborn ideas, it nevertheless has a highly developed brain .... This brain is inherited from its ancestors; it is the deposit of the psychic functioning of the whole human race.... In the brain the instincts are preformed, and so are the primordial images which have always been the basis of man's thinking—the whole treasure-house of mythological motifs" (CW 8, ¶589). Frances Wickes writes: "Children and adults may sometimes have dreams that convey an extremely important message of the collective unconscious" (p. 289). She adds, however, that such dreams are rare in children, who seldom experience fateful moments involving the intervention of the collective unconscious (pp. 289f.). Charlotte Geitel writes: "The introverted do not want to overcome the unconscious. For all intents and purposes, they do not want to detach themselves from the unconscious at all, but would prefer to remain forever with the mother, the personification of the unconscious" (*Reich der Seele*, v. 2, pp. 99f.). "They are attached more strongly than others to the eternal primordial ground, the collective unconscious, which is both a blessing and a curse" (ibid., p. 100). Neumann's intention to develop his hypothesis further is suggested in a handwritten scrap of paper, found among the pages of his typescript, which reads in part: "Das Vorwissen der Kinder (Children's foreknowledge) 133." (Assuming "133" is a page number, it refers to this passage in Neumann's typescript.)]

88 *EN*: Cf. Volz, p. 383, on Philo. [The relevant passage reads: "Philo weaves allegorical threads through his account: if the animals could become tame, he thinks, then the animals in us would be tamed even more, which would be the greater good; or rather, the animals in us must first be tamed, and only then will the wild animals lose their courage."]

89 In the Testament of Naphtali, concerning the last times: "The one who does not do the good, men and angels will curse . . .; the devil will inhabit him as his own instrument. Every wild animal will dominate him, and the Lord will hate him" (Charlesworth, v. 1, p. 814).

90 Sibylline Oracles, Book III, lines 790–92: "Roving bears will spend the night with calves, the flesh-eating lion will eat husks at the manger like an ox, and mere infant children will lead them" (Charlesworth, v. 1, p. 379) – Ed.

91 *EN*: Cf. Volz, p. 364. [Although Neumann omits quotation marks, this passage is quoted nearly verbatim.]

92 Handwritten Greek: eternal life.

93 Latin: of its own kind, completely different.

94 This reference to the hiddenness of the divine anticipates Neumann's discussion of a central concept in Hasidism: "the revelation of the hidden divinity." Cf. *Roots II*, pp. 20ff.

95 *Seelen-Lehre*: alternatively, "doctrine of the psyche." The German word *Seele* may refer to either psyche or soul; its translation depends on context. The present context allows for either interpretation. Cf. *Roots II*, pp. 59, 99f, 138ff.

96 *EN*: *Bab Tlm: Baba Bathra*, 10b. ["Joseph the son of R. Joshua . . . had been ill and fell in a trance. After he recovered, his father said to him, 'What vision did you have?' He replied, 'I saw a world upside down, the upper below and the lower above.' He said to him, 'You saw a well-regulated world'." (*Bab Tlm: Baba Bathra*, trans by M. Simon, Soncino).]

97 *Hinter- und Untergrund der Welt*: The metaphor of a psychological "background and underground" refers to the hidden reality of introverted experience. The term "background," in this sense, recurs frequently in the first chapter of Neumann's *Hasidism*. Cf. *Roots II*, pp. 4, 9, 12, *et passim*.

98 Spoken by Faust to Mephistopheles in "The Mothers' Scene," in Goethe's *Faust*: Part Two, Act One, Scene 5 (trans. by Philip Wayne. London: Penguin Books, 1959, p. 78).

99 *EN*: Cf. C. G. Jung, "Die Erlösungsvorstellungen in der Alchemie" ("Ideas of Redemption in Alchemy"), *EJ 1936* [CW 12,3,III]; "Einige Bemerkungen zu den Visionen des Zosimos" ("The Visions of Zosimos"), *EJ 1937* [CW 13,2]; *Psych & Rel* (1938) [CW 11,1]. [In his 1937 lecture, Jung writes that alchemists experience processes in the material world corresponding to their philosophical conceptions: "Since Zosimos, like all the other alchemists, is convinced not only that his philosophy can be applied to matter but that processes also take place in it which corroborate his philosophical assumptions, it follows that he must have experienced, in matter itself, at the very least an identity between the behaviour of matter and the events in his own psyche" (CW 12, ¶409).]. Jung's first Terry Lecture, "The Unconscious Mind," discusses the impact of unconscious irruptions on both individuals and nations, including the emergence of the "Wotan" possession that he observed in the dreams of Germans after World War I (*Psych & Rel*, 1938, p. 33 and notes 15–17, pp. 118f.). (Cf. CW 11.1, ¶1–55).

100 Latin: stone. In this passage, Neumann uses alchemical terms familiar from Jung's writings. (Cf. CW 12 and CW 13.)

101 Latin: work.

102 *JHWHs Wirksamkeit in der Zeit*: lit. YHWH's effectiveness in time. Neumann frequently uses the term *Wirksamkeit* in relation to YHWH. Here it is translated as "working," elsewhere as "power."

103 *EN*: See Volz, p. 188. [Volz writes: "Strangely enough, the son of man is not a very active personality in the imagery of these passages, despite possessing all the characteristic features. . . . This has to do (cf. Dan 12:1) with the style of apocalypticism, which likes to use the passive and lets 'things happen' instead of letting figures act."]

104 *Vor-Bild* (*Vorbild*) (lit: "pre-image"): model, example, pattern, standard, prototype. Neumann's hyphen emphasizes the word's root meaning.

105 Hebrew: Egypt.

106 *EN*: Glatzer, *Tannaiten*, op. cit., p. 32. [Neumann misquotes the title of Glatzer's second chapter, "Aktivierung der Geschichte" ("Activation of history").] [A handwritten scrap of paper, found among the pages of Neumann's typescript, suggests his intention to explore this theme: "JHWH, Gottes Anteil in der Zeit (YHWH, God's participation in time), 139."]

107 The *tannaim* were scholars (rabbis) whose period dates from the end of the first century BCE through the end of the second century CE. The greater part of the Mishnah, the basic material of rabbinic Judaism, is attributed to these sages (Schiffman, 1991, p. 10).

108 *Aktivierung der Geschichte*: Glatzer's phrase (cf. n. 106 above) is correctly quoted here.

109 *EN*: *Tannaiten*, op. cit., p. 47. [The remainder of this paragraph is consistent with Glatzer's argument.]

110 On the tannaitic view of history, Glatzer writes "that historicization within the tannaitic theory of history is not performed on foreign ground but on one's very own, by

being inserted into the historical context, where it becomes meaningful only within the divine plan underlying all events" (ibid., p. 49).

111 Latin: consider the end.

112 Cf. *Roots I*, pp. 83ff.: "The historical form of the certainty of salvation."

113 Cf. *Roots II*, p. 44, where the same passage occurs: "For the Jew of antiquity, a miracle was the experience of YHWH's way of working, the indefinable character of which breaks through the world's rational lawfulness."

114 In the passage known as the Covenant with Abraham (Gen 15), God promises that the people's time of servitude will be limited to 400 years (Gen 15:13f.). And in the story of the Exodus from Egypt, it is said that their servitude has lasted 430 years (Ex 12:40).

115 Latin: in one action.

116 Neumann observes that in the canonical (pre-apocalyptic) writings, YHWH's appearances are discontinuous with human history, breaking in from a different plane of existence.

117 Daniel 7:13: "I saw in the night visions, and behold, with the clouds of heaven there came one like a son of man, and he came to the Ancient of Days and was presented before him." Enoch 46:2f.: "And I asked . . . 'Who is this, and from whence is he who is going as the prototype of the Before-Time?' And he answered and said to me, 'This is the Son of Man, to whom belongs righteousness, and with whom righteousness dwells. And he will open all the hidden storerooms; for the Lord of the Spirits has chosen him, and he is destined to be victorious'" (Charlesworth, v. 1, p. 34). In IV Ezra 13:3: "And I looked, and behold, this wind made something like the figure of a man come up out of the heart of the sea. And I looked, and behold, that man flew with the clouds of heaven" (ibid., p. 551).

118 "*Menschensohn*": as used in Daniel, the designation "son of man" is not a messianic title, but means "human being." In this context the phrase is lower case. When it appears in Neumann's text as a title, it is capitalized.

119 *eines Menschenaehnlichen*: Neumann paraphrases Buber's translation of Daniel 8:15: "mit den Wolken des Himmels kam einer wie ein Menschensohn" ("with the clouds of heaven came one like a son of man").

120 Charlesworth, v. 1, p. 551.

121 *EN*: *Anani*, "Man of the Clouds." Similarly, *Bar Nafbe*, "Son of the Cloud." Cf. Zobel, *Gottes Gesalbter* (God's anointed), p. 342. These are Talmudic names for the messiah, like *Shalom*, "Peace." [After careful research, Tamar Kron and David Wieler advise that the Aramaic term, *bar nafbe*, occurs in none of the published editions of Zobel's *Gottes Gesalbter*.]

122 Latin: in a nutshell.

123 IV Ezra 7:118–20: "O Adam, what have you done? For though it was you who sinned, the fall was not yours alone, but ours also who are your descendants. For what good is it to us, if an eternal age has been promised to us, but we have done deeds that bring death? And what good is it that an everlasting hope has been promised us, but we have miserably failed?" (Charlesworth, v. 1, p. 541).

124 *EN*: Jung [1936], "Richard Wilhelm: In Memoriam," *Geheimnis*, 2nd edn. [Jung writes that Wilhelm was changed inwardly by the Chinese spirit: "This deep transformation was certainly not won without great sacrifice, for our historical premises are so entirely different. The keenness of Western consciousness and its harsh problems had to soften before the more universal, more equable nature of the East; Western rationalism and one-sided differentiation had to yield to Eastern breadth and simplicity" (CW 15, ¶93). Here Jung does not mention introversion or intuition, but Neumann makes the connection.]

125 *EN*: Jung [1921] *Psychologische Typen* (*Psychological Types*, CW 6) hereafter: *Types*). [Cf. Jung's descriptions of extraverted and introverted intuition, CW 6, ¶610–15; 632–7.]

126 *EN*: Here and below, cf. *Types*. [Jung's definition of the inferior function: CW 6, ¶763f.]

127 French: reality function.

128 *EN*: Cf. Gunkel's commentary in Kautzsch [1900], IV Ezra, op. cit., p. 338. [On compassion for sinners, cf. IV Ezra 7:102–8:62, Kautzsch, pp. 376–83.]

129 Charlesworth, v. 1, p. 530.

130 *EN*: Auerbach [1938], *Wüste und Gelobtes Land*, v. 2, p. 262.

131 *EN*: Baldensperger [1903], *Die messianischen-apokalyptischen Hoffnungen des Judentums* (*Messianic and apocalyptic hopes of Judaism*), p. 87.

132 *EN*: Cf. p. 15 above. [Cf. Neumann's Introduction to the Work, *Roots I*, p. 9, quoting Baer's (1936) *Galuth*, p. 93: "Essentially, this Judaism remained as it had been two thousand years before, or at least, if it had developed, it had developed only in nuances. It still upheld the same eschatological concepts of history, with the chosen people at its center" (*Galut*, English edition, 1988, p. 109).]

133 I Maccabeans 9:27: "Thus there was great distress in Israel, such as had not been seen since the time that prophets ceased to appear among them."

134 IV Ezra 14:45ff.: "And when the forty days were ended, the Most High spoke to me saying, 'Make public the twenty-four books that you wrote first and let the worthy and the unworthy read them; but keep the seventy that were written last, in order to give them to the wise among your people. For in them is the spring of understanding, the fountain of wisdom, and the river of knowledge'" (Charlesworth, v. 1, p. 555).

135 IV Ezra 14:47. Translation based on Metzger's version in Charlesworth (ibid.), slightly altered to match Neumann's wording.

3

THE DANGEROUS ENDING OF THE YHWH–EARTH TENSION

1. Breaking the tension between YHWH and earth

The Gnostic threat

The entire psychology of this time is strongly influenced by Gnosticism, which, as we now know, took hold of the whole Near East as a religious movement, penetrating as far as India in the east and deep into Europe in the west. This is not the place to engage the scientific discussion of the ways Gnosticism influenced the Jewish worldview and was influenced by it; historical connections exist every-where, and questions of origin and priority are secondary to our purpose. But the YHWH–earth tension that is sometimes manifest among the apocalyptic writers certainly comes close to Gnosticism, where the connection between deity and world is broken into an irreversible dualism.

It is not our task to present even an outline of the Gnostic worldview.[1] Nevertheless, anticipating later concerns, we should take this opportunity to offer some basic psycho-logical comments on it. First of all, as we have emphasized, this movement is still very much alive in the modern Jew. Beyond that, essential Jewish psychological attitudes may be brought to light by differentiating them from the Gnostic worldview.[2]

A fundamental trait of all Gnostic systems is the radical rejection of the world. The basic assumption of Gnosticism is that light exists in the depths. Whether it falls there through sin, descends voluntarily, or suffers a defeat, light in the depth has an embryonic, fragmentary consciousness. Finding itself within the world of the unconscious, it views this depth, this *tehom*–Tiamat[3] aspect of the world, as a totality. The structure of *hyle* (matter) is repeatedly identified with the drive structure of the unconscious, the prevailing power of materiality, and the earthly dimension that causes unconsciousness.

Whether this structure is characterized as subterranean fire, evil lust, and desire, as serpent, dragon, and Egypt, as darkness, evil, insurrection, gloom, or hatred, it is always clear that the power of the unconscious, here represented as the world, is hostile to consciousness. Exactly the same is true when we see, in the tremendous mythical projection of Gnosticism, how the destiny of light, the element of consciousness, is represented in the world. Revelations of worldly life come to the unworldly light fragment in images of falling, sinking, captivity, sleep, numbness, drunkenness, separation from home, fear, wandering, and home sickness. The conditions of the Gnostic experience are expressed in metaphors of scattering and self-alienation, and in feelings of being surrounded and threatened by the hostile noise of the world.

These Gnostic projections represent with unsurpassed intensity a primal problem of all human existence: namely, what it means to exist as a small fragment of consciousness amid the overpowering and devouring powers of the world and the unconscious.

The principle of the redeemed redeemer, which we find throughout Gnosticism as a basic theme of the doctrine of salvation, is the fundamental principle of all consciousness. It is the redeeming power of higher consciousness. As a call from outside, from the realm of light, it summons the ego to free itself from its entanglement with the unconscious and to become conscious of itself, to gather itself, and thus to return home. That is, it is a call to achieve as a reality the human being's original state of belonging to the world of higher consciousness, the realm of light.

If space allowed, it would be inviting and illuminating to study in depth how the dualism of consciousness and unconsciousness recurs in the dualism of divinity and world. The most topical contents and problems, with which we are actively engaged today, as the contents and problems of depth psychology, may be found projected on the mythical level.

Only two themes are highlighted here, because they will prove important to us later. The descending act of redemption, which Gnosticism always characterizes as redemption through knowledge, corresponds to what appears today in countless dreams and images as the act of consciousness descending into the unconscious. This descent of consciousness is surely archetypal and can be found in innumerable mythologies, for, ultimately, wherever redemption comes from above, what is meant is this act of redemption going into the unconscious.

An exceptional danger accompanies this descent, however: the imminent loss of consciousness. This enormous danger, that light will be overwhelmed by darkness, has never been as formative as it became in Gnosticism. For there, as was common at the time, the stance of consciousness was felt to be unequal to the immense superiority of irrational unconsciousness. This inequality was felt to be great and fundamental, in a way that we know—but then reliably—only at times of tremendous upheaval, when the light of individual consciousness threatens to be smothered by the storm of world events.

The danger of intuition

Associated with the problem of the descending redemptive act is the further problem of "the capacity of unconscious contents to become conscious,"[4] that is, the fact that latent conscious qualities exist to some extent in the unconscious.

Awakened from outside by the intervention of the descending act of consciousness, these qualities are brought into cooperation with the one who redeems consciousness. Characteristically, Gnosticism—like all movements at this time—is not about universal redemption, which would represent a "transformation of unconscious contents."[5] Instead, it concerns only a redemption of those parts capable of "re-remembering back," that is, those parts that originate in consciousness, and whose conscious structure, which has become latent, is actualized here.

So we are dealing with an exact mythological prototype of psychic structure as viewed by psychoanalysis. The instinctual structure of the unconscious constitutes the resistance to redemption through consciousness. This redemption refers largely to contents that were once conscious, that have entered the sphere of the unconscious, and that must once again be wrested from it by the descent of redeeming consciousness.

The second theme, which we should touch upon at least briefly, concerns the relation of the "Self"[6] to the ego. In the hymn dedicated to it, the Self is the pearl.[7] Here again, Gnostic language employs an archetypal symbol, the ubiquitous collective symbolism of the elusive precious object, the treasure in the unconscious. This is what lies at the heart of the struggle. This pearl is part of the realm of light that was dragged off to Egypt. It is the spark that, having been reacquired and rescued, now guarantees the return, the homecoming, out of the world and into the land where light originates. This pearl is well known from the modern person's experience of the unconscious; it is a familiar symbol of the Self as the totality of the psyche.[8,9]

Psychologically, this Self has all the qualities that we know from Gnosticism as properties of the realm of light. It has the character of the transpersonal, transcendence, the wholly other, enlightenment, separation, alienness, etc., especially when, as in Gnosticism, it contrasts with a negatively awakened unconscious, the nature of which is for the most part destructively desirous.

The crucial factor that Gnosticism shares with all ancient mystery religions is redemption through the ego's identification with the Self. This identification leads to a flooding with contents that cannot be assimilated by the expansion of consciousness and the ego. It ends in a radical transformation of the life principle, corresponding to deification, as in all the ancient mystery cults that are known to us.[10]

This deification has its parallel in all ecstatic–mystical experiences. It is the result of a radical introversion, which, beyond the stage-by-stage awakening of the many-layered unconscious, ends by dissolving the individual, ego-governed personality structure. Always and everywhere, this process of radical introversion involves the same phenomena, in that the collective unconscious is always awakened and encountered layer by layer, with corresponding experiences of heavens and hells, demonic spirits, and circles of gods. It finally culminates, through progressive de-personalization,[11] with the ego's dissolving in the Self.

Individual experiences, such as the ecstatic experiences of the mystics, belong to the substance of this deification process, as do systematic teachings such as those of yoga,[12] where whole groups of disciples follow this path. In yoga, these processes are initiated during a person's lifetime. The corresponding method of the *Bardo Thödol*,[13] on the other hand, strives to reach out beyond life, to teach one who has died how to avoid rebirth by accomplishing the identification of the ego with the Self, which here appears as the "primary clear light."[14]

As we see in Gnosticism, however, and especially in Manichaeism, this transformation of the life principle transforms only ego consciousness. The psyche as a whole is not transformed. In deification, the fragments of light are separated from the elements of darkness, and this process of selection is identical in the individual, in humanity, and in nature. The dark parts, however, are merely isolated; they are not part of what is transformed. In Gnosticism, and also in large parts of Christianity, the irredeemability of evil—a crucial problem, for example, in IV Ezra[15]—remains an essential fact of human existence. Deification, occurring only through the identification of the ego with the Self, leaves the dark side of the world out of the process of transformation.

But with this resigned dualism, half the world is sacrificed. And this half of the world even presents itself here, in contrast to the realm of light, as the totality of what we call the world. In the end, therefore, by the sacrifice of the inferior function—evil, the other side[16]—the basic problem, the problem of opposites, has once again been shattered, but not resolved.

The ego that is identified with the Self always experiences the world as negative. This experience inevitably leads to a progressive annihilation of the world, that is, to a sacrifice of the outer world[17] and of extraversion. In other words, it leads to the elimination of the creative polarity between ego and Self, outside and inside, world and God.

Gnosticism and Judaism

Ego consciousness, which emerged as an organ of orientation toward and experience of the world, always sides with the outer world, to which in a certain sense it belongs. In this respect it contrasts with the Self. Thus, every time the ego is dissolved by the Self, the possibility of experiencing the world is also dissolved. In this way—and this is the conscious aim of Gnosticism—the creation of the world is undone. From this perspective, the final position of Gnosticism, and thus Gnosticism as a whole, was clearly unacceptable to Judaism.

Even when the world is perceived in apocalyptic and negative terms, it remains created by God. No matter what hostile and averted attitude toward it the apocalyptic writers may take, the world remains not only the arena but also the subject of the debate. The world remains relevant as a reality, whether for grace or for judgment. Ultimately, therefore, it is not a question of redemption from the world, but of redemption in the world.

The negative aspect of the world can never be detached from the sphere of human decision-making and responsibility, because the human being is established to rule over the world, that is, to make it fruitful, consistent with the tension between YHWH and the world.

The Gnostic perspective is impossible for Judaism because, as mentioned earlier, the remoteness from God is so fundamental in Semitism that the ego's identification with the Self, its deification, becomes extremely difficult. Despite their substantial resemblance, the distance remains between divine and human, Self and ego. Indeed, this distance provides the space for divine experience in the first place, which Buber has formulated in terms of encounter and dialogue.[18]

The ancient Jewish idea of the purity of nature,[19] which affirms the world as a divine creation and attributes its negative aspect to what is negative in the human being, is irreconcilably opposed to the Gnostic rejection of the world. This Jewish position sets up consciousness as the authority responsible for the state of the world. Consequences flow from this, including ethics, affirmation of the here and now, and the recognition of a principle of justice that becomes known in the course of history.

Gnosticism does not hold itself responsible, as a matter of ethical consciousness, for the negativity existing in the world nor for the sense of a fall from an original, higher state. Rather, it underpins its own disastrous condition with a cosmic prehistory, in which the human being and humanity as a whole are blamelessly entangled. "Hence the revolt against the world, refusal to accept it, and refusal to accept oneself."[20]

Despite its Gnostic tendency, Judaism cannot adopt this stance. That is why the Gnostics' hatred of the Old Testament is not unfounded, for it contends, emphatically and against all likelihood, for the goodness of creation. The Jew essentially takes on the responsibility for evil, even to an almost unbearable extent, as we shall see. And yet, despite the enduring tension between good and evil, he insists on the possibility of living in and accepting the world.[21]

This finds beautiful expression in the aforementioned passage about the "Education of the Child."[22] For when the human spirit (the pre-existent soul) is summoned to enter into the drop of semen from which its earthly body is to be formed, it says:

> "Lord of the world, I have satisfaction in the world, in which I have been since the day on which I was created; if it is your will, then do not let me enter into this foul-smelling drop, for I am holy and pure." Thereupon, however, the Lord, praise be unto him, says to him: "The world into which I lead you is better than the world in which you are, and when I formed you, I formed you solely for this drop."[23]

The same thing happens again when the time has come for the child to be born into the world from its mother's "three abodes." As the angel says:

> You were formed in your mother's body against your will, and against your will you shall be born.[24]

These words show just how strongly Jewish consciousness, too, suffers from the world and experiences its subjection to the overwhelming destiny of living. Above this, however, in the strongest imaginable contrast to Gnosticism's hostility to the world, stands the reality of life, which alone gives meaning to everything spiritual and to the existence of spirits. Now, it would seem obvious that the soul itself, the pre-existent spirit, thinks Gnostically, as it were, simply resigning itself to the superior power of the divine. Characteristically, however, when after a difficult life this very angel comes up to the human being to lead him out of the world, the same weeping can be heard as when the angel called the human being to birth.

Transition is the cause of human terror. Out of spiritual perseverance or inherent inertia, no one wants to surrender any level of his lived existence, spiritual, embryonic, or human. The divine decree exercises dominion over just this restricted human insight and this limited reaction, when it orders the human being to fulfill himself in the creation, the here and now.

This espousal of creation is the fundamental, irrevocable contrast between Judaism and Gnosticism. It also explains the radical reversal of values that Gnosticism, in its hostility toward creation, attempts with regard to Judaism and the Old Testament. Seen in this way, the Gnostic equation YHWH = demiurge = devil is as logical as the positive evaluation of all the negative instances of the Old Testament, from the serpent and Cain to Esau, and the demonizing of all the figures belonging to YHWH, from the patriarchs to the prophets.

Despite which, and disregarding historical connections with Persian dualism and pre-Gnostic trends, the Gnostic devaluation of the body has penetrated deep into Judaism. Initially, however, the Gnostic identification of evil with the flesh was not found within Judaism, but was only later established by Christianity. The idea of the devil as the lord of this world is Gnostic–Christian; only against him does the Johannine–Gnostic dictum become understandable: "My kingdom is not of this world" (John 18:36).

Within Judaism, that is, also within the apocalypse, this Gnostification never went so far. The demonic power of evil, whether at work in the individual, in the history of humanity, or in Jewish history, is always and fundamentally an instrument in the hand of YHWH, the lord of the *whole* world. Although the opaqueness of evil's association with YHWH is often confusing and ensnaring, and God's willing of evil can cause the deepest conflicts and the most destructive doubts, the devil never becomes a counter-god. The paradox lies in YHWH's ownership of evil, his two-sidedness, which often seems to obscure his hidden unitary character.

Thus, the concept of original sin, in its Christian intensification, is foreign to ancient Judaism. Despite the formulation of the seed of evil, sown in Adam, or of evil matter, which already gave rise to sin in Adam—a strongly Gnostic idea— indeed even despite the original sin starting with Adam (IV Ezra 7:118),[25] that brought death and cursed the soil, freedom of choice always, crucially, remains possible for the individual. This, however, means that Judaism leaves open the possibility of an autonomous human self-redemption from evil. Unlike Gnosticism, it does not make an extra-human intervention for the sake of humanity the indispensible prerequisite of redemption.

Alongside these notions, which seemingly lean toward Gnosticism, the writings of the apocalypticists contain such pointed Jewish and anti-Gnostic statements as these:

"In the same manner that a mountain has never turned into a servant, nor shall a hill become a maidservant of a woman; likewise, neither has sin been exported into the world. It is the people who have themselves invented it" (1 Enoch 98:4).[26] Or: "For, although Adam sinned first and has brought death upon all who were not in his own time, yet each of them who has been born from him has prepared for himself the coming torment. And further, each of them has chosen for himself the coming glory" (Baruch 54:15). And: "But each of us has become our own Adam" (Baruch 54:19).[27]

The difficulty of becoming free from evil is not only acknowledged here, but even overemphasized, because corruptibility and sinfulness are as strong as the natural principle of the body. One needs to realize that the ethical threat for this time arose from the body's sheer instinctiveness, that is, from the unconscious, insofar as it represents the human drive structure. We refer here to our earlier reflections on the connection between the dimension of earth and nature and the sexual–orgiastic.[28]

The characteristic of hell is the same as that of the negative unconscious. In this view, earth lies on hell like a lid on a pot,[29] or—in a more recent formulation—as consciousness lies on the "sub"conscious, or the cerebral cortex, the seat of consciousness, on the cerebral matter and the brain stem, representing the unconscious. This equation of hell with the unconscious is verified—not that this would be necessary—by the other ways hell is symbolized, as darkness and depth, abyss, chasm, cave, grotto, maw, mouth, oven, dragon, etc. This entire symbolism, which we come across to this day in mysteries, myths, fairytales, dreams, fantasies, and poems, is a highly meaningful variation on the symbol of the uterus as the place of origin. It has its negative character—as hell—to the extent that the unconscious is the source of the unconscious powers that devour consciousness. But the same symbolism, for instance, the uterus as a place of mystery and revelation, has a highly positive character wherever the creative force of the unconscious gives birth to new contents.

The original attachment to nature in the Old Testament led to divine visions on earth, both in the process of individual destiny and in the people's historical process, that is, it led to the projection of the unconscious into reality. In the period of the apocalypse and Gnosticism, however, the human structure underwent a change, in that consciousness moved sharply away from the unconscious. The dissociation between these systems became so extreme that the powers of the unconscious only seldom extended into the here and now, and this world became a far more isolated world of consciousness.

Previously, in the tension between YHWH and earth, the two faces of the unconscious appeared entirely in this world and were resolved there, but since then, these two sides have moved further apart, which seems to have set free both human consciousness and the world of the here and now. This world is set free, a fact that expresses itself in that the divine influence no longer appears with the plastic immediacy of a theophany, as it did, for instance, with the angels whom Abraham invited for a meal. The divine retreat into the world of heaven and hell is a retreat into the invisible. Not that the reality of those worlds means less to a person living in these times than the reality of the angels did to Abraham in the story, but it is another, more psychic, form of reality.

It is as if the character of what we now regard as a psychic quality, as the unconscious, moved inward only gradually, as diverse stages of projection unfolded. Originally, this unconscious influence was cloaked in the character of the outer world, like a thing[30] of the world. Later, it still had a worldly character, but now, as belonging to the other world, it was concrete like a world of objects[31] but independent of this world. Later still, it appears in our time as a psychic world, that is, as an objective inner world, once again with the character of the world, namely, of an object-world that exists independent of the subject, the collective unconscious, except that now it is projected into the inner space, the psychic space, and no longer, as before, into the outer space of the world.

In innumerable creation myths, the son separates the cohabiting primordial parents and places the father as a heaven above himself, and the mother as an earth beneath himself.[32] According to the same archetype, around this time human history once placed the unconscious as a hell beneath itself and another time as a heaven above itself. In the middle, between these polar influences of the two-sided unconscious, stands the human being in this world, with consciousness and its world. As a result, as we have seen, the situation of the world had to be interpreted as both a distancing of heaven and a strengthening of the demons, that is, as being influenced more and more by the negative aspect of the unconscious.

This constellation of the collective unconscious underlies the entire period. It is evident both in Gnosticism and in the apocalypses. Both Gnosticism and Gnostic-influenced Christianity set themselves against hell, in the equation: world = body = matter; and, for heaven, in the equation: hereafter = consciousness = spirit. Against these, however, Judaism refuses to resolve YHWH's basic polarity, as in the opposition of YHWH and earth. Rather, it insists on a structure of YHWH that includes the two-sidedness of the world. "I am the Lord, and there is no other: I form light and create darkness, I make weal and create evil; I the Lord do all these things" (Is 45:7).[33] And then, advancing to the synthesis of the dual structure: "Shower, O heavens, from above, and let the skies rain down righteousness; let the earth open, that salvation may spring up, and let it cause righteousness to sprout up also; I the Lord have created it" (Is 45:8).[34]

This duality also becomes evident in the much-maligned materialism of the Jewish doctrine of resurrection, which insists on the resurrection of the *body*. It does not matter which paradoxical formulation this leads to, whether the reunification of souls and bodies, the awakening of the old body, or the formation of a new one. All these formulations just symbolize a commitment to the two-sidedness that began in creation and that still supports the world's existence. In other words, they represent the connection between the other-worldly spirit and the this-worldly body, the double aspect of both the world and YHWH.

The process of Gnostification unquestionably plays a major role in Judaism, especially in medieval Judaism. But as long as the tension between YHWH and the world is viewed as the energetic basis for the existence of the world and the individual, that is, as long as Judaism draws its most important life impulses from the tension between reality and possibility, the Gnostic answer to the problem of life, through sacrifice, cannot remain conclusive.

It is true that Judaism's increasingly ascetic and world-rejecting tendencies stand unconsciously under the sign of Gnosticism. But when Hasidism emerges, as a late but powerful movement, it shows that anti-Gnostic and anti-ascetic forces of life have become strong enough to assert themselves. Later, we shall explore the extent to which Gnostic themes once again appear, in a completely altered form, in Hasidism itself.

In this connection, we must not overlook how strongly the situation of exile predisposes Judaism toward the Gnostic worldview. All aspects of Gnosticism, which apply generally to the human being and his consciousness of being lost— existence in a foreign land, captivity, the fall, subjection to the rule of strangers, longing for homeland, being separated from origins, fragmentation—all of these and countless other Gnostic themes characterize not only Jewish existence in general, but also, very specifically, the facts of Jewish history. It is as if the Jewish exile had been put into the world to exemplify the Gnostic point of view. Similarly, it is no coincidence that the Gnostic theme of the king's lost son[35] is taken up, spun out, and repeated countless times by Jewish midrash.

Within Judaism, what worked against this extraordinary Gnostic threat was everything that was misunderstood on the Gnostic–Christian side as works righteousness, materialism, and enslavement by the law. If we have tried to trace the contrast in ancient Judaism between the orientation of prophetic introversion and the dependence of materialist, pagan extraversion, and if we have had to consider how fateful the exclusion of inner experience was for the religious existence of Judaism, then we must also do justice to the other side for its important role in preserving the substance.

2. Shrinking the tension between YHWH and earth: The anti-Gnostic threat

The apocalypse certainly represents a positive religious breakthrough in Judaism, the breakthrough of direct inner experience. But it also poses a Gnostic danger, the danger of intuition, with its substance-dissolving character.

The moment when Hebrew prophecy, with its reality-critical, counter-empirical nature, presented its new revelation as a new demand, new change and new development to the weakened substance of the people's foundation, that is, the moment when ancient Judaism lost its nature-bound overemphasis on the earth, at that moment the prophetic–apocalyptic irruption could become the greatest threat.

Working against this danger are the forces of Judaism that are attached to reality, those forces, the excessive growth of which had originally brought forth Hebrew prophecy as a counter-movement. With the destruction of the Temple and the downfall of the empire, that which had previously enhanced existence suddenly changed and became a danger, and what until now had prevented development, now preserved existence.

The exclusion of inner experience

The inner vitality of Judaism had once been supported by the conflict and cooperation of its different positions, but this relationship changed fundamentally when the body politic began to decay. Just as a strong introversion in the balanced individual, one whose adaptation to reality is maintained and preserved, is not only unthreatening but leads to fruitful tensions, so the aggressive force of inner revelation, as represented by prophets and apocalyptic writers, enhances the development of a people whose reality is closely associated with nature, that is, a people possessing land and landscape, commerce and politics, customs and art.

But just as a strong introversion can have disastrous effects on a weak character, or one unadapted to reality, even leading to the disintegration of personality, so the preponderance of aggressive men of introspection may affect a people not rooted in reality, causing psychic epidemics and the downfall of the entire people.

For a people with a normal habitus, one that is rooted in the soil and existing independently, such psychic epidemics can usually be balanced out by the historical process. The regenerative powers of such a people, or of some of its parts, will gradually prevail. But things are different in the abnormal situation of the Jewish people.

In pseudo-messianic movements, the apocalyptic tendency erupts violently and leads to mass movements, as happened, for example, with Sabbatai Sevi.[36] In that case, the subsequent collapse is so catastrophic that it literally challenges the people's continued existence.[37] To a decisive extent, the Jews lacked the counterbalance that was put up against corresponding chiliastic movements in the west. There, thanks to their natural situation, large segments of the population did not need the world either to open up or to change; they were sufficiently stabilized (or, as one says today, saturated) here on earth.

For the Jews, with their negative experience of history, any existential certainty was stigmatized as provisional, and every apocalyptic situation that promised to cancel the exile, the basis of inner and outer provisionality, had to be generally affirmed, so that it ended in a mass movement, seizing the entire people. Once the messianic situation turned out to be pseudo-messianic, however, this willingness to give up the conditions of actual existence as merely provisional had disastrous consequences. It left the people not only disappointed in their expectation of salvation but also disillusioned about the circumstances of actual existence. Their willingness to give up these circumstances made their situation of exile more transparent, and, along with that, it exposed the hopeless provisionality of Jewish existence as a whole.

It is not our task to trace in detail how these setbacks led in part to nihilism. Nor would this be possible, because, apart from some few hints in this direction on the topic of Sabbateanism and Frankism,[38] the sectarian movements that led to a falling away toward Islam and Christianity,[39] these developments have remained completely unresearched, as have many other developments within Judaism. It is only important for us to see how all these trends and developments came to be synthesized and overcome in Hasidism.

The forces preserving the people were needed now to curb all those inner powers that would have shaken the existence of the people to its foundation, which anyway was merely artificially maintained. This development, which began after the Babylonian exile and became prominent after the destruction of the Temple,[40] is to some extent the positive side of Judaism. Even the cessation of revelation with Ezra and Nehemiah should not be seen simply as a result of the rigidity that follows when any church is formed. Nor does it merely reflect a Jewish over-emphasis on the earth. Rather, once again, in the face of the weakened existential situation, it corresponds to the tendency to preserve substance; thus it amounts to a form of national discipline.

Law and rabbinism

Even the strengthening and development of the *halakha*, the lawful regulation of everyday conduct, is more than a symptom of rigidity in rules and carefully thought-out ways of acting. Glatzer rightly observes: "The kingdom of God, whose assertion is opposed by contemporary history, finds its realm in the quasi-private sphere of human life. Thus, the *halakha* constitutes a domain that confesses its absolute commitment to the kingdom of God and regards itself as the nucleus of the messianic kingdom."[41]

This development can readily be followed in the assessment of the *bat kol*.[42] After the end of official prophecy, the *bat kol*, the daughter voice or heavenly voice, was still at first a form of direct revelation, which from time to time passed judgment in specific cases and intervened correctively as a higher authority (*Bab Tlm: Yoma* 9b).[43] The *bat kol* rose above the law, and "what it pronounced, even if it opposed explicit provisions of the law, was deemed sacred and binding."[44]

A diametrically opposed spirit speaks in the following passage, which clearly emphasizes the rejection of direct revelation:[45]

> On that day R. Eliezer brought forth every imaginable argument, but they did not accept them. [. . .] Again he said to them: "If the *halahah* agrees with me, let it be proved from Heaven!" Whereupon a Heavenly Voice cried out: "Why do ye dispute with R. Eliezer, seeing that in all matters the *halahah* agrees with him!" But R. Joshua arose and exclaimed: "*It is not in heaven.*"[46] [. . .] We pay no attention to a Heavenly Voice, because Thou hast long since written in the Torah at Mount Sinai, *After the majority must one incline*[47] (*Bab Tlm: Baba Mezia* 59b).[48]

Besides the tremendous danger that it poses, this rejection of direct revelation, this "repudiation of YHWH,"[49] which later prompted deliberations on whether the *bat kol* should not be regarded as soothsaying and therefore prohibited, also has an extremely positive aspect.

At a time when the revelatory relationship is disturbed and almost abolished, the original covenantal character, which once constituted the basic relationship between YHWH and the people, has now been converted into law. The unified consciousness of the majority of teachers, the national elite, is said to be the immanent seat of divinity, which not even this group is capable of dethroning. This sacral awe before the highest form of human consciousness, as represented by most of the great teachers, also means something completely different from democracy: human consciousness here appears as God's partner. The synthetic act of the human–God relationship is now interpretation, the conscious elucidation of the God-given Torah. Only thus should the words allegedly spoken by YHWH, when he suffered a similar rejection, be understood: "My children have defeated me. They are in the right."[50]

The primacy of consciousness rests on the fundamental teaching of Judaism, which places the conscious person's responsibility for the people, humanity, and the world at the center of world history. From this source, it draws its moral vigor, but equally its radical hostility toward all the dark wisdom of paganism and toward the uncontrollable influence that delivers a weak consciousness to the superior power of the unconscious. This primacy of consciousness also subjects the bearer of revelation, the prophet, to control by reality, and to the strength and clarity of consciousness, for, as we have seen, the ranks of prophecy are ordered such that the clearer consciousness is, the higher the inspirational rank, whereas dream states and twilight states occupy the lowest rank. Ranked highest, however, and embodied in Moses, is conversation with God in the waking state, by day, in the clearest state of consciousness.

This dignity of human consciousness, against all the transpersonal forces that rise from the unconscious and claim to show the way, has very serious implications in an age of limited consciousness and flooding by the unconscious. Primitive psychology is characterized by the constant endeavor to protect the small light of consciousness against the overwhelming influences of the unconscious. Similarly, an age that is threatened by Gnosticism must safeguard the integrity of teaching and consciousness against the danger of unchecked direct revelations. Although this is a positive part of the development of any church, it tends to degenerate into dogmatic paralysis and the repression of all new revelation as heresy.

But within Judaism, deprived of its natural foundation, this danger became almost a historical necessity, when the law became an artificial seedbed. Talmudism is the successful attempt, although at the cost of untold victims, to turn the world of laws into a construction replacing the natural basis. With this world of laws, the Jewish people could continue to exist without losing its character as a people. The greatness of this attempt, unique in human history, to place a people's existence entirely on an intellectual basis, has never been quite understood, because only the artificiality of its methods was seen, and never the heroic nature of the venture.

The life of the Jewish people spans several millennia and is still developing. Here, the attempt is made, through interpretation, to fold the people's life backward into the given, revealed world of the law, and also, using a highly artificial interpretation of the law, to maintain a lively contact between the old revelation and the changed necessities of everyday life. On the face of it, this effort is characterized largely by formalism and word splitting, but behind these is a wholly different endeavor, a recognition of the world and of history as an unfolding revelation, to be understood with the interpretive help of human consciousness. Thus, there is a tireless movement back and forth between daily necessity and revelatory text, between textual passage and everyday life, in an ongoing effort to tighten the weave of the world-penetrating revelation.

This is not the place to show how all of this became bogged down, or how primordial forces and counterforces were activated, especially in the Kabbalah. But it is important to observe that for the Jewish person the galut involved, inevitably, a disastrous loss of instinct. There was a gradual falling away from the great affinity of the *Tanakh*[51] with nature and with the whole abundance of plastic forces,[52] as seen in the struggle between prophetic introversion and a pagan-extraverted attachment to the world. The Jewish people had belonged unconsciously to the natural world, their destiny influenced by the passage of seasons, landscapes, elements, and festivals, shaping people through their self-evident embeddedness in natural life. Now, to the degree that the Jewish destiny became more and more a matter of foreign landscapes, changing countries, and life in cities and ghettoes, this unconscious integration into the natural world was lost.

Despite all attempts at assimilation, the profoundest desire of which was to quench this thirst for nature and the homeland, what emerged was a form of secondary nomadism. For behind every attempt to settle down lurked the compulsion to continue wandering, and over every deep breath of rest hung the threat of expulsion.

Here and there, in many places and among many peoples, long periods of rest permitted the Jew to strike seemingly firm roots. But this hardly mattered, for, wherever it happened, in Palestine or Spain, Russian Poland or Germany, even if a new instinctive wave surged, releasing creative forces, the people's experience, the historical experience of deep pain caused by tearing up roots, always hovered in the background, as a warning and an anxiety, behind all the joy of being settled.

This continuous inner state of war, the constant compulsion to hold one's consciousness tightly and observe one's neighbors with care, to know when they would be ready to break out and sate themselves on the blood of Jews, this tense consciousness on the part of the whole people, lasting for thousands of years, decisively reshaped its character.

The ways of presenting themselves that the Jewish people assumed and lost, to be replaced with new ones, were exceedingly varied and highly individual, and we cannot begin to give an account of them. In a general way, however, it can be stated—with a few important exceptions—that the oppositions we traced in the Old Testament under the symbol of YHWH–earth tension, oppositions that became deeper for the post-exilic apocalyptic writers, now fell apart, and the substance of Jewish existence dwindled as a result.

The loss of earth, inner and outer

On the one hand, what followed was a "stepping out of history," a total renunciation of any national, secular, political ambition. With the loss of land, state, and natural rootedness in this world, the course of history became irrelevant for Judaism. Until the arrival of the last days, which would reverse this loss, the historical situation was merely provisional, based on the sacrifice of the natural, external world. The external world shrank down to everyday life, to the sheer necessity of continuing to live, and to establishing the outer possibilities of survival, individually and collectively. The orientation to this world was fed, to be sure, by the small trickle of a constructed relationship with the revealed law. But it lacked ideas and development; it was haphazard and rootless, corresponding to the now emerging secondary nomadism, over which always hung the destiny of provisionality.

Passing through a church state of priestly theocracy, the original theocratic tendency had regressed to a pragmatic fulfillment of the Law. Behind this, originally, was the attempt to bring theocracy into everyday life on a purely spiritual basis. The moment the law became the basis of national, ethnic, economic, and religious existence, all together, this attempt was bound to rigidify, and the theocratic motive retreated behind the pragmatic one.

Beside this loss of the outer world, however, stands a parallel loss of the inner world, because inner revelation had been excluded and the consciousness of increasing decline was equated with the decline of God's direct relationship with Israel. The guilt leading to the galut had made a new revelatory relationship between YHWH and the people impossible. Only the old revelation remained valid, and anything and everything had to be related to it.

This cut-off was possible, insofar as it could be enforced, thanks to the very fact that the galut made a regression to the collective inevitable. A religious individualism had already begun to emerge before the destruction of the Second Temple, compensating for the priestly theocracy. At the same time, the wave of apocalypticism had broken forth from within. But the destruction of the collective foundation now led to a violent recollectivizing, for this alone made it possible for the people to go on existing.

To "hear" direct revelation presupposes that one is securely embedded in the depth of the collective, and at the same time that one is naturally related to nature and its stillness. It is no coincidence that the life of the shepherd, the solitary figure in nature, is the prophet's great, perennial situation, from the tribal patriarchs to Joseph, and from Moses to David and Amos.

To a substantial extent, the loss of this relatedness also meant the loss of hearing, that is, of direct revelation as originally understood by Hebrew prophecy. Inner experience now became dangerously individual, no longer being embedded in the people and the landscape, and isolation prevailed. On this basis, the increasing rejection of inner revelation is easier to understand. It means, however, that what consciousness gained in intensity, the inner dimension lost in depth. Now, for the first time, with the loss of the compensatory experience of earth, nature, and world, the Jewish person became predominantly rationalistic and moralistic, and his spiritual emphasis turned into intellectualism.

Secondary nomadism, in its situation of rootlessness, attempted to create an artificial basis of existence in doctrine, which emerged as a substitute for the land, for *Eretz Israel*. Thus, it radicalized "life in foreign lands,"[53] making it impossible to reconcile the opposition between spirit and earth.

Of particular importance in this respect is the loss of the feminine side of consciousness in favor of radical masculinization, an extreme emphasis on active and rational components. This is particularly evident with regard to introversion. Originally, Judaism had consciously emphasized an inner, feminine stance toward the irradiating impulse and the word of God. This stance had been symbolized most strongly in the image of the people as the bride of God.[54] This attitude of stillness, maintaining silence and preparing oneself for inner experience, poses no contradiction to the active assimilation and realization that are then demanded, but this attitude now began to disappear. Even introversion became active, speculative, and rational, geared toward working through what was found, rather than being expanded by a new thing breaking in.

It is difficult to give an overview of this process in relation to the outer world, for what was lost was the capacity to be shaped by the landscape, by history, and by the world. To be sure, the repeated accomplishment of active adaptation was an incredible achievement, but with that came a barely conceivable seclusion from the world, within which Judaism existed as an enclave. Constantly assimilating to a new environment, and actively appropriating the foreign world into one's own, never led to being fundamentally transformed by this foreign world. After all, in its existential plight, the Jewish people had to reject any transformation by the foreign as a threat of destruction. And, at the same time, it had to seek to develop the capacity for active reception. This masculinizing of Judaism, in the sense of active receptivity, as a symptom of its loss of the outer and inner world, led to the suppression of every affirmation of feeling and of nature, and produced the extremely rigorous and grim attitude toward the world that is generally confused with Jewishness as such.

With the curbing of introversion and the loss of the world, the mind becomes aligned more and more with the conscious principle. At the same time, the law is emphasized, and masculine aspects are valued more and more highly. Having heaped all values upon the intellect, what followed was the strongest possible repression of the opposite principle. Nature, world, earth, and woman were progressively repressed and negativized. The feminine assumed an increasingly Lilith-like character and became a demonic seducer, very much in the ascetic, Gnostic–Christian, world-denying sense.

This medievalism of the Jewish person and his subterranean Christianity cannot occupy us here. But it is important to reiterate that this medievalism was necessarily more radical and disastrous than that of the western peoples, for galut Judaism lacked, as a means of compensation, both the pagan foundation of these peoples and their shared attachment to the earth, which could not be entirely buried by

Christianization. Provided the life of a people is rooted in nature, even if state and trade, art, philosophy, and religion are forced to develop in certain directions, distorted, or refined, there is always the possibility, indeed the certainty, that compensation from the depths of the unconscious will break through in the individual and the collective. Not even a church can completely obstruct the living stream of inner revelation, which blazes a path for itself in counter-movements and ultimately, despite all, transforms the character of the collective.

In the case of the Jewish people's foundation, diminished by the loss of the inner and outer world, this natural movement of the pendulum, which governs every people's development by the opposition of forces, could be allowed only small oscillations. Otherwise, the people's whole existential foundation would have been threatened with collapse.

A certain balance, which prevented the disaster of paralysis, was achieved by the people's breaking up into many parts, scattered over many countries, the different developmental paths of which stimulated each other's growth. On the other hand, powerful horizontal movements, such as the messianic movements or the Kabbalah, which seized all parts of the people at once, prevented the people as a whole from becoming too decentralized.

The loss of instinctive ties, together with an over-emphasis on the conscious principle, inevitably brought about an extensive loss of relationship with that part of the collective unconscious that all peoples find projected in nature.

Heaven and earth, water source and stone, lightning and storm, these are never anonymous things. Rather, they possess, for every people, the specific character of belonging, as shown in the designations "mine" and "ours." Thus, through the projection of the people's own essential contents, the changed natural object is experienced from within. Above all, earth here is not earth, but the earth of *Eretz Israel*, into which an endless stream of relatedness has entered, from the patriarchs to the destruction of the Second Temple. Only the longing of the patriarchs and their wanderings, the people's conquests, battles, and defeats, the buried ancestors and the blood that was shed, the Canaanite influence, the resacralization in cult and law, only all of this, from the pagan cultic dances around the tree on the high place to the cave in Carmel where Elijah hid, all these currents of the libido and history of the people caused the earth archetype, which lives as a primary matrix[55] in the collective unconscious, to become a Jewish reality, which says: our land and our earth.

And so it is with everything else. It is not that one must knowingly perform an act of historical remembrance here, but all of this resonates in the unconscious, giving background and substance and the mysterious element of belonging and relation, which is the only basis of a real experience. Of the irrational forces that become visible in feeling, a substantial part is nurtured by this numinous attachment linking the individual and the people with the homeland, with whose history they have been connected since time immemorial.

A significant layer of archetypal contents consists of natural symbols and is experienced unconsciously through their projection onto natural objects. The natural object seems to have no specific character of its own, and it ought to be irrelevant whether an oak or a sycamore, for instance, symbolizes the tree. In reality, however, this is not so. As is well known, the fixation on childhood impressions plays a major role in this regard, because an abundance of formative influences is finalized during this stage of life, in which the collective unconscious is especially plastic. But over and beyond the personal dimension of a single life, every people possesses its primal experiences, activated in customs and practices, art and history, fairytales and legends, which form an unmistakable canon of original symbolism.

3. The secret victory of the mother archetype[56]

The early stages of every religion abound with sacred places, stones and water sources, trees and mountains, which constitute, in their totality, the specific animation of local nature. Religious development in the Old Testament had tried to overcome this numinous relationship with nature, but only a one-sided theological orientation fails to recognize that behind monotheism a background of living places and symbols always remained at work. Abraham's tree, Rachel's tomb, the mountains of Gilboa, the waters of Gideon, an endless web of lived relationships lay on the entire land and entered naturally into every symbol that emerged from the unconscious, into the prophets' images and the teachers' midrashim.

With the galut, all of this became remote and an object of yearning. Over the foreign nature in which the Jew was forced to live fell the ban and taboo of hostility and expulsion, as the Talmud tells us in this uncanny sentence: "When a person walks in a field and studies, and then interrupts his study and says, 'What a beautiful tree this is,' he is guilty of death."[57]

The dominance of rational consciousness

The defense against the overwhelming mother archetype spread from YHWH's dominance to a radical attempt at repression, assisted by the prophetic emphasis on consciousness. The mother archetype, however, retained its vitality for a long time, because its unconscious projection onto earth, Zion or Israel, provided the necessary counterweight to the emphasis on ethical consciousness. Reality, as a natural given, whether consisting of economic and political circumstances or of the people's prevailing nature, always softened YHWH's fatherly claim, to the extent that the contrast turned into a fruitful interplay between complementary pairs of forces.

Later, when the fullness of life was lost, the principle of consciousness became radically dominant and was restricted to the rational principle, whereas the feminine aspect was consciously excluded. Once this had happened, as always in such cases, there followed a terrible subterranean revenge. Banished entirely into the unconscious, the mother archetype crept secretly, thus doubly dangerously, into the purely masculine world of Judaism. This was doubly dangerous, of course, because being unaware of danger also makes a counter-reaction impossible.

Whenever primordial forces are driven out of the conscious sphere, they re-enter that sphere in an altered guise from the background, except that now, tainted by the negative conscious attitude, they also reveal their negative aspects.

The Torah and the mother archetype

Under the rule of Torah—that is, the law, which gradually comes to mean the dogma of the law—there follows a decline toward the mother archetype. This decline is masked, however, by the teaching, placed in the foreground, that YHWH's will is being carried out.

In this process, the typically masculine mode of YHWH's activity, its revolutionary, irruptive power, disruptive to consciousness, was lost. With the dogma of the law began the new rule of the mother archetype, encompassing, nurturing, intoxicating, infantilizing, and castrating toward active expansion.

Just as turning the figure of Moses into a priest obscured his prophethood, the fact that the dogma, as law, bore or seemed to bear YHWH's impress impeded the insight that the dangerous mother goddess, in a new guise—dangerous because she prevented the development of consciousness—had victoriously taken over the Jewish people. The mother archetype always represents the conservative attitude of preserving the status quo. This is something taught by every church, concretizing the mother archetype. By contrast, YHWH's irruptive force—like every principle that urges toward the expansion of consciousness—seeks constant change, flexibility, and readiness for combat.

The highly complicated nature of Jewish development resided in the fact that the apparent radicalization of the masculine principle, involving the loss of feminine counterforces (people, home, earth), necessarily led to the unconscious intrusion of the feminine aspect, because without it no life is possible.

This feminine aspect was projected onto the Torah, the law, which was supposed to form the basis of the people's life, taking the place of its natural basis. Over the millennia, however, the growing prevalence of the law over YHWH's prophetic authority, that is, the gradual ascendance of the mother archetype and its devouring of the Jewish people, proceeded entirely unconsciously. One might even say that it proceeded on the opposite premise.

Being unconsciously devoured by the dragon of the Torah stands under the theme of YHWH's rule of consciousness. And in exactly the same way, the attempt in our present day to reactivate the principle of YHWH follows from the conscious theme of activating the unconscious, the mother archetype.

How the principle of YHWH became latent

In Judaism, the feminine aspect of creativity, the "feminine part of the deity," is not symbolized by the Torah, but by the *Shekhinah*.[58]

With the destruction of the Second Temple and the expulsion of Israel into the galut, it is said that the *Shekhinah*, the indwelling presence of God in Israel, the personified feminine aspect of the deity, also goes into the galut and wails for reunion. This symbol seems to contain the key problem of all Jewish existence. For this separation of the lamenting and banished *Shekhinah* from the divine, this separation of the lamenting and banished Israel from YHWH, symbolizes and expresses the disastrous fact that galut-Judaism is disconnected from its creative primal ground.

This separation, corresponding psychologically to the dissociation of consciousness from the primal creative powers of the collective unconscious, was expressed symptomatically within Judaism by the exclusion of direct religious experience and also by the provisional paralysis of adherence to the law.

But a great movement of awakening, still unrealized by Judaism, prepared the decisive revolution of Judaism in which we stand today. This movement, which broadly delineates directions of inner rebirth, is Hasidism.

Notes

1 *EN*: See Jonas, *Gnosis*, op. cit. [Apparently referring to the whole first volume of Jonas's work.] (Cf. above, *Roots I*, p. 88, n. 52.)

2 *EN*: On the history of the Gnostic influence on Judaism, particularly on the Kabbalah, see the writings of Gershom Scholem. Due to its inaccessible nature, non-specialists have left aside the entire problem of the Kabbalah, which is unquestionably of crucial importance for our problem of inner revelation. [In the present work, Neumann refers only sparingly to Scholem's already voluminous writings on Jewish mysticism, most of them published in Hebrew. This comment on the neglect of the Kabbalah clearly paraphrases Scholem's introduction to his 1936/1937 essay, "Zum Verständnis des Sabbatianismus" ("Understanding Sabbateanism"), cited below.]

3 *tehom*: Hebrew, "the deep." Tiamat was also the Babylonian name of the female chaos monster. The two words are linguistically connected.

4 No source is cited. Neumann would have known Jung's discussion of Khidr as a Self-symbol, which describes the ego's response to "the superior guidance of the self" (cf. CW 9i, ¶247).

5 Possibly referring to Jung's *Beziehungen*, which Neumann frequently cites elsewhere. Cf. CW 7, *Two Essays*, "Preface to the 2nd edition," p. 123; also ¶341f. and ¶398. Another source familiar to Neumann at the time of writing was Jung's *Wandlungen*, especially Chapter 7, "Das Opfer" ("The sacrifice"). (Cf. CW 5, *Symbols of Transformation*, especially ¶91 and ¶669).

6 In Jung's terminology, the archetype of the Self is variously described as the transcendent function, the God-image in the psyche, or the supra-personal center of the personality, which calls the individual to wholeness. (Cf. also notes 8 and 9 below.) It should be noted that here, in Neumann's first mention of the Self, it is discussed in relation to the ego. Neumann's ground-breaking concept, the ego–Self (or Self–ego) axis, is anticipated in this work. (Cf., for example, "*Ruach* and *Tiferet* as ego–Self," *Roots II*, pp. 81ff.)

7 *EN*: See Jonas, "Das Lied von der Perle." [Cf. *Gnosis*, pp. 320–8.]

8 *EN*: See Jung, *Wandlungen*, op. cit. [Neumann may have in mind a passage comparing Mithras and Christ to the sun (1925 edition, pp. 96ff.; CW 5 ¶156ff.). No references to the "pearl" or the "Self," as such, appear in the first three editions of *Wandlungen*, which remained unchanged from 1912 through 1937, but the revised fourth edition refers to the pearl (CW5, *Symbols of Transformation*, 1953, ¶509f.). When writing the present work, Neumann may have seen an early draft of that passage.]

9 *EN*: Cf. *Beziehungen*, op. cit. [Jung's theory of the Self emerges in his 1928 edition, pp. 203ff, where he writes, in Hull's translation: "I have called this centre the self.... the self has as much to do with the ego as the sun with the earth" (CW 7, *Two Essays*, ¶399f).]

10 *EN*: Apuleius, *The Golden Ass*. [In Apuleius's narrative, Psyche's ordeals lead to her deification. This archetypal story was later explored by Neumann in his 1956 monograph,
Amor and Psyche.]

11 *Ent-Persönlichung* (*Entpersönlichung*): Neumann adds a hyphen, evidently for emphasis.

12 *EN*: Evans-Wentz, *Yoga und Geheimlehren Tibets* (*Yoga and the secret teachings of Tibet*), cf.
especially Book 3. [The third book is titled *Der Pfad des Wissens: Der Yoga der sechs Lehren*
(*The Way of Knowledge: The yoga of the six teachings*).]

13 *EN*: *Das tibetanische Totenbuch* (*The Tibetan book of the dead*), ed. Evans-Wentz. With an
introduction by C. G. Jung. [Jung's introduction, titled "Psychological Commentary,"
includes this passage, in Hull's translation: "In the initiation of the living, . . . this 'Beyond'
is not a world beyond death, but a reversal of the mind's intentions and outlook, a psychological 'Beyond' or, in Christian terms, a 'redemption' from the trammels of the world
and of sin. Redemption is a separation and deliverance from an earlier condition of darkness and unconsciousness, and leads to a condition of illumination and releasedness, to
victory and transcendence over everything 'given'" (Evans-Wentz, ed., 1960, pp. xl–xli).
Cf. also CW 11, ¶841.]

14 In Tibetan Buddhist teaching, the "primary clear light" appears at the moment of death
(ibid., Book I, Part I, pp. 89ff).

15 On the ultimate irredeemability of evil, cf. IV Esra 7:102 through 8:62 (Kautzsch, op. cit.,
1900, pp. 376–83).

16 *der anderen Seite*: an oblique reference to Jung's concept of the shadow, which the ego
views as negative, and as other.

17 *Weltseite*: when discussing psychological orientations toward interior or exterior reality,
Neumann often uses nouns based on *Seite* (lit. "side," "aspect"). (Cf. above, *Roots I*, p. 19,
n. 18.) Here, *Weltseite* (lit. "world aspect") refers to the material dimension or outer reality.

18 Buber's theme of encounter and dialogue is central to his 1923 work, *Ich und Du* (*I and
thou*). His view of the separation between the divine and the human is, however, more
paradoxical than Neumann implies here. Alluding to two of Rudolf Otto's concepts,
Buber writes: "Of course, God is 'the wholly other'; but he is also the wholly same: the
wholly present. Of course, he is the *mysterium tremendum* that appears and overwhelms;
but he is also the mystery of the obvious that is closer to me than my own I" (Buber, *I
and Thou*, op. cit., p. 127).

19 *EN*: See above, p. 60. [*Roots I*, p. 37, "The Affirmation of Nature and Nature's Purity."]

20 *EN*: Puech, "Der Begriff der Erlösung im Manischaeismus" ("The concept of redemption in Manicheism"), *EJ 1936*. [Puech's lecture is in three parts, pp. 183–286. Despite
Neumann's quotation marks, the above statement does not appear verbatim; but similar
content occurs on pp. 239f. and p. 243.]

21 Cf. "Life in this world," *Roots II*, pp. 90ff.

22 *EN*: See above, p. 133, n. 3 [*Roots I*, p. 93, n. 85. Neumann quotes from Wünsche, *Aus
Israels Lehrhallen*, v. 3, pp. 214ff.]

23 Wünsche, 1907, op. cit., pp. 214f. [Cf. *Midrash Tanhuma Yelammedenu*, Chapter 11 (Ex
38:21–40:38), "These Are the Accounts," section 3: "At that time the Holy One, blessed
be He, says to the soul: Enter the semen that is in this one's hand. The soul opens its
mouth and cries out: 'Master of the Universe, I have always been satisfied with the place
in which I dwelt from the day you created me, why do You desire that I enter this putrid
drop? Now I am holy and pure, but then I will be cut off from the place of Thy glory.'
Thereupon the Holy One, blessed be He, replied: The place which you are to enter is
better for you than the place where you have dwelt. From the moment I created you it
was only for this drop of semen" (p. 654, trans. by Berman).]

24 Ibid., pp. 215f. [Paraphrased from *Midrash Tanhuma Yelammedenu*, op. cit.: "You know, my
son, that you were formed against your will; against your will you will be born; against
your will you will die; and against your will you are destined to give an accounting
before the King of Kings, the Holy One, blessed be He" (p. 656, trans. by Berman).]

25 Cf. above, *Roots I*, p. 101, n. 123.

26 Charlesworth, v. 1, p. 78.

27 Ibid, p. 640.

28 Cf. above, "The Near East and the significance of the Mother Goddess," *Roots I,* pp. 15ff.

29 *EN:* Volz, p. 328. [Volz writes: "One knows how large *Gehinnom* is, namely, sixty times greater than Eden, 216,000 times greater than earth; thus earth behaves toward hell 'as the lid does toward the pot.' One can therefore say: the size of hell is beyond all measure."]

30 *Dingwesen:* lit. "thing-being." Mark Kyburz advises that this term is found in the works of Husserl and Heidegger, commonly translated "thing."

31 *Objektwelt:* lit. "object-world." Noted by Mark Kyburz as a Heideggerian term.

32 Neumann's generalization holds in many ancient cosmologies, but not in the Egyptian, where the sky is symbolized as a female figure.

33 Neumann quotes the 1934 B&R translation, with slight changes: "ICH [JHWH] bins und keiner sonst: der das Licht bildet und die Finsternis schafft, der den Frieden macht und das Übel [Böse] schafft. ICH [JHWH] bins, der all dies macht." B&R systematically use capitalized personal pronouns in place of the Tetragrammaton (YHWH), a choice that Neumann does not imitate. He also changes their "Übel" to "Böse" (arguably a more emphatic word for "evil"). "Böse" is a word that Jung often uses, in contexts that overlap with Neumann's, for example, his 1940 Eranos lecture on the Trinity (cf. CW 11, ¶247).

34 Neumann's quotation diverges significantly from the B&R edition.

35 Cf. *Roots II,* pp. 46ff.: "The Theory of Sparks."

36 Sabbatai Sevi (Zevi) (1626–1676): Rabbi and Kabbalist of Spanish descent, born in Smyrna. He traveled as a would-be messiah to Salonica, Cairo, and Constantinople, where he converted to Islam. He died in Smyrna. The Sabbatean movement continued after his death as a heretical sect within Judaism. (Cf. G. Scholem, *Sabbatai Sevi: The Mystical Messiah,* 1973.)

37 *EN:* Mentioned in Scholem, *Schocken Almanach 5697.* [G. Scholem, 1936/37, "Zum Verständnis des Sabbatianismus" ("Understanding Sabbateanism"), op. cit., pp. 36f. *The Schocken Almanach* was founded in Berlin in 1933 by the publisher, Salman Schocken, and moved to Jerusalem in 1939.]

38 Movement named for Jacob Frank (1726–1791), a Polish Sabbatean leader, who traveled and taught, claiming to be the reincarnation of Sabbatai Sevi. He rejected the Talmud, embraced elements of Christianity, and was expelled by Jewish authorities in Poland.

39 *EN:* Scholem 1936/37, op. cit., p. 37.

40 Referring to the Second Temple, destroyed in 70 CE.

41 *EN:* Glatzer, op. cit., p. 44.

42 Hebrew: lit. "daughter of a voice," or echo.

43 In the *Bab Tlm: Yoma* 9b, we read: "After the later prophets Haggai, Zechariah, and Malachi had died, the Holy Spirit departed from Israel, but they still availed themselves of the Bath Kol" (*Bab Tlm: Yoma,* trans. by L. Jung, Soncino).

44 *EN:* Homburger, "Bath-Kol," *Real-Enzyklopedie,* v. 2. [Citation not found. *Paulys Realencyklopädie* has no entry for "Bath-Kol."]

45 Neumann introduces the passage with a summary, identifying the rabbi in the story: "When Elieser ben Hirkanos could not make his opinion prevail, in a dispute over a questionable legal interpretation, he called on the judgment of heaven . . . ." The remainder of the quotation is more or less consistent with the Talmudic passage.

46 Neumann omits a portion of this passage, in which it is explained that the Torah has been given at Mount Sinai and therefore is no longer in heaven. (Cf. Deut 30:12.)

47 Neumann explains, paraphrasing: ". . . the Law expressly orders that, in doubtful matters, the decision shall accord with majority vote."

48 *Bab Tlm: Baba Mezia,* trans. by H. Freedman, Soncino.

49 *EN:* Bergel, *Mythologie der alten Hebräer,* v. 1, p. 9 [Neumann slightly paraphrases this passage: "The law is only given to the inhabitants of the earth, and only they can decide on it by means of a majority / in such cases no attention should be paid to the *bat kol*

[heavenly voice]' (*Baba Mezia*, 59b). Later on, YHWH also often had to put up with such rejection. On one such occasion, he said: 'My children have defeated me. They are in the right'."]

50 Ibid. The final line from Bergel's passage, quoted above, paraphrases a statement in the *Bab Tlm: Baba Mezia*, 59b, op. cit.

51 Hebrew: holy writings; Bible. The word is based on the initial letters of the words naming the three major parts of the scriptures: *Torah* (law), *Nevi'im* (prophets), and *Ketuvim* (writings).

52 *plastische Kräfte*: Neumann's meaning is not immediately clear. "Plastic" may be meant in the sense of "physical" or "natural."

53 "*Seins in der Fremde*": the phrase may be Neumann's. No citation is given.

54 Cf., for example, Isaiah 62:56.

55 *Nurmatrize*: compound German noun, formed from *nur* ("only") and *Matrize* ("matrix," "mother-form," related to the French word *matrice*, "womb").

56 Cf. above, *Roots I*, pp. 15ff., "The Near East and the significance of the Mother Goddess"; p. 41, paragraph beginning, "The exclusion of the feminine principle from the cult"; pp. 62ff., "YHWH and the Mother Goddess." Cf. also Jung, "Psychological Aspects of the Mother Archetype" (*EJ 1938*, pp. 403–44; CW 9.i, 4).

57 The saying occurs in *Pirke Avot* (*Sayings of the Fathers*) 3:7: "Rabbi Yaakov said, 'Were one to be walking on the road while studying and then stop one's studies to say, "How beautiful is this tree! or "How nice is that field!" such a person would be considered by the Torah to have sinned against one's own soul" (*Pirke Avot: A Modern Commentary on Jewish Ethics*. Ed. and trans., L. Karaviz and K. M. Olitzky, p. 40).

58 Cf. above, *Roots I*, p. 81 and note.

4

AUTHOR'S APPENDICES

Appendix I: Methodology   138
Appendix II: The foundation stone and the waters of the deep   140
Appendix III: The composition of the Pentateuch   144
Appendix IV: Earth and the symbols of the elements   147
  Wind symbolism   148
  Body-soul and blood   150
  Earth and bull   153
  Circumcision and Passover   155
  Lilith   157

Appendix I: Methodology[1]

Our interpretation of the biblical text faces a difficult task, here and elsewhere, because we do not consider the text to be established by any historical-critical or text-critical theory of stratification, nor by any orthodox tradition of revelation. We consider the text to be psychologically real, and at the same time we attempt to understand it as a core text, that is, as the account of an original experience of the people, which has been worked through and worked on.[2] We do not ignore the existence of secondary, tendentious adaptations; we interpret these, too, as genuine psychic phenomena, worthy of serious inquiry.

Nor do we misunderstand the text allegorically. Rather, we understand its symbolic elements as giving information about the lived event or its experienced power, as the redactor[3] consciously or unconsciously imagined it. If biases are woven into the text, we do not focus on the supposedly disillusioning fact that this is a revision, in the sense of a distortion. Rather, we recognize in this reworking a genuine working through.

There is said to be a historical connection, for instance, between the account of the Golden Calf and the Israelite bull-worship that came much later. Although we accept this connection, we also see it as crucially important that a revelation that was unbearable for the people is presented here in connection with a regression, the worship of the Golden Calf. This connection among revelation, regression, and prophetic intervention is deliberate and historically credible, even if the symbolism of regression has been taken from a later historical period and juxtaposed with the much earlier revelation on Sinai.

Now, this Sinai account may be the secondary mythologization of an older core narrative. The genius of this account is, however, that the problem of the people's emergence was seen together with the problem of revelation, and the redactor, understanding this problem as a politically topical phenomenon of his time, gave it historical force.

The legitimacy and limits of symbolic interpretation in the Old Testament would need a study of its own,[4] which would have to devise a methodology for the psychological interpretation of texts. Our work favors a structural interpretation, that is, an interpretation that analyzes events and the attitudes evident in them. For this psychological interpretation, cultural–historical and historical aspects are primary, but, in addition, the relationship between consciousness and the unconscious is also central. Our analysis of the texts focuses on this relationship in particular, because Judaism itself emphasizes the place of consciousness in intellectual and religious history.

The Old Testament texts are expanded through midrashic literature, etc., in ways that are only illustrative, not systematic. On the one hand, these texts are a product of the same deep layer of the collective unconscious that is manifest in the Old Testament, and, on the other, they reveal a reflective, assimilating conscious attitude, which could be said to have paved the way for our interpretation.

In addition to interpreting structures, our study also interprets symbols. This interpretation applies first to the symbolism occurring directly in speech, proclamation, symbolic acts, visions, and dreams.[5] Second, it applies to that which apprehends depicted events symbolically. It is crucial to establish the legitimacy and limits of this second perspective, especially if we reject a symbolic understanding of historical reports. Layers of two kinds need to be distinguished. Prehistory, understood as mythologizing history, is strongly symbolic, and the closer to Genesis it stands, the more symbolic it is. There is no doubt about the symbolic meaning of the Genesis accounts. But the mythologizing reports of the patriarchs also include a wealth of symbolic material. Despite the historical truth they contain, which deserves to be given growing emphasis, their symbolic material is not only capable of interpretation, but also demands it. This is self-evident for all visionary accounts, all theophanies and visions, from Balaam's donkey to Jacob's struggle with the angel, from the vision of the thornbush to Moses' Sinai experience. All these texts are phenomena of the inner dimension, even if they are presented in projected form as visions or hallucinations, or externalized as outer events.

Historical collective events require a more complex interpretation, however, especially in traditional accounts. Here, we must interpret, first, whatever share of historiographical thinking is evident in their form and working through. Then we must interpret the collective material itself, as reports of collective experiences. It will not always be possible, certainly, to distinguish these layers, But, in any case, a psychology limited to the individual is inappropriate here, whereas the phenomenology of the collective unconscious and the consultation of primitive psychology are crucially important.

Going by its structure, the account of the Golden Calf, for example, can be understood only in relation to the collectively unconscious processes of the Sinai event. At the same time, in the context of the problem of Moses, its treatment is complicated by the contrast between prophetic authority and priesthood. The material of the traditional account, the struggle between Moses and the people, reflects the basic problem of prophecy. The contrast between prophet and priest, meanwhile, almost certainly originates in a late period and belongs to the reworked layer of the basic text. It would be fundamentally mistaken to believe that, because this reworked layer is late, the edited text as a whole can be left uninterpreted. The account belongs to an early time and bears all the symptoms of the events of such a time. In the context of revelation and its dangers, the dynamics of the collective unconscious, which are becoming clear in this core account, virtually prove that the account is genuine. Here, historical truth becomes demonstrable through the psychological authenticity of the report. The psychic phenomena that are depicted here in great specificity are familiar from the depth psychology of early peoples. They appear nowhere else on such a scale.

Thus, historical truth proves here to be something extremely complicated and complex, no longer based simply on agreement with archaeological finds, but also essentially on the possibility of relative attribution to the psychological reality of an era. For instance, the connection between the revelation on Sinai and the Golden Calf is inconsistent with the psychological reality of the Solomonic age. That connection, as derived from the account, is no longer comprehensible for a far more consciously developed time; therefore, it did not originate then. This account dates from an era still largely dominated by the collective psyche. But it was later worked on by a group, who fully grasped its implications and shaped it in terms of the contemporary problems of their era.

For example, at a time when the basic conception of prophecy was valued, the mythologizing reality of the account was redacted (not distorted) in such a way that prophetic factors, already present in the core text, were accentuated. Thus, if the core Mosaic text had been clearly reworked in a priestly, Aaronite, or Levitical sense, by introducing the figure of Aaron beside that of Moses, now this redactor, whose primary emphasis was on prophecy, accentuated the contrast between Aaron and Moses. And by correcting the Levitical–priestly revision, in a sense he also restored the core text, with its prophetic and Mosaic character, on a new level.

Our attempt to understand the text strives in the same direction as textual redaction itself. Both are seeking to actualize the text and its accounts for a historical situation. Historiography comes into existence only when a historical era recalls its past. This historiography is genuine if does not distort what is found, but establishes the historical line of cause and effect leading from what is found to the present. The biblical text is a result of such a concern for self-understanding. That is why the core text, its reworking and its interpretation must coalesce, because merely understanding an account already represents an interpretation, and every interpretation is necessarily influenced by where the interpreter stands.

Appendix II: The foundation stone and the waters of the deep[6]

The midrashim about the foundation stone and the waters of the deep present us with several variations on the same theme, namely, the binding of the hostile and chaotic forces of the unconscious by consciousness, or by the law that it constitutes.

This law, the Torah, is identical with the stone, shard, or pot on which God's unpronounceable name is inscribed. In the magically binding formulae of names and words, we see an early embodiment of that which gives the binding power of consciousness the same crucial, chaos-dispelling, and life-saving importance that it still possesses for the modern person.

One midrash says:

> When the Lord divided the upper waters from the lower ones when he created the world, the water of the abyss gushed forth and streamed westward so that no dry land could be seen. Soon afterwards, the Lord made a small shard, upon which he scratched the undisguised name forty-eight times, and this piece of clay became God's seal, with which he locked the mouth of the abyss. If the water now tries to gush forth from the depths, it is checked by the seal and flows back into the deep.[7]

When David discovers this seal while laying the foundation stone of the Temple and then lifts it from the deep, despite every warning to the contrary, a tremendous danger arises, which only great effort can avert, for:

The water of the depths shot up and became rampant and wanted to flood the world so that it would once again turn into chaos.[8]

Another text about the creation of the world includes the following account of the foundation stone, an image that is a parallel to the shard bearing God's name:

It is written that the Lord placed a rock upon the abyss. He engraved his real name upon that rock with forty-two signs and thus covered the mouth of the abyss, so that the waters would not gush up from it. But when the generation of the Flood sinned, the Lord removed the rock and all the wells of the great deep erupted.[9]

In the same context, it says:

And the Lord erected the world upon the foundation stone, upon the stone from which everything begins, and which thereafter stood in the Holy of Holies;[10] and this is the navel of the world.[11]

An interesting variation on the theme of the foundation stone, which David removed when he established the Temple, clarifies relationships even further. On one occasion, David finds a ceramic jar instead of the foundation stone or the shard of clay. The jar or clay shard says to David:

'This was not my place from the beginning. But in the hour in which the world split apart, I was placed here. If you do not believe me, try to lift me up. The great deep lies beneath me.' Then David raised the clay seal, and the abyss broke open and threatened to devour him.[12]

The foundation stone (jar) and the seal of YHWH are identical and have two functions. Downward, they must lock the mouth of the abyss and prevent the primordial waters from gushing upward into the world and transforming it into chaos. Upward, however, they form the navel of the world, upon which stands the Ark of the Covenant in the Holy of Holies, or they lie as subterranean seals in the foundation of the Temple.

But, for the Temple and the Ark of the Covenant to stand upon this foundation stone, it must show itself to symbolize the law, the task of which, sealed with YHWH's name, is to avert the terrible threat of chaos, the flooding by the unconscious.

The capstone was laid "because the world split apart." This theme of duality and splitting[13] established the principle of opposites, the duality of the world, but thus also the splitting into the polarities of good and evil, above and below, right and left, conscious and unconscious. The flooding from the abyss is caused by the extraordinary tension between consciousness and the unconscious. Unless a saving intervention occurs, this flooding inevitably leads to the end of the world, the drowning of consciousness. This saving intervention is the laying of the foundation stone, the seal, the law, which tames and binds the forces of the unconscious and locks the mouth of the abyss.

Resonating in the "mouth of the abyss" (the *tehom*)[14] is the ancient mythical theme of the struggle against Tiamat-Rahab, the dragon of the abyss. The archetypal theme of the dragon-fight, of the Titans banished to the abyss and of the bound Midgard serpent, still exists even in the Bible in some few passages (Job 26:12; Ps 74:13; 89:11; Is 27:1, 51:9) and is revived in the midrash.[15] Thus, the meaning of the abyss, which is identical with the negative aspect of the unconscious, is related most closely to the principle of evil, as we see in the texts below.

The connection of Azazel, goat, dark power, shadow, and sin has been discussed elsewhere.[16] Here, it is important only to mention the principal insight gained there: that the goat sent away on Yom Kippur to Azazel, who is a form of the devil, and the goat which is offered at the new moon, represent the sacrificed "evil aspect."

One commentary on the new moon sacrifice remarks: "A goat as a sin-offering to YHWH—to atone for the sin of the grave of the abyss."[17] An annotation on this passage explains that the "grave of the abyss" is "the sin that is known to none but God."[18] Thus, what is referred to as the "grave of the abyss" is an atonement offering for unconscious sin. Corresponding fully to this idea, a passage in the Book of Enoch reads:

> And secondly the Lord said to Raphael, "Bind Azaz'el [the lord of evil] hand and foot (and) throw him into the darkness!" And he made a hole in the desert which was in Duda'el [God's kettle] and cast him there; he threw on top of him rugged and sharp rocks. And he covered his face in order that he may not see light.
>
> *(I Enoch 10:5)*[19,20]

In the grave of the abyss lives Azazel, the lord of evil, the evil aspect of the unconscious. This very aspect, unconscious sin, must be atoned for at the new moon and on Yom Kippur by sacrificing the goat, which in itself represents evil. This goat is sent to Azazel on Yom Kippur, which renders the people's sin *unconscious*. Thereby YHWH's forgiveness makes the sin "disappear."

As we have shown elsewhere,[21] Yom Kippur involves the sacrifice of the negative aspect. Worth adding in this respect is that, ultimately, this sacrifice represents only a repression; in fact, it can represent nothing else. Evil is not "accepted"; rather its negative force is kept down by the foundation stone, the law, upon which stands the world. No real transformation of evil is possible by this means, as proven by the disasters that occur whenever this foundation stone is removed. This happens, for instance, in the Flood. The sin of the generation of the Flood, "YHWH's removal of the foundation stone" (see above), and the eruption of the wells of the abyss, all of this is actually a single process, in that sinning is equated with breaking the law, removing the capstone, being flooded by the unconscious.

For the law always represents the bulwark of consciousness erected against the affectivity, aggression, and destructive force of the unconscious.

Whereas all of this is easily understandable, a striking and seemingly senseless variant traces the yawning abysses and the threat of chaos back to the revelation on Sinai.

Once again, in establishing the Temple, David finds the clay jar that seals the abyss. In reply to David's question, the jar says:

> I lie here as the seal on the abyss. David asked: Since when have you lain here? The jar replied: Since the hour when the Lord spoke these words on Mount Sinai: I am the Lord, your God. Then the world quaked and the chasms yawned. But I was obliged to cover them and came hither.[22]

As we have seen, the chaotic force of the unconscious involves the anonymous dynamics of forces, the overwhelming energy of which lowers consciousness and causes it to sink catastrophically in the ocean of the unconscious. Such processes are evident in orgiastic–religious collective movements and instinctual irruptions. Another phenomenon occurs, however, when a new content appears, more powerful than consciousness, but it is not consciously taken in. Energetically, this is quite similar to the phenomenon of flooding, but this situation has a different index. In the first case, consciousness must avert the unconscious content, but, in the second, its task would be to assimilate that content.

In both cases, failing to accomplish the task leads to ruin, because the energetic force of consciousness is insufficient against the greater power of the unconscious constellation. The first case signifies death by regression, a sinking in the state of negativity, the defeat of a higher principle by a primitive, inferior one. The second, in contrast, typifies the "sacred death," being carried off by the divine; here, the irruption of the higher ranking dissolves the lower ranking rather than transforming it.

This second death is the death of the gods' favorites, the rapture; it is also the death of Nadab and Abihu.[23] But the first death is that which is suffered by the people through its regression with the Golden Calf.

The great power of irrupting divinity makes the abysses yawn; it creates the threat of doom. But in the transcendent function of the law, the seal of the abyss, and the tablets of the covenant, the tension of opposites is overcome and the abyss is closed.[24]

The threat of chaos, exorcized by this synthesis, therefore reappears immediately when this synthesis is destroyed, which is what occurred when the tablets were smashed. This smashing, rather than representing an arbitrary act by Moses, follows necessarily from the people's regression with the Golden Calf.

As the midrash formulates it:

> The hour when Moses smashed the tablets of the covenant, the waters of the ocean broke their bounds and wanted to flood the world. Then Moses took the calf and burned it. Afterwards, he exclaimed to the floodwaters: O, ye

waters, what are you doing! The ocean spoke: The world could only persist by virtue of the Torah, which stood upon the tablets. But this Torah was betrayed by the Children of Israel when they made the Golden Calf, and so we want to destroy the world. And Moses said: Now then, may all those who committed this sin be consigned to you. He scattered the ashes over the ocean, but the waves did not abate. And so Moses mixed the water with the ashes of the calf and gave it to the Children of Israel to drink. Forthwith, the wrath of the ocean was stilled.[25]

It is highly illuminating to see how this Zoharic text equates Moses' struggle with YHWH's wrath and his struggle with the wrath of the ocean, the flood of the unconscious. The meaning of the narrative is clear: it is Moses' endeavor to save the people. Just as Abraham negotiates with God to rescue Sodom and Gomorrah, Moses negotiates with the ocean to rescue the sinful people. First, he explores whether destroying the calf will be enough. Then, he offers the death of those who made the calf. But it is not until he offers the ordeal of the entire people that "the wrath of the ocean was stilled." The catastrophic split, the abyss of the people's unconscious, can only be stilled when all truly "adulterous parts" are destroyed by the ordeal.

There is an obvious connection between this Zoharic text, where Moses' action tends toward grace, the biblical text, where Moses prevents YHWH's wrath from destroying the whole people (Ex 32:32), and the subsequent theophany of God's grace (Ex 33:12f.). This connection sheds light on the Old Testament understanding of God, which is most emphatically misunderstood by Christian theology. This understanding cannot be explored here in detail, but it will become evident to anyone who approaches the text without bias.

Appendix III: The composition of the Pentateuch[26]

It is understandable that a priesthood with a codified ritual opposed the basic conception of prophecy.[27] But, as this early prophetic structure of the texts has remained unrecognized until now, the only textual revision emphasized was the one that introduced the priestly Zadokite element into the text, in order to subordinate the Levitical element. The corrections and falsifications of the priestly Zadokites, who traced their genealogy to Aaron, whom they had turned into Moses' brother,[28] can be found in all those passages referred to by biblical criticism with the letter "P."[29] These passages—contrary to the line shown above—stress the significance of Aaron and his sons.

The subordination of the Levites to the Aaronites is a verifiable fact. It belongs, as is well known, to the Deuteronomic centralization in Jerusalem, by which the earlier high priests were subordinated as Levites to the Jerusalemite Zadokite Temple priests.

But whereas it is clear what Aaronite–Zadokite priests are, it is far less obvious what is really meant by "Levites." As "belonging to YHWH" (Num 3:11, 8:16,

18:6), the Levites inherit nothing, because YHWH is their inheritance. They are substitutes for the firstborn, who were YHWH's original property. This tribe, and especially the family of Moses, is characterized by a predisposition toward social contact with God.

According to Auerbach's deductions, Abiathar is the last of the Elides.[30] He is a descendant of Moses[31] and author of the historical work, which, as "J,"[32] makes up our text to a considerable extent. Deriving the Shiloh priesthood from Moses, with *Urim* and *Thummim* and the Tent of Meeting as its estate, makes the line of Moses, as Levites, into hereditary bearers of an oracular prophecy, by sheer virtue of these inherited oracular objects. They constitute the shrine in Shiloh, just as their counterparts do for the shrine in Dan,[33] likewise founded by one of Moses' direct descendants.[34]

From this perspective, Abiathar's work of history has a Levitical emphasis. This *Levitical* emphasis, in stark contrast with its priestly–Zadokite revision (which is, of course, Aaronite), needs a brief explanation. It has a tribal and family accent, which distinguishes the Levites from the rest of the people as "Mosites."[35] It also includes the separation of the firstborn, originally God's chosen ones—the people's primary, anonymous prophetic disposition is still evident here—as represented by the tribe of Levi. Those who gathered around Moses after the episode of the Golden Calf, and were "with YHWH," are regarded as Levites in precisely this sense, although in fact most of them were presumably members of Moses' close family, whose exposure to his power was greatest. On all accounts, the Levites invoke this deed as the actual founding act, from which they could derive the privileged role that they played among the people thereafter.

The end of Exodus, which concludes with Moses' transformation into a mana-personality, continues without a break in the third chapter of Numbers,[36] where the Levites take the place of the firstborn of the people.[37] Probably linked directly with this is the law of the Nazirites, that is, the subordination of those dedicated to YHWH, the "lay priests," to the priests—originally Levites. Like them, these replaced the firstborn and now bless those dedicated to God, namely, those to whom they are meant to mediate YHWH's blessing. (Here as elsewhere, the inserted verses 2–3,[38] "about Aaron and his sons," are a later anti-Levitical revision by the Zadokites.) In Numbers 8:5 follows the appointment of the Levites by Moses and their separation from the people, with strikingly few Aaronite revisions. The fact that the account continues directly with the pillar of clouds and the setting forth from Sinai (Num 9:15–23; 10:11f.) proves that these chapters immediately follow the events in Exodus, the Sinai account.

Originally, Korah's rebellion[39] was doubtless directed against Moses. Only later did a biased Zadokite revision inflect this event into a Levitical rebellion against Aaron. This bias, however, is entirely transparent. The rebellion of the alleged "Levite" is followed so obviously by the appointment of the Levites that one biblical scholar observes: "The entire passage sounds like a first induction or even an explicit commissioning of the Levites. And this tallies with verse 4,[40] which attempts an etymological interpretation of their profession."[41] Contrary to the folk-prophetic tendency, it is precisely the Levitical orientation of the line of Moses that re-establishes itself after the claims rivaling his have been rejected. The famous "staff of Aaron" (Num 17:6–11) is actually a Levitical staff. Here, as throughout the Levitical text, although Aaron is a Levite and Moses' brother, he is completely subordinate to the latter. It was only later that the Zadokites, as Aaronites, opposed the line of Moses, representing the Levitical tradition.

The dominating will of the priestly Zadokites clashes with the Levites' claim to monopoly, which had been established by the Levites and especially by Moses' family, based on the principle of a hereditary prophetic priesthood, as the historical case of the Elides shows. Characteristically, however, not only the Levites and the family of Moses but also the Zadokite priests derived their claims from Moses, by tracing their Aaronite descent to Moses' brother. This brother also appeared as a minor figure in the Levitical texts, his importance being enhanced by textual redactions.

The struggle between the Aaronites, as cultic priests, and the Levites, as hereditary prophets headed by Moses' family, finally led to the Deuteronomic compromise. This compromise involved gathering the Levites at the Temple in Jerusalem and completely subordinating them to the Aaronites. Assembling the high priests as "Levites" for Temple- worship represents a compromise between Aaronites and Levites, who were united in their suppression of folk-prophetic individuals. Many of these high priests were apparently *nevi'im*, anonymous prophets and seers possessed by YHWH, along the lines of the previously emphasized, folk-prophetic tendency of Moses in the texts, insofar as there were no regressions to Canaanite paganism. Aaronites and Levites necessarily competed in their efforts to eliminate the idea of charismatic anonymity and to replace it with privileged castes and institutions.

The prophetic redaction, emphasizing the text's folk-prophetic tendencies, stands opposed to both these directions and therefore sees the opposition between Aaronites and Levites, which is found in earlier revisions, as thoroughly fitting.

Having inserted everywhere the subordination of the Levites under "Aaron and his sons," the Aaronite–Zadokite revision of the basic Levitical text reaches its high point in the extreme anti-Levitical thrust, inflecting Korah's rebellion into a Levitical uprising against Aaron. But along with this pro-Aaronite and anti-Levitical tendency, another highly remarkable line also becomes evident, which one can describe only as anti-Aaronite.

The series of negative Aaronite passages begins with the Golden Calf and Aaron's failure.[42] In Leviticus 10 follows the death of Aaron's sons. Then comes Aaron and Miriam's complaint (Num 12), in which the primacy of the prophet Moses, already emphasized by his descent from Sinai (Ex 34:30), is established, whereas Aaron is utterly rejected. Here, as elsewhere, Moses' intercession on behalf of Aaron contrasts with the latter's irresponsible, castigating attitude toward the people. The next chapters need to be reviewed in a manner still to be discussed, especially regarding the power of Aaron, who appears entirely as Moses' functionary (Num 17). The death of Aaron and Miriam (Num 20) is striking, to say the least. Striking because the death of both occurs at the same time and is recounted in the *same* chapter, and also because their complaint against Moses (Num 12) and YHWH's outburst of wrath against them are reported immediately before their death. There are good reasons for suspecting that this death was originally seen as a consequence of their revolt against Moses.

The anti-Aaronite series, stemming from the Levitical core text, once again emphasizes Moses. But it also has a strongly prophetic accent, which not only underscores Moses' prophetism but also, in a clear sideswipe at his family, highlights the primacy of YHWH's free charismatic choice. For this reason, the anti-Levitical correction, which turns Korah and his group into Levites who are destroyed by YHWH's fire, is preserved beside its anti-Aaronite counterpart, which lets Aaron's sons, Nadab and Abihu, perish in YHWH's fire. For the prophetic redaction, even the Mosaic descent of the Elides, the Shiloh priesthood, confers no charismatic privilege. The hereditary Mosaic and Levitical prophetic priesthood counts as little here as the claim of the Zadokite line of priests. Abiathar[43] is probably the early reviser and redactor of basic Levitical texts and traditions, and he may have been influenced directly by the prophet *Samuel*, to whose figure, as the center of these prophetic revisionary tendencies, everything points.

Samuel emphatically opposes the Elides, and thus also the hereditary prophecy of the descendants of Moses and Levi. Yet he also represents YHWH's free charismatic election, as shown in the story of Saul and David. Granted, the connection between Abiathar and Samuel is not obvious in the text, but it is hinted at, both in Abiathar's deadly antagonism toward Saul and in his flight to David, Samuel's ally. As the last descendant of Moses, his antagonism to the Zadokites (2 Sam 8:17, 20:25; 1 Chron 18:16) corresponds to the antagonism of Moses' family toward its Zadokite–Aaronite opponents.

But if it is true that the folk-prophetic tendency goes back to Abiathar, rather than to one of the text-redacting students of the prophet Samuel, then in him we would be dealing not only with a historiographical but also with a religious genius. And his transformation under Samuel's influence, from a hereditary–prophetic and Levitical persuasion to a folk-prophetic and charismatic one, would determine and anticipate essential lines in the development of Jewish intellectual history.

It is meaningful that clear traces of the struggle between prophetic tendencies and Levitical–Aaronite counter-tendencies can be found precisely where the original text presents the struggle between Moses and the counter-currents persisting among the people.[44]

Appendix IV: Earth and the symbols of the elements[45]

In Appendix IV, material that seems very disparate is arranged in a continuous cycle, although its various parts belong to different sections of the text. All the comments in this appendix concern the symbolism of the YHWH–earth conflict. This material could be liberally extended; what is presented here is only enough to illustrate the textual context.

The first part includes midrashic texts that outline the meaning of the spirit-wind, especially in its contrast with earth, that is, as a part of the collective symbolism of the elements, with wind-and-fire symbolism on the one side and earth-and-water symbolism on the other.

The next two sections deal with the dimension of earth and nature, as related or unrelated to the spiritual domain. Comments on blood, in its connection with earth and with *nefesh*,[16] the body–soul, can provide only a hint. The second part of our work, on the psychological significance of Hasidism, will discuss in greater detail the theory of the soul and its connection with the Kabbalah. Here, that theory is only mentioned, insofar as it characterizes one aspect of the YHWH–earth relationship.

The section dealing with the connection between circumcision and the Passover is already closely linked to the previous part, because of the importance of the role played here by blood. Even more crucial, however, is how our main topic becomes visible there, that is, the way the natural sphere is institutionally placed under the dominance of YHWH.

The dominant principle of spirit and wind appears at the beginning of this appendix and returns at the end, in the protective effect of the Passover ritual and circumcision. Especially in this context, the ascendency of the YHWH principle is proven when it abandons mere opposition to the earth and, by pervading nature, establishes a new union between YHWH and earth, above and below, spirit and nature.

In the last section, which presents material on the Lilith problem, the aspect of "earth as threat" is addressed from another angle, namely, the significance of the negative feminine in Judaism.

Wind symbolism

The theme of the fundamental duality of the world is reflected in one text under the motto, "Everything comes into being only through unification and opposition," a principle that reaches its full expression in the Kabbalah. In this text we read:

> Two things exist that were not created; they are the wind and the water; they were there from the beginning, just as it is said: the wind of the Lord[47] hovered above the waters.[48]

The polarity of consciousness and the unconscious is symbolized here by the contrast between the elements of wind and water. But then the text goes on to say:

> God is one, and no other thing stands beside him; and it is the same with the wind. It, too, has no counterpart and nothing else belongs to its kind. You cannot grasp it, you cannot beat it, nor burn it, nor discard it. You may say: but the tube keeps the wind inside. But no! For look, you are holding the tube, and along comes someone and asks: what is inside? You say: the wind. He says: what kind of thing is that, is it black or red, white or green, can it

be purchased on the market? You have no answer. If you open the mouth of the tube, the wind goes forth. But you cannot see it. Even more, it bears humans and moves heaven and earth. . . . Now you will see that the whole world is filled with the wind. It alone carries the world. It is the highest, it was at the beginning of all things.[49]

This naive allegory emphasizes all those aspects that have made the wind powerfully symbolic since time immemorial. Also, it sounds like a brotherly expansion of a sentence in the Gospel of John: "The wind blows where it chooses, and you hear the sound of it, but you do not know whence it comes or whither it goes" (John 3:8).[50] The contrast of water and spirit, which plays the decisive role in Gnosticism and in the Gospel of John, is developed further in the Jewish midrash and in Kabbalistic symbolism. Only future research will decide whether this is a case of Judaism being influenced by Gnosticism, or whether basic Semitic elements of Gnosticism unfolded parallel to Judaism, or whether, as seems most likely, both occurred side by side. In any event, it is striking that Gnostic elements make a powerful appearance in the unconscious of the modern Jew.[51]

Between earth and water, on the one hand, and fire and air (wind), on the other, there exists an association that cannot be obscured by a certain ambiguity in the symbolism of the elements. The unity of wind-and-fire symbolism becomes obvious, for example, in the New Testament, in the outpouring of the Holy Spirit,[52] symbolized by small flames that transform those affected into *pneumatikoi*, people of the spirit, which means, however, into people who belong to the sphere of air and wind.

A similar but slightly different idea speaks to us in the following passage:

Three things were already in existence before the world: water, wind, and fire. The water became pregnant and gave birth to darkness. Fire became pregnant and gave birth to light. Wind became pregnant and gave birth to wisdom. These elements also govern the world. Wind and wisdom, fire and light, darkness and water.[53]

It is impossible to demonstrate here that this passage belongs to Gnostic speculation about Sophia. But the connection is clear, in the depiction of Sophia as the daughter of the wind, the Holy Spirit, with whom she is identified.

The uniqueness of the *ruach*–wind dimension is made absolutely plain here, however, as a basic concept, in that the wind appears as a symbol connecting and sublimating the fundamental opposites of consciousness and the unconscious. The structure of this passage corresponds perfectly to the reality that YHWH stands beyond the opposites of spirit and earth, and that he only temporarily seems to identify with one dimension and enter into it, namely, the dimension of the spirit.

Water-darkness and fire-light, as unconsciousness and consciousness, are the basic polarities of the energetic life of the soul, and thus of the world. But the wind and its offspring, wisdom, regarded as one part of the prevailing trinity, are essentially distinct from the other two parts, for in them the elemental symbolism of darkness and light is overcome. Wisdom, which gives meaning to the unconscious and to consciousness, constitutes a domain beyond the elements, because it activates the higher level of that which is always meant by YHWH, a content that stands behind all symbolism of the unconscious and cannot be identified with its parts, but represents its relatedness to the wholeness of meaning as such.

Earlier we noted that, with the beginning of creation, duality was placed under the primacy of the wind. Here, in the trinity, the element of wind and wisdom mediates between light-fire and darkness-water. Characteristically, the earth, which would one expect as the fourth element, is missing. About the psychological meaning of this missing Fourth, see the writing of C. G. Jung.[54] Here, apparently, earth is contained in the "water-and-darkness" domain of the unconscious. The Sefer Yetzirah says:

> Three mothers in the world: heaven,[55] earth, wind. In the beginning, heaven was created from fire, earth from water, wind from air, which mediates between fire and water.[56]

Here the mediating position of wind is once again clearly formulated, as the position of wind, spirit, the wise Sophia, between light–fire–heaven and water–darkness–earth.

It should be mentioned that the position of the wind between heaven and earth corresponds at every point to the position of the *Shekhinah* between YHWH and the world, that of the moon between the sun (as YHWH) and the earth, and that of Israel between YHWH and the peoples.[57]

Here we must once again emphasize that we are fully aware we are juxtaposing texts from very different periods. For our purposes, however, the question of historical context or foreign influence[58] is unimportant. What matters is the pervasiveness of the symbolism and its historical impact.

Body-soul and blood

Beside the *ruach*-breath soul, there is the *nefesh*-blood soul. The statement, "The blood is the soul (*nefesh*)" (Deut 12:23), is commented on by another assertion, "The soul (*nefesh*) of the flesh is in the blood" (Lev 17:11; cf. Gen 9:4).[59] Blood, the body's principle of life, may not be consumed. It is taboo in a particular sense, because as the incarnation of the body, blood belongs to the earth. It must therefore be poured onto the earth (Lev 17:13; Deut 12:24) and covered with earth. Likewise, the blood from circumcision is covered with earth, and circumcision is performed over earth or water.[60] This relationship of earth and blood is probably ancient. The idea even pervades the story of Abel's slaying by Cain (Gen 4:10), for the earth's reaction to the stain of spilled blood is decisive here.

The earth spits out those who behave negatively, including those who disrespect the connection of blood and earth. Inherent in this fact is a normative cooperation between YHWH and earth, which should never be overlooked. The earth reacts according to YHWH's law; earthly nature turns against the sinners who commit unnatural deeds. This cooperating earth is a higher earth, being YHWH affiliated. But on closer inspection, even the "earth as threat" stands under YHWH's law of justice, imposing his judgment on those who sin against his directives.

The eating of blood, the blood orgy, is doubtless one of many forms of earth-worship and divinatory earth-ecstasy. This is clearly confirmed by a collection of prohibitions, including those against the "foreskin" of trees (see above),[61] the consumption of blood, and soothsaying (Lev 19:26). On the other hand, the acknowledged sacredness and meaningfulness of blood, in short its taboo character, especially suits it for the decisive role in sacrifice. Its offering atones. In a sense it is the quintessence of corporeality, and thus it mediates in a substantial way between YHWH and humanity. By the smearing or sprinkling of blood the priest is ordained, the people and the leper are reconciled, and the covenant between YHWH and the people is sealed (Ex 24:6, 29:12f.; Lev 8:30, 14:7, etc.).

This meaningful quality of blood is the essential reason why animal sacrifice is privileged over plant sacrifice. The fact that animal sacrifice is natural among nomadic peoples is not crucial in this respect. It would stand to reason that, once the people had settled, plant sacrifice could also have begun to play a crucial role. Sociological explanations of the pre-eminence of animal sacrifice are also inadequate, and an emphasis on the "nomadic ideal" is illuminating only if it is understood more deeply and comprehensively than has been customary.

The vegetative obviously also has an earthy character, because for any kind of plant life, the connection with the soil is ever present. But other layers of the unconscious are associated with animal life, the quintessence of which, blood, appears as the body's soul. Human drives, and those of nature as a whole, as well as the affectivity that so deeply takes possession of the body, are connected in an elemental way with the region of blood[62] and its vitality. Unlike the calm steadiness and down-to-earth rootedness of vegetative existence, the animal embodies the motility and emotionality of roving instinct and blood-thirsty drivenness. To this day, bodily instincts in the human unconscious are still symbolized by animals, and the relationship of instincts with the various deep regions of the body corresponds strikingly to different animal species. Warm-blooded creatures characteristically represent the highest, most advanced product of natural development, and the region of blood is the highest region of the unconscious, pushing up beneath the threshold of consciousness. Consciousness, with its sense of security, is unsettled most obviously and insistently by the affects and drives radiating from this region.[63]

Animal sacrifice predominates, therefore, wherever there is some insight into the strength and vitality of the region of blood. This is certainly the case with a strongly instinctual people like the *Bnei Israel*. Two themes, taken together, influenced animal sacrifice: the strong taboo-ladenness of blood against the background of the animal drives, and blood as the quintessence of the animal, the highest product of nature. We need not decide here whether sacrifice corresponds to an offering of this zone or to a communion, creating a connection between the bodily system and YHWH by the magical–cultic means of blood sacrifice. Blood is offered to YHWH because, as the seat of bodily life, it is the most precious good that can be offered to the tribal God, the lord of the tribe. To him is owed the best, whether of cattle or property, be it the firstborn, one's only son, or one's own life.

It would be highly revealing to trace the association of the various part-souls and parts of the soul with the elements and bodily regions, to the extent that this connection was made in Judaism. A few brief remarks must suffice here. The concept that the soul exists in five parts, which we find partially elaborated in the Kabbalah, is already present in the midrash.[64] Here, the following souls are distinguished: the *nefesh* as the principle of blood and life; *ruach* as the ascending and descending principle of wind and spirit; *neshama* (see above, *nishmat hayim*)[65] as the rational soul; *yehida* as the unitary soul in contrast to the polarity of the body; and *haya* as the soul of life, which, ascending in sleep, draws life from above.

We cannot address the association of parts of the soul to the spheres and levels of the world, but what interests us, in the Kabbalah's complicated theory of the soul, is the opposition of wind and earth. So it is important to mention the following. The *nefesh* soul represents the principle of vitality in its transience. Subordinated to it is the domain of vegetative and animal life, which contrasts with the principle of *ruach*–wind–spirit, and *neshama* rationality.[66] The *nefesh* soul originates in the earth;[67] it resides in the liver and governs the blood system.[68] The breath soul, *ruach*, as the principle of moral decision-making, is seated in the heart, because breath, which is regarded as emanating from the heart, defines its essence. Thus, it is also the principle of the word.

In terms of elemental symbolism, water and earth are associated with *nefesh*, as are the moon and the feminine.[69] The hierarchy of the elements, parts of the soul, and regions of the world are important in this connection. For the Kabbalah, the *nefesh* typically "possesses no light as such; she[70] is closely associated with the body, whose nutrition and functions she governs. As it is said (Proverbs of Solomon 31:15), she distributes the food for her house and the day's work among her maids. The house—that is . . . the body, which is fed; the maids are the limbs, which obey the *nefesh*. Above the *nefesh* rises the *ruach*, who governs the former, gives her laws, and illumines her as far as necessary."[71]

Over the course of the Jewish history of ideas, the system of body, earth, and nature was radically subordinated to the principle of YHWH, wind, and spirit. But the animating wind, the *ruach*, is already at the foreground of the Genesis text, in the breath of life, which gives Adam his soul and spirit, making him the ruler and center of the world, as much as in the fact that the world is created by the word, the breath that speaks meaning, the *logos*.

Thus, the opposition of the principle of YHWH with that of earth is repeated in the opposition of *ruach* and *nefesh*. But in this connection, the dimension of earth and blood, when properly aligned, also has a positive character.

Earth and bull

The domain of earth is by no means negative from the beginning, although in factual–historical terms it is widely regarded as infected. As Adam had been established as ruler over the soil, *adama*,[72] the curse that struck him also afflicted the earth (Gen 3:17). At all events, the Jew's supposed alienation from earth cannot be traced back to this curse. The fact that the "earth as threat" plays such a major role in Judaism merely reflects its power within the Jewish system of life. Nevertheless, in Jewish thinking, the fact that human beings are dominated by the earthy dimension of the unconscious is only secondary. In primary reality, that is, according to the way human beings were created, the earth is coordinated and subordinated; an original cooperation exists between YHWH and earth for the benefit of the world and its people. The midrash formulates this as follows:

> But when the earth heard God's saying [that human beings should multiply and fill the earth], it trembled and spoke to its Creator: O, Lord of all worlds, my strength will not suffice to feed the multitudes of people. The Lord spoke: I and you, we both want to feed these multitudes. So they divided their labor between them. The Lord took upon himself the night, and gave the day to the earth. What did the Lord do? He created the sleep of life. The human being lies quietly asleep all night. Sleep is his food and healing, life and refreshment. The soul, it is said, fills the human body; but in the hour when people are asleep, it rises and draws its life from above.
>
> But the Lord stands by the earth and soaks it with his rain; and it bears fruit and gives sustenance to all creatures.[73]

For this midrash, it is characteristic not only to give the earth second place beside YHWH, in what we have called "cooperation," but also to avoid the too-easy symbolism of associating YHWH only with heaven. In contrast to the cooperation of pagan–cosmic deities, where heaven and earth are juxtaposed as relatively equivalent principles, here a completely different association has been chosen for YHWH and earth.

The outer world of day and sunlight belongs to earth, whereas to YHWH is assigned the inner aspect of the world, night and sleep, but thus also the realm of revelation and the soul. This intersecting symbolism beautifully and unobtrusively shows that the world lives from within. YHWH, as the life-giving and fructifying principle, nurtures the soul and earth at night. From there flows life, and "fruit and food."[74]

So long as the secure pairing of the polarity, above–below, YHWH–earth, has not broken apart but remains guided by the YHWH principle and is "fruitful," the human being who is yoked into this polarity is also productive, neither alienated from earth nor forsaken by YHWH.

This changes when the earth gains dominance, because the human being lives in *participation mystique* with the unconscious layer symbolized by the earth. What follows, reactively, is the rejection of the dimension of earth, now represented by the threat of the Golden Calf. This *participation mystique* with the earth and its rejection can once again be exemplified by turning to the symbol of the bull.

The calf or bull is an archetypal symbol of the earth's fertility. The fact that in Canaan the bull meant fertility is known from the bull-idols of Baal that were worshiped in Israel. In the Mithraic mysteries, bull sacrifice has the same meaning as the sacrifice of the fertile aspect of the world. Dionysus, as a bull, also symbolizes the phallic aspect of earth—compare the bull as an astrological earth-sign—just as in India Shiva's bull, Nandin, symbolizes the primordial sexual power and lust of the creative god. In this respect, the phallic cult and ecstatic–sexual orgiasticism mostly belong together, as phallic cults demonstrate throughout human history. Even if the bull appears and is sacrificed in the mother cult,[75] he nevertheless represents male potency offered to the Great Mother, just as the Galli, the priests of Cybele, the Great Mother, were obliged to offer it in self-castration.

One passage in the Zohar[76] suggests that the Golden Calf is regarded there as the embodiment of this world, disconnected from the divine, in contrast with the deity's hidden part. Here again, the calf represents the dimension of earth, unpenetrated by divinity.

Thus, it is also natural that the lord of darkness resembles a bull or a three-headed bull.[77] Likewise, legends about the death of sinners,[78] upon whose forehead or between whose shoulders traces of a calf's hoof were found, identify the calf with the devil.[79]

This also explains the resulting midrashic association of wine with the devil. Wine, the noble product of the earth, and as such sacred to the world, also occupies a pre-eminent role in Jewish feast days. Its rejection occurs, along with the rejection of all divination, when it is consumed as an attempt to awaken the unconscious at the expense of the conscious system. Those dedicated to God, the Nazirites, had to abstain from wine and grapes in any form. The Rekabites[80] did the same, in contrast to Canaanite earth worship. Even the prohibition of wine in Islam seems to go back to this nomadic rejection of the orgiastic aspect of earth.

This rejection applies to the earth's seductive aspect, which renders unconscious. It emerges directly from the fact that the symbol of the bull and the calf also appears as a positive symbol when it is not separated from YHWH but occurs in connection with him.

Thus, the bull is apprehended as one of the figures—lion, eagle, bull, human—in the *Merkavah*[81] of God's throne in Ezekiel (1:5–10), which is widely known as the subject of speculation in one section of the Kabbalah. The angel Ridya[82] also has the form of a calf. This angel is "charged with watching that the earth is soaked by the heavenly rains from above and by the waters of the deep from below." He stands "between the lower deep and the upper deep."[83]

Bull-symbolism is preserved here, but in the form of a fertility that emanates from YHWH, as a servant, an angel, integrated into the hierarchy of the divine economy. Joseph's identification with the bull must be understood, likewise, on the earthly plane. As the savior from famine, as YHWH's servant, he symbolizes fertility, and even his dead body guarantees the fertility of Egypt.[84]

Circumcision and Passover

Whereas the previous sections of this appendix have concentrated mainly on the symbolism of the elements and related problems, this section considers another matter. Our previous findings are nevertheless significant for what follows.

Our attempt to demonstrate the connection between circumcision and Passover refers to various customs to illustrate the meaning of the term "grafting," how the YHWH aspect seizes the earth–body aspect, or rather combines itself with it. In this respect, it is crucial to show that, and how blood acts and must act as a mediator. For, as a principle in relation to the body, it has a spiritual character, whereas, in relation to the principle of *ruach* or spirit, blood epitomizes corporeality.

To avoid complicating matters further, we exclude the problem of the firstborn, which seems to have been linked with the Passover ritual at a later stage. However, the "bridegroom of blood" passage (Ex 4:24–26) is evidently a very old text, which is of the greatest import in understanding the connection between circumcision and Passover. It describes YHWH's attack on Moses immediately after his return from Egypt,[85] because the latter had neglected his son's circumcision.[86]

The following passage indicates the link between these rituals:

> When circumcising a boy, one must smear some of the blood that is shed during the *milah*[87] on his feet [. . .] the blood smeared on the foot is the sign of the *milah* about which God has spoken.[88]

Just as a sign of the covenant is mentioned here, so it is elsewhere:

> And the blood shall be a sign on your houses.[89]

Here, foot translates more appropriately as leg. The rite of circumcision, with the bloody genital and the blood-smeared legs, thus exactly parallels the smearing of blood on the two doorposts and the lintel prescribed by the Passover ritual, especially because the "lintel" is what "protrudes above,"[90] and thus corresponds exactly to the genital.

The meaning of blood is decisive here.[91] Without its substantiality, it is impossible to fulfill this sacred bond. Even a circumcised child, that is, one born without a foreskin, must be circumcised, because "the blood of the covenant must drip down."[92]

The Passover festival is regarded as the remnant of a wedding rite carried out between YHWH and Israel, in which is demonstrated that YHWH belongs to the people wedded to him.[93] An analysis of the Easter ritual, which corresponds to Passover, as a wedding ritual, can be supplemented not only with the Zoharic passage mentioned by Eisler,[94] but also with a reading, especially on Passover, of the Song of Songs, which has always exemplified the symbolism of YHWH's marriage with Israel.

But the connection between *milah* and Passover is confirmed by the bridegroom-of-blood passage, which can be understood only in this context.

YHWH falls upon Moses, but his wife, Zipporah, circumcises their hitherto uncircumcised son, smears the blood on his legs (see above), and says: "Indeed, a bridegroom of blood are you to me. Thereupon he released him" (Ex 4:25–26). The threat of death is thus successfully averted by circumcision and the smearing of blood, just as smearing blood on the doorposts and lintel on Passover successfully averts the threat of death for the firstborn.

Zipporah's statement, "Indeed, a bridegroom of blood are you to me," refers of course to YHWH.[95] She speaks these words on behalf of her son, whom she circumcises, in his substitution to YHWH. Through this act of circumcision she fulfills the ritual of the marriage covenant with YHWH. Therefore we read: "Then she said 'a bridegroom of blood' upon the circumcision" (Ex 4:26). In this way, the endangered, because uncircumcised, son, and his equally endangered parents, especially Moses, find refuge and protection with YHWH: "Thereupon he released them."[96]

In puberty rites, as is well known, there is commonly a link between circumcision and marriage, in that the circumcision performed in such rites is a ritual prerequisite for the marriage ceremony. The fact that Zipporah, the Midianite, utters the words, "A bridegroom of blood are you to me," while circumcising, is often considered a residue of such puberty rites. Indeed, based on this passage, some have even argued that circumcision was adopted from the Midianites.

The circumcision performed in puberty rites, however, involves an initiation, through which the individual becomes a fully fledged member of the collective and thus also capable of marriage. At an early stage in Judaism, on the other hand, circumcision, as an act performed on the child, was already distinguished from the adolescent initiation that accepts the thirteen year old, as *bar mitzvah*,[97] into the collective and makes him a "son of the law."

This passage seems to mean that the Midianite Zipporah uses the concept "bridegroom of blood," which she knows from puberty rites, in a *new* way, relating and transferring it to the child circumcision, initially unfamiliar to her, that is demanded by YHWH. This is the meaning of the unequivocally clear sentence: "She said 'a bridegroom of blood' upon the circumcision."

The individual is accepted into the covenant with YHWH by means of the same ancient ritual through which, in other circumstances, the individual was accepted into the collective. In both cases, the rite of circumcision is associated with marriage, except that here the act of circumcision signifies the consummation of the marriage with YHWH himself.

This connection with YHWH through circumcision has the same meaning for the individual as Passover does for the people, namely, protection against YHWH's own negative forces. Characteristically, circumcision appears in Mosaic law only in connection with Passover. The one passage where it is still mentioned (Lev 12:2) is related to the impurity of the woman in childbirth, which belongs in the context of the Lilith problem.

The ultimate confirmation of the connection between circumcision and Passover is found in the fact that no uncircumcised male may participate in the

Passover. This is why, on Passover, Joshua circumcised those born in the wilderness (Josh 5:2, 10), for only those united with YHWH as individuals by the *milah* may become part of his collective union with the people.

Another fact supports this connection: both the night before circumcision and the night of Passover are called *leil shimurim*, a night of watching[98] (Ex 12:42). The threat of death is greatest in both nights. In the night before circumcision, this is because the hostile powers make one final attempt to overpower the child, who is as yet unprotected by marriage with YHWH, and only prayer protects the child on this night against the threat of Lilith.

The contrast to the night of Passover points once again to this very connection. In that night, even though God's angel of death passes by on this night of danger, the protection is so great that those united with YHWH through circumcision and the Passover ritual are completely safe. On this night, no Jew prays the *Shema Israel*,[99] which otherwise protects and separates him from the nocturnal threat of the unconscious and evil spirits. This night, the only one without the *Shema* is the night of protection, of YHWH's nuptial union with Israel. In it, chosenness is fulfilled in substance, as the great event of selection in Egypt makes clear.

Lilith

We have already mentioned Lilith twice. We must now place the relationship between Lilith, the negative feminine principle, and circumcision in a larger context. These texts and the complex of this relationship are more important than our abbreviated account can show. Judaism's stance toward women and also, as Part Three will show,[100] the modern Jew's attitude toward the feminine are largely influenced by these basic views.

Circumcision, as an action upon a child, was already separated in early Judaism from adolescent initiation, to which it originally belongs and by which the thirteen-year-old male is accepted into the collective. The meaning of young men's puberty rites is always that the youth is born into the collective of men, masculinity, and spirit, through a process of transformation and rebirth. On the one hand, the young boy is declared a man and admitted to the sexual realm, but, at the same time, he is also initiated into the traditions and rites of the tribe, that is, its spiritual tradition, and must now fulfill a spiritual–male task as a community functionary within the tribal collective. He has his place in the collective, and the duties and rights of the community of men now apply to him.

Until puberty, the child, the male child as well, has lived largely within the motherly domain, and its very life is assigned to the sphere of women. One essential purpose of puberty rites is to dissolve the *participation mystique* between mother and son, and thus to make him inwardly capable of sexuality. In the process, his childhood can be ended, the feminine *imago*[101] can be separated from the mother, and the liberated image of the feminine can now be projected onto a same-age female partner.

In a primitive culture, the development of the individual is to some extent divided by the puberty rites into two phases. First is the matriarchal phase, which, characterized by the dominance of the mother image and *participation mystique* with her, stands under the sign of the unconscious. Then comes the patriarchal phase, in which the male individual steps out of the mother's domain and, under the dominance of the father image, and, in *participation mystique* with him, activates and lives the masculine–spiritual aspect.

The separation of circumcision from adolescent initiation, bringing it forward to the eighth day of the child's life, arises from the tendency to push back the female–maternal aspect in favor of the paternal one. This means, however, that the dimension of YHWH and spirit is meant to be strengthened at the expense of the earth and the unconscious. As we know, over the course of a fateful development in Judaism, which we shall consider later, this led to taking the male Jewish child from his mother, starting in his third year of life, to "study." As a result, the heightening of the conscious aspect was certainly taken to extremes, at the cost of the unconscious aspect. (This direction, inaugurated by Judaism, is not as absurd as it seems at first. It follows the exact same lines as every other cultural development, a fact that is evident from the modern practice of separating children from the maternal milieu at the age of six and placing them within a male intellectual one. Incidentally, the rise of the kindergarten movement is gradually pushing this development forward to an even earlier stage.)

The fact that the separation of circumcision and adolescent initiation is actually intended in this sense is made clear by the following: A relic of adolescent initiation is found in Judaism in the *bar mitzvah*, the ceremony in which the thirteen-year-old boy becomes a son of the law and an adult, who must now fulfill all the duties and rights of the religiously valid Jew. This ceremony replaces the previous circumcision of the thirteen year old in a puberty rite, as is still related in Genesis.[102]

Whereas the obligation to marry was once associated with this time, it was the only duty that was later moved, with the deorientalizing of Judaism, to the eighteenth year of life, whereas all other duties come into force with the *bar mitzvah*. Until this time, it suffices that the *father* is responsible for the son, by virtue of their *participation mystique*. At his son's *bar mitzvah*, the father therefore recites a prayer of thanks for being relieved of this responsibility.[103] On the other hand, however, the following sentence applies: "Until the age of thirteen, the son is struck for his father's sin; thereafter, every one dies for his own misdeed."[104]

The relationship between Lilith and circumcision is plainly the underlying cause for the fact that, when the thirteen-year-old is circumcised and enters into the covenant with YHWH, this effects his separation from the feminine principle and his entrance into *participation mystique* with the masculine–spiritual domain, represented by the father.

The seven days spent by the child with its mother, until he is taken away from her on the eighth day, are the seven days during which the mother is unclean (Lev 12:2f.).[105] This uncleanness, which is transferred to the child and initially prevents circumcision, originates in the taboo ladenness of the zone of sexuality and blood, through which the child passes at birth. A boy delivered by a cesarean section can and must be circumcised immediately.[106] In this light, it is understandable that the offering for the covenant with YHWH, seen as parallel to sacrifice, can be brought only on the eighth day.

This paralleling with sacrifice suggests an expanded concept. The law prescribes that the firstborn of animals, ox and sheep, may be offered to YHWH only on the eighth day because the animal should stay with its mother for seven days (Ex 22:29). The same is true for circumcision, which represents the sacrifice of the firstborn.[107] Even the animal belongs to its mother for seven days and may be offered to YHWH only on the eighth. Here, too, we find an expanded principle of impurity, in that the *participation mystique* with the negative–feminine zone of sexuality and blood, established by the birth process, initially prevents an association with YHWH. That the impossibility of offering the newborn to YHWH before the eighth day stems from a cosmic rather than a statutory principle of purity is also proven by the fact that circumcision was fixed on the eighth day between Abraham's time and the giving of the law, during which period no law of purity existed.[108]

But the principle of the impure fruits in the first three years, the so-called "foreskin of the trees," is crucial in this respect. Fruit, as already explained,[109] is impure because the dimension of earth and water is prevalent in this time. This means, however, that the feminine earth–water principle is still dominant in the growth of trees and fruits, which is caught between the polarities of earth and water and sun (fire) and air. At first, the taboo of being earth-born still clings to the young fruit and makes it impure. Thus, in the fourth year, the fruits are offered as sacred to YHWH, and humans may use them starting only in the fifth. The parallel with the threefold rhythm is obvious: first, impurity through *participation mystique* with the negative aspect of earth; second, offering to YHWH, sacrifice of the firstborn and circumcision; and third, entrance into normal life within the confines of the law. Humans, animals, and plants all have the same precondition for the sacred life: being taken into YHWH's possession.

The initial dominance of earth and water always requires the completion of a sacred rhythm of seven, before the animal or the child may be offered to YHWH. As the midrash formulates it: "Thus God spoke: Bring no sacrifice before me until the Sabbath has passed by it: no seven days pass without a Sabbath, and thus no circumcision may be performed without a Sabbath touching the land."[110]

To go fully into the meaning of the Sabbath and the sacred number seven goes beyond our discussion here. Clearly, however, the Sabbath incarnates the principle of YHWH and spirit, which is superior to the earth. Constellated in the Sabbath is the opposition between YHWH's sacred day of rest and the everyday earthly working week, in the sense that rest here always signifies a closeness to YHWH. Therefore, the eighth day stands under the sign of seven, and circumcision may be performed only then.

As mentioned earlier, however, the night before the circumcision is a critical time, because hostile forces then endeavor to seize the child. Especially menacing in this regard is Lilith, the child-eater, a female demon. She threatens the days before the circumcision, during which the child still lives in *participation mystique* with its mother, who is unclean during this time.

The threat is generally seen as being greatest on Friday. As the day on which God created the evil demons,[111] it stands in a specific and dangerous contrast to the sacredness of the Sabbath. It was therefore considered a day of misfortune. Just as the Sabbath plays a positive role as a precondition for circumcision, Friday evening plays a specifically negative one. Thus, to this day, the Jews of Cairo, for instance, use peas to protect a male child against Lilith on the Friday evening before the circumcision. Like all vegetables in hulls, peas are used as a superstitious sacrifice to demons, to protect the child.[112]

Lilith is more significant than her succubus character would initially lead one to suspect. In the Middle Ages, succubi were thought of as demonic female creatures who fornicate with men in their dreams. The origin of Lilith is ancient. Numerous incantations for her exorcism have survived in Babylonian sources,[113] and early reports say that the sleeping cannot resist her embrace.[114] Likewise, the Talmud says: "He who sleeps alone in the house is possessed by Lilith."[115] Her character as a succubus, as a demonic being who pollutes dreams at night,[116] makes her a fitting embodiment of the spiritual–female power that stirs sexual desire and fornication; she appears in this guise in the Kabbalah.[117] But Lilith is more than this: in the texts, she far exceeds the figure of a female fiend, for which certain groups of spirits are named.[118]

The female demon who preys on the newborn is archetypal, as the Greek Lamiae and Roman Striges, the Arabic Ghoul, and the Armenian Al suggest.[119] Similarly, the Mandeans believed that Zachriel, yet another Lilith, crouches on the bed of pregnant women.[120]

Lilith's essential characteristic as a demon is not her devouring of children, however, but her profound hostility toward men. In her hatred of the masculine, she incarnates the negative aspect of the feminine per se. Killing the male child and seducing men to greed and fornication are merely two sides of the same thing. She is said to be the mother of Ahriman,[121] the queen of demons, the inciter of the serpent. And just as the last, lowest, and most worldly of the ten Kabbalistic spheres is feminine, the *Shekhinah*, the divine immanence, the feminine aspect of the deity, so in the corresponding spheres of impurity, the last and lowest sphere, parallel to the *Shekhinah*, is Lilith,[122] the feminine aspect of Satan.

The negative connection of the feminine with blood, and thus with the earth, is most evident in the archetypal uncleanness of the woman, who menstruates and gives birth. The taboo effect here seems to arise from the male "castration complex,"[123] which is activated by the bloody female genital. But it is only the archetypal background that makes this complex so meaningful.

Lilith carries this negative aspect. Hers is "the time of the waning moon, when its light diminishes and become deficient."[124] The whole world, not only the world of women, stands under the sign of the waning moon, in an impaired state that is symbolically "menstruation," and in which the negative principle of the world is strengthened. This is why all Jewish festivals are celebrated on the waxing moon.[125] Menstrual blood, through whose emission the woman "cleanses" herself, is the principle of uncleanness, and so it is even said that "Lilith is the blood from the cleansing of the *Shekhinah*."[126]

Whereas the *Shekhinah* is the positive moon, indeed the full moon, Lilith is the black moon.[127] In this connection, the course of the moon represents a cosmic process of the earth, into which all natural life on earth is yoked. The relationship between menstruation and Lilith follows not only from the fact that, archetypally, the menstrual period is also a time of uncleanness, but even more from the fact that, in Judaism, the waning moon and female menstruation are set forth as factually belonging together. That the connection between Lilith and menstruation was still alive in the Jewish Middle Ages is evident from the following story: "A man frequently noticed drops of blood on a tree, which resembled those of a menstruating woman; he therefore wanted to chop down the tree, but a learned man warned him against doing this, because he would lose his life, since Lilith was certain to inhabit this tree."[128]

Whereas the *Shekhinah* represents the positive anima-aspect of the feminine, Sophia, Lilith stands for the negative aspect. As such, she appears as the queen of the city of Saphir,[129] which is associated with the tales about the Queen of Sheba, the ruler of the female demons. The negative anima, so evident in the Middle Ages, which experiences woman as a temptress, enchantress, witch, and demonic conqueror, plays a major role in the psychology of the Jew, greater than that played by the positive anima, for reasons that are deeply related to our topic, the opposition between YHWH and earth.

This negative anima is also archetypal, an essential component of the negative aspect of the mother goddess. For the "terrible mother" corresponds, in a child's consciousness, to the experience of the terrible woman. Standing behind this Ishtar aspect of the feminine,[130] another danger repeatedly threatens the man's spiritualconscious dimension: the aspect of the unconscious as a danger, "the earth as threat." Whether this danger manifests itself fundamentally in the temptation by Eve, or negatively as Potiphar['s wife],[131] Delilah, and Salome, or positively as Ruth, Yael, Judith, and Esther, the superior power of the feminine is placed in the foreground time and again, whether seductively through intelligence, sweet temper and guile, or rapaciously, as a beauty that exploits the man's desire.

(From the dimension of feminine worldliness, the "castration complex" threatens the spiritual world and spiritual development of men, not only mythologically but often also in psychological reality, especially in the psychology of the second half of life. The characteristic reversal here goes so far that sexual abstinence quite often constitutes the potent stance, whereas falling prey to female sexuality, and abandoning the spiritual aspect for its sake, is branded and punished by the unconscious as regression, indeed as castration. This is significant, because this perspective, which is a partially correct perspective on the second half of life, later became disastrously totalized in Judaism and medieval Christianity.)

The midrash, which tells of Lilith, Adam's first wife, is characteristic in this respect: [132]

> When the Holy One had created the first human being, he said: it is not good for the man to be alone. And so he made him a wife from the earth (*adama*), like unto him, and called her Lilith. They immediately started quarrelling.

She said: "I do not want to lie below." But he said: "I do not want to lie below, but on top, and it befits you to be below, and me on top." She said: "We are equal, because we both come from the earth," and neither wanted to obey the other. When Lilith realized this, she spoke the *Shem ha-Meforash*, God's unspeakable name, and flew into the air of the world.[133]

Further on, the text mentions where Lilith located herself: "She was found standing in the sea, in the torrential water."[134]

The thoroughly Gnostic aspect of another text,[135] in which Lilith, as the wife of Satan and the daughter of primordial evil, desires *Adam Kadmon*[136] and wants to copulate with him, belongs to another level, however, and need not be discussed here.[137]

Lilith's manifold relationship with Adam is important. Before the creation of Eve, her behavior corresponds to that in the above passage. After the creation of Eve, the form of Adam and Eve's relationship in paradise makes her envious and desirous, but her attempt to disturb the couple ends with her banishment to the depths of the ocean.[138] In another version, in which she incites the serpent to seduction, her intention succeeds only too well. In the third stage, after the Fall and the expulsion from Paradise, she has intercourse with Adam, and demons, spirits, and ghosts are begotten from this marriage.[139]

The first Lilith is plainly enough the earth-woman. Unlike Eve, who was later created out of Adam, she refuses her subordinate place below Adam. The seduction by the serpent is also attributed to Lilith, as mentioned, and with this seduction Eve also gains a position "on top." She takes over in a negative way, and later she is therefore subordinated to Adam by the curse, whereas previously she was placed beside him as a "helper corresponding to him,"[140] that is, as a principle with equal rights.

This is not the place to examine the meaning of the feminine in Judaism. But it is characteristic that the struggle with the feminine principle of earth is placed here, at the very beginning of the world, and also that, in a tragic and ironic twist, Adam's second wife repeats and carries on the role of his first wife, Lilith, even though Eve comes from a different place of origin, not the earth but Adam's own rib.

Strikingly, however, this Lilith, the earth-woman, is not how one would at first imagine an earth-woman. There is nothing primitive about her. Instead, she proves to be infinitely superior to poor Adam and, as we shall see, not only to him. She is the great sorceress. She employs God's unspeakable name, the sacred instrument of great magic, and she lives in the sea, the waters of the deep, which not even the angel's summons could entice her to leave. The connection of this feminine aspect of the earth-woman with the magical–divinatory domain and the negative "waters of the deep"[141] can hardly be expressed more explicitly.

The negative, unconscious-rendering aspect of this female figure is characterized by the infertile, consuming desire that she represents and arouses. Already the Babylonian Liliths "stirred human passion, only to prevent its gratification."[142] Symbolically, this character of passionate desire is represented by the young Lilith, the elder woman's double, who is described as follows: "From head to navel, this

Lilith resembles a beautiful woman; from the navel down, however, she is nothing but fire and flames."[143]

The fiery character of this Lilith's lower half is different in a specific way from, for instance, the fish-character of mermaids and the lacerating bird-character of the Sirens. Common to all these types is the difference between the lower body and the upper, female–human part, but, in each case, the specific kind of inhumanity is an essential distinguishing trait.

A part of Lilith—and here our discussion comes full circle—is her succubus character, here meaning the "unfruitfulness and deviance" of the passions. It is sexual arousal and flooding that does not reach its object, but is infertile and blind, as it were, and leads to a sexual self-poisoning of the soul. Adam, avoiding Eve, begets demons, spirits, and ghosts with Lilith. It is the sexual fantasy that, held fast by the anima, does not enter life, but awakens the negative aspect of the unconscious. This also explains the archetypal idea of the demonically unclean effect of infertile semen in pollution[144] and masturbation. (Compare this also with the belief that a mandrake grows from the semen of the hanged man.) The often-stated connection between earth and divination is once again affirmed here, as is the sexual affinity of these spheres.

Judaism's rigorous sexual morality is also directed by the primacy of consciousness. That the direction of sexuality toward procreation stands under the sign of YHWH[145] is confirmed by circumcision, which subordinates the natural orientation to YHWH's intention. An objectless sexuality, or one that is directed away from the object, for instance, a sexuality offered orgiastically to the earth or to a *baal*,[146] for any purpose—even the purpose of fertility—belongs to idolatry and magic, just like a deviant and perverse sexual orientation. All of these deviations and detours lead to the negative domain of earth, that is, to Lilith, and awaken the unconscious at the expense of consciousness.

That sexual orgies, offerings of semen, perverse practices, etc., belonged to the cult of Canaanite–Near Eastern deities, and therefore had to be rejected, should not be understood merely in a historical connection. Rather, one must understand this and how the fundamental opposition of YHWH and earth stands behind this struggle, as the opposition between a principle of consciousness and spirit, cooperating with the unconscious, and an unconscious that subordinates consciousness to itself. Lilith's demand to "be on top" is fundamental, and it is fundamentally rejected.

Strikingly enough, contemporary astrology[147] characterizes Lilith, the black moon, in the same categories as those we have elaborated here. The connection between Kabbalistic–occult traditions and astrology is very close.

Astrology claims the existence of a rarely observed black moon, which is called Lilith and is supposedly linked genetically with the earth and the moon. Its effect is described as follows: "Its signs are psychic perversions of all kinds, especially affecting the erotic zone: bestiality and sadism are the worst." Lilith's human embodiment is an "atavistic reminder of primeval stages."[148] Here, the sexual, magical character of the negative anima becomes plainly evident in its infertile yet arousing and confusing aspect. Here, too, Lilith is the real adversary of consciousness and its most profound threat.

Notes

1 In Neumann's typescript, this appendix is related to the beginning of the first section of Chapter One: "The Near East and the significance of the Mother Goddess" (*Roots I*, pp. 15ff.).

2 *verarbeitete und bearbeitete*: Neumann's pair of adjectives, which may also be translated "assimilated and edited," seems deliberately chosen on account of their shared root: *Arbeit* (work). In the following paragraph, these words reappear as nouns: "eine Bearbeitung … eine echte Verarbeitung" ("a reworking … a genuine working-through"). Here Neumann may be imitating a rhetorical feature in biblical Hebrew, the *Leitwort* (guiding word), about which Buber writes ("*Leitwort* Style in Pentateuch Narrative," in B&R, *Scripture and Translation*, pp. 114ff.).

3 *Redaktor*: the word here includes the meaning of "editor," but extends beyond it. Biblical redactors, in the view espoused by Buber and others, unified the existing layers of the scriptural text by rearranging, combining, and to some extent even rewriting. Buber reports that his fellow translator, Franz Rosenzweig, as a "profound joke," liked to say "that the abbreviation *R* stood not for *Redaktor* but for *Rabbenu*, our teacher" ("Zu einer neuen Verdeutschung der Schrift," Beilage zum ersten Band, *Die fünf Bücher der Weisung*, p. 7n).

4 *EN*: *Jakob und Esau* I, III. [In the first chapter of *Jacob & Esau*, a discussion of the symbolic understanding of texts occurs, for example, on p. 44. In the third chapter, cf., for example, pp. 55f.]

5 *EN*: Cf. Häussermann op. cit. [Presumably a reference to "Die Deutung des Symbols" in *Wortempfang und Symbol in der alttestamentlichen Prophetie*, pp. 41–102. (Cf. *Roots I*, p. 38, n. 84.]

6 Neumann assigns his Appendix II to an early section of Chapter One, "The revelation on Sinai and the people's failure." Specifically, it follows "The Golden Calf" (*Roots I*, pp. 23ff.). It evidently grew out of an early version of Neumann's first chapter. In an early typescript, the statement originally preceding the first paragraph of this appendix reads: "To introduce the problem of the confrontation between the forces of the unconscious, which we intend to explore in key passages of the Pentateuch, we have chosen a selection of midrashim grouped around this problem, namely, the midrashim about the foundation stone and the waters of the deep."

7 *EN*: *Sefer ha-Maasiyoth* 157; cf. Bin Gorion, *Sagen der Juden*, v. 5, p. 132.

8 Ibid.

9 *EN*: Midrash ha-Neelam in *Zohar Hadash* and *Sefer Rasiel,* p. 14a; cf. Bin Gorion, v. 1, p. 36.

10 *im Allerheiligsten*: in the Holy of Holies, i.e., the innermost chamber of the Davidic Temple. Here, where the Ark of the Covenant was kept, only the high priest was permitted to enter, and that only once a year.

11 *EN*: Midrash ha-Neelam in *Zohar Hadash* and *Sefer Rasiel*, p. 14a; cf. Bin Gorion, v. 1, p. 36.

12 *EN*: Midrash Samuel 26b; cf. Bin Gorion, v. 5, p. 134. [(Cf. *Roots I*, p. 21, n. 29.]

13 *EN*: *Jacob & Esau*, Chapter 1, pp. 11ff.

14 Hebrew: oceanic depth, abyss, chaos. In Babylonian mythology, the deep (*tehom*) is personified in the monster and goddess Tiamat.

15 *EN*: cf. Jeremias, *Das alte Testament im Lichte des alten Orients*, where one finds, on p. 57, a good example of revealing an archetypal theme, without, however, overemphasizing the reciprocal influence. [In this passage, Jeremias quotes Proverbs 3:19f., in a version which reads: "… dadurch, daß sie (*die Weisheit*) ihn (*Jahve*) erkennt, haben sich die *Tehemot* gespalten …" ("[at the creation] … when Wisdom knew YHWH, the depths were divided …").]

16 *EN*: *Jacob & Esau*, Chapter 1, pp. 11ff.

17 *EN*: Sifre to Numbers 14:5. [No corresponding passage has been found.]

18 *EN*: Midrash Lekach Tob: cf. Bin Gorion, *Sinai & Garizim*, p. 187n.

19 Charlesworth, v. 1, p. 17. When quoting ancient texts, Neumann sometimes adds interpretation, as here, translating the names Azaz'el and Duda'el.
20 *EN*: Baer's "correction" is mistaken. The stones belong on top of Azazel, thus echoing
   the theme of the foundation stone. [Neumann's reference is probably to an unidentified
   passage in Baer's *Galut*.]
21 *EN*: *Jacob & Esau*, Chapter 1, pp. 28 ff.
22 *EN*: *Jer Tlm: Sanhedrin* 29a; also *Bab Tlm: Sukkah* 53a; cf. Bin Gorion, *Sagen der Juden*,
   v. 5, p. 133. [The passage is from *Sagen der Juden*, v. 5. Bin Gorion's Talmudic refs are
   accurate (ibid., p. 472). Citation not found in *Jer Tlm: Sanhedrin*. In *Bab Tlm: Sukkah*
   53a, we read: "When David dug the Pits, the Deep arose and threatened to submerge
   the world. 'Is there anyone,' David enquired, 'who knows whether it is permitted to
   inscribe the Name upon a sherd, and cast it into the Deep, that its waves should sub-
   side?'" (*Bab Tlm: Sukkah*, trans. by I. Slotki, Soncino).]
23 Cf. *Roots I*, p. 64.
24 *EN*: A Zoharic text referring to the myth of the foundation stone generalizes it as follows: at a time when people speak the truth, "the stone rises and receives the truth; it
   turns around and places itself upon the abyss. The world is made constant; telling the
   truth made the world constant." Conversely, lying makes the waters rise and scatters
   the sacred signs on the stone: "The waters strive to rise, to spread across the world, and
   to turn it into what they used to be." Here, mythical events are further typified and
   become the symbol of a Gnostified struggle of truth against the dark power of the
   primarily negative unconscious. See Zohar to Exodus 20:7 in Glatzer, *Sendung und
   Schicksal*, p. 49. [Glatzer's chapter title: "Wahrheit und Lüge: Aus dem Sohar" ("Truth
   and lies: From the Zohar"). The passage to which Glatzer refers is found in Zohar II
   91b. Cf. also Appendix A, *Roots II*, p. 185.]
25 *EN*: Zohar to Exodus 32:19f; cf. Bin Gorion, *Sagen der Juden*, v. 4, p. 265. [Zohar II 113b
   to Exodus cited, ibid., p. 387. Cf. also Appendix A, *Roots II*, pp. 185f.]
26 Appendix III originally followed the section in Chapter One titled "Prophecy, false
   prophecy, pagan prophecy" (*Roots I*, pp. 32ff.).
27 The immediately preceding passage in Chapter One reads: "This original line, which
   can still be demonstrated in the text, is blurred by the battle between the Levites and
   the Aaronite-Zadokite priests, who both oppose the prophetic conception of YHWH's
   direct charismatic choice" (*Roots I*, p. 35).
28 *EN*: See Auerbach, *Wüste und Gelobtes Land*, v. 1, pp. 95f.
29 "P" is an abbreviated reference to the "priestly source." Neumann shows his acquaint-
   ance with source criticism, a form of biblical exegesis developed by German Protestant
   theologians during the nineteenth century. The theory distinguishes four sources or traditions underlying the Hebrew scriptures, and names them by their initials: J (Yahwist),
   E (Elohist), D (Deuteronomic), and P (Priestly).
30 *Eliden*: direct descendants of Eli.
31 *EN*: Auerbach, op. cit., pp. 95f.
32 "J" is an abbreviation for the "Yahwistic" source, deemed by source-critical scholars to
   be the oldest of the scriptural sources.
33 On the creation of ritual objects at the shrine in Dan: "Now the man Mikha had a
   house of God; he had made an *efod* and *terafim* and had given-mandate to one of his
   sons, so that he had become a priest for him" (Judges 17:5, trans. by Everett Fox). The
   efod was an outer garment worn by the High Priest, which here carries the sense of
   "image." *Terafim* are "usually understood as household idols or figurines" (Fox, 2014,
   p. 235n).
34 *EN*: Cf. Auerbach, op. cit., pp. 28ff., on Judges 17:7ff.
35 "*Moschiden*": direct descendants of Moses. This word, parallel to *Eliden*, *Aroniden*, etc.,
   is occasionally found in German biblical commentaries of Neumann's period. The
   English equivalent, "Mosites," is rarely if ever used.
36 Cf. Numbers 3:11ff.

37 *EN*: See the discussion above, concerning the omission of inserted passages about the law. [Cf. *Roots I*, pp. 32f.]

38 Neumann's text reads *Vers 23*, apparently a typing error. The reference is to Numbers 3:2f.

39 This passage occurs in Numbers 16.

40 Numbers 18:4 begins, in Fox's translation: "They are to be-joined to you . . . ." Richard Corney advises that the first verb, "be-joined," has the same Hebrew root—לוה—as the name Levi. (Cf. also Gen 29:34.)

41 *EN*: Holzinger, Introduction to Chapter 18 (Kautzsch). [The quoted passage is found in Emil Kautzsch's German translation of the Old Testament, *Die Heilige Schrift des Alten Testaments* (1894; 4th edn, 1922, ed. by Bertholet). Heinrich Holzinger, a Protestant scholar, wrote the general introduction for v. 1 (pp. 1–7), and his notes and commentaries are interspersed in the first four books of the Pentateuch. This statement occurs in his commentary to Numbers 18:1–24 (4th edn, v. 1, p. 228).]

42 *EN*: See above, p. 41, n.3. [*Roots I*, p. 25, n. 42.]

43 Cf. *Roots I*, p. 32, n. 65.

44 The following paragraph, crossed out by the author, originally concluded Appendix III: This clarification distinguishes the primacy of the prophets' charismatic choice against false prophecy, which here appears as the claims of laymen (Dathan and Abiram), Levites (Korah), Aaronites (Aaron), and the family of Moses (Aaron and Moses). All of these competing claims are rejected in favor of the man Moses, the genuine and sole bearer of the executive power of YHWH, the Leader-God.

45 In Neumann's typescript, Appendix IV belongs to the second major section of his first chapter, "YHWH and the earth principle." He locates it after the sub-section titled, "YHWH as lord of fertility" (*Roots I*, pp. 43f.).

46 *nefesh*: a term in Hebrew for "soul," related etymologically to "throat," but having a variety of meanings. (Cf. *Roots I*, pp. 150ff.: "Body-soul and blood." Also cf. *Roots II*, pp. 25, 69, 72ff.)

47 *ruach Elohim*, the phrase, from Genesis 1:2, may be read as "the Spirit of the Lord" or "the wind of the Lord."

48 *EN*: Bin Gorion, *Sagen der Juden*, v. 1, p. 31 (referring to Midrash Themura in *Beth ha-Midrash*, v. 1, pp. 106f., and to *Sefer Yetzira*). [References are as listed in *Sagen der Juden*, v. 1, p. 352. Without knowing which editions of *Beth ha-Midrash* and *Sefer Yetzira* Neumann cited, these passages cannot be verified.]

49 Ibid.

50 Neumann quotes an unidentified translation. This phrasing is from the RSV.

51 *EN*: See Part Three. [At the time of writing, Neumann intended his third part to be devoted to ". . . the problem of the modern Jew. Illustration of historic–collective contents in dream and fantasy material," etc. (Neumann, 11 May 1940, *J-N Corresp*, p. 141).]

52 As in the account of Pentecost, e.g., Acts 2:1–4.

53 *EN*: Midrash ha-Neelam in *Zohar Hadash*, p. 6a. Cf. Midrash Bereshit Raba 124, Bin Gorion, *Sagen der Juden*, v. 1, p. 37 [Cf. *Sagen der Juden*, v. 1, p. 352.]

54 *EN*: Jung, *Psych & Rel*, pp. 71ff and 85ff. [Neumann cites the first English edition. Cf. CW 11.1, ¶103ff and ¶119ff.]

55 *Himmel*: the word in German means both "sky" and "heaven." Throughout this section, it may be read as "heaven." In this paragraph, however, where "*Himmel*" is part of the created world, "sky" may be a better reading.

56 *EN*: Erich Bischoff, *Die Elemente der Kabbalah, Erster Teil: Theoretische Kabbalah* (hereafter: Bischoff), p. 68. [In Bischoff's translation, this verse is found at Chapter 3, Mishna 4. In a contemporary English translation, it is found at Chapter 3, Mishna 3: "Three mothers Aleph, Mem and Shin in the world; breath, water and fire. Heavens were created first of fire, earth was created of water. Air, created from breath, tips the balance between them" (*Sefer Yetzira*, 2010, trans. by J. H. Worch, pp. 214f.).]

57 *EN*: Cf. Part Two. [*Roots II*, pp. 80, 170.]

58 *Fremdbeeinflussung*. Neumann makes no attempt to isolate biblical texts within their historical period, nor does he closely interrogate the archeological evidence about cross-influences between cultures in the ancient Near East. Instead, he draws on all available parallels to illustrate common symbolic patterns.

59 As noted, the Hebrew word *nefesh* has more than one meaning. In this paragraph, emphasizing the meaning "soul," Neumann's quotations read, following B&R: "'*Das Blut ist die Seele' (Nefesch)*"; "*Die Seele (Nefesch) des Fleisches ist im Blut.*" [In B&R: "*Denn die Seele des Fleisches, im Blut ist sie...*".] We have translated these lines according to Neumann's text. Fox's translation reads: "[T]he blood is the life" (Deut 12:23); "[T]he life of the flesh—it is in the blood" (Lev 17:11). In Genesis, the parallel reads: "[F]lesh with its life, its blood, you are not to eat!" (Gen 9:4).

60 *EN*: Bin Gorion, *Sagen der Juden*, op. cit.; also *Sinai und Garizim*, pp. 469f.

61 Cf. *Roots I*, p. 37, under "Affirmation of Nature and Nature's Purity." Cf. also *Roots I*, p. 159.

62 *Blutregion*: in this passage, discussing the symbology of blood, Neumann repeatedly uses *Region* and its compounds to refer metaphorically to the interwoven realities of body and psyche. Of this passage, Nancy Furlotti comments: "[Neumann] is referring to the 'realm' of affect with its red, potent energy and life-force.... Blood is the life-force that enlivens all life, including people and the gods.... All early cultures had to struggle to contain the affects/instincts seen as blood" (N. Furlotti, 20 July 2017).

63 *EN*: See C. G. Jung's introduction to *The Tibetan Book of the Dead*, especially his comments on the *Sidpa Bardo* and the adequacy of Freud's theory of sexuality, pp. 22f. [For example, Jung writes: "One rather wishes that Freudian psychoanalysis could have happily pursued these so-called intra-uterine experiences still further back ... beyond the *Sidpa Bardo*" (CW 11.7, ¶842). He continues: "Freudian psychoanalysis, in all essential aspects, never went beyond the experiences of the *Sidpa Bardo*; that is, it was unable to extricate itself from sexual fantasies and similar 'incompatible' tendencies which cause anxiety and other affective states" (ibid., ¶843).]

64 *EN*: *Midrash Bereshit Raba, Sefer Haggadah*, v. 3, p. 17. [Without knowing the edition to which Neumann refers, the passage cannot be located.]

65 Cf. *Roots I*, p. 40.

66 *EN*: Scholem, "Kabbala," in *Encyclopaedia Judaica* (hereafter *Enc Jud*), v. 9. (Scholem's major article on Kabbalah is found in *Enc Jud*, v. 9 (1932), cols 630–732. Neumann here summarizes a passage from cols 704f.]

67 *EN*: *Pirkei* of Rabbi Elieser, *Enc Jud*. [Evidently referring to a passage in Scholem's article on "Kabbala": "*nefesh* is even thought of (by Pirke R. Elieser and some philosophers) as a transient vital principle originating in the earth" (ibid., col. 705). A general description of the so-called "*Pirkei* (chapters) of R. Eliezer" is in *Enc Jud*, v. 1 (1928), under "Aggadische (Haggadic) Literatur," cols 1030f. In *Enc Jud*, v. 6 (1930), "Eliezer ben Hyrkanos," cols 461ff., R. Eliezer is described as being among the leading *tannaim* at the end of the first, beginning of the second century CE. In the post-Talmudic period, eighth century, the "*Pirkei* of R. Eliezer" were attributed to him (col 466).]

68 *EN*: Molitor, *Philosophie der Geschichte oder über die Tradition in dem alten Bunde und ihre Beziehung zur Kirche des neuen Bundes. Mit vorzüglicher Rücksicht auf die Kabbalah* (*A Philosophy of history. On tradition in the Old Covenant and its relation with the Church of the New Covenant. With special attention to the Kabbalah*), v. 3, pp. 521ff.

69 *EN*: Ibid., p. 299.

70 The association of *nefesh* with the feminine is evident in the quotation from the Zohar that follows. The context is a passage from Proverbs about the good wife.

71 *EN*: Zohar II 142a; from Bischoff, p. 111. [Both the *nefesh*, which Bischoff calls the *Sinnenseele* ("sensual soul"), and the *ruach*, which he calls the *Geistseele* ("spirit soul") are personified. Cf. Appendix A, *Roots II*, p. 186.]

72 Hebrew: soil, ground. In the account of Adam's creation (Gen 2:5–7), the word "soil" (*adama*) appears in three consecutive verses: God sees that someone is needed to till the soil; moisture rises to water the soil; and God forms a human being (*adam*) from dust of the soil.

73 *EN*: Fragment in the *Pirkei* of Rabbi Eliezer XII, supplemented by Midrash Bereshit Raba XIV,9; cited in Bin Gorion, *Sagen der Juden*, v. 1, pp. 115f. [Bin Gorion's attributions are found on p. 355.]

74 *EN*: *Jakob und Esau*, Chapter 1. [Neumann's reference is unclear.]

75 *EN*: Przyluski, "Ursprünge und Entwicklung des Kults der Muttergöttin" ("Origins and development of the Mother Goddess cult"), *EJ 1938*, pp. 11–57.

76 *EN*: Zohar I 2a; cf. Bischoff, v. 1, p. 136. [This passage reads, in part: "He (the hidden one = *Ein Sof*) is present and not present, deep and hidden. And his name (being absolute, undetermined) is '*mi*' (who?). . . . Therefore, in the (story of the) sin of the Golden Calf (Ex 32:4), it is rightly written: 'This (*eleh*) is your God (*elohekha*).' And as the '*mi*' unites with '*eleh*,' the name (of God) always unites with the (lower) levels, and on this secret rests the universe!" Cf. Appendix A, *Roots II*, p. 182.]

77 *EN*: *Pesikta Rabbati* 20, 95a and *Sefer Rasiel* 14b and 36a; cf. Bin Gorion, *Sagen der Juden*, v. 1, pp. 6, 44, 45. [*Pesikta Rabbati* text is found on p. 6, and *Sefer Rasiel* text on pp. 44f.]

78 *EN*: *Jer Tlm:Yoma* 39a; *Bab Tlm:Yoma* 19b; cf. Bin Gorion, *Sinai und Garizim*, p. 473. [*Jer Tlm:Yoma* 39a is about blood sacrifice at Yom Kippur. In *Bab Tlm:Yoma* 19b we read: "Some sort of noise was heard in the Temple Court, for an angel had come and struck him down on his face to the ground, and his brethren the priests came in and they found the trace as of a calf's foot on his shoulder . . ." (*Bab Tlm:Yoma*, trans. by Leo Jung, Soncino).]

79 *EN*: On the goat and bull, cf. *Jakob und Esau*, I. [The goat is discussed in *Jacob & Esau*, Chapter 1 (e.g., pp. 10–17); the bull is not mentioned.]

80 Cf. *Roots I*, p. 45, n. 120.

81 Hebrew: chariot. The word does not actually occur in the passage in Ezekiel 1, where the four faces (lion, bull/ox, eagle, human) are described. The vision is of a burning, wheeled structure that carries God's throne through the heavens; therefore it is given the name *Merkavah*.

82 In Persian mythology, Ridya is the angel in charge of rain (*Bab Tlm: Ta'anith*, trans. by J. Rabbinowitz, Soncino, 25b, n.5).

83 *EN*: *Bab Tlm: Ta'anith* 25b. Cf. parallel passages in *Bab Tlm:Yoma* 20b. Cf. also Rashi's commentary on this passage, and Bin Gorion, *Sinai und Garizim*, p. 473. [In *Bab Tlm: Ta'anith* 25b: "R. Eliezer said: 'When on the Feast of Tabernacles the water libations are carried out, Deep says to Deep, "Let thy waters spring forth. . . . I myself have seen Ridya, who resembles a three years' old heifer; he stands between the lower deep and the upper deep; to the upper deep he says, 'Distil thy water and to the lower deep he says, 'Let thy waters spring forth'." (*Bab Tlm: Ta'anith*, trans. by J. Rabbinowitz, Soncino). Parallel not found in *Bab Tlm:Yoma* 20b.]

84 *EN*: See the cycle of legends around Joseph's shrine (Bin Gorion, *Sagen der Juden*, v. 4, pp. 183 ff.).

85 Neumann's error. This episode in the Exodus narrative (Ex 4:24ff.) occurs when Moses is on his way back to Egypt. An astonishing element in the narrative is YHWH's threat to Moses' life, which René Malamud sets in the context of initiation into the mystery of the Great (Spirit) Father ("Gedanken zu Exodus 4:24," *Drei Aufsätze*, 2017, p. 290).

86 Another possible reading is that Moses himself is uncircumcised, and his infant son's emergency circumcision is efficacious for him as well (*Oxford Annotated RSV*, p. 72, note on Ex 4:25).

87 Hebrew: the covenant (of circumcision)

88 *EN*: Bin Gorion, *Sinai & Garizim*, p. 465.

89 *EN*: Ibid. [Cf. Ex 12:23.]

90 *EN*: Gesenius, *mashkof: Wörterbuch des Hebräischen*. [In the 1810 edition of Gesenius's *Hebrew Dictionary* we find, on p. 663: "מַשְׁקוֹף: *Oberschwelle . . . das Gebälke über der Thür*

(lintel . . . the beam above the door). 2 Mos. 12, 7.22.23." Neumann's phrase, "was oben hervorragt" (which protrudes above), does not appear in the dictionary entry.]

91   EN: Cf. Appendix IVb. [*Roots I*, pp. 150ff.]

92   *EN: Bab Tlm: Shabbath* 135a; cf. Bin Gorion, *Sinai & Garizim*, p. 463.

93   EN: Cf. Eisler's suggestion: "Das Rätsel des Johannes-Evangeliums" ("The riddle of the Gospel of John"), *EJ 1935*, p. 495, on Trumbull-Clay's "threshold covenant." [Evidently a reference to a book by H. Clay Trumbull, *The Blood Covenant*, in which "threefold covenant" is a central theme. Perhaps misreading "threefold," Eisler refers to "Trumbull-Clay's 'Threshold Covenant' . . . the analysis of Easter blood-rites."]

94   *EN*: See above, Zohar III 258b. [On marriage ritual. Cf. *Roots II*, Appendix A, p. 188.]

95   The Hebrew text is ambiguous. Other scholars read that Zipporah touches Moses' legs with their son's blood and calls Moses her "bridegroom of blood" (cf. Everett Fox, *The Five Books of Moses*, p. 279, note to Ex 4:25).

96   Neumann's paraphrase of Exodus 4:26, quoted above.

97   Hebrew: lit. "son of the commandment."

98   The usual meaning of the phrase is "a sleepless night." Erel Shalit advises that, in the context of the night of Passover, during the Israelites' flight from Egypt, the watching or guarding is understood to be performed by God.

99   Hebrew: "Hear, O Israel." Signaling the central prayer of Judaism: "Hear, O Israel, the Lord thy God, the Lord is one."

100 Neumann anticipates Part Three, which he did not complete.

101 Latin: image. Here the term refers to the son's inner picture of his mother, inevitably influenced by the Mother archetype, which must be distinguished from the personal mother, as an individual in the outer world.

102 EN: Genesis 20. [Apparently an error. A more likely reference would be Genesis 17, in which Abraham and all the males in his camp are circumcised, including his thirteen-year-old son, Ishmael (Gen 17:23–7).]

103 *EN*: Midrash Bereshith, cited by Bin Gorion, *Sinai & Garizim*, p. 103.

104 *EN*: Midrash Ruth, cited by Bin Gorion, ibid., p. 104.

105 In Fox's translation of Leviticus, this verse, like others naming the condition commonly translated as "impurity" or "uncleanness," is rendered using the Hebrew word, *tamei*. He notes: "[T]he term is not well served by negative translations, such as 'impure' or 'unclean'; the Hebrew signifies that something is in a charged state and must not come in contact with the sanctuary" (Fox, *The Five Books of Moses*, p. 525, n. 2).

106 *EN*: Rashi's commentary on *Bab Tlm: Shabbath* 135a; cited by Bin Gorion, *Sinai & Garizim*, p. 105.

107 *EN*: Cf. commentaries and references in Bin Gorion, ibid., p. 102.

108 *EN: Bab Tlm: Shabbath* 135a and Rashi's commentary; cited in Bin Gorion, ibid., p. 105.

109 *EN*: See above, p. 61. [*Roots I*, p. 37: "Affirmation of nature and nature's purity."]

110 *EN*: Midrash Vayikra; cf. Bin Gorion, *Sinai & Garizim*, p. 102.

111 *EN: Bab Tlm: Abboth* 5, 6; *Sifre* II 355; *Pesahim* 54a. Cf. Blau, *Das altjüdische Zauberwesen* (*Magical beings in ancient Judaism*). [In Ludwig Blau's first chapter, we read: "God created the evil spirits on Friday" (p. 11). Blau's annotation to this sentence appears to be the source of Neumann's Talmudic citations. In Mishnah 6 of *Abboth*, we read: "Ten things were created on the eve of the Sabbath at twilight . . . and some say also, the destroying {spirits} . . ." (*Bab Tlm: Abboth*, trans. by J. Israelstam, Soncino). In *Pesahim*, we read: "Our rabbis taught: Ten things were created on the eve of the Sabbath at twilight. . . . Others say, the harmful spirits (demons), too" (*Bab Tlm: Pesahim*, trans. by H. Freedman, Soncino). Jim Rosenbloom advises that two Hebrew editions of *Sifre* were available when Blau wrote. Without knowing the intended edition, his citation to *Sifre* cannot be confirmed.]

112 *EN*: Grunwald [1909], *Mitteilungen zur jüdischen Volkskunde*, v. 9, p. 12.

113 *EN*: "Lilith," *Enc Jud* [S. A. Horodezky, "Lilit," *Enc Jud*, v. 10 (1934), cols 972–4.]

114 *EN*: Soldan & Heppe, *Geschichte der Hexenprozess*, v. 1.

115 *EN*: *Bab Tlm: Shabbath* 151b. ["R. Hanina said: One may not sleep in a house alone, and whoever sleeps in a house alone is seized by Lilith" (*Bab Tlm: Shabbath*, trans. by H. Freedman, Soncino).]

116 *EN*: Scheftelowitz, *Altpersische Religion und Judentum: Unterschiede, Übereinstimmungen und gegenseitige Beeinflussungen* (*Ancient Persian religion and Judaism: Contrasts, similarities, and mutual influences*), p. 30.

117 *EN*: Zohar I 27b. [Cf. Appendix A, *Roots II*, pp. 182f.]

118 *EN*: Targum on Deuteronomy 32:24. [This verse does not directly mention Lilith, but it names several groups of demons: "From the midst of the Babylonian captivity I shall exile them to Media and to Elam. Those of the house of Agag shall oppress them, who are comparable to demons swollen with hunger and like destroyer demons consumed by birds and like midday demons afflicted by evil spirits and demons of the night inflated with evil spirits" (*The Aramaic Bible: Targum, Pseudo-Jonathan*, v. 5b: *Deuteronomy*, trans. by E. G. Clarke, p. 93).]

119 *EN*: Scheftelowitz, *Altpalästinischer Bauernglaube in religionsvergleichender Beleuchtung* (*Ancient Palestinian folk-belief, in the light of comparative religions*), p. 5, n. 1.

120 *EN*: Lidzbarski, *Johannesbuch der Mandäer* (*The Mandaean book of John*), v. 2, p. 11; cf. Scheftelowitz, *Altpalästinischer Bauernglaube*.

121 *EN*: *Bab Tlm: Baba Batra* 73a. Lilith is called the mother of Hormin (a demon) or of Hormiz (Ormuzd) (*Bab Tlm: Baba Batra*, trans. by M. Simon, Soncino).

122 *EN*: Cordovero, *Pardes Rimmonim*; cf. "Lilith," *Enc Jud*. [In his encyclopedia article, Horodezky quotes Cordovero: "The last of the ten spheres of uncleanness is named for her." He also comments on the heaven-disturbing hostilities between Lilith and other female demons (*Enc Jud*, v. 10, col. 973).]

123 Although Jung's work on complexes was well established at the time of writing, the concept of a castration complex was primarily identified with Freud's psychology. Neumann's use of quotation marks distances him from Freud's phrase. His next sentence, emphasizing archetypal theory, reframes the concept within a Jungian orientation.

124 *EN*: Scholem, "Kapitel aus dem Sohar" (chapter from the Zohar), p. 77.

125 *EN*: Molitor, *Philosophie der Geschichte*, v. 3, op. cit., pp. 204f.

126 Neumann provides no source for this story.

127 *Schwarzmond*: in esoteric religion, designating the new moon or the dark of the moon.

128 *EN*: *Sefer Hasidim*, cited in Scheftelowitz, *Altpalästinischer Bauernglaube*, op. cit., pp. 22f.

129 *EN*: Cf. Targum on Job 1:15; also Homburger, "Lilith," *Realenzyklopädie*. ["When Lilith, the Queen of {Sheba} and of Margod fell upon them suddenly and led them away, and they killed the young men . . ." (*The Aramaic Bible: Targum, Pseudo-Jonathan*, v. 15: *Job*, trans. by C. Mangan, pp. 25f.). The reference to Homburger's article is puzzling. *Paulys Realencyklopädie* (1926), contemporary with Neumann's writing, contains no article on Lilith.]

130 *EN*: Jeremias, *Das alte Testament im Lichte des alten Orients* (*The Old Testament in the light of the ancient Near East*), p. 434.

131 *Potiphar*: The word "wife" (*Frau*) is omitted in Neumann's typescript, but the reference is clear (Gen 39:6–20).

132 *EN*: August Wünsche, "Otijoth Ben Sira," cited in Bloch, *Priester der Liebe*, p. 235f. [The Bloch citation is confirmed, but the Wünsche source is unclear.]

133 *EN*: Bloch, *Priester der Liebe*, pp. 235f.

134 *EN*: Bin Gorion, *Sagen der Juden*, v. 1 p. 324.

135 *EN*: Ibid., p. 325 (from the Zohar).

136 Hebrew: the primordial man. Cf. *Roots I*, p. 51, n. 136; cf. also *Roots II*, pp. 69ff., 81, *et passim*.

137 *EN*: On the principle of the darkness striving toward *Adam Kadmon*, cf. Jonas, *Gnosis*, pp. 290ff. [In Jonas's chapter, "Das manichäische Erlösungsdrama" (The Manichaean redemption drama), section titled "Ewigkeit und Finsternis" ("Eternity and darkness").]

138 *EN*: Bin Gorion, *Sagen der Juden*, v. 1, p. 325 (Zohar).

139 *EN*: Hayyim Vital, "Lilith," *Enc Jud*, op. cit. [Horodezky's article "Lilith" contains a quotation from *Ez ha-Hayyim* (*Tree of Life*) by Hayyim Vital (1542–1620, leading disciple of Isaac Luria), from which Neumann takes the final two statements in this paragraph. Cf. *Enc Jud*, v. 10, col. 973.]

140 Genesis 2:18: "Now YHWH God said: It is not good for the human to be alone, I will *make* him a helper corresponding to him" (E. Fox, trans.).

141 *EN*: Cf. Appendix II, p. 187. [*Roots I*, p. 140: "The foundation stone and the waters of the deep."]

142 *EN*: On Lilith, see Vital, *Enc Jud* [Cf. note 139, above.]

143 *EN*: *Chesed l'Avraham* VI; cf. Bin Gorion, *Sagen der Juden*, v. 1, p. 327.

144 *Pollution*: the involuntary emission of semen.

145 *EN*: On YHWH as lord of fertility, cf. p. 74 [*Roots I*, pp. 43ff.]

146 Hebrew: pagan deity.

147 *EN*: Alfred Fankhauser, *Das wahre Gesicht der Astrologie*, pp. 73f.

148 Ibid.

EDITORIAL NOTE

Working with the materials for this book, I observed something about Neumann's writing method. His handwriting was nearly illegible. Perhaps for that reason, he typed up his own manuscripts, using sheets of carbon paper to produce a master copy, with three carbon copies. The existence of four identical typescripts allowed him to revise his work by hand. When he finished revising one of the lower carbon copies, he transferred his changes to a better one, revising again in the process. Last of all, he entered final revisions, either neatly printed or else typed on slips of paper and pasted into the master copy. This "fair copy" was presumably meant for the publisher.

So, Neumann created multiple, nearly identical copies of his manuscript, all of which he kept. Thanks to his painstaking method, his thrift in keeping duplicate copies, and his family's careful oversight, today we have the benefit of being able to compare different versions of his work. More than once, when transcribing this book, I could decipher Neumann's nearly illegible handwritten revisions only by studying an alternate copy.

The most dramatic instance arose with "Life in this world," the missing 36-page section in Part Two, printed as Chapter Three of *Hasidism*. This chapter exists today because I was able to reconstruct it from Neumann's poorest carbon copy, amended by comparison with his earlier version of Part Two.

In recent years, the existence of multiple, nearly identical copies produced an anomaly, one that may be typical of the vicissitudes that beset old and valuable manuscripts. Documents for Parts One and Two, essentially identical to those on which this work is based, are now privately owned by a company in California, which bought them at auction in 2006. The auction catalogue described them as follows:

> Two volumes . . . some typed and manuscript corrections on strips of paper
> affixed to the typescript, cloth-backed card wrappers, repairs to a few pages

with translucent adhesive tape, some small tears, browning, creasing to second title, small tears to wrappers.

(Sotheby's, London, 2006)

Although the unnamed buyers have declined to respond to repeated inquiries, no
harm resulted for the present work, because the complete, original materials were
still accessible. As explained, multiple copies of Neumann's typescripts, held by the
Erich Neumann Estate, were available for editing. I might have liked to compare
passages in these typescripts with the same passages in the auctioned copies; but as
it turned out, such comparisons were not essential.

I could not have prepared this book for publication without help from several
learned consultants. Erel Shalit had intended to be my primary consultant, in addition to overseeing the whole endeavor, but he fell ill, tragically, a few months
after our work began. Through illness and treatments, he used his strength strate-
gically, establishing the work's editorial direction in essential ways. For example,
he pondered and then accepted the title I proposed for the work, and later the
volume subtitles. He reviewed English-language options for transliteration from
Hebrew, and we worked together to set transliteration conventions for the work.
At a crucial point, Erel made it clear that the translation must be flexible, because
Neumann's youthful style required vigorous editing. He invited Professor Moshe
Idel to write the Foreword for Volume Two. As his last editorial contribution, in
January 2018, Erel sent out a set of electronic images, Neumann's "Torah" water-
colors. From these paintings, after his death, Nancy Furlotti and I selected the two
cover images.

The Roots of Jewish Consciousness is heavily annotated, for good reasons. The
challenge of bringing a work from the early twentieth-century German–Jewish
thought-world into the English-language world of today required extensive annotation. To mention only one example, in the early 1930s, when the Hitler era
began, the German language went through a transition. For instance, at Neumann's
time of writing, the word *völkisch* still had its old meaning, "national" ("pertaining
to a people"), as well as its newer one, "nationalist" (or, in Nazi jargon, "racially
German"). In his "Introduction to the work," Neumann uses the term twice in
one sentence, giving it both meanings (*Roots I*, p. 2, n. 4).

While working as translator, Mark Kyburz contributed to annotations and
helped the editorial process in other ways, with a fine copy-editor's eye. And,
as noted in the Acknowledgments section, several other scholars have responded
to my queries over the past three years, generously lending time and attention to
this project.

A special challenge arose early in the editorial process, because Neumann's personal library is lost. His books were given away years ago, and their whereabouts are
no longer known. To track down his many citations to German-language works that
are, in some cases, rarely read today, I turned at various times to the resources of the
Dorot Reading Room at the New York Public Library, the libraries of the Jewish
Theological Seminary and the Leo Baeck Institute, and—frequently, in the last

eighteen months—the vast Judaica collection at the library of Brandeis University, where I found invaluable help in the office of head librarian and Hebraist, Jim Rosenbloom.

In the annotations to this work, Neumann's original notes are introduced with his initials: *EN*. Editorial additions to his notes are enclosed in square brackets. Unsigned notes are by the editor, with occasional contributions from Mark Kyburz. Unless otherwise marked, all German-to-English translations are the collaborative work of Mark Kyburz and Ann Conrad Lammers. Mark, who translated Neumann's *Jacob & Esau*, began the translation process for the present work by systematically comparing key terms in *The Roots of Jewish Consciousness* with the translations of those terms in Neumann's previously published works. Over time, he prepared initial drafts of almost every document of *Roots*. He then graciously allowed me to revise his English texts, to bring them to a stylistic standard that I strongly felt, with support from Nancy Furlotti and Erel Shalit, was appropriate for this publication. As a consequence, Mark and I have collaborated intensively on every part of *Roots*, balancing our shared concern for accuracy and faithfulness to the original with the need for accessible, idiomatic, and readable English.

When it came to Neumann's quotations from published sources in German, we found three situations requiring special attention. First, when quoting the Bible, he favored the translations of Buber and Rosenzweig, then newly published, which have a distinctive character. Second, when quoting from the *Zohar*, Neumann draws from three German translations, which vary in their interpretations of the medieval Aramaic texts. Third, he quotes copiously from Buber's *Die chassidischen Bücher* (*Hasidic tales*). Mark and I had to decide how best to honor the author's choices, as we brought these and other quoted materials into English.

Dr. Everett Fox's biblical translations, *The Five Books of Moses* (1983, 1997) and *The Early Prophets* (2014), represent the best equivalent we could find of the translations undertaken in the 1920s by Martin Buber and Franz Rosenzweig. Dr. Fox's English version follows approximately the same principles as those of Buber and Rosenzweig, because it is meant to be read aloud and conveys—as far as possible—the aural and poetic qualities of the original Hebrew texts. As the B&R translations differ from other German Bibles, the voice in Fox's translations is different from that of other English-language translations.

Daniel Matt's English translations of the *Zohar*, in the Pritzker Edition, are now widely accepted as standard. In contrast, Neumann alternates among three German editions of the *Zohar*, all of them freely paraphrased and based on now-dated research. The advice of Tamar Kron and Erel Shalit was to substitute Matt's translations for our renderings of these passages. By following this suggestion, however, we would have introduced another problem. Neumann was deliberate in his use of sources, sometimes comparing one version with another. If his choices had been hidden behind a "standard" version, his nuances and associations would have been lost. Our compromise, therefore, was to be faithful in translating the passages Neumann quoted, while also—to the extent possible—printing Daniel Matt's versions of corresponding passages at the end of *Roots II* (Appendix A).

Neumann quotes heavily from Buber's collected stories of great Hasidic teachers, *Die chassidischen Bücher*, published in 1927/1928. For English versions of these passages, we were fortunate to have the two-volume translation by Olga Marx, *Tales of the Hasidim: The Early Masters* (1947), and *The Later Masters* (1948). Marx reorganizes Buber's text, however. Her edition includes passages from his other books, while omitting passages from *Die chassidischen Bücher*. Passages not found in *Tales of the Hasidim* are translated by Kyburz and Lammers. Neumann's citations to Buber's book are maintained as he gave them. *Tales I* and *II* are also cited when appropriate.

While we worked on the English edition, Neumann's book was being translated into Hebrew by Tamar Kron and David Wieler, whose judicious suggestions and corrections have often made our English translations more accurate. Dr. Kron is a Jungian analyst and a leading professor of Jewish mysticism. With her guidance, I located several elusive passages in the Talmud and Mishnah. It was she who first referred me to the Pritzker *Zohar*, and who helped me direct an artist's recreations of Neumann's drawings of the Sefirotic Tree.

BIBLIOGRAPHY

I. Primary sources

This section shows works cited by Erich Neumann in the text and notes of Volumes One and Two of *The Roots of Jewish Consciousness*. Translations and related editions, including abbreviated references to Jung's Collected Works (CW), appear immediately after the editions to which they correspond, enclosed in square brackets.

A few sources that Neumann regularly consulted and quoted are missing from this list, including his German edition of the Talmud. In the absence of his personal library, it is hard to say which of the then-available editions should be listed here. Editions of the Talmud consulted by the editor are listed under **Secondary sources**, together with sources cited by contributors to *Roots I* and *II*.

Apuleius, Lucius, *Der Goldene Esel: Metamorphosen*, translated by August Rode, Berlin: Propyläen, 1920. [Originally published 170 CE.]
[— *The Golden Ass, or Metamorphoses*, translated and introduced by E. J. Kenney, London and New York: Penguin Classics, 1999.]
Auerbach, Elias, *Wüste und Gelobtes Land*, v. 1: *Geschichte Israels von den Anfängen bis zum Tode Salomos*, v. 2: *Geschichte Israels vom Tode Salomos bis Ezra und Nehemia*, Berlin: Schocken, 1938.
Azulai, Avraham b. Mordecai, *Chesed l'Avraham*, Amsterdam: Emanuel Athias, 1785.
Baader, Franz, *Franz von Baaders Vorlesungen und Erläuterungen zu Jacob Böhmes Lehre*, edited by Julius Hamberger, Leipzig: Bethmann, 1855.
Baer, Yizchak, *Galuth*, Berlin: Schocken, 1936.
[— *Galut*, translated by Robert Warshaw, Lanham, MD: University Press of America, 1988.]
Baldensperger, Wilhelm, *Die messianischen-apokalyptischen Hoffnungen des Judentums*, 3rd edn, Strassburg: Heitz & Mündel, 1903.
Baudissin, Wolf Wilhelm Graf von, *Kyrios als Gottesname im Judentum und seine Stelle in der Religionsgeschichte*, v. 3, 4, Giessen: Eißfeldt, 1929.

Baumann, Hans, "Tier und Pflanze als Symbole," *Zentralblatt für Psychotherapie und ihre Grenzgebiete*, v. 10.3, Leipzig: Hirzel, 1938, pp. 149–65.

Baynes, H. G., *Germany Possessed*, introduction by Hermann Rauschning, London: Jonathan Cape, 1941.

Bergel, Joseph, *Mythologie der alten Hebräer*, v. 1, Leipzig: Friedrich, 1882.

Bin Gorion, Micha Josef, *Die Sagen der Juden: Von der Urzeit*, v. 1; *Ssefer Hamaassioth CLVII*, v. 5; *Ssefer Jezira*, v. 1, Frankfurt am Main: Rütten und Loenig, 1913.

— *Sinai und Garizim: Über den Ursprung der israelitischen Religion, Forschung zum Hexateuch auf Grund rabbinischer Quellen*, Berlin: Morgenland, 1926.

Birnbaum, Salomo, *Leben und Worte des Balschemm nach chassidischen Schriften, Auswahl und Übertragung von Salomo Birnbaum*, Berlin: Welt, 1920.

Bischoff, Erich, *Elemente der Kabbalah, Teil I: Theoretische Kabbalah. Das Buch Jezira, Sohar-Auszüge, Spätere Kabbalah. Übersetzungen, Erläuterungen und Abhandlungen*, Berlin: Barsdorf, 1913.

Blau, Ludwig, *Das altjüdische Zauberwesen*, Budapest: Jahresbericht der Landes-Rabbinerschule in Budapest, 1898. (2nd edn, Berlin: Lamm, 1914.)

Bloch, Chajim, *Priester der Liebe: Die Welt der Chassidim*, Zürich: Amalthea, 1930.

[— *Aus Mirjams Brunnen*, introduction by Salcia Landmann, Darmstadt: Melzer, 1966.]

Brecher, Gideon, *Das Transzendentale, Magie und magische Heilarten im Talmud*, Wien: Klopf & Eurich, 1850.

Buber, Martin, *Des Baal-Schem-Tow Unterweisung im Umgang mit Gott*, Hellerau: Hegner, 1927.

— *Die chassidischen Bücher*, Berlin: Schocken, 1928.

[— *Tales of the Hasidim*, Volume One: *The Early Masters*, translated by Olga Marx, New York: Schocken, 1947.]

[— *Tales of the Hasidim*, Volume Two: *The Later Masters*, translated by Olga Marx, New York: Schocken, 1948.]

[— *Tales of the Hasidim. I. The Early Masters; II. The Later Masters*, translated by Olga Marx, Foreword by Chaim Potok, New York: Schocken, 1991.]

— *Ich und Du*, Leipzig: Insel, 1923.

[— *I and Thou*, translated by Walter Kaufmann, New York: Scribner, 1970.]

— *Königtum Gottes*, v. 1: *Das Kommende*, Berlin: Schocken, 1932/1936.

[— *Kingship of God*, 3rd edn, translated by Richard Scheimann, New York: Harper & Row, 1967.]

— *Moses*. משה, Jerusalem: Schocken, 1945.

[— *Moses: The Revelation and the Covenant*, New York: Harper & Brothers, 1958.]

— *Reden über das Judentum: Gesamtausgabe*, Berlin: Schocken, 1932.

— *Der Weg des Menschen: nach der chassidischen Lehre*, Heidelberg: Lambert Schneider, 1948, 1960.

[— *The Way of Man According to the Teaching of Hasidism*, translator unidentified, Secaucus, NJ: Citadel, 1966.]

Buber, Martin und Rosenzweig, Franz, *Die Schrift*, v. 1: *Die Fünf Bücher der Weisung* (Im Anfang, Namen, Er rief, In der Wüste, Reden); v. 2: *Künder: Bücher der Geschichte* (Jehoschua, Richter, Schmuel, Könige); v. 3: *Künder: Bücher der Kündung* (Jeschajahu, Jirmejahu, Jecheskel, Die Zwölf), Berlin: Schocken, 1934.

— *Die Schrift und ihre Verdeutschung*, Berlin: Schocken, 1936.

[— *Scripture and Translation*, translated by Lawrence Rosenwald, with Everett Fox, Bloomington and Indianapolis, IN: Indiana University Press, 1994.]

Cassirer, Ernst, *Philosophie der symbolischen Formen*, v. 2, *Das mythische Denken*, Berlin: Bruno Cassirer, 1925. [Facsimile edition, Darmstadt: Primus, 1997.]

[— *The Philosophy of Symbolic Forms*, vol. 2, *Mythical Thought*, translated by Ralph Manheim, preface and introduction by Charles W. Hendel, New Haven, CT: Yale University Press, 1955.]

Chantepie de la Saussaye, P.D., Bertholet, A., Lehmann, E., et al., *Lehrbuch der Religionsgeschichte*, v. 1, Tübingen: Mohr, 1925.

Cordovero, Moshe, *Pardes Rimmonim*, Safed, Israel: [n.p.], 1548.

Diels, Herman (trans), *Herakleitos von Ephesos*, Berlin: Weidmann, 1909.

Eisler, Robert, "Das Rätsel des Johannes-Evangeliums," *Eranos-Jahrbuch 1935*, Zürich: Rhein, 1936, pp. 323–512.

Ermann, Adolf, *Die Literatur der Ägypter: Gedichte, Erzählungen und Lehrbücher aus dem 3. und 2. Jahrtausend v. Chr.*, Leipzig: Historische Buchhandlung, 1923.

Evans-Wentz, W. Y., ed., *Das Tibetanische Totenbuch*, mit Einleitung von C.G. Jung, Zürich: Rascher, 1935.

[— ed., *The Tibetan Book of the Dead*, with Psychological Commentary by C. G. Jung, London, Oxford, New York: Oxford University Press, 1960.]

— ed., *Yoga und Geheimlehren Tibets*, v. 3, München: Barth, 1937.

Fankhauser, Alfred, *Das wahre Gesicht der Astrologie*, Zürich & Leipzig: Orell Füssli, 1932.

Franck, Adolphe, *Die Kabbala, oder die Religions-Philosophie der Hebräer*, aus dem Französischen übersetzt, verbessert und vermehrt von Adolf Gelinek, Leipzig: Hunger, 1844. [2nd edn, Berlin: Lamm, 1913.]

Freud, Sigmund, *Der Mann Moses und die monotheistische Religion*, Amsterdam: Allert de Lange, 1939.

Geitel, Charlotte, "Das introvertierte Kind," *Reich der Seele: Arbeiten aus dem Münchener psychologischen Arbeitskreis*, v. 2, edited by G. R. Heyer, München: Lehmanns, 1937.

Gesenius, Heinrich Friedrich Wilhelm, "Mischkaf," *Neues Hebräisch-deutsches Handwörterbuch*, Leipzig: [n.p.], 1815/1823/1828.

Glatzer, Nahum Norbert, *Untersuchung zur Geschichtslehre der Tannaiten*, Berlin: Schocken, 1933.

Glatzer, Nahum Norbert & Strauss, Ludwig, *Ein jüdisches Lesebuch. Sendung und Schicksal. Aus dem Schrifttum des nachbiblischen Judentums*, Berlin: Schocken, 1931.

[— *Time and Eternity: A Jewish Reader*, translated by Olga Marx, New York: Schocken, 1946.]

Goethe, Johann Wolfgang, *Faust: Zweiter Teil*, Aarau: Sauerländer, 1832/1960.

[— *Faust: Part Two*, translated by Philip Wayne, London: Penguin, 1959.]

Goldberg, Oskar, *Die Wirklichkeit der Hebräer: Einleitung in das System des Pentateuch*, Berlin: David, 1925.

Goldschmidt, G,."Alchemie der Ägypter," *Ciba-Zeitschrift*, no. 57: *Der Ursprung der Alchemie*, Basel und Leipzig: Gesellschaft für Chemische Industrie in Basel, 1938.

Grunwald, Max, ed., *Mitteilungen zur jüdischen Volkskunde*, v. 9, Berlin: Calvary, 1909.

Gunkel, Hermann, trans, "Das vierte Buch Esra," *Apokryphen und Pseudepigraphen des Alten Testaments*, v. 2: *Die Pseudepigraphen des Alten Testaments*, edited by E. F. Kautzsch, Tübingen: Mohr, 1900, pp. 331–401.

Häussermann, Friedrich, *Wortempfang und Symbol in der alttestamentlichen Prophetie: Eine Untersuchung zur Psychologie des prophetischen Erlebnisses*, Giessen: Töpelmann, 1932.

Heiler, Friedrich, *Das Gebet: Eine religionsgeschichtliche und religionspsychologische Untersuchung*, 2nd edn, München: Reinhardt, 1920.

Hennecke, Edgar, ed., *Neutestamentliche Apokryphen, in Verbindung mit Fachgelehrten in deutscher Uebersetzung und mit Einleitungen*, 2nd edn, Tübingen: Mohr, 1924.

Heyer, Gustav Richard, *Organismus der Seele*, München: Lehmanns, 1932.

Heyer, Gustav Richard and Seifert, Friedrich, eds, *Reich der Seele: Arbeiten aus dem Münchener psychologischen Arbeitskreis*, v. 1, 2, München: Lehmanns, 1937.

Heyer, Lucy, "Erinyen und Eumeniden: Der Kampf zwischen Geist und Erde in der antiken Tragödie," *Reich der Seele: Arbeiten aus dem Münchener psychologischen Arbeitskreis*, v. 1, edited by G. R. Heyer and F. Seifert, München: Lehmanns, 1937, pp. 39–51.

Holzinger, Heinrich, "Einleitung, Numeri 18," *Die Heilige Schrift des Alten Testatments*, v. 1, translated by Emil Kautzsch, 4th edn, edited by Alfred Bertholet, Tübingen: Mohr, 1922, p. 228.

Hornstein, Maria, "Der Mensch und sein Tier," *Reich der Seele: Arbeiten aus dem Münchener psychologischen Arbeitskreis*, v. 2, edited by G. R. Heyer and F. Seifert, München: Lehmanns, 1937, pp. 119–58.

Horodezky, Samuel A., "Baal-Schem-Tob (בעש״ט), Israel ben Elieser," *Encyclopaedia Judaica: Das Judentum in Geschichte und Gegenwart*, v. 3, edited by Jakob Klatzkin, Berlin: Eschkol, 1929, col. 835–42.

— "Lilith," *Encyclopaedia Judaica: Das Judentum in Geschichte und Gegenwart*, v. 10, edited by Jakob Klatzkin, Berlin: Eschkol, 1934, col. 972–4.

— *Mystisch-religiöse Strömungen unter den Juden in Polen im 16.–18. Jhdt*, Leipzig: Engel, 1914.

— *Torat ha-magid mi-Mezerits ve-sihotav*. תורת ה ״מגיד״ ממזריטש ושיחתיו (The teaching of the Maggid of Meseritz and his conversations), Berlin: Ajanoth, 1923.

— *Torat Rabi Nahman mi-Bratslav ve-sihotav*. תירת רבי נחמן מברצלב ושיחיתיו (The teaching of R. Nachman of Bretzlav and his conversations), Berlin: Ajanoth, 1923.

Jeremias, Alfred, *Das alte Testament im Lichte des alten Orients: Handbuch zur biblisch-orientalischen Altertumskunde*, Leipzig: Hinrich, 1906.

Jonas, Hans, *Gnosis und spätantiker Geist*, v. 1: *Die mythologische Gnosis*, with foreword by Rudolf Bultmann, Göttingen: Vandenhoeck & Ruprecht, 1934.

Jung, C. G., *Analytische Psychologie und Erziehung: Drei Vorlesungen gehalten in London im Mai 1924*, Heidelberg: Kampmann, 1926. [Reprint, 1936.] [CW 17,3]

— *Die Beziehungen zwischen dem Ich und dem Unbewussten*, Darmstadt: Reichl, 1928. [CW 7,2]

— "Bruder Klaus," *Neue Schweizer Rundschau*, August 1933, pp. 223–9. [CW 11,6]

— *Diagnostische Assoziationsstudien*, v. 2: *Beiträge zur experimentellen Psychopathologie*, Leipzig: Barth, 1909. [CW 2,9]

— "Einführung," *Das Geheimnis der Goldenen Blüte: Ein chinesisches Lebensbuch*, Übersetzt und erläutert von Richard Wilhelm mit einem europäischen Kommentar von C. G. Jung, München: Dorn, 1929, pp. 7–88. [2nd edn, Berlin: Dorn, 1936.]

— "Einführung," *Das Tibetanische Totenbuch*, edited by W. Y. Evans-Wentz, Zürich: Rascher, 1935, pp. 15–35. [CW 11,11]

— "Einige Bemerkungen zu den Visionen des Zosimos," *Eranos-Jahrbuch 1937*, Zürich: Rhein, 1938, pp. 15–54. [CW 13,2]

— "Zur Empirie des Individuationsprozesses," *Eranos-Jahrbuch 1933*, Zürich: Rhein, 1934, pp. 201–14. [CW 9.i,11]

— "Die Erlösungsvorstellungen in der Alchemie," *Eranos-Jahrbuch 1936*, Zürich: Rhein, 1937, pp. 13–112. [CW 12,3,III]

— "Zum Gedächtnis Richard Wilhelms," *Das Geheimnis der goldenen Blüte: Ein chinesisches Lebensbuch*, 2nd edn, edited by R. Wilhelm and C. G. Jung, translated by R. Wilhelm, Berlin: Dorn, 1936, pp. ix–xviii. [CW 15,5]

— *The Integration of the Personality*, translated by Stanley M. Dell, New York: Farrar and Reinhart, 1939. [CW 9,i, CW 12, CW 17.]

— "Die Lebenswende," *Seelenprobleme der Gegenwart*, Zürich: Rascher, 1931, pp. 248–74. [CW 8,16]

— "Psychological Analysis of Nietzsche's Zarathustra: Notes on the Seminar." Unpublished, typed transcriptions of English-language seminars, edited by Mary Foote, 1934–1939.

— "Psychologische Grundlagen des Geisterglaubens," *Über die Energetik der Seele*, Zürich: Rascher, 1928, pp. 200–24. [CW 8.11]

— *Psychologische Typen*, Zürich: Rascher, 1921. [2nd edn, 1930.] [CW 6]

— "Die Psychologischen Aspekte des Mutterarchetypus," *Eranos-Jahrbuch 1938*, Zürich: Rhein, 1939, pp. 403–44. [CW 9.i,4]

— *Psychology and Religion: The Terry Lectures*, New Haven, CT and Oxford: Yale University Press, 1938. [CW 11,1]

[— *Psychologie und Religion: Die Terry Lectures, gehalten an der Yale University*, translated by F. Froboese and T. Wolff, Zürich: Rascher, 1940.]

— *Seelenprobleme der Gegenwart*, Zürich: Rascher, 1931. [CW 4, CW 6, CW 8, CW 10, CW 15, CW 16, CW 17.]

— "Die Struktur der Seele," *Seelenprobleme der Gegenwart*, Zürich: Rascher, 1931, pp. 114–75. [CW 8,7]

— "Traumsymbole des Individuationsprozesses," *Eranos-Jahrbuch 1935*, Zürich: Rhein, 1936, pp. 13–134. [CW 12,3,II]

— "Über die Archetypen des kollektiven Unbewussten," *Eranos-Jahrbuch 1934*, Zürich: Rhein, 1935, pp. 179–230. [CW 9.i,1]

— *Über die Energetik der Seele*, Zürich: Rascher, 1928. [CW 8,1; 8,6; 8,9; 8,11]

— "Die verschiedenen Aspekte der Wiedergeburt," *Eranos-Jahrbuch 1939*, Zürich: Rhein, 1940, pp. 399–447. [CW 9.i,5]

— *Wandlungen und Symbole der Libido: Beiträge zur Entwicklungsgeschichte des Denkens*, Leipzig,Vienna: Franz Deuticke, 1912–1925. [CW 5]

— *Wirklichkeit der Seele: Anwendungen und Fortschritte der neueren Psychologie*, with contributions by H. Rosenthal, E. Jung, W. M. Kranefeldt, Zürich: Rascher, 1934. [CW 8, CW 10, CW 15, CW 16, CW 17, CW 18.]

— "Wotan," *Neue Schweizer Rundschau*, March 1936, pp. 657–69. [CW 10,10]

Kautzsch, Emil F., *Apokryphen und Pseudepigraphen des Alten Testaments*, v. 2: *Die Pseudepigraphen des Alten Testaments*, Tübingen: Mohr, 1900.

— *Biblische Theologie des Alten Testaments*, 4th edn, Tübingen: Mohr, 1922.

Klatzkin, Jakob, ed., *Encyclopaedia Judaica: Das Judentum in Geschichte und Gegenwart*, v. 1–10 (A–Lyra), Berlin: Eschkol, 1928–34.

Lévy-Bruhl, Lucien, *Das Denken der Naturvölker*, Wien, Leipzig: Braunmüller, 1926. [Originally published as *Les fonctions mentales dans les sociétés inférieures*, 1910.]

[— *How Natives Think*, translated by Lilian Ada Clare, New York: Washington Square Press, 1966.]

— *Die geistige Welt der Primitiven*, München: Bruckmann, 1927. [Originally published as *La mentalité primitive*, 1922.]

— *Die Seele der Primitiven*, Wien und Leipzig: Braunmüller, 1930. [Originally published as *L'âme primitive*, 1927.]

Lidzbarski, Mark, *Das Johannesbuch der Mandäer*, v. 2, Giessen: Töpelmann, 1905.

Michaëlis, Edgar, *Die Menschheitsproblematik der Freudschen Psychoanalyse: Urbild und Maske*, Leipzig: Barth, 1925.

Molitor, Franz Joseph, *Philosophie der Geschichte oder über die Tradition in dem alten Bunde und ihre Beziehung zur Kirche des neuen Bundes. Mit vorzüglicher Rücksicht auf die Kabbalah*, v. 3, Münster: Theissing, 1839.

Müller, Ernst, *Der Sohar: Das heilige Buch der Kabbala, nach dem Urtext herausgegeben*, Wien: Glanz, 1932.

— *Der Sohar und seine Lehre: Einleitung in die Gedankenwelt der Kabbalah*, Wien, Berlin: Löwit, 1920.

Neumann, Erich, "Beiträge zur Symbolik des Jakob-Esau-Gegensatzes," typescript, 1934, pp. 1–99.

[— *Jacob and Esau: On the Collective Symbolism of the Brother Motif*, edited and introduced by Erel Shalit, translated by Mark Kyburz, Asheville, NC: Chiron, 2015.]

— "Das Bewusstsein und der religiöse Aspekt: Als Einleitung in einen Kurs über 'Das Unbewusste und der religiöse Aspekt'," unpublished typescript of lecture, November 1940, pp. 1–27 (now missing pp. 5–11).

— "Bewusstseins-Entwicklung und Psychologie der Lebensalter," typescript, 1943, pp. 1–27.

[— "The Development of Consciousness and Stages of Life," second lecture in four-lecture series, "The Importance of Consciousness in the Experience of Depth Psychology," *Roots II, Hasidism*, Appendix B.II, pp. 209–34.]

— "David und Saul," unpublished typescript of short story, n.d., pp. 1–15.

— "Eros und Psyche: Ein Beitrag zur seelischen Entwicklung des Weiblichen," in Apuleius, *Amor und Psyche*, Zürich: Rascher, 1952, pp. 75–217.

[— *Amor and Psyche: The Psychic Development of the Feminine. A Commentary on the Tale by Apuleius*, translated by Ralph Manheim, Princeton, NJ: Princeton University Press, 1956.]

— "Die religiöse Erfahrung in der Psychoanalyse," unpublished typescript of lecture, April 1940, pp. 1–20.

— "Zur religiösen Bedeutung des tiefenpsychologischen Weges," typescript, 1942, pp. 1–26 (missing pp. 27–9).

[— "The Religious Meaning of the Path of Depth Psychology," fourth lecture in four-lecture series, "The Importance of Consciousness in the Experience of Depth Psychology," *Roots II, Hasidism*, Appendix B.IV, pp. 256–74.]

— "Symbole und Stadien der Bewusstseins-Entwicklung," typescript, 1943, pp. 1–20.

[— "Symbols and Stages of Conscious Development," first lecture in four-lecture series, "The Importance of Consciousness in the Experience of Depth Psychology," *Roots II, Hasidism*, Appendix B.I, pp. 190–208.]

— *Tiefenpsychologie und neue Ethik*, Zürich: Rascher, 1949.

[— *Depth Psychology and a New Ethic*, with forewords by C. G. Jung, Gerhard Adler, and James Yandell, translated by Eugene Rolfe, Boston & London: Shambhala, 1969/1990.]

— "Der tiefenpsychologische Weg und das Bewusstsein," typescript, 1943, pp. 1–20.

[— "The Path of Depth Psychology and Consciousness," third lecture in four-lecture series, "The Importance of Consciousness in the Experience of Depth Psychology," *Roots II, Hasidism*, Appendix B.III, pp. 235–55.]

— *Ursprungsgeschichte des Bewusstseins*, mit einem Vorwort von C. G. Jung, Zürich: Rascher, 1949.

[— *The Origins and History of Consciousness*, with a foreword by C. G. Jung. translated by R. F. C. Hull, Princeton, NJ: Princeton University Press, 1954.]

Ninck, Martin, *Götter- und Jenseitsglauben der Germanen*, Jena: Diederichs, 1937.

— *Wodan und germanischer Schicksalsglaube*, Jena: Diederichs, 1935.

Otto, Rudolf, *Das Heilige: Über das Irrationale in der Idee des Göttlichen und sein Verhältnis zum Rationalen*, München: Beck, 1917.

[— *The Idea of the Holy: An Inquiry into the Non-Rational Factor in the Idea of the Divine and its Relation to the Rational*, translated by J. W. Harvey, London: Oxford University Press, 1923.]

— *Sünde und Urschuld und andere Aufsätze zur Theologie*, München: Beck, 1932.

Przyluski, Jan, "Ursprünge und Entwicklung des Kults der Muttergöttin," *Eranos-Jahrbuch 1938*, Zürich: Rhein, 1939, pp. 93–136.

Puech, Henri-Charles, "Der Begriff der Erlösung im Manichäismus," *Eranos-Jahrbuch 1936*, Zürich: Rhein, 1937, pp. 183–286.

Ramakrishna, Sri, *The Teachings of Sri Ramakrishna*, edited by Swami Budhananda, Calcutta: Advaita Ashrama, 1971. (Combines two volumes.)

Scheftelowitz, Isidor Isaac, *Altpalästinischer Bauernglaube in religionsvergleichender Beleuchtung*, Hannover: [n.p.], 1924.

— *Altpersische Religion und Judentum: Unterschiede, Übereinstimmungen und gegenseitige Beeinflüssungen*, Giessen: Töpelmann, 1920.

Scholem, Gershom Gerhard, *Bibliographia Kabbalistica: Die jüdische Mystik (Gnosis, Kabbala, Sabbatianismus, Frankismus, Chassidismus) behandelnde Bücher und Aufsätze von Reuchlin bis zur Gegenwart*, Leipzig: Drugulin, 1927. [Rev. edn, Berlin: Schocken, 1933.]

— *Das Buch Bahir: Ein Schriftdenkmal aus der Frühzeit der Kabbala auf Grund der kritischen Neuausgabe von Dr. Gerhard Scholem*, Leipzig: Drugulin, 1923.

— *Die Geheimnisse der Schöpfung: Ein Kapitel aus dem Sohar*, Berlin: Schocken, 1935.

— "Kabbala," *Encyclopaedia Judaica: Das Judentum in Geschichte und Gegenwart*, v. 9, edited by Jakob Klatzkin et al, Berlin: Eschkol, 1932, cols 630–732.

— *Major Trends in Jewish Mysticism*, Jerusalem and New York: Schocken, 1941.

— "Zum Verständnis des Sabbatianismus: Zugleich ein Beitrag zur Geschichte der Aufklärung," *Almanach des Schocken Verlags 5697*, Berlin: Schocken, 1936/37, pp. 30–42.

Silberer, H., *Probleme der Mystik und ihrer Symbolik*, Wien: Leipzig & Heller, 1914.

Soldan, W. G. & Heppe, Heinrich, ed., *Soldan's Geschichte der Hexenprozesse, neubearbeitet von Dr. Heinrich Heppe*, v. 1, Stuttgart: Cotta, 1880.

Steinmann, E., רבי נחמן מברסלב ("Rabbi Nachman of Brezlav"), *Davar*, 11 October 1940, Tel Aviv, p. 3.

Trumbull, H. C., *The Blood Covenant: A Primitive Rite and its Bearings on Scripture*, Philadelphia: Wattles, 1898.

Virolleaud, Charles, *L'Astrologie Chaldéenne: le livre intitulé "Enuma (Anu) ilu.Bel"* (transliteration and translation of an ancient Mesopotamian text), Paris: Paul Geuthner, 1908.

— "Die grosse Göttin in Babylonien, Ägypten und Phönizien," *Eranos-Jahrbuch 1938*, Zürich: Rhein, 1939, pp. 121–60.

Volz, Paul, *Das Dämonische in Jahwe*, Tübingen: Mohr, 1924.

— *Die Eschatologie der jüdischen Gemeinde im neutestamentlichen Zeitalter nach den Quellen der rabbinischen, apokalyptischen und apokryphen Literatur*, Tübingen: Mohr, 1934.

— *Der Geist Gottes und die verwandten Erscheinungen im Alten Testament und im anschliessenden Judentum*, Tübingen: Mohr, 1910.

— *Mose und sein Werk*, Tübingen: Mohr, 1907/1932.

von Sydow, Eckart, *Kunst und Religion der Naturvölker*, Oldenburg: Gerhard Stalling/ Sacramentum Artis, 1926.

Weber, Max, *Gesammelte Aufsätze zur Religionssoziologie*, v. 3: *Das antike Judentum*, Tübingen: Mohr, 1923.

[— *Ancient Judaism*, translated and edited by Hans H. Gerth and Don Martindale, New York: Free Press; London: Collier-Macmillan, 1952 .]

— *Wirtschaft und Gesellschaft: Grundriss der verstehenden Soziologie*, Abteilung III: *Grundriss der Sozialökonomik*, Tübingen: Mohr, 1922.

Wellhausen, Julius, *Abriss der Geschichte Israels und Juda's*, Berlin: Reimer, 1884.

— *Israelitische und Jüdische Geschichte*, Berlin: Reimer, 1894. [8th edn, Berlin & Leipzig: DeGruyter, 1921.]

— *Prolegomena zur Geschichte Israels*, 2nd edn, Berlin: Reimer, 1883.

Wickes, Frances, *Analyse der Kindesseele: Untersuchung und Behandlung nach den Grundlagen der Jung'schen Theorie*, Einleitung von C. G Jung, Stuttgart: Hoffmann, 1931.

— *The Inner World of Childhood: A Study in Analytical Psychology*, with introduction by C. G. Jung, New York: Appleton, 1927.

— *The Inner World of Man, With Psychological Drawings and Paintings*, New York: Farrar & Rinehart, 1938.

Wilhelm, Richard & Jung, C. G., eds, *Das Geheimnis der Goldenen Blüte: Ein chinesisches Lebensbuch*, translated by Richard Wilhelm, with a European commentary by C. G. Jung. München: Dorn, 1929. [2nd edn, including Jung's memorial to Richard Wilhelm, Berlin: Dorn, 1936.]

[— *The Secret of the Golden Flower: A Chinese Book of Life*, with European commentary by C. G. Jung, translated by Cary F. Baynes, London: Kegan Paul, 1935.]

Wolff, Toni, "Betrachtung und Besprechung von 'Reich der Seele'," *Zentralblatt für Psychotherapie und ihre Grenzgebiete*, v. 10, 4/5, Leipzig: Hirzel, 1938, pp. 239–78.

Wünsche, August, trans., "Von der Bildung des Kindes," *Aus Israels Lehrhallen: kleine Midraschim zur späteren legendärischen Literatur des Alten Testaments übersetzt von Aug. Wünsche, nach der Buberschen Textausgabe*, Leipzig: Pfeiffer, 1907.

Zimmer, Heinrich, *Kunstform und Yoga im indischen Kultbild*, Berlin: Frankfurter, 1926.

[— *Artistic Form and Yoga in the Sacred Imges of India*, translated and edited by Gerald Chapple, Princeton, NJ: Princeton University Press, 1984.]

II. Secondary sources

Sources used in the scholarly apparatus of *The Roots of Jewish Consciousness*.

Abelson, J., ed., *The Zohar, Soncino Edition*, v. 1–5, translated by H. Sperling and M. Simon, London and New York: Soncino Press, 1933.

The Aramaic Bible, Targum, Pseudo-Jonathan, v. 2: *Exodus*; v. 5b: *Deuteronomy*; v. 15: *Job*, translated by M. Maher, Collegeville, MN: Liturgical Press, 1987–91.

Der Babylonische Talmud, mit Einschluss der vollständigen Mišnah, v. 7, translated by L. Goldschmidt, Haag: Nijoff, 1933.

Berman, Samuel A., *Midrash Tanhuma Yelammedenu: An English Translation of Genesis and Exodus from the Printed Version of Tanhuma Yelammedenu with an Introduction, Notes and Indexes*, Hoboken, NJ: KTAV, 1996.

Bialik, H. N. and Ravnitzky, Y. H., eds, *The Book of Legends: Sefer ha-Haggadah. Legends from the Talmud and Midrash*, translated by William G. Braude, introduction by David Stern, New York: Schocken, 1992.

Buber, Martin, *For the Sake of Heaven*, translated by Ludwig Lewisohn, Philadelphia, PA: Jewish Publication Society of America, 1945.

Catane, Moshe, ed., *Bibliography of the Works of Gershom G. Scholem*, Jerusalem: Magnes Press, The Hebrew University, 1977.

Charlesworth, James H., ed., *The Old Testament Pseudepigrapha*, v. 1: *Apocalyptic Literature and Testaments*; v. 2: *Expansions of the "Old Testament" and Legends, Wisdom and Philosophical Literature, Prayers, Psalms, and Odes, Fragments of Lost Judeo-Hellenistic Works*, Peabody, MA: Hendrickson, 1983.

Corrigan, K., "Soul and the Sensible World." *Reading Plotinus: A Practical Introduction to Neoplatonism*, West Lafayette, IN: Purdue University Press, 2005, pp. 38–41.

Corney, Richard W., private email correspondence and telephone consultation, 2015–18.

Dennis, Geoffrey W., *The Encyclopedia of Jewish Myth, Magic and Mysticism*, Woodbury, MN: Llewelleyn, 2007.

Dreifuss, Gustav, "Erich Neumanns jüdisches Bewusstsein," *Kreativität des Unbewussten: Zum 75. Geburtstag von Erich Neumann (1905–1960). Analytische Psychologie*, v. 11, 3–4, edited by H. Dieckmann and C.A. Meier, Basel, München, Paris, London, New York, Sydney: Karger, 1980, pp. 239–47.

Drob, Sanford, *Kabbalistic Visions: C. G. Jung and Jewish Mysticism*, New Orleans, LA: Spring Journal Books, 2010.

Ephrayyim, Moshe Hayyim, *Degel Mahaneh 'Efrayyim*, Jerusalem: Mir, 1994.

Epstein, I., ed., *The Hebrew–English Edition of the Babylonian Talmud: Shabbath, Pesahim, Yoma, Sukkah, Ta'anith, Hagigah, Sotah, Baba Bathra, Baba Mezia, Sanhedrin, Abodah Zara, Abboth, Niddah*, translated by H. Freedman, L. Jung, J. Rabbinowitz, et al., London: Soncino, 1967–1989.

Fehlbaum, Nico, private email correspondence, 2018.

Fishbane, Michael, *The Garments of Torah: Essays in biblical hermeneutics*, Bloomington and Indianapolis, IN: Indiana University Press, 1989.

Fox, Everett, "The Book in its Contexts," introduction to Martin Buber and Franz Rosenzweig, *Scripture and Translation*, translated by Lawrence Rosenwald with Everett Fox, Bloomington and Indianapolis, IN: Indiana University Press, 1994, pp. xiii–xxvii.

— trans., *The Schocken Bible*, Volume I: *The Five Books of Moses* (Genesis, Exodus, Leviticus, Numbers, Deuteronomy): *A New Translation with Introductions, Commentary and Notes by Everett Fox*, New York: Schocken, 1983/1986/1990/1995.

— trans., *The Schocken Bible*, Volume II: *The Early Prophets* (Joshua, Judges, Samuel, and Kings): *A New Translation with Introductions, Commentary and Notes by Everett Fox*, New York: Schocken, 2014.

— private email correspondence and telephone consultation, 2015–16.

Friedmann, Dov Baer Mimezeritch, *Magid devarav le-Yaakov*, edited by Rivka Schatz-Uffenheimer, Yerushalayim: Hotsa'at sefarim 'a. sh, Y.L. Magnes, ha-Universitah ha-Ivrit, 1976. [Orig. pub., 1780.]

— *'Or ha-'Emmet*, Benei Beraq: Yahadut, 1967.

Furlotti, Nancy Swift, "Preface," *The Roots of Jewish Consciousness*, Volume One: *Revelation and Apocalypse*, edited by Ann Conrad Lammers, translated by Mark Kyburz and Ann Conrad Lammers, London and New York: Routledge, 2019, pp. **00–00.**

— private email correspondence, 2015–18.

Garb, Jonathan, *Yearnings of the Soul: Psychological Thought in Modern Kabbalah*, Chicago, IL and London: University of Chicago Press, 2015.

Gellman, Jerome, "Buber's Blunder: Buber's Replies to Scholem and Schatz-Uffenheimer," *Modern Judaism*, 2000, v. 20(1), pp. 20–40.

Greenstein, Edward L., *Essays on Biblical Method and Translation*, Atlanta, GA: Scholars Press, 1989.

Gunkel, H. and Zimmern, H., *Schöpfung und Chaos in Urzeit und Endzeit: Eine religionsgeschichtliche Untersuchung über Gen 1 und Ap Joh 12*, Göttingen: Vandenhoeck & Ruprecht, 1895.

Heschel, Abraham Yehoshu'a, *'Ohev Israel*, Zhitomir: Hanina Lipa and Joshua Heschel Shapira Printers, 1863.

Holtz, B. W., ed., *Back to the Sources: Reading the Classic Jewish Texts*, New York: Summit Books, 1984.

Hurwitz, Siegmund, "Psychological Aspects in Early Hasidic Literature," *Timeless Documents of the Soul*, edited by H. Jakobsohn, translated by H. Nagel, Evanston, IL: Northwestern University Press.

Idel, Moshe, "Foreword: On Erich Neumann and Hasidism," *The Roots of Jewish Consciousness*, Volume Two: *Hasidism*, edited by Ann Conrad Lammers, translated by Mark Kyburz and Ann Conrad Lammers, London and New York: Routledge, 2019, pp. xiii–xviii.

— *Hasidism: Between Ecstasy and Magic*, Albany, NY: State University of New York Press, 1995.

— *Kabbalah: New Perspectives*, New Haven, CT and London: Yale University Press, 1988.

— "Martin Buber and Gershom Scholem on Hasidism: A Critical Appraisal," *Hasidism Reappraised*, edited by Ada Rapoport-Albert, London and Portland, OR: The Littman Library of Jewish Civilization, 1997, pp. 389–403.

Jacobs, Louis, ed. *A Concise Companion to the Jewish Religion*, Oxford: Oxford University Press, 1999.

Jaffé, Aniela, *From the Life and Work of C. G. Jung*, expanded edition, translated by R. F. C. Hull and Murray Stein, Einsiedeln: Daimon, 1989.

Joseph, Steven, Private email correspondence, 2016, 2018.

Jung, C. G., *Answer to Job*, translated by R. F. C. Hull, London: Routledge & Kegan Paul, 1954. [CW 11,9]

— *Dream Analysis: Notes of the seminar given in 1928–1930*, edited by William McGuire, London: Routledge and Kegan Paul, 1984.

— "An Eightieth Birthday Interview," *C. G. Jung Speaking: Interviews and Encounters*, edited by William McGuire and R. F. C. Hull, Princeton, NJ: Princeton University Press, 1977, pp. 268–72.

Jung, C. G. and Kirsch, James, *The Jung–Kirsch Letters: The Correspondence of C. G. Jung and James Kirsch*, edited by Ann Conrad Lammers, translated by Ursula Egli and Ann Conrad Lammers, London: Routledge, 2011. [Rev. ed., London: Routledge, 2016.]

Jung, C. G. and Neumann, Erich, *Analytical Psychology in Exile: The Correspondence of C. G. Jung and Erich Neumann*, edited and introduced by Martin Liebscher, translated by Heather McCartney, Princeton, NJ: Princeton University Press, 2015.

Jung, C. G. and White, Victor, *The Jung–White Letters*, edited by Ann Conrad Lammers and Adrian Cunningham, London and New York: Routledge, 2007.

Kafka, Franz, *Der Prozess*, Frankfurt am Main and Hamburg: Fischer, 1960. [Originally published 1925.]

Kravitz, Leonard and Olitzky, Kerry M., trans. and eds., *Pirke Avot: A Modern Commentary on Jewish Ethics*, with foreword by W. Gunther Plaut, New York: UAHC Press, 1993.

Lammers, Ann Conrad, "James Kirsch's Religious Debt to C. G. Jung," *Jung Journal: Culture and Psyche*, Vol. 6, No. 1, Winter 2012, pp. 21–34.

Lancaster, Brian, *The Essence of Kabbalah*, London: Eagle Editions, 2005.

Leshem, Zvi, private email correspondence, 2018.

Lévy-Bruhl, Lucien, *How Natives Think*, translated by Lilian Ada Clare, New York: Washington Square Press, 1966.

Löwe, Angelica, *"Auf Seiten der inneren Stimme . . ." Erich Neumann—Leben und Werk*, Freiburg und München: Alber, 2014.

Malamud, René, "Gedanken zu Exodus 4:24," *Drei Aufsätze*, edited by Monica Malamud-Matter, Zürich: Daimon, 2017.

Matt, Daniel C., ed. and trans., *The Zohar* (ספר הזהר), *Pritzker Edition*, v. 1–12; v. 1–9 translated by Daniel Matt; v. 10–11 by Nathan Wolski, Palo Alto, CA: Stanford University Press, 2004–17.

Naor, Bezalel, *Lights of Prophecy*, New York: Union of Orthodox Jewish Congregations of America, 1990.

Neumann, Erich, "Die Angst vor dem Weiblichen," *Die Angst*, Studien aus dem C. G. Jung-Institut, v. 10, Zürich: Rascher, 1959, pp. 67–112.

[— "The Fear of the Feminine," *Fear of the Feminine and other essays on feminine psychology*, edited by William McGuire, translated by Boris Matthews, Princeton, NJ: Princeton University Press, 1994, pp. 227–82.]

— *Das Kind: Struktur und Dynamik der werdenden Persönlichkeit*, Zürich: Rhein, 1963.

[— *The Child: Structure and Dynamics of the Nascent Personality*, translated by Ralph Manheim, New York: Putnam, for C. G. Jung Foundation for Analytical Psychology, 1973.

— *Die große Mutter: Der Archetyp des großen Weiblichen*, Zürich: Rhein, 1956.

[— *The Great Mother: An Analysis of the Archetype*, translated by Ralph Manheim, Princeton, NJ: Princeton University Press, 1955. (2nd edn, 1963.)]

— "Der mystische Mensch," *Eranos-Jahrbuch 1948*, Zürich: Rhein, 1949, pp. 317–74.

[— "Mystical Man," *The Mystic Vision: Papers from the Eranos Yearbooks*, v. 6, edited by Joseph Campbell, translated by Ralph Manheim, Princeton, NJ: Princeton University Press, 1968, pp. 375–415.]

— "Die Psyche und die Wandlung der Wirklichkeitsebenen: Ein metapsychologischer Versuch," *Eranos-Jahrbuch 1952*, Zürich: Rhein, 1953, pp. 169–216.

[— "The Psyche and the Transformation of the Reality Planes: A Metapsychological Essay," *The Place of Creation*, edited by William McGuire, translated by H. Nagel, E. Rolfe, J. van Heurck and K. Winston, Princeton, NJ: Princeton University Press, 1989, pp. 3–62.]

— *Tiefenpsychologie und Neue Ethik*, Zürich: Rascher, 1949.

[— *Depth Psychology and a New Ethic*, with forewords by C. G. Jung, Gerhard Adler, and James Yandell, translated by Eugene Rolfe, Boston & London: Shambhala, 1990.] [First published, with forewords by C. G. Jung and Gerhard Adler, London: Hodder & Stoughton, 1969.]

— *Ursprungsgeschichte des Bewusstseins*, mit einem Vorwort von C. G. Jung, Zürich: Rascher, 1949.

[— *The Origins and History of Consciousness*, with foreword by C. G. Jung, translated by R. F. C. Hull, Princeton, NJ: Princeton University Press, 1954.]

Neumann, Erich, and Jung, C. G., *Analytical Psychology in Exile: The Correspondence of C. G. Jung and Erich Neumann*, edited and introduced by Martin Liebscher, translated by Heather McCartney, Princeton, NJ: Princeton University Press, 2015.

Neumann-Loewenthal, Rali, interview, Jerusalem, 29 April 2015; telephone consultations, June 2018.

Neusner, Jacob, ed. and trans., *The Talmud of the Land of Israel: A Preliminary Translation and Explanation: Yoma, Ta'anith, Megillah, Sotah*, Chicago, IL: University of Chicago Press, 1984–1990.

Omer-Man, Jonathan, private email correspondence and telephone consultation, March 2018.

Rapoport-Albert, Ada, ed., *Hasidism Reappraised*, London and Portland, OR: The Littman Library of Jewish Civilization, 1997.

Rosenzweig, Franz, "The Unity of the Bible," *Scripture and Translation*, translated by Lawrence Rosenwald, with Everett Fox, Bloomington and Indianapolis, IN: Indiana University Press, 1994, pp. 22–6.

Schiffman, Lawrence. H., *From Text to Tradition: A History of Second Temple & Rabbinic Judaism*, Hoboken, NJ: KTAV, 1991.

Scholem, Gershom Gerhard, *Bibliographia Kabbalistica: Verzeichnis der gedruckten die jüdische Mystik—Gnosis, Kabbala, Sabbatianismus, Frankismus, Chassidismus—behandelnden Bücher und Aufsätze, von Reuchlin bis zur Gegenwart*, Leipzig: Drugulin, 1927.

— *Sabbatai Sevi: The Mystical Messiah*, translated by Zwi Werblowsky, Princeton, NJ: Princeton University Press, 1973.

— "The Unconscious and the Concept *Qadmut ha-Sekhel* in Hasidic Literature," *The Latest Phase: Essays on Hasidism*, edited by D. Assaf and E. Liebes, Jerusalem: Am Oved-Magnes, 2008 (Hebrew).

Segal, Robert, private email correspondence, 2015, 2018.

Shalit, Erel, "Introduction," *Jacob and Esau: On the Collective Symbolism of the Brother Motif*, edited and introduced by Erel Shalit, translated by Mark Kyburz, Asheville, NC: Chiron, 2016, pp. xix–lvii.

— private email correspondence, 2015–18.

Shalit, Erel and Stein, Murray, eds, *Turbulent Times, Creative Minds: Erich Neumann and C. G. Jung in Relationship (1933–1960)*. Asheville, NC: Chiron, 2016.

Skolnik, Fred, ed., *Encyclopaedia Judaica*, 2nd edn, v. 1–22, New York: Macmillan Reference; Jerusalem: Keter, 2007.

Wigoder, Geoffrey, ed., *Encyclopedic Dictionary of Judaica*, New York and Paris: Leon Amiel; Jerusalem: Keter, 1974.

Worch, J. Hershy, trans., *Sefer Yetzira: Chronicles of Desire. A New Hebrew/English Translation & Commentary*, Lanham, MD: University Press of America, 2010.

Zemmelman, Steve, "C. G. Jung and Erich Neumann: Conflict, Philia, and Finding the Other in Oneself," *Jung Journal: Culture and Psyche*, Summer 2016, v. 10.3, pp. 77–83.

The Zohar, Pritzker Edition, v. 1–12, translated and edited by Daniel C. Matt (v. 1–9); translated by Nathan Wolski (v. 10–11), Palo Alto, CA: Stanford University Press, 2004–17.

The Zohar, Soncino Edition, v. 1–5, edited by J. Abelson, translated by H. Sperling and M. Simon, London and New York: Soncino Press, 1933.

INDEX

Volumes One and Two

Note: This index covers both Volumes One and Two. Volume One page numbers are introduced with a superscript 1; Volume Two page numbers are introduced with a superscript 2. Page entries followed by & *n* indicate that the note relating to that text is also relevant. Page entries followed by *n* and a number, such as 169*n*102, indicate a specific endnote of relevance.

Aaron/Aaronites, [1]20, 27 & *n*, 33, 34–35, 140, 145–147
abaissement du niveau mental, [1]48 & *n*, 53; [2]241
Abiram, [1]34
Abraham, [1]45, 51, 144, 159, 169*n*102
abyss *(tehom)*, [1]140–144
actualizing of messianism, [2]18–20, 103–104, 128, 133, 134
Adam, [1]40 & *n*, 101 & *n*, 109*n*69, 109*n*72, 120–121, 152, 153; [2]29, 78, 97, 107–108, 110, 138, 184, 185, 186–187; Lilith and, [1]161–162, 163
adama (earth), [1]40 & *n*, 153 & *n*
Adam Kadmon, [1]51 & *n*, 162; [2]155–156, 165, 167; hermaphroditic nature of, [2]81–82, 97, 130; parts of the soul and, [2]69–76, 80, 81, 82; as Self, [2]82, 111, 155–156, 169, 170, 171; *tzaddik* and, [2]123–126, 132
Adler, Alfred, [2]177, 244
adultery, [1]25, 43
aging, [2]83, 97, 126–128, 221–222, 231
Ahriman, [1]160 & *n*
air (wind) symbolism, [1]37, 38–40, 44, 148–150; [2]75, 76
Al (demon), [1]160
alchemy, [1]xxxiii; [2]191, 225; apocalypse and, [1]95–96; uroboros symbol, [2]191, 193, 194
am ha-aretz, [2]38 & *n*

analysis, stages of, [2]259–268
anamnesis, [2]240, 259
angels, [1]36 & *n*, 81, 119, 120, 154, 157; [2]93
anima/animus, [1]54 & *n*, 70*n*89; [2]xviii, 78 & *n*, 96 & *n*, 199, 209, 214, 221, 222, 244, 246–247, 248; anthropocentric worldview, [1]51, 53, 55; [2]9–10, 62, 115, 133–134, 137, 147; modernity and, [2]23
animal level, [2]59–60, 61–62, 63, 155
animals: *participation mystique* with, [2]57 & *n*, 192; sacrifice of, [1]37, 151–152, 154, 159; symbolism, [1]92, 94, 154; [2]57, 227; *see also* uroboros
anti-Semitism, [1]5, 9
apocalypticism: alchemy and, [1]95–96; danger of, [1]123–125; destiny and, [1]99–100; end of direct revelation and, [1]78, 79–82; messiah as unifying symbol, [1]100–105; messianism and, [1]87–90, 124; psychological meaning of eschatology, [1]82–87; rebirth archetype and, [1]90–95; redemption in time and, [1]96–99
archetypes, [1]4, 99–100; [2]218–219, 242
Ark of the Covenant, [1]78, 141 & *n*
art, [2]176, 202
asceticism, [1]19; [2]36, 38, 98–99, 100, 103, 122–123, 136, 196
Assiah, [2]67

assimilation, ¹5–6, 127, 129; ²173–179
astrology, ¹63, 163
Athena, ²198 & *n,* 199
atomization, ²163–164, 173, 174, 178
Auerbach, Elias, ¹32 & *n*
autonomy, individual, ²10–12
auto-suggestion, ²57
Azazel, ¹142
Azilut, ²67, 68

Baal, cult of, ¹16, 154, 163
Babylonian exile, ¹11*n,* 76–77, 105*n*4
Balaam, ¹34 & *n,* 35
bar mitzvah, ¹156 & *n,* 158
barrenness, ¹43–44
bassar (flesh), ¹40, 90
bath, ritual, ²41
bat kol, ¹125
Baudissin, Wolf Wilhelm Friedrich von,
    ¹22, 51–52, 53, 65*n*5
Behemoth, ¹92 & *n*
belief, primacy of, ²91
Beriah, ²67
Besht *see* Israel ben Eliezer
    (Baal Shem Tov)
biblical criticism, ¹5, 7, 138–140, 144–147,
    164*n*3, 165*n*29
Binah (reason), ²68, 69, *70, 71,* 72, 79
birth, ¹93, 119–120; ²29
black moon, ¹161, 163
blood: animal sacrifice and, ¹46, 151–152;
    body-soul and, ¹150–152; ²72–74;
    circumcision and, ¹150, 155–156;
    impurity and, ¹158, 159, 160
blue light (Zohar), ²83–84
body: affirmation of, ²38; negative views
    of, ¹120, 122; ²172 & *n*; resurrection of,
    ¹122
body parts, symbolism of, ¹152; ²72–74, 75,
    187–188
body-soul *(nefesh),* ¹40, 166*n*46; ²72, 73–75,
    78, 84, 186; blood and, ¹150–152; life
    stages and, ²127; Self and, ²83; vitalist
    concept of, ²25
brain, *neshama* and, ²72, 75
breath *see ruach* (breath)
breath of life *(nishmat-hayim),* ¹40, 152
bridegroom of blood (biblical narrative),
    ¹60 & *n,* 155–156
bride of God, ¹129
bronze serpent, ¹30, 34
brotherhood, ²198, 199; *see also* hostile
    brothers archetype
Buber, Martin, ¹6, 22, 42, 66*n*24,
    71*n*107, 134*n*18; ²48*n*2, 21; approach
    to Hasidism, ¹xxxiv–xxxv; ²xiii–xiv,

xv–xvi, xvii; influence on Neumann,
    ¹xxxiv–xxxv, xl*n*37
bull symbol, ¹154
Bunam, Rabbi, ²11, 12, 14, 62
Burgkmair, Hans, ²71, 76 & *n*
burning bush (biblical narrative) *see*
    thornbush revelation

Canaanite religion, ¹16–17, 42, 154, 163
castration complex, ¹160 & *n,* 161
catalepsy, ²67
cathartic phenomenon, ²225
certainty, need for, ¹57
Chabad movement, ²171–172, 180*n*24
chaos, ¹91, 141, 143
childbirth, uncleanness of, ¹159, 160
children: psychology of, ¹131; ²210–215,
    239–240; separation from maternal
    milieu, ¹158; ²195, 213; wisdom of,
    ¹93–94 & *n;* ²29, 30
choice, freedom of, ¹120; ²45–46, 77–79,
    102, 107–109, 110–111
chosenness of Israel, ¹42–43, 52, 54, 63
Christianity, ¹2, 5; ²163–165; Gnosticism
    and, ¹5, 118, 120, 122; grapevine
    metaphor in, ²132–133 & *n;* heaven and
    earth in, ¹90; Judaism and, ¹5, 18, 51,
    53, 78, 90, 101–102, 120, 122, 124 & *n,*
    129; ²163, 164–165; messianic figure in,
    ¹101–102; ²163; rejection of the feminine
    in, ¹4, 129, 161
chthonic deity, cult of, ¹16
circle symbol, ²231, 272
circumcision, ¹37, 42, 43, 59, 60, 150,
    158–160, 163; Lilith and, ¹158–160 of
    Moses' son, ¹65*n*15, 156 & *n,* 168*n*86;
    Passover and, ¹155–157
Civilization and its Discontents (Freud),
    ²223 & *n*
collective guilt, ¹76, 77
collective unconscious, ¹3–4, ¹122;
    asceticism and, ¹19; childhood and, ¹131;
    cultural content of, ¹130–131; early
    humans and, ¹93; ecstatic states and,
    ¹17, 19–20, 117; ²67, 241; emotional
    component of, ²200–202, 224; Sinai
    revelation as projection of, ¹23; universal
    nature of, ¹3–4, 131; wisdom of, ¹93
color symbolism, ²82, 83–84
communion, sacrament of, ¹92
community, Hasidism and, ²9
compassion *(Rahamim),* ²69, *70,* 76, 132, 150
concretizing of unconscious contents, ¹54–55
consciousness, primacy of, ¹50, 53, 60, 61–62,
    126, 154; Jewish sexual morality and, ¹163
consciousness, responsible, ¹xl*n*31, 49

continuity, Jewish, [1]8–9
contraction *(tzimtzum):* as principle of creation, [2]6–7; in time, [2]17–18
covenant, Israel-YHWH, [1]43, 50–51, 52 & *n,* 54, 59, 61–62, 78, 81, 101, 151; circumcision and Passover as signs of, [1]155–157, 158
cow symbol, [2]57
creation *see* world
creation, contraction as principle of, [2]6–7
creation myths, [1]122
creative obsession, [2]241–242
creativity, [2]40, 42
cultural stages, nature and, [2]56–59
Cybele, [1]154

dancing, [1]16; [2]94
Dan, shrine in, [1]145 & *n,* [1]165*n*33
darkness symbolism, [1]91, 92 & *n,* 121, 149–150; [2]196–197
Dathan, [1]34 & *n,* 35
David, King, [1]36, 140–141, 143, 147
death: impurity and, [1]37; Tree of Death, [2]84; while praying, [2]42; of the world, [1]91
death sentences, [1]24 & *n,* 25
deification, [1]101, 117, 118, 119
Delilah, [1]63, 161
demiurge, [1]120; [2]28
demons, [1]81, 94, 120; [2]27–28; child-eating, [1]159, 160; Lilith, [1]157–163
depth psychology: context and overview of, [2]239–240; dream series and, [2]269–273
destiny, archetypal experience and, [1]99–100
deus absconditus, [1]xxxii, 38
deviant sexuality, [1]163
devil (Satan), [1]89–90, 90, 120, 142, 154; [2]93
Diaspora *see galut,* psychology of
Din (judgment), [2]29, 30–31, 69, *70, 71, 72,* 76, 81, 82, 130, 132
Dionysus, [1]154
direct revelation: end of, [1]79–82; individual religiosity and, [1]77–78; latent capacity of individuals for, [1]27–30, 32–35; [2]10, 129; as messianic motif, [1]88; rejection of, [1]20–21, 27, 30, 32, 125–126, 128; [2]149; responsible consciousness and, [1]48–49; "stepping out of history" and, [1]128–129; [2]18
diversity, value of, [2]7, 8, 9
divination, [1]30–31 & *n,* 47, 49, 53, 54, 63, 154
divine attributes, human beings and, [2]152–156; *see also* Sefirotic Tree
dogmatism, [1]56–57, 132; [2]165–166
Dov Baer of Leovo, Rabbi, [2]172 & *n*

Dov Baer (Great Maggid) of Meseritz, Rabbi, [2]xvii, 15, 33, 41, 99, 104, 107, 112, 139, 143–144, 152–153
dragon archetype, [1]142; [2]197–198, 199, 213, 215, 232; *see also* uroboros
dream-ego, [2]245, 261
dreams: collective unconscious and, [1]94 & *n*; Hasidic parable about, [2]11; interpretation of, [2]261–262, 264, 267, 268–273; revelation in, [1]48, 53; spiritual experience of, [2]26–27; succubi and, [1]160
Dreifuss, Gustav, [1]xxxvi
dualism, [1]115–116, 118, 120, 122–123, 148; [2]141–142

early humanity *see* primitive humanity
earth, [1]91; affirmation of, [1]37–41; blood and, [1]150–151; dependence on humankind of, [1]55; earth-*adam,* [1]40 & *n,* 153 & *n*; exile and loss of, [1]129–130; fertility and, [1]43–44; heaven and, [1]46, 90, 100–105; [2]34, 75, 111, 114, 141; Mother Goddess and, [1]15–16, 40–41, 54, 62–63, 122, 154; [2]195; principle of, [1]36; symbolism, [1]150–154; [2]75; as threat, [1]41–43; veneration of, [1]15–17; [2]56–58; willingness to abandon ties to, [1]45–46
Easter, [1]155
ecstatic states, [1]17, 20, 50, 53–54, 154; [2]67, 241; Hasidism and, [2]32–35, 41, 67, 83, 94–95, 102, 114, 137, 144
Edom, [2]73, 74
ego: attributed to *ruach*-soul, [2]107; choice and, [2]36, 79; instinct and, [2]201; Self and, [1]117–119; [2]124–126, 127, 136, 147, 151, 152, 153
ego-consciousness: ascent of the soul and, [2]66–69; meditation and, [2]67, 68; psychic conditions and, [2]240
ego-Self, [2]79 & *n,* 81–85
ego-stability, [1]19–20, 49–53, 60–61, 49–53
Egypt: exodus from, [1]83–86, 91, 97 & *n,* 98 & *n*; mythology, [2]209
Ein Sof, [2]22
elements, the: primitive humanity and, [2]56; symbolism of, [1]147–154; [2]75–76
Eli, descendants of, [1]145 & *n,* 147
Elijah soul, [2]13–14, 19–20
emancipation, [2]4, 173, 176, 177
end of time *see* apocalypticism
Enlightenment, [2]173–174, 177–178
Eretz Israel, [1]41, 129, 130
Erinyes, [2]199, 208*n*11
Ernst, Cassirer, [2]192
Esau, [1]44
eschaton, rebirth archetype and, [1]90–95

Essenes, [1]78 & *n*
eternal life, [1]91, 94 & *n*
Eumenides, [2]198, 207, 208*n*11
Eve, [1]162; [2]30–31 & *n*
evil, [1]82, 83, 90, 119, 162; [2]105, 118*n*74;
    body and world as, [2]172, 180*n*26; as
    feminine, [2]30–31, 96, 97; Gnostic view
    of, [1]120; good within, [2]105–106, 107,
    110, 118*n*69, 142; Hasidic view of, [2]97,
    101–107, 111–114; Kabbalistic view
    of, [2]30–31; knowledge of good and,
    [2]107–108, 110; problem of, [1]118; [2]30–31,
    107; and wholeness, [2]111
evil spirits *see* demons; devil (Satan)
evil urge, [2]93, 102, 110, 116*n*20
Exile, Babylonian, [1]76–77, 105*n*6; *see also
    galut*
exodus from Egypt, [1]83–86, 91, 97 & *n*,
    98 & *n*
extraversion, [1]46, 118, 123; [2]125; of the
    Jewish person, [2]173, 174, 175; and
    memory loss, [2]177; progressive, [2]32,
    227; in western people, [2]237–238
Ezekiel, [1]76 & *n*; [2]72, 155

faith in God, [2]xvi, 43–44 & *n*, 112–113
false messiah, [1]124 & *n*
false prophecy, [1]32–36, 47–48
fate, [1]61 & *n*, 63; [2]40, 41
fate *(moira)*, [1]61; [2]28, 62 & *n*
father archetype, [1]158; [2]203, 211–212,
    124–125, 127, 214–215
fear of God, [2]95–96, 152–153
feeling function, [2]78, 234*n*34; suppression
    of, [1]129
female sexuality, [1]63, 161, 162–163
feminine aspect of God *see Shekhinah*
feminine principle, [1]96–99, 131–132,
    157–163; [2]197–199, 203; children,
    maternal sphere and, [1]157–159; [2]213–214;
    Mother Goddess and, [1]15–16, 40–41, 54,
    62–63, 122, 154; [2]195; *nefesh* and, [1]152;
    negative, [1]4, 63, 157–163; rejection of, [1]4,
    129, 131–132; *see also* anima/animus
fertility, [1]15–16, 17, 43–44, 154
festivals, [2]41
fire: apocalypse and, [1]87 & *n*, 91; as metaphor
    in sparks theory, [2]60, 102; symbolism of,
    [1]22–23, 37, 38–39, 149–150, 163; [2]36, 68,
    75, 84, 101, 196–197, 225; veneration of,
    [2]56; YHWH's theophany and, [1]22–23,
    38–40, 66*n*34, 69*n*84, 87; [2]83, 106
firstborn, sacrifice of, [1]60, 145, 152, 156, 159
flesh *(bassar)*, [1]39, 40, 90
floods/flooding, [1]59, 141–144
forbidden fruit, [1]92, 93; [2]107

"foreskin" of trees, [1]36, 69*n*82, 51, 159
forgiveness of sin, [2]103
fornication, [1]160
foundation stone and the waters of the
    deep (midrash), [1]140–144, 165*n*24
Fox, Everett, [1]11*n*28, 69*n*80
Frankism, [1]124 & *n*
freedom of choice, [1]120; [2]45–46, 77–79,
    102, 107–109, 110–111
Freud, Sigmund, [2]176, 212, 177;
    Civilization and its Discontents, [2]223,
    234*n*32; *Moses and Monotheism,* [2]180*n*35;
    on psychology of myths, [2]194
Friday, [1]160
Friedman, Dov Baer of Leovo, [2]172 & *n*
Friedmann, Dov Baer of Meseritz *see* Dov
    Baer (Great Maggid) of Meseritz, Rabbi
fruitfulness, [1]92, 153
future, primacy of, [1]103

galut, psychology of, [1]8–9, 127–131,
    132–133; [2]136, 165–166, 168–169
Garden of Eden, [1]68*n*, 93 & *n*; [2]28 & *n*;
    see also paradise, restoration of
Gedulah (greatness), [2]69, 70, 76
Gehenna, [1]92 & *n*
Genesis, [1]139, 152
Gevurah (strength), [2]69, 70, 76
Ghoul, [1]160
Glatzer, Nahum, [1]97 & *n*, 107*n*33,
    107*n*34, 125
glorification of the blessed, [1]93
Gnosticism, [1]5, 88, 103, 115–123, 133,
    149; [2]25–26, 108; Hasidism and,
    [2]140–144; Judaism and, [1]119–120
goat sacrifice, [1]142
God: attributes of, [2]152–153; dependence
    on human beings of, [1]62; [2]148–149;
    hiddenness of, [2]22, 23, 65, 105, 120–121;
    human identity with, [2]151–156;
    paradoxical nature of, [1]61; presence in all
    things, [2]46–48; remoteness of, [1]81, 119;
    throne of, [1]154; [2]72; *Tiferet* attributed to,
    [2]80–81; *see also Shekhinah;* YHWH
goddesses, [1]15–16, 40–41, 54, 62–63, 122,
    154; [2]195
Golden Calf, [1]21, 23–24, 25, 26, 28, 31, 32 &
    n, 33–34, 55, 138, 139–140, 143–144, 154
good and evil, knowledge of, [2]107–108, 110
good, as counterpart of evil, [2]30, 142
Grace *(Hesed),* [2]29, 30, 35, 95
grace of God, [2]152–153
grafting, symbol, [1]43, 59
grapevine symbol, [2]132, 159*n*
Great Maggid *see* Dov Baer (Great Maggid)
    of Meseritz, Rabbi

greatness *(Gedulah)*, [2]69, *70, 76*
Gunkel, Hermann, [1]103, 106*n*29, 107*n*31, 114*n*128

Haggai, [1]78
halakha, [1]125
hallowing of nature, [1]37 & *n*, 42 & *n;* [2]142
Hannah, [1]43
Hasidism: affirmation of body and world, [2]38–39; anthropocentric worldview, [2]62, 115, 133–134; asceticism and, [1]122; decline of, [2]171–173; Gnosticism and, [2]140–144; Jewish antiquity and, [2]133–136, 144–145; Kabbalah and, [2]xiii, xv, xvii, 20, 23–24, 35; rabbinism and, [2]36, 38, 85, 166; scholarly approaches to, [1]xxxiv–xxxv; [2]xiii–xvii; theory of sparks in, [2]46–48; transvaluation of, [2]165–171; value of the simple person in, [2]90–92, 113
Häussermann, Friederich, [1]72*n*
haya, [1]152
hearing the divine, [1]52–53
heart, symbolism, [2]72, 73–74, 75, 76
heaven and earth, [1]46, 90, 91, 100–105, 121–122, 153; [2]34, 75, 111, 114, 141
sefirot, element and parts of body attributed to, [2]75, 76
heavenly food *(manna),* [1]92
hell, [1]121–122
hereafter, [1]36, 88, 91, 100
hermaphroditism, [2]97; *of Adam Kadmon,* [2]81–82, 97, 130; of children, [2]214; principle of, [2]81–82, 96–97, 130–131
Heschel, Rabbi Abraham Yehoshu'a, [2]xvii–xviii
Hesed (grace), [2]29, 30, 35, 52*n*, 69, *70, 71, 76,* 81, 130, 165
Heyer, Gustav Richard, [2]85*n*4
Heyer, Lucy, [2]208*n*11
Hezekiah, [1]30
hidden light, [1]93–94; [2]64, 103, 112; *The Hidden Light* (Buber), [1]85, 110*n*43
hiddenness of the divine, [2]22, 23, 64, 105, 120–121
high priests, [1]67*n*46, 144, 146
history, activation of, [1]97, 112*n*106; apocalyptic view of, [1]83–84, 96–100
Hod (splendor), [2]*70, 71, 72*
Hokhmah (wisdom), [2]68, 69, *70, 71*
holiness in all things, [2]16, 22, 23, 24, 46, 47, 48, 60, 91, 103–104, 105–106
Holy of Holies, [1]141 & *n*
holy spirit, [1]53–54, 70*n*90, 79, 92, 135*n*43; [2]10, 144; Sophia as, [1]149
Holy Spirit: Christian usage, [1]39 & n, 53–54, 149

hostile brothers archetype, [2]243–245
human beings: anthropocentric worldview and, [1]51, 53, 55; [2]9–10, 62, 115, 133–134, 137, 147; creation of, [1]40; dependence of God on, [1]62; [2]148–149; as God's image, [1]51; [2]56; identity with God, [2]151–156; incommensurability with divine of, [1]61–62; individuality of, [2]6–7; as redeemers, [2]141, 142, 143, 145, 146; subordination of nature to, [1]42
human body, symbolism of, [2]75–76
human consciousness, [1]1–4
hypostases, [1]81

Idel, Moshe, [1]xxxiv & *n*, xxxv & *n*, xli*n*42; [2] xxvii & *n*; foreword by, [2]xiii–xviii
idolatry, [1]25, 41, 163; [2]74; concretization as, [1]55; Golden Calf event, [1]23–24, 25
impurity, [1]37, 69*n*80, 159; [2]142
incarnation, divine, [2]5
Indian spirituality, [1]4, 154; [2]5–6, 22, 271
individual: achievement of wholeness, [2]14–17; autonomy of, [2]10–12; as divine vessel, [2]11–12; Elijah soul and, [2]13–14; importance of, [2]7–10, 103, 169–170; latent prophetic capacity of, [1]27–30, 32–35, 54; [2]10, 129; messianic stage of, [2]10, 19, 103
individual autonomy, [2]10–12
individualism, religious, [1]51–52, 76, 77, 79–81, 96
individuality, [1]76–77; [2]8–10, 11–12, 16
individuation, [1]95; [2]13–14, 140, 170, 210, 222, 223, 225, 249, 251, 252
inhibitions, [2]202; *see also* instinct
initiation rites, [1]156 & *n*, 157–158 & *n;* [2]126, 214–215 & *n*, 221, 231, 240, 244
inner experience, exclusion of, [1]124–125, 128–130
inner revelation, [1]87, 89; [2]10–11
inner sequence of spiritual realm, [2]21, 23–24
inquiring of God, [1]30
instinct, [1]151; [2]200–201, 202, 218; reconnection with, [2]225
intangibility of YHWH, [1]52
intellectualism, [1]129; [2]90, 136
internalizing process, [1]88
intoxicants, [1]17, 20, 154
introversion, [1]46, 111*n*124, 117, 129; [2]67–68, 124–126; dangers of, [2]27–28; of libido, [1]19; meditation and, [2]21–22; night world and, [2]26–27; of sacrifice, [2]104–105
introverted intuitives, [1]102–103; [2]224
intuition, danger of, [1]116–118
Isaac, [1]43, 45
Isaiah, [1]21

I-Self, [2]79 & *n*
Ishtar, [1]161
Islam, [1]154
Israel and Judah, kingdom of, [1]81 & *n,* 105*n*6
Israel ben Eliezer (Baal Shem Tov), [2]33, 46, 48*n*1, 53*n*149, 99–100, 104, 105, 133, 134
Israel, covenant with YHWH, [1]43, 50, 52, 155
Israel, Land of, [1]41, 65*n*4, 129, 130

Jacob, [1]44, 69*n*68; [2]73, 74
Jacobs, Louis, [2]xv
Jeremiah, [1]42, 78
Jerusalem, destruction of, [1]76
Jesus of Nazareth, [1]45, 94, 101; [2]163
Jethro, [1]31, 33
Jewish antiquity, Hasidism and, [2]133–136, 144–145
John, Gospel of, [1]149
Jonah, [1]62, 74*n*168
Joseph, [1]154
Joshua, [1]21, 34, 157
joy, [2]92–95
Judah and Israel, kingdom of, [1]81 & *n,* 105*n*6
Judaism, Gnostic influence on, [1]133
judgment *(Din),* [2]29, 30–31
Jung, C. G.: anima/ animus concept, [1]54 & *n;* [2]158*n*54, 209, 214, 222; on archetypes, [2]xvii, 218, 244; *Beziehungen zwischen dem Ich und dem Unbewussten,* [1]28 & *n,* 62 & *n,* 68*n*50, 133*n*5; [2]8 & *n,* 147 & *n,* 158*n*54, 158*n*66, 190 & *n,* 239 & *n;* on castration complex, [1]160 & *n;* on divinity and religion, [1]6, 38, 62; [2]248; Erich Neumann and, [1]xii–xv, xxix–xxxiii; [2]xxvi; *Geheimnis der goldenen Blüte,* [1]6 & *n,* 113*n*124; [2]271 & *n;* on individuation, [2]221, 222, 223, 230, 249, 266; Kabbalah, interest in, [2]xvi; on the Self, [1]117, 133*n*6, 133*n*9; [2]266; on symbolism, [2]226, 228, 229, 271; typology of, [2]199, 217, 223; *Wandlungen und Symbole der Libido,* [1]71*n*104; [2]53*n*168, 233*n*18

Kabbalah, [1]152, 154, 163; [2]7, 20–21, 23–24, 85, 136, 153, 169; *Adam Kadmon,* [1]51 & *n,* 162 & *n;* [2]97, 69–75; levels of the world and *sefirot,* [2]66–69; Lurianic, [2]98–99; principle of male-female polarity, [2]130–131; problem of evil and, [2]30; rabbinism and, [2]85; Sefirotic Tree, [2]96–97; stages of life and, [2]126–127; *tzimtzum,* [2]6–7
kadosh, [2]271 & *n*
Kafka, Franz, [1]87 & *n,* 108*n*48; Neumann's essays on, [1]108n49

Keter (crown), [2]69, *70, 71, 72*
kingdom *(Malkhut),* [2]68
Kirsch, James, [1]xxxix*n*26, xl*n*31, xli*n*47
knowledge, [2]90–91, 99–100; of good and evil, [2]107–108, 110; original, [1]93–94; [2]29, 30, 31; uncertainty and, [2]95, 105, 144, 143
Korah, [1]34, 145, 147; [2]12

Lamiae, [1]160
Land of Israel, [1]65*n*4
Last Judgment, [1]80, 82–83, 84–86, 87–89, 90–95
law, [1]29–30, 31, 42, 56–57, 58–59, 60–61, 104, 125–127, 132; [2]166, 175
Law, Tablets of the, [1]23, 24–25, 28
Leah, [1]43
leil shimurim (night of watching), [1]157 & *n*
Leitwort (guiding word), [1]138*n*2; [2]53*n*147
levels of nature, [2]56, 59–63, 65
levels of the world (Kabbalah), [2]66–69
Leviathan, [1]92, 110*n*73
Levites, [1]25, 26, 27, 34, 35, 45, 67*n*44, 67*n*46, 144–145
life, principle of, [2]47
life stages, [2]124–128
light symbolism, [1]92–93, 94, 115–116, 117, 149–150; [2]74–75, 196–197, 271
Lilith: as negative female, [2]96; opposition to *Shekhinah,* [2]74
liver, *nefesh* and, [2]72, 73–74, 75
"living God," YHWH as, [1]40
logos (word), [1]53, 152
love for God, [2]95–96
love of God, [2]152–153
Lurianic Kabbalah, [2]54*n*191, 86*n*41, 88*n*95, 98–99
Luria, Rabbi Isaac, [2]49*n*5

magic, [1]4, 80, 86, 162; [2]149
Malachi, [1]78
male deities, [1]16, 40
male-female symbolism, [1]40, 92; [2]30–31, 60–61, 72, 76, 80–82, 193
male psychology, feminine archetypes and, [2]195, 197–199
Malkhut (kingdom), [2]xvii, 68, 76–77, 130, *70, 71,* 80; as feminine aspect of God, [2]146; as feminine symbol, [2]97; Self and, [2]83
mana-personality, [2]8, 191; Moses as, [1]28 & *n,* 31; *tzaddik* as, [2]123, 171
mandala symbol, [1]92; [2]231, 272
Mandeans, [1]160
Manichaeism, [1]118; [2]141, 142
manna, [1]92 & *n*
"man of the clouds," [1]89, 100 & *n,* 101

marriage of Israel and YHWH, [1]43, 59, 155, 156

marriage, sexual polarity and, [2]150

Marx, Karl, [2]176

masculinization, [1]129

mass-psychological experiences, [1]19, 49; [2]192, 240; *see also* ecstatic states

matter, inferiority to spirit, [2]20–21, 22, 23, 24, 38, 65–66

meaning, level of, [2]62–63, 65

meditation, [2]21–24, 25, 137; ecstatic state and, [2]32; stages of, [2]66–68

melancholy, [2]74, 93, 94, 97–98

Mendel of Kozk, Rabbi, [2]172, 180*n*29

menstruation, [1]160–161

mental illness, [2]240

mercy of God, [2]152–153

Merkavah, [1]154, 168*n*81; [2]72, 269 & *n*

messiah figure, [1]81–82, 89–90, 94, 96; Christian conception of, [1]101–102; [2]164–165; false, [1]124; as unifying symbol, [1]91, 100–103; [2]164

messianism: actualizing of, [2]18–20, 103–104, 128, 133, 134; apocalypse and, [1]75, 82, 87–90, 96, 124

Midianites, [1]156

midrash, [1]152 & *n*

midrashim: birth of the child, [2]29; foundation stone and waters of the deep, [1]140–144; Jacob's head and the sacred stones, [2]59; Lilith, [1]161–162

mineral level, [2]59, 61, 65

miracle, YHWH and, [1]62; [2]43–46

Miriam, [1]34, 146–147

Mithraism, [1]45, 154

modern humanity: atomizing and collectivizing of, [2]235–236, 251, 257, 265; collective unconscious and, [2]262–263; "compartmental psychology" of, [2]237; lack of wholeness, [2]220–221; numinous experience and, [2]249–254; outward orientation of, [2]237, 263; primitive tendencies within, [2]245–246, 262; recovery of wholeness, [2]224–225; symbols and, [2]226, 227, 228, 229

moira (fate), [1]61; [2]28, 62 & *n*

Molitor, Franz Joseph, [1]37, 69*n*81

moon symbolism, [1]152, 160; [2]80

moral choice, [2]77–78, 110–111

morality, ego-stability and, [1]49

Moses: biblical redactors and, [1]144–147; capacity to speak directly with God, [1]*18*, 48, 126; circumcision of son, [1]155, 156 & *n*; descendants of, [1]32, 145; elevation of, [1]27–28, 31; Golden Calf and, [1]23–26; mana-personality

of, [1]145; messiah figure and, [1]91, 100; prophecy and, [1]27–36; ritual ordeal and, [1]25–26; Sinai revelation, [1]17, *18,* 20–21, 23, 27; Tablets of the Law, [1]23, 25, 143–144; thornbush revelation, [1]23 & *n;* [2]106

mother archetype, [1]131; [2]96, 194, 199, 211–213, 214–215; children and, [1]157, 158; [2]210–215; dogmatism and, [1]132; [2]169, 170; parts of the soul and, [2]124–125, 127; *Shekhinah* as, [2]80; son-lover figure and, [2]195, 197–198; Torah and, [1]132; *see also* Mother Goddess

Mother Goddess, [1]15–16, 40–41, 42, 43, 44, 54, 62–63, 122, 154, 161; [2]195

mother symbol, cow as, [2]57

Mount Nebo, [1]35

Mount Sinai revelation, [1]17–19, *18,* 20, 21–22, 23, 24

mystery religions, [1]45, 93, 117, 154

mysticism, [1]46, 52; [2]5

mythology, [2]194, 196–198, 199, 205–206

Nachmanides, [1]30

Nachman, Rabbi, [2]14, 22, 27, 40, 41, 45, 91, 101–102, 133, 134, 172, 41, 180*n*

Nadab and Abihu, [1]64, 84, 143, 147

name of God (YHWH), [2]79

nature: affirmation of, [1]37–41, 119; [2]38–39, 59, 142; alienation from, [1]21–22; hallowing of, [1]37 & *n*, 42 & *n;* [2]142; miracle and, [2]43–46; *participation mystique* with, [2]192; realms and levels of, [2]56–63, 65; veneration of, [2]56; YHWH manifesting through, [1]*18,* 86, 87, 21–23, 37–39; YHWH's power over, [1]50, 86; *see also* earth

Nazirites, [1]145, 154

Near-Eastern religions, [1]15–17; [2]163, 195

nefesh (body-soul), [1]40, 166*n*46; [2]72, 73–75, 78, 84, 186; blood and, [1]150–152; life stages and, [2]127; Self and, [2]83; vitalist concept of, [2]25

nefesh-hayah (living being), [1]40

Neoplatonism, [2]78, 88*n*77, 141

neshama, [1]152; [2]26, 72, 75; life stages and, [2]126–127; selfhood and, [2]79, 83

Netzach (eternity), [2]70, 71

Neumann, Erich, [1]xxiv–xxv; approach to Hasidism, [1]xxxiv–xxxv; [2]xiv, xxvii, xv–xviii; Carl Jung and, [1]xii–xv, xxix–xxxiii; decision not to publish, [1]xxix–xxxi; publication of work, [1]xxxvi–xxxvii; scholarly influences on, [1]xxxiv–xxxv, xxxvi

neuroticism, [1]58; [2]178, 240

New Year, [2]37–38, 41
Nietzsche, Friedrich, [1]36
niggun, [2]58
night of watching *(leil shimurim),* [1]157
night symbolism, [1]153
night world, [2]26–32, 36
Nineveh, [1]62 & *n*
nishmat-hayim (breath of life), [1]40, 152
Noah, [2]113
nomadism, secondary, [1]127–128
nothingness, principle of, [2]21, 22, 28, 35–43, 66, 68
novelty, fear of, [1]57
numbers, sacred, [1]159; [2]51*n*70, 76–77, [2]82
numinous experience, [1]44–45, [2]249–250

object projection, [1]86
ocean symbolism, [1]100–101; [2]5, 73–74
Oedipus complex, [2]211, 212–213, 222
Oedipus myth, [2]197–198
Ohel Moed, [1]30, 69*n*73
Olam-ha-Azilut, [2]34 & *n*
old age, [2]83, 97, 126–128, 221–222, 231
Old Testament, [1]138–147, 144–147; bias against, [1]5
oracles, [1]30, 31, 68*n*59, 68*n*60, 145
ordeal, ritual, [1]24–26, 25, 26, 66*n*37, 144
Oresteia, [2]197, 198, 207
original knowledge, [1]93–94; [2]29, 30, 31
Otto, Rudolf, [1]39; [2]249

paganism, [1]16–17, 35, 41, 42–43, 151, 153
parable, role of, [2]120–121
Paraclete, [1]103
paradise, restoration of, [1]91–95
paradox, YHWH and, [1]43, 44–45, 61, 84
parent-child relationship, [2]210–213, 214–215, 222
participation mystique, [1]25 & *n*, 41, 42, 55, 56, 60, 76, 153–154, 157–158, 159; [2]28, 46, 56–57; defined, [1]67*n*38; [2]56–57, 191; early humanity and, [2]198, 199, 200; of parents and children, [2]210–211; sacred objects and, [2]57
passion, [2]32–33, 100–101, 102, 143
Passover, [1]43, 60, 97
Paul, Saint, [1]101
peace, apocalypse and, [1]90, 94
pearl symbol, [1]117
Pentateuch, [1]138–147
perfection, male-female union as, [2]78, 81–82, 130–131
persona, [2]209
personalization, [2]204, 205–206; *see also* secondary personalization

phallic symbols, [1]4 & *n,* [1]154
pilpul, [2]166, 179*n*10
Pinchas, [1]34
plagues, [1]24, 25, 33, 60, 84, 86
plant level, [2]59, 61
plant sacrifice, [1]151, 159, 160
pneuma-soul, [2]75
pneumatic experience, [1]87
pneumatikoi, [1]149
possession, psychic, [1]22, 23, 46–47, 53
prayer, [1]30; [2]41–42, 113–114, 137
present moment, absoluteness of, [2]17–18, 103
priesthood, [1]27, 57, 67*n*, 151; Hasidism and, [2]166–167; priestly law, [1]55, 56–57, 58–59; prophecy and, [1]32–35, 58–59, 79, 144–147
primitive humanity, [1]2–4, 19, 23, 41, 49, 59; [2]192–195, 198, 199–206, 220; original knowledge and, [1]93–94; primal experience and, [2]245–246; puberty rites and, [2]214–215; symbols and, [1]3–4; [2]226, 227–228, 229; procreation, [1]163
"procreative" union of *sefirot,* [2]80, 81, 82, 130
profane, sacred and, [2]103–104
projection (psychology), [2]57
prophecies, fulfillment of, [1]76 & *n*
prophecy, [1]44–46; decline of, [1]78–82, 79; as distinct from divination, [1]46–49, 53–55, 61–62; ego-stability and, [1]49–53; latent capacity of individuals for, [1]27–30, 56–57; [2]10, 32–35, 129; nature of, [1]46–49; as protection against the conscious, [1]57–60; theocracy and, [1]75; true *vs.* false, [1]32–36, 47–48, 79
Protestantism, [2]163, 165
puberty, rites of, [1]156 & *n,* 157–158 & *n;* [2]126, 214–215 & *n,* 221, 231
purity of nature, [1]119; [2]59, 142

queen symbol, [2]80, 81

rabbinism, [1]125–127; [2]7, 136, 138; Hasidism and, [2]166, 171–172, 173
Rachel, [1]43
Rahamim (compassion), [2]69, *70,* 76, 132
rainbow symbol, [2]82
Ramakrishna, Sri, [2]5
rapture, apocalyptic, [1]143
rationalism, [1]129–130, 131–132; [2]7, 108, 136, 165–166
rationality, [2]199, 217, 219
rational soul *(neshama),* [1]152, 26, 72, 75
reality, transcendence of, [2]65–66
reason *(Binah),* [2]25–26, 68
rebirth of world, [1]88, 90–92, 96; [2]36–37

rebis, [2]230 & *n*

redeemer, [1]51, 116; human being as, [2]141, 145, 146; *tzaddik* as, [2]132–133

redemption, [1]80, 95, 117, 120; [2]141; Christian doctrine of, [2]103; of divine sparks, [2]47, 48, 58–59, 62, 81, 121, 130; ethical stance *vs.* magical formulae, [1]80; as function of human beings, [2]64; God's hiddenness and, [2]22; individual responsibility for, [2]19; Near-Eastern religion and, [2]163; self-redemption and, [2]65; through sin, [2]100–101, 107; time and, [1]96–99

Rekabites, [1]45, 154

religious experience, [2]248–250

religious individualism, [1]76, 77, 78, 79, 80, 96, 101; [2]164

renewal of world, continual, [2]36–39, 40–43, 105

repentance, [1]74*n*166; [2]100–104, 107, 133, 147–148

resurrection, [1]89, 91, 122

revealed Torah, [1]61

revelation *see* direct revelation; prophecy

Ridya, [1]154 & *n*

rites of initiation, [1]156; [2]191–192, 216, 231, 240, 244

ritual bath, [2]41

rituals, effectiveness of, [1]60

Rizhyn, Rabbi of, [2]11

rootlessness, [1]128, 129, 130; [2]174, 175

Ropshitz, Rabbi of, [2]10

ruach (breath), [1]149, 152; [2]72; heart and, [2]72, 73–74, 75; life stages and, [2]127; as the middle, [2]76–78; Self and, [2]83; *tzaddik* as embodiment of, [2]129; of YHWH, [1]39–40, 53 & *n*

Sabbateanism, [1]124–125; [2]175

Sabbath, [1]37, 159–160; [2]37 & *n*, 41

sacrament of communion, [1]92

sacred and profane, [2]103–104

sacred cow, [2]57

sacred objects, *participation mystique* and, [2]57

sacred stones, [2]56, 59

sacrifice, [1]46, 142, 151–152; introversion of, [2]104–105

sacrificial meal, [1]92

Sadigura (Hasidic dynasty), [2]172 & *n*

saints, temptations of, [1]80, 94; [2]110

salvation, [1]80, 81, 82, 83–86, 88, 89, 91, 94, 96–99 ; [2]45, 82, 150; in history, [2]128, 163, 168–169; through the symbol, [2]228; through the *tzaddik,* [2]132

Samson, [1]36, 63

Samuel, [1]43, 147

Saphir, [1]161

Sarah, [1]43

Satan, [1]82, 89, 90, 94,160; [2]28, 93

Saul, King, [1]63; [2]144

savior, [1]81

Schatz Uffenheimer, Rivka, [2]xv, 53*n*138

Scholem, Gershom, [1]xxxiv–xxxv, xli*n*47; approach to Hasidism, [2]xiv–xv, xvii

scientific worldview, [1]79; [2]236–239

seal of YHWH, [1]140, 141

secondary personalization, [1]49; [2]205, 206, 208*n*26, 210, 211, 212, 215, 222, 239, 240

Second Temple: destruction of, [1]6, 8, 76, 128, 130; and theocracy, [1] 76, 77–79, 105*n*4, 105*n*6, 128

secularization, [1]58, 75; [2]173–174

seduction, feminine, [1]63, 160, [1]161

Sefer Yetzirah, [1]150; [2]51*n*70, 75, 87*n*66

sefirot, [2]21, 51*n*70, 67–72, 75–85, 132–133

Sefirotic Tree, [2]69–72, 76–78, 82

sekel, [2]25–26, 51*n*86

Self, [1]79–80, 82–83, 133*n*6; as *Adam Kadmon,* [2]169, 171; ego and [1]117, 118, 119; [2]83, 106, 136, 151, 152, 153, 266; Jung's theory of, [1]117, 133*n*6, 133*n*9; [2]266; maturity and, [2]124, 126–128; as unifying symbol, [2]230–232; *see also* transcendent function

self-affirmation, [2]93

self-consciousness, [1]79; [2]90–91

selfhood, [2]192

self-realization, [2]13–14, 32; messianic stage and, [2]18–20

self-redemption, [2]65

self-renewal, [2]40, 41–43

self-transformation, [2]64, 66

serpent: bronze, [1]30; of paradise, [1]162; [2]107–110; transformative, [2]*109*; as uroboros, [2]191, 193, 194, 196, 197, 199, 211, 212, 230, 231, 232

seven, number, [1]37, [2]82

sexuality: abstinence, [1]19; deviance, [1]163; female seduction and, [1]63, 160–163; orgiastic cults, [1]16, 17, 53, 154, 163; ritual impurity and, [1]158–159, 160–161

sexual symbolism, [1]60–61, 76, 80, 81, 97, 130–131

shadow personality, [2]225, 244–245

Sheba, Queen of, [1]161

shedim (evil spirits), [2]28

Shekhinah, [1]81, 106*n*24; as feminine aspect of God, [1]132–133, 150, 160, 161; [2]36–37,

63, 80, 83, 97 145–147; as *Malkhut,* [2]80; opposition to Lilith, [2]73–74; *sefirah* of, [2]70; as world, [2]81

Shema Israel (Hear, O Israel), [1]157 & *n*

Simeon ben Lakish, Rabbi, [1]85

Simon bar Yochai, Rabbi, [2]150

Sinai revelation, [1]17, *18,* 20, 21–22, 23, 24, 27, 32–33, 143

sin/sinners, [1]103, 120–121, 142, 154; [2]91–92, 98, 100–101, 103, 107

sister archetype, [2]198–199

sleep/sleeping, [1]153, 160; [2]25–26, 36–38, 101–102

snake *see* serpent

Sodom and Gomorrah, [1]144

solitude, [2]12, 26, 27, 125, 126, 144

Solomonic Temple, [1]105*n*4; [2]49*n*11

Song of Songs, [1]155

son-lover figures, [2]195, 197–198

son of man, [1]100–102

Sophia, [1]149, 150

soul, [1]39, 148; [2]25; ascent of, [2]63–66; levels of, [2]55–59, 63–66; *nefesh,* [2]25, 69, 72–73; *neshama,* [2]25, 26, 69, 72–75; night as regenerative for, [2]36–37, 38; *ruach,* [2]69, 72, 74–75, 76–84; sparks and, [2]58; transformation of, [2]69–75; transmigration of, [2]58; *yehidah,* [2]79

soul, parts of, [1]152; *Adam Kadmon* and, [2]69–76; associated with parts of body, [2]72; elements attributed to, [2]75–76; life stages and, [2]126–127, 128; transformation and, [2]69–75; unity among, [2]82–83

sparks, divine, [2]16–17, 55–56, 58, 102; ascent of, [2]63–66; Hasidic *vs.* Gnostic, [2]140–141, 142–143; redemption of, [2]58–59, 60, 62, 81, 107, 112, 141, 142, 146–147; theory of, [2]46–48

speech, as defining human trait, [2]60

spirit *(ruach)* of God, [1]39–40, 53–54, 149–150

spirit, superiority of, [2]20–21, 22, 23, 24

spiritual realm, inner sequence of, [2]23–24

splendor *(Hod),* [2]70, 71, 72

stages of life, [2]124–128

stones, sacred, [2]56, 59

storm symbolism, [1]22, 66*n*34, 87

strength *(Gevurah),* [2]69, 70, 76

Striges, [1]160

succubi, [1]160, 163

suffering, [2]111, 112, 133

sun symbolism, [1]4; [2]80, 81symbolic level, [2]62–63, 66, 120

symbolism, [1]4, 22–23,138–139; [2]57–58, 85*n*4, 191, 226–229

Tablets of the Law, [1]23, 24–25, 26, 28

taboos, [1]19, 24, 25, 151, 158, 159; [2]57, 202

talking being, level of, [2]62

talmid hakam, [2]7 & *n*

Talmud, [1]160; [2]155

Talmudic law, [1]125–127

Tanakh, [1]127

tannaim, [1]107*n*33, 112*n*107

temptation, [1]80, 94; [2]107–108, 110

temptress, negative feminine as, [1]161, 162

Tent of Meeting, [1]82, 145

theocracy, [1]30, 58, 75, 76, 77, 78, 81, 88, 89, 95, 102, 105*n*

theophany, [1]20, 24, 38, 60, 87; [2]21

Therapeutae, [1]78 & *n*

third eye, symbol, [2]271

thornbush revelation, [1]23 & *n;* [2]106–107

thought: as defining human trait, [2]60; inner sequence and, [2]23–24, 25

throne of God, [1]154

Tiamat-Rahab, [1]142

Tiferet (beauty), [2]69, 70, 71, 72, 95, 96, 132; as central activity, [2]78–81; colors of, [2]82; as ego-Self, [2]81–85; identification with YHWH and humanity, [2]80–81; as the middle, [2]76–78; *tzaddik* as embodiment of, [2]129; union with *Malkhut–Shekhinah,* [2]83

time: absoluteness of present moment, [2]103; affirmation of, [2]31; apocalypse and, [1]96–101; contraction in, [2]17–18; salvation in, [1]91; as the working level of the unconscious, [1]98–99; YHWH's working in, [1]97

Torah, [1]23, 29, 61, 67, 106*n*15, 123, 126, 138, 139, 140; [2]18–19, 166; "dragon" of, [1]132, [2]171–172; mother archetype and, [1]132

transcendent function, [2]229, 230, 248, 252; *see also* Self

Tree of Death, [2]84

tree of knowledge, [1]93

Tree of Life *see* Sefirotic Tree

trees, "foreskin" of, [1]37 & *n,* 159

tree symbolism, [2]22, 82, 132–133; *see also* Sefirotic Tree

trial, ritual, [2]25, 26

typological differentiation, [2]209

tzaddik, [1]51; [2]7–9, 128–129; *Adam Kadmon* and, [2]123–126, 132–133; care of souls and, [2]8–9; continuous attachment to God, [2]113, 145; as embodiment of oneness, [2]131–132; as embodiment of *Tiferet* and *ruach,* [2]129; God-like, [2]148; hiddenness of, [2]120–123; "in a fur coat,"

[2]35, 92, 122; individual autonomy and, [2]10–12; mana-personality of, [2]123, 171; as mediator, [2]135; power over evil spirits, [2]28; as redeemer, [2]132–133; *sefirah* of, [2]70; as soul doctor, [2]131–132
tzaddikism, [2]129–133, 171
tzelem, [2]79–80, 82
tzimtzum, [2]6–7, 12, 18, 21, 22, 23, 24, 29, 31, 103, 149

uncertainty: fear of, [1]57; as Hasidic value, [2]90, 105
uncleanness, [1]37 & *n*, 158–159, 160–161, 163 & *n*, 169*n*105; [2]46–47
unconscious contents, concretizing of, [1]54–55
unifying symbols, [1]23, 24, 25, 29, 91, 100–105; [2]130, 229, 240, 248
unity, principle of, [2]111
Urim and *Thummim,* oracle, [1]30, 68*n*59, 68*n*60, 78, 145
uroboros, [2]191, 193, 194, 196, 197, 199, 211, 212, 230, 231, 232
uterus symbol, [1]121

vegetative level, [2]59, 61
vine symbol, [1]42–43; [2]132–133 & *n*
visions, collective, [1]19, 23
visions, revelation in, [1]52–53
vitality, concept of, [1]40; [2]24–26, 55–56, 47
Volz, Paul, [1]94, 97, 108*n*46

waters of the deep, foundation stone and (midrash), [1]140–144, 165*n*24
water symbolism, [1]140–141, 152; [2]41, 75
Weiss, Joseph, [2]xv
Wellhausen, Julius, [1]61
Western consciousness, [1]3; [2]206–207, 209, 210; *see also* modern humanity
white light (Zohar), [2]84
wholeness, individual, [2]15–17
will, development of the, [2]209
wind (air) symbolism, [1]37, 38–40, 44, 148–150; [2]75, 76
wine, [1]45, 154
wisdom, [1]93, 149–150; [2]28, 29, 30, 39–40
wisdom *(Hokhmah),* [2]68, 69, 70, 71
witches, [1]4, 162
women: fertility and, [1]43–44; uncleanness and, [1]159, 160
word *(logos),* [1]53, 152

words, spiritual power of, [2]23
"working faith," [2]44
world: acceptance of, [2]111–114, 115, 122; affirmation of, [2]38, 93, 142–143; anthropocentric, [1]51, 53, 55; [2]9–10, 62, 115, 133–134, 137, 147; death and rebirth of, [1]90–94, 96; detachment from, [2]125–128; Gnostic *vs.* Jewish views on, [1]118–119; Hasidic concept of, [2]35–43, 45–47, 62; hiddenness and visibility of, [2]26–28, 63–64; levels of (Kabbalah), [2]66–69; levels of nature and, [2]59–63; nothingness and, [2]35–36; path of mediation and, [2]20–24; rejection of, [1]103, 115–116; [2]141, 175; renewal of, [2]36–39; as *Shekhinah,* [2]81; as symbol, [2]114–116, 120; transcendent reality of, [2]65–66; *tzimtzum* and, [2]6–7

yehidah, [1]152; [2]79
Yesod (foundation), [2]70, 71, 72, 76, 80, 132, 159*n*67
Yetzirah, [2]67
YHWH: covenant with Israel, [1]43, 50, 52, 54, 155; earth-principle and, [1]36–44; infinity and intangibility of, [1]52, 81; as lord of fertility, [1]43–44; Mother Goddess and, [1]16–17, 62–64; Moses and, [1]18, 48, 126; nature of, [1]44–46; phenomenology of irruptions, [1]18, 21–23, 37–39, 86; remoteness of, [1]44, 81, 95; seal of, [1]25, 140–142; spirit *(ruach)* of, [1]39–40, 53–54, 149–150; transcendence of, [1]81; unpredictability of, [1]61, 84, 98–99; vitality and, [1]40; working in time, [1]96–97; *see also* God
Yom Kippur, [1]142; [2]98, 134

Zachriel, [1]160
Zadokites, [1]144, 145, 146
Zalman, Rabbi, [2]29, 31
Zechariah, [1]78
Zion, [1]41
Zipporah, [1]156
Zohar, [1]154; [2]36–37, 73, 75, 79, 83–85, 93, 150; Neumann's sources, [2]181; Pritzker edition, [2]181–189; Soncino edition, [2]182–183
Zusya, Rabbi, [2]14, 20, 94 & *n*, 118*n*69, 89 & *n*, 124

SCRIPTURAL INDEX

Note: This index covers both Volumes One and Two. Volume One page numbers are introduced with a superscript 1; Volume Two page numbers are introduced with a superscript 2.

Bible

Gen 1:10, [2]93
Gen 2:18, [1]161; [2]30
Gen 3:17, [1]153
Gen 4:10, [1]150
Gen 5:2, [2]82
Gen 6:9, [2]113
Gen 9:4, [1]150
Gen 12:1, [1]45; [2]124
Gen 12:6, [1]17
Gen 15:13f, [1]98
Gen 17:23–7, [1]158
Gen 18:25, [1]51
Gen 19:24, [1]22
Gen 20:7, [1]51
Gen 25:22, [1]30
Gen 32, [1]36
Gen 39:6–20, [1]161
Ex 2:11f, [1]36
Ex 2:12, [1]29
Ex 2:23, [1]84
Ex 3:2ff, [1]23
Ex 3:9, [1]84
Ex 3:15, [1]86
Ex 4:10, [1]29
Ex 4:10–17, [1]36
Ex 4:24–26, [1]155, 156
Ex 4:28, [1]29
Ex 5:24–26, [1]60

Ex 6:12, [1]86
Ex 7:1, [1]91
Ex 12:1, [1]86
Ex 12:40, [1]98
Ex 16:15, [1]92
Ex 18:13, [1]30
Ex 18:13–23, [1]31
Ex 18:14ff, [1]29, 30
Ex 18:16, [1]30
Ex 19:10–12, [1]19
Ex 19:16, 18, [1]20
Ex 19:21, [1]20
Ex 19:23, [1]20
Ex 20:15–16, [1]20
Ex 20:17, [1]20
Ex 20:18, [1]20
Ex 20:19, [1]20
Ex 20, [1]20
Ex 22:29, [1]159
Ex 24:6, [1]151
Ex 29:12f, [1]151
Ex 32:1, [1]25
Ex 32:2–6, [1]27
Ex 32:7–14, [1]18
Ex 32:10f, [1]29
Ex 32:10–14 [1]27
Ex 32:14, [1]24
Ex 32:19, [1]24
Ex 32:20–24, [1]27
Ex 32:26–29, [1]26

Ex 32:32, [1]27, 51
Ex 32:35, [1]24
Ex 33:7, [1]30
Ex 33:12–23, [1]29
Ex 34:30, [1]28, 146
Lev 8:30, [1]151
Lev 9:24, 10:2, [1]22
Lev 10, [1]146
Lev 12:2f, [1]156, 158
Lev 14:7, [1]151
Lev 16:16, [2]46, 106
Lev 17:11, [1]150
Lev 17:13, [1]150
Lev 19:18, [2]106
Lev 19:23, [1]37
Lev 19:26, [1]151
Num 3:2f, [1]145
Num 3:11, [1]144–145
Num 5:12–31, [1]25
Num 8:5, [1]145
Num 8:16, [1]144–145
Num 9:15–23, [1]145
Num 10:11f, [1]145
Num 11:1, [1]22
Num 11:27, [1]21
Num 11:29, [1]21, 33
Num 12, [1]146, 147
Num 12:6–7, [1]48
Num 16, [1]145
Num 16:1–35, [2]12

Num 17, [1]146
Num 17:6–11, [1]146
Num 18:4, [1]145
Num 18:6, [1]144–145
Num 20, [1]146
Num 20:12, [1]35
Num 21:9, [1]30
Num 22–24, [1]34
Num 23:9, [1]9
Num 25:20, [1]59
Num 40f, [1]33
Deut 4:19–20, [1]63
Deut 4:25, [1]83
Deut 9:24, [1]35
Deut 10:12, [2]96
Deut 12:23, [1]150
Deut 12:24, [1]150
Deut 18:15, [1]35
Deut 18:15–18, [1]21, 28–29
Deut 20, [1]85
Deut 32:17, [1]44
Deut 32:22, [1]22
Deut 32:24, [1]160
Deut 33:9, [1]45
Josh 5:2, 10, [1]157
Judg 6:21, [1]22
Judg 9:37, [1]17
Judg 13:20, [1]22
1 Sam 2:12–34, [1]84
1 Sam. 2:27–36, [1]33
1 Sam 9:9, [1]30
1 Sam 10:6, [2]144
1 Sam 10:10, [1]63
1 Sam 11:6, [1]63
1 Sam 16:15, [1]63
1 Sam 19:10, [1]63
1 Sam 19:23ff, [1]63
1 Sam 28:7, [1]63
2 Sam 8:17, [1]147
2 Sam 20:25, [1]147
1 Kgs 2:26f, [1]33
1 Kgs 17:4, [2]14
1 Kgs 18:24, [1]22
1 Kgs 18:38, [2]84
1 Kgs 38, [1]22
2 Kgs 5:24, [1]17
2 Kgs 8:8, [1]30
2 Kgs 18:4, [1]30
1 Chr 18:16, [1]147
2 Chr 7:1, [1]22
Job 1:15, [1]161
Job 1:16, [1]22
Job 26:12, [1]142

Ps 18:9, [1]22
Ps 39:12b, [2]125
Ps 71:9, [2]38–39
Ps 72:17, [1]90
Ps 74:13, [1]142
Ps 89:11, [1]142
Ps 104:4, [1]22
Ps 108:2, [2]149
Prov 3:6, [2]105
Prov 31:15, [1]152
Eccles 1:7, [2]37
Is 5:2, [1]43
Is 6:3, [2]16, 46
Is 21:2, [1]21
Is 27:1, [1]142
Is 30:34, [1]22
Is 31:3, [1]40
Is 34:9, [1]22
Is 43:2, [1]22
Is 45:7, [1]xxxii
Is 45:7, [1]122
Is 45:8, [1]122
Is 51:9, [1]142
Is 65:5, [1]22
Is 66:1, [1]78
Jer 2:21, [1]42
Jer 5:14, 17:4, [1]22
Jer 23:16f, [1]47
Jer 28:9ff, [1]47
Jer 31:31, [1]78
Jer 35:6f, [1]45
Lam 3:23, [2]36, 39
Ezek 1:5–10, [1]154
Ezek 1:26, [2]72
Ezek 8:2, [1]81
Ezek 18:20, [1]76
Dan 4:12, [2]82
Dan 7:9, [1]81
Dan 7:10, [1]22, 87
Dan 7:13, [1]89, 100
Dan 8:15, [1]100
Dan 10:13, [1]82
Hos 2:18ff, [1]50
Amos 5:6, 7:4, [1]22
Jonah 3:10, [1]62
Mal 3:19, [1]85
Mal 4:2, [1]85
Mark 1:13, [1]94
Mark 12:13–17, [2]65
John 2:4, [1]26
John 3:8, [1]44
John 15:4f, [2]132
John 18:36, [1]120
1 Cor 13:2, [2]44

Apocrypha and Pseudepigrapha

1 Macc 4:46, [1]104
1 Macc 9:27, [1]104
1 Enoch (Ethiopic Apocalypse of) 8:3, [1]92
1 Enoch 10:1, [1]92
1 Enoch 10 :5, [1]142
1 Enoch 10:6, [1]82
1 Enoch 10:13, [1]82
1 Enoch 14:9, [1]81
1 Enoch 33 :3, [1]109n67
1 Enoch 46, [1]100
1 Enoch 46:2f, [1]113n117
1 Enoch 48, [1]92
1 Enoch 48 :6, [1]108n57
1 Enoch 48 :37, [1]89
1 Enoch 60 :24, [1]92
1 Enoch 62 :7, [1]89
1 Enoch 71 :5, [1]81
1 Enoch 71 :15, [1]90
1 Enoch 96 :3, [1]92
1 Enoch 98 :4, [1]121
1 Enoch 101 :1, [1]90
2 Enoch (Slavonic Apocalypse of) 8:2–6, [1]109n68
IV Ezra 4:26f, [1]103
IV Ezra 5:6, [1]82
IV Ezra 6:40–52, [1]92
IV Ezra 6:52, [1]92
IV Ezra 7:30, [1]91
IV Ezra 7:105, [1]80
IV Ezra 7:118–20, [1]101
IV Ezra 7:118, [1]120
IV Ezra 7:121, [1]92
IV Ezra 8:2, [1]81
IV Ezra 8:52, [1]92, 109n72
IV Ezra 13:3, [1]100
IV Ezra 14:45ff, [1]104
IV Ezra 14:47, [1]105
2 Baruch (Syriac Apocalypse of) 3:7, [1]91
2 Baruch 21:6, [1]81
2 Baruch 29, [1]92
2 Baruch 29:4, [1]92
2 Baruch 29:7, [1]92
2 Baruch 29:8, [1]92
2 Baruch 46:4, [1]81
2 Baruch 54:15, [1]121

2 Baruch 54:19, [1]121
Testament of Moses
10:1, [1]82
Testament of Moses 10:9,
[1]90, 109[n]60
Life of Adam and Eve 36,
[1]92, 109[n]72

Babylonian Talmud

Bab Tlm Shabbath 135a,
[1]155 & [n]92, 158 & [n]106,
159 & [n]108
Bab Tlm Shabbath 151b,
[1]160 & [n]115
Bab Tlm Pesahim 54a, [1]90
& [n]61, 160 & [n]111
Bab Tlm Yoma 9b, [1]125
& [n]43
Bab Tlm Yoma 19b, [1]154
& [n]78
Bab Tlm Sukkah 53a, [1]143
& [n]22
Bab Tlm Ta'anith 31a, [1]92
& [n]75
Bab Tlm Ta'anith 25b,
[1]154 & [n]83
Bab Tlm Hagigah 12a,
[1]93 & [n]82; [2]31 &
[n]113Bab Tlm Sotah 6b,
[1]24 & [n]37
Bab Tlm Baba Mezia 59b,
[1]125

Bab Tlm Baba Bathra 73a,
[1]160 & [n]121
Bab Tlm Baba Bathra, 10b,
[1]95 & [n]96
Bab Tlm Sanhedrin 46b,
[2]155 & [n]164, 253 & [n]32
Bab Tlm Sanhedrin 97a,
[1]91 & [n]67
Bab Tlm Abodah zarah, 3b,
4a, [1]85 & [n]40
Bab Tlm Abboth 5, 6, [1]160
& [n]111

Jerusalem Talmud

Jer Tlm Yoma 39a, [1]154
& [n]78
Jer Tlm Yoma 92, [1]78 & [n]16
Jer Tlm Megillah 73a, [1]92
Jer Tlm Sotah 3:19a, [1]24
& [n]37
Jer Tlm Sanhedrin 29a,
[1]143 & [n]22

Zohar

Zohar I 2a, [1]154, 168[n]76;
[2]182
Zohar I 19a,b, [2]36–37,
52[n]134, 182
Zohar I 27b, [1]160 & n117;
[2]182–183
Zohar I 51a, [2]77, 84, 183

Zohar I 51b, [2]84, 183–184
Zohar I 55b, [2]82, 89[n]99, 184
Zohar I 191a, [2]155,
161[n]162, 184
Zohar II 12a, [2]155, 184
Zohar II 20a, [2]69, 184
Zohar II, 70b, [2]155 &
[n]161, 184
Zohar II 76a, [2]155 & [n]163,
171, 185
Zohar II 91b, [1]143,
165[n]24; [2]185
Zohar II 113b, [1]143–144,
165[n]25; [2]185–186
Zohar II 142a, [1]40 &
[n]101, 152 & [n]71;
[2]74–75, 186
Zohar II 176b, [2]81 & [n]96, 186
Zohar II 205b, [2]155,
162[n]166
Zohar III 10b, [2]80 &
[n]93, 186
Zohar III 48a, [2]155 &
[n]160, 186–187
Zohar III 65a, [2]79 & [n]80, 187
Zohar III 104a, [2]79 & [n]87, 187
Zohar III 144a, [2]72, 187
Zohar III 144b, [2]75, 87[n]65
Zohar III 232a,b, [2]73 &
[n]52, 187–188
Zohar III, 234a, [2]73, 188
Zohar III 258b, [1]155 &
[nn]93–94 ; [2]188
Zohar III 296a, [2]82 &
[n]100, 188–189

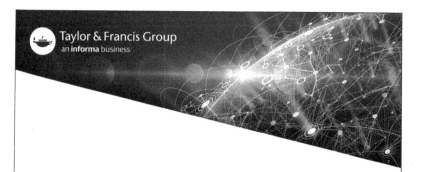